The Press in the Middle East and North Africa, 1850–1950

Politics, Social History and Culture

Edited by
Anthony Gorman and Didier Monciaud

EDINBURGH
University Press

Edinburgh University Press is one of the leading university presses in the UK. We publish academic books and journals in our selected subject areas across the humanities and social sciences, combining cutting-edge scholarship with high editorial and production values to produce academic works of lasting importance. For more information visit our website: edinburghuniversitypress.com

© editorial matter and organisation Anthony Gorman and Didier Monciaud, 2018
© the chapters their several authors, 2018

Edinburgh University Press Ltd
The Tun – Holyrood Road
12 (2f) Jackson's Entry
Edinburgh EH8 8PJ
www.euppublishing.com

Typeset in 11/15 Adobe Garamond by
Servis Filmsetting Ltd, Stockport, Cheshire

A CIP record for this book is available from the British Library

ISBN 978 1 4744 3061 6 (hardback)
ISBN 978 1 4744 3063 0 (webready PDF)
ISBN 978 1 4744 3064 7 (epub)

The right of the contributors to be identified as authors of this work has been asserted in accordance with the Copyright, Designs and Patents Act 1988 and the Copyright and Related Rights Regulations 2003 (SI No. 2498).

Contents

List of Tables — v

Introduction — 1
Anthony Gorman and Didier Monciaud

I The Press as National Voice

1 News Publishing as a Reflection of Public Opinion: The Idea of News during the Ottoman Financial Crises — 31
Gül Karagöz-Kızılca

2 Disruptions of the Local, Eruptions of the Feminine: Local Reportage and National Anxieties in Egypt's 1890s — 58
Marilyn Booth

3 The Arabic Palestinian Press between the Two World Wars — 99
Mustafa Kabha

4 *Falastin*: An Experiment in Promoting Palestinian Nationalism through the English-language Press — 126
Fred H. Lawson

II   The Rise of the Journalist

5   Press Propaganda and Subaltern Agents of Pan-Islamic Networks in the Muslim Mediterranean World prior to World War I   153
Odile Moreau

6   The Publicist and his Newspaper in Syria in the Era of the Young Turk Revolution, between Reformist Commitment and Political Pressures: Muhammad Kurd 'Ali and *al-Muqtabas* (1908–17)   176
Kaïs Ezzerelli

7   From Intellectual to Professional: The Move from 'Contributor' to 'Journalist' at *Ruz al-Yusuf* in the 1920s and 1930s   207
Sonia Temimi

III   Critical, Dissident Voices

8   The Anarchist Press in Egypt before World War I   237
Anthony Gorman

9   The Ethiopian War as Portrayed in the Italian Fascist and Antifascist Press in Tunisia   265
Leila El Houssi

10   A Voice from Below in the 1940s Egyptian Press: The Experience of the Workers' Newspaper *Shubra*   288
Didier Monciaud

IV   The Press as Community Voice

11   The Lamp, Qasim Amin, Jewish Women and Baghdadi Men: A Reading in the Jewish Iraqi Journal *al-Misbah*   323
Orit Bashkin

12   From a Privileged Community to a Minority Community: The Orthodox Community of Beirut through the Newspaper *Al-Hadiyya*   345
Souad Slim

Notes on the Contributors   371
Index   376

Tables

3.1	City of origin of Palestinian journalists	112
3.2	Political affiliation of Palestinian journalists	116
3.3	Circulation of Arabic Palestinian newspapers, 1929–39	117
8.1	Anarchist newspapers, periodicals and *numeri unici*, Egypt, 1877–1914	255
10.1	*Shubra* editorial committee, 1942–3	291

Introduction

Anthony Gorman and Didier Monciaud

The press occupies a crucial place in the modern history of the Middle East and North Africa. Its interest and significance lies in its importance not only as a medium of representation that a society produces *of* itself but also of what a society produces *for* itself. An understanding of its historical development is therefore vital to an appreciation of many processes of political, social and cultural change and of the evolution of public opinion and the debates surrounding social and cultural identities in the Middle East.

The Middle East and North Africa region offers a rich range of materials for a study of the press. In the hundred years from 1850 to 1950 it emerged as a medium of expression and chronicler of political developments punctuated by a record of dynamic contact and conflict within local societies and with European imperialism, initially in the latter nineteenth century and subsequently with the break-up of the Ottoman Empire and the decolonisation process that immediately followed World War II. During this time intensive, energetic debates were conducted and political struggles waged over the nature of political community, definitions of social classes and the character of cultural identity. The period sees the rise of nationalist movements where the press played a central role in supporting the nationalist cause but also a more complex part in articulating different perspectives on political, cultural and social questions. Essential to an understanding of political history and its representation, the press was also a participant in and subject to political circumstances, at times benefiting from the opportunities offered by free public debate while in other situations being subject to repressive legal regimes. Ultimately, the period ends with formal independence granted across much of the region when a rich tradition of political and cultural contest framed by a context of colonial domination and anticolonial struggle moves to a phase where newly installed national regimes sought to mediate and impose their own agenda on the role of the press. It therefore offers a rich opportunity to explore the press as a forum and an agent in a period of dynamic transformation.

The number of newspaper titles produced in the region over the period 1850–1950, while almost impossible to quantify precisely, is staggering in its profusion and diversity.[1] From the late nineteenth century on, there was an explosion in publishing that took many different forms, of daily newspapers, weekly magazines, illustrated periodicals, high-brow journals and popular rags, of numerous fleeting and fewer long-established titles, variously scientific, literary or satirical in tone, from local papers to reviews, from community organs to political tribunes, from educational journals and professional beacons catering to specialised interests in politics, culture and economics, published in at least a dozen different local and foreign languages in single and sometimes multilingual editions. The context of the first age of globalisation in the nineteenth century integrating the region into the world economy and the rise of the colonial project created opportunities for these very different press endeavours.

This emergent print culture affected the transmission of ideas and knowledge despite modest levels of literacy across the region while the mass of published periodical material spoke of a series of connected societies that were redolent with a strong desire to express themselves, to give voice to their individual elements and constituents, and to consume news, commentary and various literary forms. This creative polyphony of social voices and kaleidoscope of published textures, of original material, of translations, reproductions, adaptations, of text, caricatures, illustrations and photographs provides a fascinating and multifaceted subject of study.

This volume emerged from a workshop held at the Ninth Mediterranean

Research Meeting at the European University Institute in Florence in March 2008 which brought together a diverse range of scholars working on different aspects of the Middle Eastern press. The papers presented there, and subsequently developed and included here, share a common concern with the complex social, political and cultural aspects of the press in the period before 1950 and an engagement with its dynamic and multidimensional character. Based on a detailed reading of press material and drawing on archival research, they cover a significant geopolitical range with cases studies across the region, from the heartland of the Ottoman Empire to the post-Ottoman Arab world of Egypt, Palestine, Iraq and North Africa. Chronologically, they straddle the financial crises of the Ottoman Empire in the 1870s and the long confrontation with European colonialism, from the period of colonial expansion before World War I to the interwar period under the veneer of the mandatory administrations in Palestine and Iraq. Comprising the work of both Anglophone and Francophone scholars (four chapters have been translated from original French versions), the contents of this volume offer a range of scholarship across at least two academic language communities that are not always in close dialogue.[2]

Historical Background

The beginnings of the press in the Middle East can be dated to short-lived French-language publications that appeared in Istanbul and Cairo at the very end of the eighteenth century. More than twenty years later press activity took on renewed impetus with the state playing a critical role in sponsoring the earliest newspapers. Government presses in Istanbul and in Cairo, particularly the celebrated Bulaq press, served as key sites of production.[3] These early official newspapers were closely tied to state projects, dealing mostly with administrative and legal issues and read almost wholly by members of the elite, bureaucracy and the military. Noteworthy among these early titles were *al-Waqa'i' al-Misriyya* (Cairo, 1828), the *Moniteur ottoman* (Istanbul, 1831) and *Takvim-i Vekayi* (Istanbul, 1831). During the second half of the nineteenth century there was a shift to a developing private sector and independent newspapers. From the 1850s, as Beirut then Cairo became thriving urban centres, political, intellectual and cultural debates began to take place concerning key issues of the time such as colonial domination and the relationship of the region to the West, questions of political identity, of Ottomanism, Arabism and Islam, of social and cultural issues, of science and the economy. In Istanbul in 1860 the launch of *Tercümân-ı Ahvâl* by Agah Effendi and İbrahim Şinasi and of the Arabic-language *al-Jawa'ib* by Ahmad Faris Shidyaq the following year were important landmarks. In due course a similar phenomenon across the region from Morocco to Iran brought about by political changes underwrote the emergence of an effervescent press. In the critical period from the middle of the nineteenth until the middle of the twentieth century it both exemplified and in part documented the political, social and cultural development of the region against the backdrop of the decline of Ottoman power, growing foreign influence and the awakening of alternative agendas in a global context where the national question and political independence became central.[4]

The rise of the print media in the Middle East was the result of a number of technological, social and economic factors. Developments in press technology were accompanied by a great expansion in transport and communication systems, such as the extension of the telegraph, railway and steamboat services, which facilitated greater speed of information and fostered a greater demand for public discussion. As a new medium, the press enabled changes in social practices and became an important tool for the transmission of ideas in the region.[5]

The rise in literacy as a result of new educational programmes served as another important foundation for the flourishing of the press.[6] In the Ottoman Empire, education had expanded first during the Tanzimat period and even more so during the reign of 'Abd al-Hamid II. This process nurtured a new educated class linked to the modernisation process which opened the way to reconfigurations of identity assisted by the new media forms.[7] The lack of precise figures for popular literacy and the circulation figures for individual newspapers means it is difficult to determine accurately press readership or the audience of specific titles. Nevertheless, the number and range of newspapers particularly from the end of the nineteenth century onwards, when printing became particularly influential, indicate a broad and diverse matrix of popular engagement, even if this influenced various elements of society unevenly and in different ways.[8] Print publications were even able to extend their audience and reach the functionally illiterate through public and collective readings in coffeehouses and other venues. Rapid social changes and a deep transformation occurred through the rise of printing, as in Palestine in the first part of the twentieth century, penetrating most spheres of social community life.[9] The dynamics produced by the emergence and the impact of a print industry, the expansion in the number of public libraries, and the increasing publication of books, pamphlets and newspapers which gave greater opportunities for reading can fairly be called a revolution.

The emergence of a private, independent press in the second half of the nineteenth century meant the state no longer directly controlled the public space that was opening up to an increasingly diverse range of social representation, contestation and criticism. It quickly moved to contain this new freedom. In 1864 the Ottoman press law (based on a French template) inaugurated a local tradition of press regulation by stipulating qualifications on press ownership and restrictions on freedom of speech.[10] Other authorities followed: the Egyptian Publications Law of 1881 brought in harsher financial penalties and in time imprisonment as a punishment for press malefactors. The early years of the British occupation may have provided a period of relative freedom after 1882 but the authorities would launch a robust crackdown in 1909 to deal with the rising nationalist movement and other critics.

In the post-Ottoman era, the policy of state control of the press continued as successor states and mandatory administrations further tightened the regulatory regime in the name of defending the social order. Although freedom of the press was often explicitly guaranteed in the constitution, so was the authority of the state to suspend it by invoking emergency powers as was the case with Egypt, Syria, Lebanon, Jordan and Iraq.[11] The suspension and banning of publications and the imprisonment of journalists became increasingly common. In Egypt dedicated prisons for those who ran afoul of the press laws were legislated for although never built.[12] In mandatory Palestine, official warnings and press suspensions were routinely decreed under the 1933 Press Ordinance and subsequent Emergency Regulations.[13] In the 1930 Iraqi constitution state regulation of the press was codified and policed after independence by the establishment of a Press Bureau. The 1954 press law, passed following the hostile public response to the signing of the Baghdad Pact, made clear to Iraqis the limitations of freedom of speech.[14]

The relationship between state authorities and newspapers was never simply coercive, however.[15] As the press became a more influential and public medium, governments required its services as a channel of communication by which to win the support of, or at least neutralise, the literate population. In pursuing this aim, contacts between government officials and editors were cultivated, favours granted and subsidies disbursed to those editors and owners willing to play the required role. Newspapers for their part needed access to sources of information, favours from government officials and on occasion financial assistance. For these reasons, despite the restriction of licences, increased use of censorship and banning of newspapers, plurality and freedom of expression in the press remained a relatively significant phenomenon until the 1950s when the rise of authoritarian regimes saw greater restrictions on press freedom and, in some cases, nationalisation.

In the period 1850–1950, the press in the Middle East and North Africa is particularly notable for its linguistic diversity. Arabic and Turkish, as the majority languages, developed growing readerships in their respective regions while resident ethnic and religious communities, such as Jews, Armenians, Greeks and Italians, sustained a vibrant and often multilingual press. The Greek- and Armenian-language presses were the product of long-established communities in Anatolia, Greater Syria and Egypt. More complex was the profile of Jewish newspapers published in various languages (among them Arabic, Hebrew, Judeo-Arabic, Ladino and French). Other press languages owed more to the impact of European political and cultural influence, however. French-, English- and Italian-language newspapers, because of their imperial affiliations and their reception by different social groups usually among the local elites and middle class, were well represented across the region. An influential lingua franca during the nineteenth century, Italian was significantly displaced over time by French, which became the prestigious foreign and socially elite language in the Levant, a testimony to its cultural standing and commercial importance, and in the Maghrib on the basis of colonial authority and the presence of Francophone settlers.[16] English-language newspapers such as the *Egyptian Gazette* (Cairo, est. 1880–) and the *Iraq Times* (Baghdad, est. 1914) were by-products of direct British authority in the region. Although mediated through the matrix of colonialism, these different language-reading communities were not insulated from one another even if communication between them was undoubtedly regulated by the knowledge of languages and influenced by community and class considerations. Active interconnections and news and debate flowed between them. Indeed, in such a multicultural, polyglottal milieu it was not unusual for a newspaper to carry articles in more than one language,[17] or to be published in different language editions.[18]

The role of those who produced newspapers has been seminal in the history of the press. In its early years, particularly in the case of official publications, these were often bureaucrats and functionaries. With the proliferation of private newspapers, other professionals including lawyers, doctors, teachers and businessmen took up journalism as a part-time activity. For political activists, cultural commentators and budding intellectuals the press served as a favoured means of exercising influence and gaining prestige even if it rarely served as a means to a secure livelihood.[19] Political journalists were active from the second half of the nineteenth century, with the Young Ottoman circle, but it was perhaps not until after World War I that the professional journalist began to be recognised as an established occupation. More specialised roles such as reporters, correspondents, columnists, cartoonists and photographers in turn would gain recognition. Yet even after this time, skilled amateurs or generalist writers continued to contribute to newspapers, particularly small-scale publications.

The rising status of journalism was manifested in other significant ways.[20] The formation of journalist associations provided both a measure of the standing of the profession and a potential vehicle for exercising influence in the interest of its members or for even broader political ends. Egypt led the way with initial attempts to establish such a body before 1914. By the late 1930s two separate associations, the union of Egyptian women journalists and an association of foreign-language journalists, had been formed although the first official journalist syndicate was not formally recognised in law until 1941 and in Syria a year later. Nationalisation of the press, as happened in Egypt in 1960, meant journalists gained the economic security of government employment but compromised their freedom of expression.

The institutionalisation of journalism as an academic subject was another marker of its professional standing.[21] In the earlier period the field had attracted people from a great range of backgrounds but during the interwar period there were moves to provide for more structured training and a standard set of skills. Journalism itself was first taught at higher education level at the American University in Cairo in 1936 while in 1939 an Institute for Editing, Translation and Journalism was opened as part of the College of Arts at Cairo University, subsequently becoming a regular department in 1954. Mahmud Azmi, a lawyer by training with a considerable record as founder and editor of a number of Egyptian newspapers, was named first director of the Institute with Ibrahim 'Abduh, prolific historian of the Egyptian and Arabic press, serving as his assistant and successor.[22]

Literature Review

The scholarly literature on the Middle Eastern press is impressive in its breadth and diversity even if the very uneven survival of primary sources has hampered anything like a full consideration of many aspects of its history. Despite the great number of newspaper titles documented during the period under examination, studies that have appeared have most often focused on key newspapers and reviews, partly because the nationalist struggle, however configured, has dominated the historiography of the region and partly because many of the less mainstream publications have not survived, or access to them and relevant archival material has been limited.

Almost every historian of the early period of the Arabic press is indebted to the work of Filip de Tarrazi,[23] and for Egypt to Martin Hartmann[24] and Ibrahim 'Abduh,[25] which, while none are complete, are indispensable references. More recently, the website *Jara'id*, a listing of nineteenth-century Arabic periodicals, has proved an invaluable addition in establishing a more accurate catalogue of the press.[26] Discursive studies of the press in the Middle East are numerous but often quite limited in focus. In English the work of Ami Ayalon still stands out as the only broad and scholarly survey of the origins and development of the Arab press in the Middle East (although not the Maghrib). In his examination of the period from the beginning of the nineteenth century until the end of World War II, Ayalon situates the press in its historical context, providing a general view of relations between the state and private publishers, and dealing with practical issues of periodical production.[27]

Beyond this a great number of studies have addressed more specific themes. The majority, particularly the Arabic-language literature, have been framed regularly in terms of the development of the press within a national narrative. Studies on the press of Egypt,[28] Iraq,[29] Saudi Arabia,[30] the Gulf States,[31] Syria and Lebanon,[32] and Palestine,[33] as well as the Maghrib,[34] Yemen[35] and Iran,[36] trace the history of the press in conjunction with a process of the construction of national identity and intellectual maturation often in the context of the struggle for independence. Some works have taken a more specific focus and scrutinised the relationship between the press and key issues such as the national movement or national question,[37] critical events in the national narrative,[38] or in relation to the rise of Zionism.[39] Others have employed domestic political currents as a point of reference, whether mainstream nationalist parties like the Wafd,[40] or oppositional movements of the leftist[41] or Islamist press, to present a sub-theme within the national struggle.[42] Individual mainstream newspapers, both celebrated and less well-known titles,[43] or different press genres such as cultural reviews,[44] satirical works[45] and illustrated magazines,[46] have in turn proved fruitful avenues of research.

The specialisation of the press allowed for the development of specific audiences and a forum for the articulation of particular issues. Studies of the women's press, whether produced by women and/or for women, have established themselves as a prominent theme in feminist scholarship. Ijlal Khalifa's pioneering work during the 1960s on the feminist press in Egypt[47] was not immediately followed up but when scholars, for the most part working in the West in the 1990s, began to examine the stirrings of the feminist movement in Egypt at the end of the nineteenth century in detail the women's press was an obvious place to turn.[48] Other studies have appeared since exploring the theme of the expression of the female voice in the press, or the representation of women in the mainstream press.[49] Community newspapers, or those with a communal focus, have been a fertile avenue of enquiry for exploring the often tense and conflicting points of orientation between religious and national identity. Studies of the Jewish press, perhaps more than any other category, have engaged with the tension between community and nation, particularly with the rise of Zionism, in articulating that identity.[50]

The multilingual dimension of the press in the Middle East and North Africa has been well recognised in the literature even if this has been engaged most often by addressing individual language categories rather than by an integrated study of the nature of this diversity.[51] As indicated above, studies of the Arabic press have proliferated in recent decades. From studies of the foreign-language press, the French-language press, which enjoyed the widest circulation across the region and particularly so in the Maghrib, has been foremost,[52] while works on the Italian-language press have tended to be limited by their focus on the local community or the interests of the Italian state.[53] Similarly the Greek-language press, largely overlooked by non-Greek historians, has been routinely celebrated by scholars of Hellenism but often without broader terms of reference.[54] The Jewish press has, by contrast, been given a fuller consideration of context,[55] but the multilingual character of the Middle Eastern press per se has been little the subject of any specific study.[56]

The journalist has featured much less as a subject of academic literature and more often in the self-authored works of the individual journalist or newspaper editor.[57] More commonly, the memoirs of political activists who worked as journalists in pursuit of their political programme have provided valuable material even if these are routinely dominated by political and personal agendas.[58] However, academic studies on the role of political journalists such as the Constitutional Liberal, Muhammad Husayn Haykal, and Muhammad Hasanayn Haykal, confidant of Nasser, have shown the possibilities that such an approach offers.[59]

Guiding Questions and Themes

Scholarly research has developed and integrated the history of the press into a political and cultural history around three axes: the press as a vector of history, as an agent of history and as a source that allows an understanding of the transformation of societies. The circulation of regular published texts became a vital element in the constitution of a public sphere in Middle Eastern societies from the late nineteenth century through the gathering of 'public' communities in time as well as in space via the interaction with readers and their experiences of open debates. While the Habermasian conception of the 'public sphere of society' proposed the emergence of a hegemonic bourgeois public,[60] and Benedict Anderson put forward the phenomenon of common text consumption supported by print capitalism as the foundation of what he called 'imagined' national communities,[61] more recent conceptions of the public sphere have moved away from the construction of a hegemonic mainstream to a more complex model of overlapping, intersecting and competing publics.[62]

The press was a crucial site for the proposal and dissemination of these new agendas. Processes of dialogue and discourse entailed ideas which eventually culminated in political platforms, ideologies and national or subaltern awareness. New identities took shape in the heat of a time of huge change with the protest against colonial powers and the development of nation states. Competing counter-publics or subaltern perspectives sought to challenge or complement mainstream conceptions of the public. The emergence of a women's press serves as a prime example. Publications dealing with women's issues appeared during the Tanzimat period but a women's press only appeared in Egypt in the 1890s, promoting new images of women in society, from conservative to liberal voices, and discussing a broad range of issues such as gender roles, feminism and political rights.[63] By the early twentieth century female activists such as Malak Hifni Nasif in Egypt could participate much more easily in debates mediated by print than ever before. Other subaltern voices would establish their own press: labour and political movements, and religious and community associations.

The periodicity of newspapers created a special kind of relationship between readers and publication. Unlike other printed forms, the newspaper is both fixed and changing. Its features, such as its title, format of text and serialisation of material, have served both to distinguish and to establish a continuity between its separate issues.[64] The relationship thus established between and among senders and receivers of ideas and information, as well as the mechanisms of reception and the perception of media forms, are an important dimension to this dynamic. In this equation the public was neither homogenous nor passive.

The press in the Middle East therefore offers a great diversity of research themes, some already well established in studies of political history but others relatively new, such as the phenomenon of the local, community and oppositional press, the construction and contest between social norms and cultural trends and the character of journalism. The contributions in this volume speak to a number of these overarching concerns and themes that recognise that the press, far from being restricted to the narrowly defined political field, extends to a wide spectrum of representation that engaged with issues of cultural values, community identity, gender roles and social status and has served as a forum for the exchange, contest and consolidation of ideas.

Fundamental to an understanding of political history and its representation, the press has played a seminal role in the construction and transformation of culture. As a regular source of public information it allowed new urban populations to find their way in metropolitan spaces, to participate in social life and to equip themselves with a memory of events. From the end of the nineteenth century, the logic of an emerging industrial culture increasingly provided tools that established or consolidated cultural practices and collective imaginations in Middle Eastern societies. Such a critical role calls for an examination of how the press constituted a relatively autonomous sphere and favoured the emergence of norms and representation of 'society', and yet also provided a forum for those norms.

In this process, the press was not only a vehicle for the representations emerging from these debates but also an actor in expressing national interests and aspirations (Karagöz-Kızılca, Booth, Kabha, Lawson), community voices (Bashkin, Slim) and non-elite networks (Gorman, Monciaud).

Despite or because of the broad social and cultural spectrum within which it operated, the relationship of the press with state authority remains a critical theme. State strategies of surveillance, censorship, suppression and other forms of harassment were regularly adopted to deal with unwelcome criticism. As the studies here show, the state adopted a variety of postures towards the press, from its use as a tool to justify government policy (El Houssi) to a repressive attitude towards those critical, dissident voices that sought, or were perceived to have sought, to undermine its legitimacy (Moreau, Gorman, Monciaud) or ultimately be coopted by it (Ezzerelli). Its practitioners have been variously fined, imprisoned, deported and rewarded for their efforts.

Language serves as a fundamental element of political and cultural representation. Collectively the volume engages with a number of press languages, including those of the majority population of the region (even if underrepresented among the literate public), namely Ottoman Turkish and Arabic, as well as Greek, Italian, English and French, which were published by local resident communities or operated as a function of imperial influence. In some contexts Ottoman Turkish (Karagöz-Kızılca) and Arabic (Booth, Kabha) was the language of emerging national publics in response to colonial interests and foreign pressures. The ways in which different languages were employed suggest a much greater complexity of politics and culture than a simple indigenous–foreign dichotomy. Italian, French and Greek could be the language of anti-state, anti-capitalist internationalist discourse (Gorman), English the language of local nationalism (Lawson), Italian of politically opposed interests (El Houssi); Arabic a language of labour affirmation (Monciaud), of community and diaspora (Slim), community and nation (Bashkin) or of political compromise (Ezzerelli).

Never wholly separate from political currents, social attitudes or cultural values, the emergence of the professional journalist represented a process of maturation that brought influence, social status and a relative autonomy to its best practitioners. In the studies presented diverse profiles of newspaper men are featured, from the committed activists of the earlier period – the commentariat of the Young Ottomans (Karagöz-Kızılca) – to political agents (Moreau), dissident labour militants (Gorman, Monciaud) and aspiring public intellectuals (Ezzerelli). In time and with greater specialisation, journalism came to recruit from a broader spectrum from middle-class men of letters (Bashkin) to political and economic commentators (Lawson, Slim) and journalistic dynasties (Kabha) who became more securely established as members of a recognised profession, or more specialised, as feature writers, reporters, cartoonists with their work regarded increasingly as a familiar literary genre (Temimi).

Structure of this Volume

In their examination of political, social and cultural life in the Middle East and North Africa in the period 1850–1950 each of the case studies engages in different and critical ways with the above-mentioned themes, with individual chapters grouped together in four sections according to more specific concerns.

Part I The Press as National Voice

Part I engages with the articulation of a national voice in the press during times of volatility and transformation and the context of national crises: the financial difficulties of the Ottoman Empire in the third quarter of the nineteenth century; the perceived national, social and moral crisis in *fin-de-siècle*

Egypt, and the political conflict in Palestine during the crucial interwar period.

Gül Karagöz-Kızılca's 'News Publishing as a Reflection of Public Opinion: The Idea of News during the Ottoman Financial Crises' examines the financial crises of the Ottoman Empire and how through press representations, social, political and economic reformists advocated for a 'public' that would unify fragmented and multiple actors to improve Ottoman society. Within this emerging structure, the Ottoman press, which was still in its early stages of development, was used to establish a new political and social order. This chapter analyses how dissident newspapers published in Istanbul, namely *Tasvir-i Efkar*, *İbret*, *Hadika* and *İstikbal*, significantly influenced the establishment of a politically and economically engaged public. In conceptualising newspaper representations of the economic crises as an outcome of conflicting interests, it resituates the tension existing not only between state and society but also among varied interests. By scrutinising how interpretations of the financial crises competed, coexisted and were utilised to promote certain interests, it reveals how newspapers provided an arena of contestation for diverse groups and individuals.

In 'Disruptions of the Local, Eruptions of the Feminine: Local Reportage and National Anxieties in Egypt's 1890s', Marilyn Booth demonstrates that inscriptions of female images in Cairo's late nineteenth-century nationalist press were part of a discursive economy shaping debates on how gender roles and gendered expectations should shift as Egyptians struggled for independence. The chapter investigates content and placement of 'news from the street' in *al-Mu'ayyad* in the 1890s. On the relatively new newspaper scene, these terse local reports – equivalent to *faits divers* in the French press – contributed to the construction of an ideal national political trajectory. While representations of women serve as the primary example, the *faits divers* genre itself shapes a politics of newspaper intervention on the national scene. An emerging advocacy role of newspaper correspondents makes the newspaper a mediator in the construction of activist reader-citizens. As portrayed in the pages of *al-Mu'ayyad*, female subjects in the public sphere are a disruptive force (adult female) and a cherished national commodity (schoolgirl). Such images surface not only through front-page news stories and editorials but also through *hawadith*, dedicated columns and announcements of institutional progress.

In 'The Arabic Palestinian Press between the Two World Wars' Mustafa Kabha discusses the development of the Arabic press during the years 1929–39. This period saw the emergence of the Palestinian national movement as it crystallised into an entity in its struggle with the Zionist movement and the British mandatory administration to prevent the fulfilment of the programme for a Jewish national home, and sought to convince Britain to grant independence or some measure of autonomous rule to Palestinian Arabs, as it had done in Iraq and Egypt. The press played a critical role in this process, from its beginnings in the mid-1920s through a period of growing strength following the events of 1929 which peaked during the Great Strike of April–October 1936. In its examination of the development of the Palestinian national movement and its cultural and social characteristics, the chapter addresses the background of the growth of the press, the reading public, the operating political forces and the extent of press influence in the shaping of public opinion in Palestinian society.

In '*Falastin*: An Experiment in Promoting Palestinian Nationalism through the English-Language Press', Fred H. Lawson offers a focused study on the Jaffa-based daily *Filastin*, arguably the most influential Palestinian newspaper of the 1920s and 1930s, published in Arabic by 'Isa al-'Isa and edited by Yusuf Hanna. In 1925, an English-language edition, *Falastin*, was launched initially consisting entirely of denunciations of Zionist activities and appeals to the British authorities for redress with little news reporting. As time passed, however, both its tone and content changed in significant ways. News reports displaced blanket condemnations on the front pages, while complaints to the authorities gave way to stories that offered reasons for the mandatory government to take action. Such shifts reflected not only the growing journalistic professionalism of the staff of *Falastin* but also a transformation in the attitude of Palestinian nationalists towards both the British and the broader international community. As it became clear that British officials and public alike would have to be persuaded to recognise Arab grievances, *Falastin* adopted a more argumentative, and less bombastic, style and became more precise and detailed in its reporting by providing accounts that could be documented and verified. Surveying the evolution of the English-language edition of *Falastin* enables one to trace crucial trends in the discursive strategies whereby literate Palestinians engaged with actual and potential adversaries during the formative phase of the Arab–Israeli conflict.

Part II The Rise of the Journalist

Part II focuses on the practitioners of journalism. The early press attracted political and social activists, amateurs and community workers. Over time as newspapers became more established as a literary form, the status of the journalist as a professional became more recognised and secure.

In her chapter 'Press Propaganda and Subaltern Agents of Pan-Islamic Networks in the Muslim Mediterranean World prior to World War I', Odile Moreau explores movement and circulation across the Mediterranean and seeks to contribute to a history of proto-nationalism in the Maghrib and the Middle East at a particular moment prior to World War I. Her discussion is particularly concerned with the interface of two Mediterranean spaces: the Middle East (Egypt, Ottoman Empire) and North Africa (Morocco), where the latter is viewed as a case study where resistance movements sought external allies as a way of compensating for their internal weakness. Applying methods developed by Subaltern Studies, and linking macro-historical approaches, namely of a translocal movement in the Muslim Mediterranean with an actor-centred perspective, she explores how the Egypt-based society, al-Ittihad al-Maghribi, used the press as an instrument for political propaganda, promoting its Pan-Islamic programme and its goal of uniting North Africa. An active agent of this society, Aref Taher, a former Turkish officer and head of the Turkish Military Mission in Morocco in 1909–10, served as newspaper correspondent to the Egyptian *al-Mu'ayyad*, which published a series of articles vehemently attacking French intervention in Morocco.

In his chapter 'The Publicist and His Newspaper in Syria in the Era of the Young Turk Revolution, between Reformist Commitment and Political Pressures: Muhammad Kurd 'Ali and *al-Muqtabas* (1908–17)' Kaïs Ezzerelli examines the career of Muhammad Kurd 'Ali (1876–1953) and his daily newspaper *al-Muqtabas*, founded in Damascus in December 1908 following the Young Turk Revolution. Close to the Syrian reformists, who comprised his readers and editorial team, Kurd 'Ali contrived to make *al-Muqtabas* one of the most widely read and influential Arabic dailies in the region. During World War I Kurd 'Ali and his newspaper faced the dilemma: either to be condemned by or to participate in Ottoman propaganda. Based on a close reading of *al-Muqtabas*, public archives and contemporary testimonies related to this family enterprise, this chapter focuses on the relationships between Kurd 'Ali and his newspaper, his readers and collaborators, as well as his ties with the political powers of that time.

In 'From Intellectual to Professional: The Move from "Contributor" to "Journalist" at *Ruz al-Yusuf* in the 1920s and 1930s', Sonia Temimi examines the prosopography of those who 'made' *Ruz al-Yusuf*, an Egyptian weekly magazine founded by the actress Fatima al-Yusuf in 1925. It addresses two specific issues: first, the presentation of an intellectual milieu through an examination of the authors who contributed to *Ruz al-Yusuf* from 1925 to 1937. Among these were 'Abbas Mahmud al-'Aqqad, an intellectual with multiple interests, and Muhammad al-Tabi'i, a clerk who developed into a gifted editor and journalist. A detailed study of their biographies and lived histories reveals generational similarities rooted in a particular political context and demonstrates how journalism was in the process of being defined by the aspirations, personal histories and aims of its practitioners. The second theme concerns the professionalisation of journalism and explores whether professional journalism necessarily means the development of a 'news press' following the Anglo-Saxon model or the French 'opinion press' model. *Ruz al-Yusuf*, a satirical magazine that fits more easily within the second category, is a good example to illustrate how searching for 'scoops' became so important that it affected professional journalistic practices.

Part III Critical, Dissident Voices

Part III focuses on a number of critical, non-elite voices in the press: the anarchists in Egypt before World War I who projected a new radical and internationalist vision of society; the fascist and antifascist forces in Tunisia in the 1930s that held forth in the debate over Italian imperial policy in North Africa during the Abyssinian war; and the emergence of a genuine voice in the labour movement in Egypt in the 1940s which sought to project a place for workers in a national framework.

In his chapter 'The Anarchist Press in Egypt before World War I', Anthony Gorman traces the development of the radical secular press from its first brief emergence in the 1870s until the outbreak of World War I.

First active in the 1860s, the anarchist movement gradually expanded its membership and influence over subsequent decades to articulate a general social emancipation and syndicalism for all workers in Egypt. In the decade and a half before 1914, its press collectively propagated a critique of state power and capitalism, called for social justice and the organisation of labour, and promoted the values of science and public education in both a local context and as part of an international movement. In seeking to promote a programme at odds with both nationalism and colonial rule, it incurred the hostility of the authorities in addition to facing the practical problems of managing and financing an oppositional newspaper.

In her chapter 'The Ethiopian War as Portrayed in the Italian Fascist and Antifascist Press in Tunisia', Leila El Houssi interrogates the confrontation between fascist and antifascist elements within the Italian community in French Tunisia through an analysis of the attitude of the local Italian-language press to the 'Ethiopian Question'. Through the daily newspaper *L'Unione* and the weekly *L'Alba*, Italian fascist propaganda focused its efforts on downplaying the impact of the 'notorious' Laval–Mussolini agreements of January 1935 and cast the conquest of Ethiopia as a prelude to more important conquests, even of Tunisia itself. It was challenged by the open condemnation of an antifascist front (anarchists, republicans, communists and Gustizia e Libertà) in Tunisia who, in the pages of the weekly magazine *Domani* and the clandestine newspaper *Il Liberatore*, accused the regime of being interested more in the profits of industrial capitalism than in the interests of Italian citizens resident in the country.

In his chapter 'A Voice from below in the 1940s Egyptian Press: The Experience of the Workers' Newspaper *Shubra*', Didier Monciaud examines the emergence of a labour newspaper in the context of the industrial struggles of the 1930s and 1940s in the Cairo suburb of Shubra-al-Khayma, a stronghold of the textile sector and scene of a dynamic workers' movement. The fight for official recognition and better economic conditions was only part of the workers' struggle. From April 1942 until January 1943 the General Union of Mechanical Textile Workers of Shubra al-Khayma (GUMTWSK) produced a weekly, *Shubra*, one of the few papers in Egypt managed and edited by trade unionists and aimed specifically at an audience of workers. This chapter examines the workers' voice expressed in the ideas, values and conceptions of labour, discussing the launch and management of the newspaper before dealing with its content, focusing on specific issues such as textile labour in Egypt, union matters, 'labour culture' and conceptions of the national struggle.

Part IV The Press as Community Voice

Part IV addresses the relationship between press, community and culture by examining two particular cases, the Iraqi Jewish community in Baghdad and the Orthodox community of Lebanon, during the decade of the 1920s. Within the framework of two different mandatory regimes, British and French respectively, each provides a fascinating example of how religious communities sought to maintain their identity and yet engage with expanding horizons in the post-Ottoman context during a time of great political change.

In 'The Lamp, Qasim Amin, Jewish Women and Baghdadi Men: A Reading in the Jewish Iraqi Journal *Al-Misbah*', Orit Bashkin provides a detailed reading of a Jewish Iraqi publication which appeared in Baghdad between the years 1924 and 1929 and has been characterised both as a Zionist mouthpiece and a testimony to the success of Arab nationalism. In seeking to resolve this apparent contradiction, the chapter examines the issues which dominated *al-Misbah*'s pages in order to highlight the identity of the paper and to enrich our understanding of the nature of the Iraqi press under the British Mandate. The chapter addresses two discursive circles – the Iraqi and the Jewish – and proposes that *al-Misbah* conveyed an unmistakable Iraqi and Arab identity. Despite the editor's Zionist inclinations, the conversations between readers and writers acquired a life of their own and the paper, in fact, promoted a new Arab Jewish identity. The themes discussed by *al-Misbah*, moreover, illustrate how Jews sought to use the state's institutions established under the Mandate as venues for the cultivation of non-sectarian and democratic citizenship.

In her chapter 'From a Privileged Community to a Minority Community: The Orthodox Community of Beirut through the Newspaper *Al-Hadiyya*', Souad Slim examines *al-Hadiyya*, the newspaper relaunched in 1921 in a dramatically different political context following the collapse of the Ottoman Empire and the installation of the French Mandate. Earlier Orthodox newspapers published by the diocese of Beirut and its community had been primarily religious and cultural in orientation. *Al-Hadiyya* took on a much more ambitious approach. Through an analysis of its leading articles, the chapter explores the political questions and the sociopolitical problems of the time, examining the astonishing range of topics covered, among them the issue of minorities, the participation of emigrants in political life, population transfers, foreign influence and the shock of the Bolshevik Revolution. Vital economic subjects were also tackled, from the Lebanese state budget to issues of the world economy.

Pressing Ahead

The period before 1950 was one of great vitality, of internal debates around identity and external struggles for liberation in the political, social and cultural life of the Ottoman Empire and the post-Ottoman Arab world. The contributions offered here provide fascinating studies of the press both as an object and an actor that engaged with a great diversity of these themes. During a time of challenge and transformation with colonial domination and different types of contest, whether political or social, different voices in the press emerged and were key tools of expression and critical producers of representation that Middle Eastern societies were producing of themselves and for themselves. In this way the press is an important window into the processes and debates surrounding political, social and cultural issues.

In the period after independence a different configuration of interests increasingly bound to the idiom of the national project saw the press become a more restricted and constrained field of expression, increasingly an organ of control, uniformity and passivity, often beholden to authoritarian rulers or subject to the compromises of state ownership. Only in recent years has this often stagnant picture of the press been challenged first by the rise of satellite television and then more recently with an online press and social media.

Notes

1. It is estimated that between 1800 and 1900 around 850–900 Arabic periodical titles were published globally (thanks to Adam Mestyan for this information and for his comments on an earlier draft of this chapter).
2. The editors would particularly like to thank Mustafa Kabha for his later con-

tribution to the volume, and Graeme Barul for his role in the translation of a number of chapters.
3. Abu al-Futuh Radwan, *Tarikh matba'at bulaq al-amiriyya* (Cairo: al-Matba'a al-amiriyya, 1953).
4. Adnan A. Musallam, 'Arab Press, Society and Politics at the End of the Ottoman Era (1799–1918)', *Al-Liqa' Journal* 25 (2005), available at <http://bethlehem-holy-land.net/Adnan/publications/EndofTheOttomanEra.htm> (last accessed 20 June 2017).
5. See Philip C. Sadgrove (ed.), *The History of Printing in the Languages and Countries of the Middle East* (Oxford: Oxford University Press, 2005); Geoffrey Roper (ed.), *Historical Aspects of Printing and Publishing in Languages of the Middle East* (Leiden: Brill, 2013).
6. Juan R. I. Cole, 'Printing and Urban Islam in the Mediterranean World 1890–1920', in Leila Tarazi Fawaz and C. A. Bayly (eds), *Modernity and Culture: From the Mediterranean to the Indian Ocean* (New York: Columbia University Press, 2002), pp. 344–64; p. 350.
7. Kemal H. Karpat, *The Politicization of Islam: Reconstructing Identity, State, Faith and Community in the Late Ottoman State* (New York: Oxford University Press, 2001), pp. 101–3.
8. Ibid., p. 134; Cole, 'Printing and Urban Islam', pp. 349–50.
9. Ami Ayalon, *Reading Palestine Printing and Literacy, 1900–1948* (Austin: University of Texas Press, 2004).
10. Donald J. Cioeta, 'Ottoman Censorship in Lebanon and Syria, 1876–1908', *International Journal of Middle East Studies* 10:2 (1979), pp. 167–86; Ipek K. Yosmaoğlu, 'Chasing the Printed Word: Press Censorship in the Ottoman Empire, 1876–1913', *Turkish Studies Association Journal* 27:1/2 (2003), pp. 15–49.
11. Ami Ayalon, *The Press in the Arab Middle East: A History* (New York: Oxford University Press, 1995), p. 260 n. 25. This was true of the constitutions of Lebanon (1926) and Syria (1930), as well as the Organic Law of Jordan (1928).
12. Anthony Gorman, 'Containing Political Dissent in Egypt before 1952', in L. Khalili and J. Schwedler (eds), *Policing Prisons and in the Middle East* (London: Hurst, 2010), pp. 157–73; p. 168.
13. Palestine Royal Commission [The Peel Commission], *Report*, 1937, p. 132; Ayalon, *Press in the Arab Middle East*, p. 100.
14. Orit Bashkin, *The Other Iraq: Pluralism and Culture in Hashemite Iraqi* (Stanford: Stanford University Press, 2009), p. 107.

15. Ebru Boyar, 'The Press and the Palace: The Two-Way Relationship between Abdülhamit II and the Press, 1876–1908', *Bulletin of the School of Oriental and African Studies* 69:3 (2006), pp. 417–32.
16. J.-J. Luthi, *Lire la presse d'expression francophone en Égypte (1798–2008)* (Paris: L'Harmattan, 2009); Gilles Kraemer, *La presse francophone en Méditerranée* (Paris: Maisonneuve et Larose, 2001); Baida Jamaâ, *La presse marocaine d'expression française, des origines à 1956* (Rabat: Faculté des Lettres et des Sciences Humaines de Rabat, 1996); Gérard Groc and İbrahim Çağlar, *La presse française de Turquie de 1795 à nos jours: histoire et catalogue* (Istanbul: Isis/IFEA, 1985).
17. One noteworthy case was *O Dodekanisos* published in Cairo during the 1930s, which regularly carried articles in four languages in each issue (Greek, Arabic, English and French).
18. Two such examples in Egypt are *Al-Ahram/Les Pyramides* (Arabic/French) (1899–1914, Cairo) and *Filistin/Falastin* (Arabic/English, Jaffa) (see Chapter 4).
19. See Dyala Hamzah (ed.), *The Making of the Arab Intellectual: Empire, Public Sphere and the Colonial Coordinates of Selfhood* (London: Routledge, 2013).
20. Donald M. Reid, 'The Rise of Professions and Professional Organizations in Modern Egypt', *Comparative Studies in Society and History* 16:1 (1974), pp. 48–51.
21. For the following, see Ayalon, *Press in the Arab Middle East*, pp. 228–30.
22. Arthur Goldschmidt, *Biographical Dictionary of Modern Egypt*, s.v. Azmi, Mahmud; J. J. G. Jansen, 'Ibrahim Abduh. (b. 1913), His Autobiographies and His Polemical Writings', *Bibliotheca Orientalis* 37 (1980), pp. 128–32.
23. Filip de Tarrazi, *Tarikh al-sihafa al-'arabiyya*, 4 vols (Beirut: Matba'at al-adabiyya, 1913–33).
24. Martin Hartmann, *The Arabic Press of Egypt* (London: Luzac, 1899).
25. Among a number of press studies, Ibrahim 'Abduh's most enduring work is probably *Tatawwur al-sihafa al-misriyya, 1798–1981*, 4th edn (Cairo: Mu'assasat sijill al-'arab, 1982).
26. '*Jara'id*, A Chronology of Nineteenth-Century Periodicals in Arabic (1800–1900)', Leibniz-Zentrum Moderner Orient, available at <https://www.zmo.de/jaraid/HTML/index.html> (last accessed 31 May 2017).
27. Ayalon, *Press in the Arab Middle East*. Ayalon has in fact published extensively on different aspects of the press and reading, most recently, *The Arabic Print Revolution: Cultural Production and Mass Readership* (Cambridge: Cambridge

University Press, 2016). Another overview on a much smaller scale but broader geographical scope is B. Lewis et al., s.v. Djarida, in P. Bearman, Th. Bianquis, C. E. Bosworth, E. van Donzel and W. P. Heinrichs (eds), *Encyclopaedia of Islam, Second Edition*, 1960–2007, online, Brill.

28. Sulayman Salih, *al-Shaykh 'Ali Yusuf wa-jaridat al-Mu'ayyad: Tarikh al-haraka al-wataniyya fi rub' qarn* (Cairo: al-Hay'a al-'amma lil-kitab, 1990); Najwa Kamil, 'Al-Sihafa al-wafdiyya 1919–1952', in Gamal Badawi and Lam'i al-Muti'i (eds), *Tarikh al-Wafd* (Cairo: Dar al-Shuruq, 2003).

29. 'Abd al-Razzaq Hasani, *Tarikh al-sihafa al-'iraqiyya* (Baghdad: Matba'at al-zahra', 1957); Fa'iq Butti, *Sihafat al-'iraq: tarikhuha wa-kifah ajyaliha* (Baghdad: Matba'at al-adib al-baghdadiyya, 1968).

30. 'Uthman Hafiz, *Tatawwur al-sihafa fi al-mamlaka al-'arabiyya al-sa'udiyya* (Jedda: Sharikat al-madina lil-tiba'a wa'l-nashr, 1976); Muhammad 'Abd al-Rahman al-Shamikh, *Nasha'at al-sihafa fi al-mamlaka al-'arabiyya al-sa'udiyya* (Riyadh: Dar al-'ulum, 1981).

31. Hilal al-Shayiji, *Al-sihafa fi al-kuwayt wa'l-bahrayn mundhu nash'atiha hatta 'ahd al-istiqlal* (Al-Manama: Matba'at banurama al-khalij, 1989); Muhammad Hasan 'Abdallah, *Sihafat al-kuwayt: ru'yah 'amma bayna al-dawafi' wa-al-nata'ij* (Kuwait: Majallat dirasat al-khalij wa-al-jazirah al-'arabiyya, 1985).

32. Ihsan 'Askar, *Nash'at al-sihafa al-suriyya. 'Ard li'l-qawmiyya fi taur al-nash'a min al-'ahd al-'uthmani hatta qiyam al-dawla al-'arabiyya* (Cairo: Dar al-nahda al-'arabiyya, 1972); Ihsan 'Askar, *Al-Sihafa al-'arabiyya fi filastin, al-urdun, suriyya wa-lubnan* (Cairo: Mu'assasat sijill al-'arab, 1982); Yusuf As'ad Daghir, *Qamus al-sihafa al-lubnaniyya, 1858–1974* (Beirut: Al-Maktaba al-sharqiyya, 1978); Juzif Ilyas, *Tatawwur al-sihafa al-suriyya fi mi'at 'am (1865–1965)*, 2 vols (Beirut: Dar al-nidal, 1982–3); Mihyar 'Adnan al-Malluhi, *Mu'jam al-jara'id al-suriyya 1865–1965* (Damascus: al-Ula lil-nashr wa'l-tawsi', 2002); Shams al-Din al-Rifa'i, *Tarikh al-sihafa al-suriyya* (Cairo: Dar al-ma'arif, 1969); Nadine Méouchy, 'La presse de Syrie et du Liban entre les deux guerres (1918–1939)', in Anne-Laure Dupont and Catherine Mayeur-Jaouen (eds), *Débats intellectuels au Moyen-Orient dans l'entre-deux-guerres. Revue des mondes musulmans et de la Méditerranée* 95–8 (2002), pp. 55–70.

33. Muhammad Sulayman, *Tarikh al-sihafa al-filastiniyya 1876–1918* (Nicosia: Mu'assasat Bisan, 1987); Mustafa Kabha, *The Palestinian Press as Shaper of Public Opinion 1929–1939: Writing Up a Storm* (London and Portland, OR: Vallentine Mitchell, 2007); Mustafa Kabha, *Tahta 'ayn al-raqib: al-sihafa al-filastiniyya wa-dawruha fi al-kifah al-watani bayna al-harbayn al-'alamiyyatayn*

(Bayt Birl: Markaz dirasat al-adab al-'arabi, 2004); 'Ayida Najjar, *Sihafat filastin wa-al-haraka al-wataniyya fi nisf qarn, 1900–1948* (Beirut: al-Mu'assasa al-'arabiyya lil-dirasat wa al-nashr, 2005); R. Michael Bracy, *Printing Class: 'Isa al-'Isa, Filastin, and the Textual Construction of National Identity, 1911–1931* (Lanham, MD and Plymouth: University Press of America, 2011).

34. Amina Aouchar, *La presse marocaine dans la lutte pour l'indépendance (1933–1956)* (Casablanca: Walladas, 1990); 'Awatif 'Abd al-Rahman, *al-Ṣiḥāfa al-'arabiyya fi al-jaza'ir: dirasa tahliliyya li-sihafat al-thawra al-jaza'iriyya, 1954–1962* (Algiers: al-Mu'assasa al-wataniyya lil-kitab, 1985); Zahir Ihaddaden, *Histoire de la presse indigène en Algérie: des origines jusqu'en 1930* (Algiers: ENAL, c. 1983); al-Zubayr Sayf al-Islam, *Tarikh al-sihafa fi al-jaza'ir* (Algiers: al-Sharika al-wataniyya lil-nashr wa-al-tawzi', 1971).

35. Muhammad 'Abd al-Jabbar Sallam, *al-Sihafa al-yamaniyya fi al-manatiq al-janubiyya* (Sana'a: Markaz 'abbadi lil-dirasat wa al-nashr, 1997); 'Alawi 'Abdallah Tahir, *al-Sihafa al-yamaniyya qabla thawrat 26 sibtimbir 1962* (Kuwait: Majalat dirasat al-khalij wa al-jazira al-'arabiyya, 1985).

36. Camron Michael Amin, 'The Press and Public Diplomacy in Iran, 1820–1940', *Iranian Studies* 48:2 (2015), pp. 269–87; L. P. Elwell-Sutton, 'The Iranian Press, 1941–1947', *Iran* 6 (1968), pp. 65–104.

37. Latifa Muhammad Salim, *Al-Sihafa wa al-haraka al-wataniyya al-misriyya 1945–1952* (Cairo: al-Hay'a al-misriyya al-'amma lil-kitab, 1987); Suhayr Iskandar, *Mawqif al-sihafa al-misriyya min al-qadaya al-wataniyya 1946–1954*, 2 vols (Cairo: al-Hay'a al-misriyya al-'amma lil-kitab, 1992, 1996).

38. Ramzi Mikha'il, *al-Sihafa al-misriyya wa-thawrat 1919* (Cairo: al-Hay'a al-misriyya al-'amma lil- kitab, 1993).

39. 'Awatif 'Abd al-Rahman, *Al-Sihafa al'arabiyya fi muwajahat al-taba'iyya wa-al-ikhtiraq al-sahyuni* (Cairo: Dar al-fikr al-'arabi, 1996); Siham Nassar, *Mawaqif al-sihafa al-misriyya min al-sahyuniyya khilala al-fatra min 1897–1917* (Cairo: al-Hay'a al-misriyya al-'amma lil-kitab, 1993).

40. Najwa Kamil, *Al-Sihafa al-wafdiyya wa al-qadaya al-wataniyya 1919–1936* (Cairo: al-Hay'a al-misriyya al-'amma lil-kitab, 1996).

41. Rifa'at al-Sa'id, *Sihafat al-yasar al-misri 1925–1948* (Cairo: Maktabat Madbouli, 1977); Rifa'at al-Sa'id, *al-Sihafa al-yasariyya fi misr 1950–52* (Cairo: Dar al-thaqafa al-jadida, 1981); Fa'iq Butti, *al-Sihafa al-yasariyya fi al-'iraq: 1924–1985* (London: n.p., 1985).

42. Shu'ayb al-Ghabbashi, *Sihafa al-ikhwan al-muslimin, Dirasa fi al-nasha'a wa al-madmun* (Cairo: Dar al-tawzi' al-islami, 1999).

43. Ibrahim ʿAbduh, *Jarida al-Ahram, Tarikh misr fi khamas wa sabaʿin sana* (Cairo: Dar al-maʿarif, 1951); Suhayr Iskandar, *Jarida Al-Misri wa al-qadaya al-wataniyya 1936–1946* (Cairo: al-Hayʾa al-misriyya al-ʿamma lil-kitab, 1986).

44. Ahmad al-Maghazi, *Al-Sihafa al-fanniyya fi misr* (Cairo: al-Hayʾa al-misriyya al-ʿamma lil-kitab, 1978); ʿAli Shalash, *Al-Majallat al-adabiyya fi misr, tatawwuruha wa duruha* (Cairo: al-Hayʾa al-misriyya al-ʿamma lil-kitab, 1988).

45. See, for example, Jamil Juburi, *Nuri Thabit: Habazbuz fi tarikh sihafat al-hazl wa al-karikatur fi al-ʿiraq* (Baghdad: Dar al-shuʾun al-thaqafiyya al-ʿamma, 1986); Hamdan Khidr Salim, *Sihafat al-sukhriyya wa al-fukaha fi al-ʿiraq: 1909–1939* (Baghdad: Dar al-shuʾun al-thaqafiyya al-ʿamma, 2010); Eliane U. Ettmüller, *The Construct of Egypt's National Self in James Sanua's Early Satire & Caricature* (Berlin: Klaus Schwarz, 2012); Marilyn Booth, 'Insistent Localism in a Satiric World: Shaykh Naggar's "Reed-Pipe" in the 1890s Cairene Press', in H. Harder and B. Mittler (eds), *Asian Punches: A Transcultural Affair* (Berlin, Heidelberg: Springer-Verlag, 2013), pp. 187–218.

46. Marilyn Booth, 'What's in a Name? Branding *Punch* in Cairo, 1908', in Harder and Mittler (eds), *Asian Punches*, pp. 271–303; Palmira Brummett, *Image and Imperialism in the Ottoman Revolutionary Press, 1908–1911* (Albany, NY: State University of New York Press, 2000).

47. Ijlal Khalifa, 'al-Sihafa al-nisaʾiyya fi misr, 1919–1939' (MA thesis, Cairo University, 1966); Ijlal Khalifa, 'al-Sihafa al-nisaʾiyya fi misr 1940–1965' (PhD thesis, Cairo University, 1970).

48. Irène Fenoglio-Abd el Aal, *Défense et Illustration de l'Egyptienne: Aux débuts d'une expression féminine* (Cairo: CEDEJ, 1988); Beth Baron, *The Women's Awakening in Egypt: Culture, Society and the Press* (New Haven, CT: Yale University Press, 1994); Marilyn Booth, *May Her Likes Be Multiplied: Biography and Gender Politics in Egypt* (Berkeley: University of California Press, 2001); Margot Badran, *Feminists, Islam, and Nation: Gender and the Making of Modern Egypt* (Princeton, NJ: Princeton University Press, 1995); Marilyn Booth, '*Woman in Islam*: Men and the "Women's Press" in Turn-of-the-20th-Century Egypt', *International Journal of Middle East Studies* 33:2 (May 2001), pp. 171–201.

49. Dhiyab Fahd Taʾi, *Tarikh al-sihafa al-nisaʾiyya fi al-ʿiraq bayna 1923 wa 2011: dirasa tawthiqiyya shamila* (Damascus: Amal al-jadida lil-tibaʿa wa al-nashr waal-tawziʿ, 2013); on Iran, see Camron Michael Amin, Selling and Saving "Mother Iran": Gender and the Iranian Press in the 1940s', *International Journal of Middle East Studies* 33:3 (August 2001), pp. 335–61.

50. See, for example, ʿIsam Jumʿa Ahmad Maʿadidi, *al-Sihafa al-yahudiyya fi al-ʿiraq*

(Misr al-Jadida, Cairo: al-Dar al-dawliyya lil-istithmarat al-thaqafiyya, 2001); Muhammad ʿAbd al-Latif ʿAbd al-Karim, *al-Sihafa al-yahudiyya fi misr qabla 1948: jaridat Isra'il namudhajan* (Amman: Dar wa'il lil-nashr wa-al-tawziʿ, 2010).

51. Ayalon, *Press in the Arab Middle East*, as well as de Tarrazi, Hartmann and website *Jara'id* focus only on Arabic newspapers. Ibrahim ʿAbduh, *Tatawwur al-sihafa al-misriyya*, discusses both Arabic- and foreign-language press.

52. Groc and Çağlar, *La presse française de Turquie*; Jamaâ, *La presse marocaine d'expression française*; Kraemer, *La presse francophone en Méditerranée*; Luthi, *Lire la presse d'expression francophone en Égypte*. See also Rouchdi Fakkar, *L'influence française sur la formation de la presse littéraire en Égypte au xixe siècle: Aux origines des relations culturelles contemporaines entre la France et le monde arabe* (Paris: Geuthner, 1973).

53. Umberto Rizzitano, 'Un secolo di giornalismo italiano in Egitto (1845–1945)', *Cahiers d'histoire égyptienne* 8:2/3 (April 1956), pp. 129–54; Michele Brondino, *La stampa Italiana in Tunisia-Storia e società, 1838–1956* (Milan: Jaca, 1998); Alessandra Marchi, 'La presse d'expression italienne en Égypte. De 1845 à 1950', *Rivista dell'Istituto di Storia dell'Europa Mediterranea* 5 (December 2010), pp. 91–125.

54. For Egypt, see Evgenios Michailidis, *Panorama* (Alexandria, 1972), and for Istanbul, Stratis Tarinas, *O Ellinikos Tipos tis Polis* (Istanbul: Icho, 2007).

55. See, for example, Sarah Abrevaya Stein, *Making Jews Modern: The Yiddish and Ladino Press in the Russian and Ottoman Empires* (Bloomington and Indianapolis: Indiana University Press, 2004).

56. But see, for example, Anthony Gorman, 'Αιγυπτιώτης-Έλλην', *ΕΛΙΑ News* 58 (summer 2001), a study of the bilingual (Greek–Arabic) monthly *Αιγυπτιώτης-Έλλην–al-Yunani al-Mutamassir* (1932–40).

57. See, for example, Fatima al-Yusuf, *Dhikrayat* (Cairo: Ruz al-Yusuf, 1953); Salama Musa, *Al-Sihafa, hirfa wa risala* (Cairo: Salama Musa lil-nashr wa al-tawziʿ, 1963).

58. Muhammad Lutfi Jumʿa, *Shahid ʿala-l-ʿasr. Mudhakkirat Muhammad Lutfi Jumʿa* (Cairo: al-Hay'a al-misriyya al-ʿamma lil-kitab, 2000); Muhammad Kurd ʿAli, *al-Mudhakkirat* (Damascus: Matba at al-Taraqqi, 1948–51).

59. Muhammad Sayyid Muhammad, *Haykal wa al-Siyasa al-usbuʿiyya* (Cairo: al-Hay'a al-misriyya al-ʿamma lil-kitab, 1996); Jamal al-Shalabi, *Muhammad Hassanayn Haykal: istimrariyya amm tahawul?* (Beirut: al-mu'assasa al-ʿarabiyya lil-dirasat wa al-nashr, 1999). For an earlier period, see Eliezer Tauber, 'The

Press and the Journalist as a Vehicle in Spreading National Ideas in Syria in the Late Ottoman Period', *Die Welt des Islams* 30 (1990), pp. 163–77.
60. Jürgen Habermas, *The Structural Transformation of the Public Sphere: An Inquiry into a Category of Bourgeois Society* (Cambridge: Polity, [1962] 1989).
61. Benedict Anderson, *Imagined Communities: Reflections on the Origin and Spread of Nationalism* (London: Verso, 1991).
62. Seteney Shami (ed.), *Publics, Politics and Participation: Locating the Public Sphere in the Middle East and North Africa* (New York: Social Science Research Council, 2009), p. 32. In this volume, see particularly Michelle U. Campos, 'The "Voice of the People" [lisan al-sha'b]: The Press and the Public Sphere in Revolutionary Palestine', pp. 237–62, who contrasts the tension of the communal and the Ottoman imperial public of 1908 generated by the local press.
63. Baron, *Women's Awakening in Egypt*; Booth, *May Her Likes Be Multiplied*.
64. Maurice Mouillaud and Jean-François Tétu, *Le journal quotidien* (Lyon: Presses Universitaires de Lyon, 1989), pp. 102–3.

PART I
THE PRESS AS NATIONAL VOICE

1

News Publishing as a Reflection of Public Opinion: The Idea of News during the Ottoman Financial Crises

Gül Karagöz-Kızılca

The meaning and utilisation of news in Ottoman society beginning from 1862 and ending with the bankruptcy of the empire in 1875 is a fascinating object of political and social history. This chapter focuses on news reports and articles in the privately owned *Tasvir-i Efkar*, *İbret*, *Hadika* and *İstikbal* that dealt with deepening economic and financial problems since they claimed to reflect the diverse voices among Ottoman publics as well as being the dissident voices of their time.[1]

In the second half of the nineteenth century, one of the most favoured ways of criticising the policies of the central government (the Porte) was through the publication of editorial articles and news reports. While the state-owned *Takvim-i Vekayi* (est. 1831) published primarily imperial edicts and reports on the promotions and travels of high-ranking bureaucrats, these first private newspapers of the empire provided news reports on current events and subjects like public health, such as the spread of plague; urban affairs, such as police reports on burglaries and stabbings; fires in Istanbul; in addition to reports on war and social and political upheavals.[2] After 1862, when private newspapers were required to publish official announcements, newspaper editors frequently wrote their own comments below the announcements on the following day and did not hesitate to criticise the government.[3]

Private newspapers rather than official publications were instrumental in the development of journalism as a profession and critical news production. Mild and bitter critiques in news reports and articles came to define the parameters of political opposition to the financial policies of the Porte. In these initial critiques, journalists vocalised the demands and concerns of their publics on financial policy and the distribution of wealth in the empire. In this articulation of public problems and demands, the conceptualisation of news changed over time as the content and layout of the papers developed. In this process, I argue that the form and structure of periodical news and commentaries undermined the production of state information.[4] Private newspapers eroded the knowledge production of the state as the readers gained access to unofficial news reports written in accessible language. This erosion was partly shaped by the periodicity of the newspapers since readers now received continual news reports on their society from a private rather than state perspective.[5] The most important aspect of these reports, however, was the approach of journalists to news writing and the ways in which they distinguished information and commentary.

In the initial section of this chapter, I will analyse how discontent with Tanzimat policies, a modernisation programme of imperial reform, affected the news-making practices and reporting styles of journalists.[6] I will then discuss the ways in which the world view of certain Ottoman journalists influenced their approach to news and show how the reporting style and the interpretation of financial and economic news in nineteenth-century Ottoman newspapers reveals the tensions within society as well as between diverse groups and the Porte.

First, I will investigate the meaning of news for the editors of *Tasvir-i Efkar*, *İbret*, *Hadika* and *İstikbal*.[7] By focusing on their news-making style, I will show how the editors of these newspapers utilised an objective news-reporting style to provide up-to-date news for their readers. Furthermore, I will discuss the possible reasons for an impartial or biased news-making style when the editors decided to cover *newsworthy* financial and economic events, and how newspaper editors utilised dispatches and articles. In addition, I will discuss how these newspapers provided news reports for diverse parts of the society and hence sought a variety of readers rather than solely fulfilling the news expectations of Ottoman elites, as argued by both the conventional and revisionist Ottoman historiographies.⁸ In this way, I aim to take to task conventional Ottoman historiography that views the press as the voice of elites rather than the expression of diverse interests and seek to show how news on Ottoman finance and economy provided a new basis to challenge state policies.

News and Journalists

As Daniel Allen Berkowitz argues, understanding the nature of news is 'like viewing a hologram'.⁹ In his view, there are many perspectives that can reveal different aspects of the same holographic picture and no single 'vantage point where the entire hologram' can entirely be viewed.¹⁰ Therefore, he suggests that in order to understand news, one should view it 'as a human construction that gains its characteristics through the social world from which it emerges'.¹¹ In this way, when Ottoman journalists presented a picture of Ottoman society in their news reports and articles, they reflected their political background, social origins, education and interests. Therefore, in order to analyse the ways in which Ottoman journalists made and utilised news and to gain a better insight into the motivations of the newspaper editors, I will explore the social, economic and political environments in which the journalist selected, wrote and framed their news for the readership.

Ottoman Journalists and Discontent with the Tanzimat Reform

The first private newspapers of the empire were published in a period shaped by fiscal difficulties, continuing wars, and insurrections in diverse parts of the empire. From the time of the Crimean War of 1853–6, the Ottoman state reluctantly but increasingly became more dependent upon foreign loans. Between the year of the first loan in 1854 and the bankruptcy of the empire in 1875, the Porte would borrow the equivalent of over a billion dollars from European markets.¹² Its inability to finance growing expenditures that were partly caused and aggravated by its centralisation policies resulted in increasing tension among diverse groups of the society.

This tension mounted with international developments, the reflections of which were felt within Ottoman society. By contrast, in the second half of the nineteenth century, a period that coincided with the emergence and development of the Ottoman press, Europe generated favourable conditions for the circulation of goods, people and capital.[13] Financiers, investors and their intermediaries were able to direct their energies and capital to areas abundant with natural resources but lacking stable governance, advanced infrastructure and technology. With the destruction of the Janissaries in 1826,[14] and the signing of the Anglo-Ottoman Trade Convention in 1838, the Ottoman Empire assured European investors of access to lands with the expectation of high profits. Yet, within the Ottoman Empire, the annihilation of the Janissaries and signing of the treaty caused mostly unvoiced annoyance among Ottoman publics, as these two acts destroyed the social and economic protection of the masses and hence the social harmony of publics. The treaty forbade monopolies in Ottoman territory and lowered import tariffs on foreign goods, enabling foreign merchants to trade more freely throughout the empire. This further eroded the shattered positions of Ottoman merchants, guilds and manufacturers, already deprived of the social and economic protection of Janissaries.[15] The acceptance of such liberal economic policies by the Porte worked to the detriment of Ottoman citizens and deepened existing tensions across society. Consequently, various groups targeted the Great Powers and their policies in the Ottoman territories by blaming Europeans for supporting free trade in the empire, despite the fact that those liberal economic policies did not affect Ottoman publics simultaneously, nor with the same intensity.[16]

Political developments in the years between 1854 and 1875 did not help ease the exasperation felt among Ottoman citizens. On the contrary, the Crimean War, the civil war of Lebanon in 1860, the Cretan insurrections of 1866–9, and the French note of 1867 supported by England and the Austro-Hungarian Empire urging the Porte to apply a more active policy in hastening the reforms, resulted in greater irritation among the Ottoman publics towards Europeans. The involvement of European powers in Ottoman politics partly stemmed from the application of the Gülhane Rescript (*Hatt-ı Sharif* of Gülhane). When the Porte proclaimed this semi-constitutional charter in 1839, it promised equality between Christian and Muslim citizens. Yet the complexity of the process and hesitations of the Porte in establishing this promised equality created unforeseen problems. These included the growing interest of the European Great Powers in the protection of Christians and hence their involvement in Ottoman internal politics, claiming that the 'sick man of Europe' had neither the ability nor the intention to provide for the well-being of its Christian citizens.[17] Such involvement created discontent particularly among Muslims who were without access to European protection or benefit from the Capitulations. As these concessions extended into economic and fiscal domains, by engaging in global trade, banking institutions and tax farming, diverse groups increasingly sought to obtain and maintain personal wealth by acquiring such privileges.[18]

Furthermore, public discontent gained even greater impetus when, as part of the Tanzimat reform, the Rescript of Reform (*Islahat Fermanı*) was proclaimed by the Porte in 1856. Issued to reaffirm the provisions of the 1839 Rescript, its main purpose was to grant equality to non-Muslims. Yet, contrary to the Porte's anticipations and hopes, instead of relieving tensions, the proclamation intensified debates over the reforms since equality had limited grounds for implementation given the lack of institutions. In the long run, however, the notion of equality increased the economic power of non-Muslims in the empire and the discontent among the Muslim population.[19] Subsequently, the reform process increased dissatisfaction with the Porte. As the sectarian clashes of 1840 and 1860 in Mount Lebanon proved, the vast majority of the Ottoman publics demanded the implementation of promised reforms, while the elites of the empire wished to maintain their traditional privileges.[20] As the Porte was not sufficiently in control of overseeing the implementation of reforms, Ottoman commoners (*ahali*) were frustrated with the reform process.[21] Similarly, the elites of the empire increasingly felt dissatisfied with the Tanzimat reforms which heralded equality before the law among its ex-subjects and new citizens and threatened their financial and political privileges. Further, the Tanzimat promise to abolish the tax-farming system in the end transferred this significant wealth resource from the local elites to the new bureaucratic elites. As the Tanzimat reforms looked to transfer local power and wealth to the central bureaucracy and bureaucratic elites, unsurprisingly this created discontent among the 'waning' elites. In this vein, the vested interests of the elites and non-elites stood in conflict over their differing expectations of the reforms. Nevertheless, their discontent with the reforms was a common reason for opposing the Porte's policies.

Well aware of the disturbances that were created by the centralisation policies of the Porte and the irritation that stemmed from the activities of European investors and their intermediaries in the empire, some Ottoman journalists embraced an ambitious journalistic project with a set agenda, namely to attempt to give a voice to unvoiced parts of society, including peasants, farmers, small merchants, petty bureaucrats, workers, beggars and landlords.[22] In claiming to fill the position previously occupied by the Janissaries, these Ottoman journalists of private newspapers expressed their contemporary political concerns.[23] They wrote on the Eastern Question, the privileges of the Great Powers, and Ottoman citizens who sought European protection and worked against the general good of the Ottoman populace.[24] Balancing the criticisms and demands of conflicting parties in the pages of newspapers was a complicated task, especially considering the contested interests of many groups such as higher- and middle-ranking bureaucrats, local notables, as well as peasants and urban workers regarding the distribution of power and wealth.

As one of the most important issues revolved around the distribution of social affluence, Ottoman journalists inevitably focused on the fiscal problems of the empire. In engaging with the perceived concerns of the many disparate groups, these journalists criticised the Porte's economic and fiscal policies on issues such as tax collecting, external debts, industrialisation, and the political, economic and judicial concessions enjoyed by Europeans. Some penned articles showing their bitter resentment towards Great Power interference in the empire, which allowed many Ottoman residents to avoid taxes. In response, the editors of *İbret* promoted Ottoman merchants' interests against those of Europeans and non-Muslim traders. In one article, the editor criticised internal tariffs as being the main impediment to the development of an Ottoman entrepreneurial class.[25] By revealing the tension between producers such as farmers and non-producers like bankers, who did not pay taxes and unfairly consumed the economic and financial resources of society, these newspapers reflected the escalating discontent that stemmed from the insufficient and uneven implementation of the Tanzimat reforms that had promised equality among the Ottoman citizens.

News Production as a Reflection of the World Views of Journalists

When the editors of *Tasvir-i Efkar*, *İbret*, *Hadika* and *İstikbal* published articles on these economic issues, they not only considered, referenced and were affected by the political, international and social environments of the empire, but they also reflected the values of their own world views, their concerns regarding the place of the empire in its surroundings and in the European world, and the voices of the different parts of the society. For the newspaper editors, the foremost political and international concern of the empire was to resist what they saw as the process of its disintegration.

This concern of journalists partly emanated from the fact that most of the newspaper editors were members of a loosely organised group, the Young Ottomans, who were dissatisfied with the delayed or mismanaged implementation of Tanzimat reforms as well as the deteriorating financial situation of the empire. As the name of the group reveals, its members emphasised their youth and the new energy that they could bring to the centuries-old empire, whose ruling members were proud to be a part of the long-established state machinery.[26] The Young Ottomans proposed liberal ideas for the implementation of new methods of governance parallel to the promises of the Tanzimat reform programme.

The methods of the Young Ottomans in challenging the traditional modes of policymaking were new as well. While not the first to criticise the Porte or search for possible ways to negotiate with it, they were the first Ottoman dissenters who utilised the press to channel their criticisms of government. Notable among these critics were İbrahim Şinasi (1826–71), Namık Kemal (1840–88), Nuri (1844–1906), Kayazade Reşad (1844–1902) and Ebüzziya Tevfik (1849–1913). All were newspaper editors: Şinasi launched *Tasvir-i Efkar*; Namık Kemal, Nuri, Reşad and Ebüzziya Tevfik published *İbret*; and Ebüzziya Tevfik published *Hadika*. Şinasi himself never became a formal member of the group, yet his ideas had a great impact on its formation. Teodor Kasap, publisher and chief editor of *İstikbal*, while not a member of the movement, was a close friend of many Young Ottomans.[27] With the exception of *İstikbal*, Ottoman historiography has viewed these newspapers as instruments used by the Young Ottomans to garner support from Ottoman publics for their political position vis-à-vis the Porte and in advocating ways to prevent the collapse of the empire.[28]

The Young Ottomans argued that the future of the Ottoman Empire could only be secured with a change in the ruling structure of the empire and, specifically, a shift from absolute to constitutional rule.[29] A lack of ideological unity among the members of the movement, however, prevented a consensus on how to achieve this change. Many advocated a possible coup against the Porte, while others rejected any kind of rebellious act. As Mardin argues in his detailed study on the Young Ottomans, although these intellectuals could be considered generally as liberals, the ideologies of these men of print differed from one another.[30]

Ottoman historians, including revisionist scholars, have not considered the Young Ottomans as real dissidents but rather as a group of intellectuals who looked to secure a share of the resources of the Ottoman bureaucracy.[31] According to this view, there existed significant structural differences between Western Europe and the Ottoman Empire. Political opposition in the Ottoman Empire differed from that in Western Europe since dissent in the West did not limit its responsibility to the salvation of empire, but rather, as in the case of the Paris Commune (1871), was mainly class-based and reflected power struggles. By contrast, the opposition movements within the Ottoman Empire lacked the ideological and political dimensions to overthrow or change existing power structures and state apparatuses.[32] Young Ottoman opposition therefore differed from its Western counterparts as the scope of political struggle was limited to factions within the bureaucratic elites and excluded social groups seeking to prevent the disintegration of the empire, that is, their struggle was aimed at the protection of the state's integrity but not the liberation of the public. According to this perspective, the only aspect of the Young Ottoman opposition similar to the methods of their Western counterparts was its use of the press, where they attempted to influence Ottoman public opinion even if it was only limited to a relatively small number of literate people.[33] Such arguments, however, fail to acknowledge Young Ottoman concerns with the well-being of Ottoman publics.

Further, like the editors, these newspaper readers are viewed as elites of the empire, both literate and educated. Even if they may have been 'elites' of the empire in educational terms, they were not part of the ruling elites. Journalists can be considered in the same way. Therefore, the world view and the rhetoric of 'non-ruling elites', which became evident through the medium of the press, included concern for issues felt by diverse groups in Ottoman society. The negative impact of tax policies on the peasants, artisans and merchants, for example, found its voice in newspapers published by these non-ruling 'elites'. I argue, therefore, that the newspapers published by these ex-Young Ottomans[34] should not merely be considered as elite organs but rather be conceptualised as tools that reflected different social elements and perspectives.

News as a Concept and Practice

The first private newspapers of the Ottoman Empire offered a skeletal narrative of major public events, including wars, foreign affairs, economic and financial developments, and domestic political news such as the promotion of bureaucrats and soldiers, edicts, and the official visits of sultans and bureaucrats. Twice a week, the chief editor of *Tasvir-i Efkar*, Şinasi, like his contemporaries in Istanbul, selected news reports on the activities of members of the upper echelons, the travels of Sultan Abdülaziz, and the promotions of bureaucrats and soldiers; however, Şinasi devoted relatively little space to such reports, and gave greater coverage to subjects that were the supposed concern of broader publics. These varied widely: reports on fires, public upheavals, taxation, crop production, commerce, and the establishment of new schools, roads and railways; news on public health issues, such as cholera outbreaks and the malpractice of various doctors and pharmacists; and a range of international news.[35] As Şinasi sorted through the news from correspondents and foreign newspapers that he collected in Istanbul, he attempted to paint a picture of the political reality of the empire for *Tasvir-i Efkar* readers. This picture had to be comprehensive enough to acquire and retain readers but also needed to be acceptable to governments that typically controlled the flow of news and the distribution of newspapers throughout the empire.[36] While the content and style of the newspaper changed over the next five years, the pages of *Tasvir-i Efkar* remained rather fragmented, with the newspaper often placing a report of an event in the editorial section.

The fragmented nature of news and the style of newspapers emanated partly from the first journalists' concepts of news and how they structured newspapers. Indeed, from the first publication of *Tasvir-i Efkar* in 1862 to the appearance of *İstikbal* in 1875, news and reporting style shifted from a rather opinion-laden form to a more modern journalistic, discursive style. The latter originated from the idea of providing information in a predominantly 'objective' tone, as journalists presenting 'facts'. As revisionist media scholars argue, however, even if news reports narrate real events, one must take into consideration the distinction between the initial physical event and the stories about the event.³⁷ Recalling Robert Darnton's contention that news is not what happened but rather stories about what happened, Ottoman journalists crafted their *selected* news stories on contemporary events with their opinions and suggestions, offering solutions to problems reported in dispatches.³⁸ News reports did not always reflect the problems of all classes and segments of the society. Rather, the dispatches of these four newspapers, like the other newspapers of the empire, published news reports based on the selection of editors that reflected their own world view more than the concerns of the general reader.

Further, the difference between news and opinion was rather blurred in the first Ottoman newspapers. The distinction between news reports and articles existed only at the layout level since editors used columns and sometimes headlines to differentiate news and editorial articles. At the level of content, however, this distinction was less clear. Rather, the latest news that was considered significant was incorporated into editorial articles as, for example, the editors of *Tasvir-i Efkar* did in reporting news on upheavals in the Balkans and Crete in the editorial section.³⁹ The style of news on finance and economy was consistent with their presentation of political news.

Reporting on Financial and Economic Events

As many revisionist media scholars contend, the distinction between news as a source of pure information and news reporting as simple narration devoid of opinion was an ideal of the journalist profession rather than a practical reality and has never really existed.⁴⁰ News compiled by Ottoman newspapers did not simply provide information on contemporary events. When a correspondent of *Tasvir-i Efkar* reported the news, he generally included his own comments on Ottoman economic and financial policy. In one instance, a report from Basra not only provided information on cereal imports but also stressed the importance of the government in developing infrastructure and the benefits of utilising the natural resources of the Mosul region. The use of natural resources included construction and operation of coal and iron mines, projects that would help develop the economic interests of the region's public.⁴¹

Such articles not only informed the readers of current political and economic events but also shaped public opinion according to the editors' perceived expectations and concerns. The news-reporting style of these private newspapers, which included the comments and judgements of the news reporters and editors, shaped almost every aspect of financial and economic news. When *Tasvir-i Efkar* informed its readers about state plans to arrange a 'monthly balance of payment sheet that explained Istanbul's customs tariffs on exports and imports', the reporter applied a discourse that included his judgement, saying that 'it has been heard that, in the future, similar sheets should be prepared for the provinces as well. If this is accomplished, the balance of trade will be established between the Ottoman Empire and Europe.'[42]

Like *Tasvir-i Efkar*, *İbret* published news on government budgets. In its report on the Ottoman budget of 1872, news and commentary were intermingled. Similar to the narrative employed by the reporters of *Tasvir-i Efkar*, the comments of the news reporter filled the news of *İbret*. The reporter informed the readership about a 'reported rumour' of a budget deficit and suggested that the government announce the real balance of payments to the Ottoman publics without 'fooling ourselves [the public]' on the budget, as had been the case the previous year in order to seek remedies for curing the deteriorating finances of the empire.[43] In this news report, giving advice to the government on behalf of the publics was a higher priority than informing the readers about the budget itself.

In another news item, the news reporter adopted a different style and informed the readers of the debts of the 'diverse empires and states' that were the mutual friends of the Ottoman Empire. Written in a less partial tone, the report provided information on the growing public debt of a range of foreign states that had obtained their loans from British bankers between the years 1862 and 1872, emphasising a 126 per cent increase in public debt over the course of those ten years.[44] While the reporter refrained from making his own comments, the emphasis on the growing debt and the ways in which the other states wasted money borrowed to cover their budget deficits from upheavals and wars, warned of a similar financial danger for the Ottomans.

News on the Ottoman economy rarely appeared without commentary in the pages of *Tasvir-i Efkar*, *İbret*, *Hadika* and *İstikbal*. From the first edition of *Tasvir-i Efkar* in 1862 to the financial bankruptcy of 1875, the reports on daily events that were purged of open comments visibly increased; however, for news on finance and economy, the commentary news-reporting style remained unchanged. Factual reports on finance and economy were inserted consistently into the editorials of *İbret*, *Hadika* and *İstikbal* that made it difficult for readers to distinguish between facts and comments. *İbret*, and in particular its editor-in-chief, Namık Kemal, published many editorial articles that provided specific information on contemporary developments. For example, in an article on imperial expenditures and incomes signed 'E.C.' (indicating editor-in-chief), the author incorporated the dispatches on the balance sheet of the year 1288 (1871).[45]

Harsher in tone, a *Hadika* editorial provided coverage of the state budget of the same year. Readers were told of the 'cruelty' of tax farmers when the state issued a tax amnesty on landholdings in regions that were affected by 'heavenly calamities'.[46] Dissatisfied with the regulations, the landholders deferred payment of their debt to the state. According to the article, although the tax farmers had four or five million kuruş (piastres) that they could farm out in their regions, by asserting that they had only a few thousand kuruş or less as their capital, the 'cruel' tax farmers unfairly requested mercy from the state and continued to postpone the repayment of their debts. Both articles were penned by Namık Kemal and appeared on almost the same day yet the rhetoric used in *Hadika* was far more bitter than that in *İbret*. Indeed, while similar in inserting news into editorials, a harsher tone in its articles was a more common practice for *Hadika*, as the newspaper and its main editor, Ebüzziya Tevfik, openly acknowledged itself as an 'oppositional' newspaper. Consequently, Namık Kemal's article was full of vehement criticism not only of the government but of also specific groups such as the tax farmers. For this reason, Ebüzziya Tevfik claimed that *Hadika* was embraced with great interest by the Ottoman publics and devoted most of its pages to editorial articles.[47]

İstikbal differed somewhat in its news-making style and approached more modern journalistic practices. Teodor Kasap, its main editor, published editorial articles in every issue but devoted more space to news reports than *İbret* and *Hadika*. While these latter two relied heavily on editorial articles in the first two of their six pages, *İstikbal* generally published news reports in its opening pages. As in the other papers, news reports on finance and the economy in *İstikbal* were not arranged in relation to journalistic concerns or rules that allowed the readers to easily find specific news reports. As editorial articles on finance and economy were of greater concern, *İstikbal* published more editorial articles on the contemporary conditions and problems of finance that included news with extended commentary than straight news reports.[48]

This style of reporting on finance and economy partly stemmed from the fact that the empire's financial problems had deteriorated to a point where it was close to financial collapse. The editors of *İbret*, *Hadika* and *İstikbal* may have analysed the empire's financial problems in detailed editorials rather than only presenting the reports as they aimed to convince their readers of the pressing need for financial precautions. Indeed, as the first issue of *İstikbal* was published amid the approaching bankruptcy, readers encountered news items on finance in editorial articles.[49] In a news report similar to an editorial article entitled 'Conditions of Yesterday's Stock Exchange', the reporter provided detailed information on the fluctuating market value of Ottoman bonds.[50] The reporter discussed the reason for this fluctuation not by providing possible financial explanations, but rather by offering his own commentary as the only logical reason, namely that the sudden decrease in the stock exchange emanated from the publication of 'various false rumours' and that there was no political reason for a drop in the market. He continued, 'we [*İstikbal*] warned the stockholders about not trusting publications' that based their information on 'stock tricks'.[51] Because they believed those publications, shareholders had started to sell their bonds.

News Publishing and Information

Commentary news reporting was partly the expected outcome of how the editors of *Tasvir-i Efkar* approached their news-publishing activities. When Şinasi petitioned the government to publish *Tasvir-i Efkar* in April 1861, he stated that the paper would focus on education and news and be published as many times as possible a week.[52] Şinasi deliberately cited education before news reporting as he wished to receive a newspaper licence without any possible intervention from the Ministry of Justice. The narrative that Şinasi used was also compatible with the discourse of the official newspaper *Takvim-i Vekayi* since one of the official motives for its publication was to help Ottoman publics increase their knowledge of current events as well as of science, arts and commerce.[53] In fact, after acquiring the right to publish

Tasvir-i Efkar, Şinasi published feuilletons, news and articles on contemporary scientific developments, as would be the case for *İbret*, *Hadika* and *İstikbal* in the following years.[54] Yet, these private newspapers were more concerned with informing and politically shaping public opinions than with educating their readers on cultural, social and scientific issues. For example, when Şinasi referred to education, he actually referred to the necessity of increasing the *political knowledge* of the readers, to make them defend their rights and, most importantly, to resist undesirable government policies. Newspaper publishing was seen as contributing to the understanding of contemporary politics and a method of resistance, rather than purely comprehending the world in a modernist sense. In this way, the educational purpose of Ottoman journalists and their contribution to developing readers' understanding of the world emanated from their political, financial and economic concerns.

Tasvir-i Efkar was the second private Ottoman newspaper published in the empire after *Tercüman-ı Ahval*. At the time of its publication in 1862, dissident voices were rather muted since there was no other publication in which they could express their views on daily politics. In referring to education both in the petition submitted to the Porte and in the lead article of *Tasvir-i Efkar*'s first issue,[55] Şinasi was able to convince the government that his intentions in publishing a paper were consistent with state objectives. While the petition did not explicitly state Şinasi's full intentions, the content and the style of *Tasvir-i Efkar* more clearly exposed the editor's perceptions about news publishing. Şinasi outlined the main reasons for publishing *Tasvir-i Efkar* in the lead article of the newspaper's first issue, namely to reflect the thoughts of the public (*halk*) on the protection of its own interests by the state and to promote a public 'which has reached a certain level of maturity to explain its thoughts'.[56] Şinasi sought the cooperation of these readers in order to criticise Porte policies, creating the impression that they would not be alone in their actions against governments, since *Tasvir-i Efkar* was ready to broaden the political knowledge of the publics.

In this discourse, the public's need for a forum (the newspaper) to explain its thoughts was emphasised. One of its editors, Ebüzziya Tevfik, noted in his memoirs that in the early days of the Ottoman press, when official and semi-official newspapers were published but a private press had yet to appear, the press was in no position to 'warn' the Ottoman public.[57] Therefore, the editors of *Tasvir-i Efkar* aimed to publish a newspaper that would place the public as the main focus of events and highlight its real interests, unlike the official newspaper. As shown here, *Tasvir-i Efkar* was conceived as a medium that would convey messages to and vocalise the views of the publics with the provision of news being secondary to giving voice and warning to those very publics.

İbret appeared in 1872, ten years after *Tasvir-i Efkar*, and in many ways inherited the news-making style of its predecessor. Unlike *Tasvir-i Efkar*, *İbret* did not include an explanatory note on the masthead of the newspaper indicating the content of the paper. It is possible that the editors of *İbret*, among whom was Namık Kemal, did not feel the need to convince the government of the 'educational' content of the paper. By comparison to *Tasvir-i Efkar*, its news commentary occupied more space than the daily or weekly reports on contemporary events; however, *İbret* still remained far from exhibiting a modern style of newspaper, which separated news from opinion.

In the pages of *İbret*, as it is clearly stated in the introduction of the newspaper, the definition of the news by the editors, Ebüzziya Tevfik, Nuri, Mahir, Reşad and Namık Kemal, had many similarities to the description offered by Şinasi. As in *Tasvir-i Efkar*, the editors of *İbret* acknowledged the significance of providing information about certain issues such as tax and economic policies of the Porte rather than events in Ottoman society. In this sense, Şinasi and Namık Kemal, like the other editors of the time, strove to inform their publics of their concerns about Ottoman policy rather than simply provide news. As the editors stated:

> the most important duty of the newspapers here [in the Ottoman Empire] is to provide the public with information about the principles of politics and progress of civilisation. Therefore, we will use this modest power [of the newspaper] essentially for this duty. Nevertheless, we will not refrain from providing news [for the public].[58]

Indeed, years later Ebüzziya Tevfik would write that *İbret* was published to discuss political and social issues, and the editors were not really interested in daily news. Furthermore, he claimed that news reports were written with a harsh tone intended to criticise the government.[59] Therefore, when the editors of *Tasvir-i Efkar* and *İbret* reported on Ottoman finance and economy, they referenced the events and financial decisions of the Porte with a predominantly commentary tone that mixed information with criticism ranging from moderate to aggressive.

The approaches employed by *Hadika* and *İstikbal* paralleled *Tasvir-i Efkar* and *İbret*'s news-reporting styles on finance and economy. While launched in 1872, the same year as *İbret*, *Hadika* devoted more space to news reports than political articles and targeted a wider readership with its more accessible discourse.[60] Yet, in terms of providing news reports that were free of commentary, *Hadika* did not differ from *Tasvir-i Efkar* and *İbret*. Like *Tasvir-i Efkar*, *Hadika* heralded itself as a daily political newspaper on its masthead. In the introductory article of the first issue, Ebüzziya Tevfik stated that without contradicting the contemporary law and regulations of the press and while respecting the 'customs and morals' of the society, *Hadika* would 'mention everything'.[61] This 'everything' included critiques of the Porte's internal and foreign policies as well as current affairs, such as drought in Anatolia, the travels of state officials, the visits of foreign consuls to the Porte, burglaries and homicides. Resembling the news style of *Tasvir-i Efkar* and *İbret*, *Hadika* aimed at providing news reports on certain events without commentary. Thus, the regular travels of the state officials and the visits of the consuls were presented with a rather objective journalistic tone; however, like *Tasvir-i Efkar* and *İbret*, the editors and the reporters of *Hadika* inserted their comments into the news on finance and economy.

Like *Hadika*, *İstikbal* devoted more space to news reports than editorials. The first editorial article of *İstikbal* expressed concern with the 'future' of the next generations of the empire.[62] For the editors of the newspaper, publishing news reports and articles was a way of constructing and securing the future of the empire. For this reason, commentary and news were blended with the news reports to create an awareness about contemporary issues. *Hadika* and *İstikbal* often reported news on economic issues, such as trade agreements between states and reports on the economic and financial problems of Ottoman publics, such as the bakery artisans, and the low level of, or unpaid, wages of workers.[63] Characteristically, news on finance and economy generally would be provided with commentary by the journalist. Furthermore, in comparison to *Tasvir-i Efkar* and *İbret*, the less complicated discourses of these two newspapers targeted a broader range of readers.⁶⁴ Beyond these common points, however, *Hadika* and *İstikbal* diverged in their news reporting. While in *Hadika*, the discourse and the content of news regarding finance and economy was inclined to have a more critical tone towards the Porte's policies, *İstikbal*'s discourse was rather cautious and even protective towards the state since in the publication days of the paper the empire came close to bankruptcy.

Conclusion

As Edward Herman and Noam Chomsky argue in their propaganda model, if one claims that newspapers look to communicate messages to various publics, one should also claim that newspapers function to inculcate individuals with the values and beliefs of the dominant ruling elite, considering that ruling elites generally control the press. For the bureaucracy, this control would be through censorship in general and specific laws and regulations in particular. For private interests, the techniques of controlling the press are varied and adjusted depending upon changing material and historical conditions. Where state bureaucracy has limited control over the press and formal censorship is absent, private interests compete with each other and 'aggressively portray themselves' as the advocates of general interests. For this reason, the critiques of the newspaper editors on subjects that would directly affect the well-being of the publics are limited in nature and leave many critical subjects untouched, such as the command and distribution of public resources. In this vein, newspapers could allow the government and private interests to shape the publics in accordance with their own interests. The control of the press by private interests against the benefit of publics, more often than not, exists in societies where the ownership of the press is monopolised and where the primary income of the press comes from advertising.⁶⁵

Although this model does not exactly fit the Ottoman case, since state censorship was not completely absent and press ownership was not monopolised by 'market forces', it might be useful for analysing how the private interests in the empire represented themselves as the advocates of Ottoman publics. Not even restrictive forms of legislation could prevent newspaper editors from enthusiastically criticising the government's policies on tax collecting, external debts and industrialisation. Further, these newspapers published by the non-ruling elites of the empire reflected diverse interests that differed from those of the elites.[66]

The editors of *Tasvir-i Efkar*, *İbret*, *Hadika* and *İstikbal* were not part of the ruling elite circles and did not represent their views. Rather, the material published in their newspapers reflected the world view of counter-elites who defended private interests by aggressively and fervently portraying themselves as advocates of general interests.[67] As the world view of these counter-elites was concerned with the criticisms of the Porte's policies on behalf of the publics and prevention of the empire's disintegration by obtaining the strong support of the Ottoman society, the way in which their journalists composed news reports and articles and represented diverse interests had to rely on the idea that providing information on the 'principles of politics' took foremost priority over news on daily events and life. Therefore, in their opposition to the Porte's policies, Ottoman journalists emphasised the problems of publics that stemmed from financial and economic difficulties. Despite the fact that these reports were written by the counter-elites of the empire, these journalists' articles and reporting style on financial issues revealed the compliance and resistance of non-elites as well.

The distribution of the empire's resources for the benefit of the public and particularly for the lower classes, however, remained exceptional and mostly untouched in these first private newspapers. Yet, in their opposition to government policies, they accentuated the deprived living conditions of peasants, merchants and lower-ranking officials, and at least aided the involvement of the lower classes in the daily discourse of political, economic and financial conflict.

Notes

1. In this chapter, the Ottoman public is contextualised not as a homogenous, stagnant entity but rather as being composed of diverse groups and individuals who were involved in practices of negotiation and resistance and, I argue, formed by fragmented and multiple agencies in nineteenth-century Ottoman society. By building particularly on Geoff Eley's work ('Nations, Publics, and Political Cultures'), this study defines the Ottoman public sphere as a composite of multiple and competing publics, an idea reflected in my use of the term 'publics' in

its plural form. For further discussion on this, see Gül Karagöz-Kızılca, 'Voicing the Interests of the Public?'

2. For reports concerning plague in Alexandria, see *Tasvir-i Efkar* no. 315 (21 Safer 1282/14 July 1865), and in Istanbul, *Tasvir-i Efkar* no. 316 (24 Safer 1282/17 July 1865); for a boat fire, *İbret* no. 97 (21 Zilkade 1289/21 January 1873); a burglary, *İbret* no. 98 (22 Zilkade 1289/22 January 1873); concerning the outbreak of war in Montenegro, *Tasvir-i Efkar* no. 2 (15 Muharrem 1279/25 March 1872).

3. See, for example, *İbret* no. 39 (24 Şaban 1289/27 October 1872); *İstikbal* no. 108 (14 Rebiülevvel 1293/9 April 1876).

4. In a series published in *Yeni Tasvir-i Efkar* in 1909, author Ebüzziya Tevfik stated that accessibility to news was limited to people from the Beyoğlu district of Istanbul who had contacts with Europeans. He argued that though at times the news was exaggerated by these people and restricted in circulation, the Ottoman public benefited from this source of information. Ebüzziya Tevfik, *Yeni Osmanlılar*, vol. 1, p. 21.

5. Sommerville (*News Revolution*, p. 9) argues that publishing periodical news means creating expectations of tomorrow's events, pushing for change in society and expectations from government, creating excitement for further news in the reader, presenting reports in terms of facts, and relating everything possible to politics. As I discuss here, such motives or agendas were, to some extent, also apparent in the Ottoman press of the period. Still, caution is needed when using Sommerville's ideas on the rise of the British press as inspiration for analysing the private newspapers of the Ottoman Empire. First, one must critically negotiate Sommerville's arguments according to the Ottoman context. According to Sommerville, the rise of the British press was overwhelmingly driven by the profit motive. In contrast, the emergence of the Ottoman press was largely linked to the development of a political culture that looked to both criticise and negotiate with the state through newspapers; publishing periodical news was predominantly about creating constant doubts or approval about government politics and policies.

6. Throughout this chapter I use the term 'news making' to refer to the ways in which Ottoman journalists selected, wrote and framed their news reports.

7. The editors of *Tasvir-i Efkar* were primarily the members of the Young Ottoman movement; *İbret* and *Hadika* were published by dissident Young Ottomans aiming to prevent the collapse of the empire. Dissatisfied with the delayed or inappropriate implementation of Tanzimat reforms and the deteriorating

financial situation of the empire, the Young Ottomans were linked through their sustained criticism of the Porte's social and economic policies.
8. See Çakır, *Osmanlıda Basın İktidar İlişkileri*; Orhan Koloğlu, *Osmanlı'dan Günümüze Türkiye'de Basın*; Brummett, *Image and Imperialism*.
9. Berkowitz, *Social Meanings*, p. 11.
10. Ibid., p. 11.
11. Ibid., p. 12.
12. Blaisdell, *European Financial Control*, p. 23; Okyar, 'Economic Growth'.
13. Kasaba, *The Ottoman Empire*, p. 44.
14. During the later eighteenth and early nineteenth centuries, Aleppo-based Janissaries were involved in the caravan business as hostellers, smiths, porters and food suppliers, as well as working as carpenters, stonecutters, house painters and boatmen; they also dominated butcher guilds in Istanbul. As Quataert shows, they also controlled the grain supply in these two cities, and shops and stores owned by Janissaries protected Ottoman urban workers against unfair state practices. See Quataert, 'Janissaries, Artisans'.
15. According to Ebüzziya Tevfik, the Ottoman public lost its rights with the abolition of the Janissaries and 'public opinion was in a deep sleep' since that event. Ebüzziya Tevfik, *Yeni Osmanlılar*, vol. 1, p. 152.
16. Karpat, 'Transformation of the Ottoman State', p. 247.
17. The attempts of the Great Powers to interfere in internal Ottoman issues by claiming themselves as the protector of a particular Christian group have their roots in the so-called Eastern Question. For further on this, see Şakul, 'Eastern Question'. For a revisionist interpretation, see Quataert, *Ottoman Empire*.
18. Particularly in port cities, Ottoman non-Muslims sought European protection to promote their economic interests and escape paying taxes. See Keyder et al., 'Port Cities in the Ottoman Empire'.
19. Karpat, 'Transformation of the Ottoman State', p. 259.
20. See Makdisi, *Culture of Sectarianism*.
21. Quataert, 'Rural Unrest'.
22. For peasant-related problems, see, for example, 'Aşar', *İstikbal* no. 54 (21 Ramazan 1292/21 October 1875); for news on workers, *İstikbal* no. 72 (16 Şevval 1292/15 November 1875); for a letter complaining of the cruelty of local landlords in Sivas region, *İstikbal* no. 102 (21 Zilkade 1292/20 December 1875); for news on beggars, 'Mesele', *İstikbal* no. 10 (30 Recep 1292/31 August 1875); on the necessity of reforms of state structures and the inadequacy of the low- and middle-ranking civil servant salaries, B. M., 'İdarece

Muhtaç Olduğumuz Tadilat', *İbret* no. 33 (15 Şaban 1289/18 October 1872).

23. Namık Kemal argued that after the Janissaries were annihilated, there were no social actors remaining in the political arena to counterbalance the power of Porte bureaucrats. *Hürriyet* 29 June 1868, quoted in Mardin, *Genesis of Young Ottoman Thought*, p. 133.

24. For the Eastern Question, see, for example, 'Şark Meselesi', *Tasvir-i Efkar* no. 465 (4 Zilkade 1283/11 March 1867); Reşad, 'Bir Mülahaza [on the unification of Slavs]', *İbret* no. 3 (11 Rebiyülahir 1289/17 June 1872); N. K. [Namık Kemal], 'Şimale Nim Nigah', *Hadika* no. 26 (17 Şevval 1289/18 December 1872). Regarding the discomfort felt by Ottomans due to the concessions granted to Europeans and Ottoman citizens with European protection, see, for example, *Tasvir-i Efkar* no. 110 (30 Muharrem 1280/17 July 1863); Kemal, 'Bir Hatıra', *İbret* no. 13 (25 Rebiyilahir 1289/1 July 1872); B. M., 'Konsoloslar', *İbret* no. 72 (15 Şevval 1289/16 December 1872); 'İngilizler', *İstikbal* no. 91 (8 Zilkade 1292/7 December 1875).

25. 'Sanat ve Ticaretimiz', *İbret* no. 57 (19 Ramazan 1289/27 May 1872).

26. Mardin, 'Yeni Osmanlı Düşüncesi', p. 43.

27. Teodor Kasap's dissident identity made him a close friend of many Young Ottomans. *İstikbal* had originally been the proposed title for Namık Kemal's publication after his return from European exile in 1872 but his licence application was rejected by the government and he was unable to establish the publication. Consequently, friends of Namık Kemal rented *İbret* and allowed him to become its main editor. Two years after its closure, Teodor Kasap launched *İstikbal* in August 1875, which continued to promote the oppositional discourse first seen in *İbret*. Tanpınar, *19. Asır Türk Edebiyatı*, pp. 351, 358.

28. See Mardin, *Genesis of Young Ottoman Thought*.

29. Indeed, Şinasi desired a constitutional monarchy for the empire. See *Tasvir-i Efkar* no. 187 (10 Zilkade 1280/17 April 1864). On similar demands and arguments in *İbret*, see Kemal, 'Hukuk-ı Umumiye', no. 18 (2 Rebiülevvel 1289/10 May 1872); B. M., Untitled, no. 68 (9 Şevval 1289/10 December 1872).

30. For example, Ali Suavi, who published *Muhbir* in Istanbul in 1866 and later in London during the exile of the group, defended the rule of the *ulema* (Islamic religious class) and gave it greater importance than the military ruling class, while Namık Kemal was closer to liberal democratic ideas and put considerable effort into introducing the concept of popular sovereignty into Ottoman political thought. Namık Kemal also argued that the separation of powers had existed

in the imperial past, with the *ulema* serving as the judiciary and the Janissaries as a countervailing force. Ali Suavi defended both physical and symbolic acts of civil disobedience, while Namık Kemal opposed any kind of act that would go beyond verbal protests against the state (Mardin, *Genesis of Young Ottoman Thought*, pp. 365–7). In practice, the ideological differences among the Young Ottomans divided the movement and led to its disintegration when Ali Suavi and Rıfat detached from the group and Namık Kemal severed his relationship with Mustafa Fazıl Paşa. For Ali Suavi, see Ebüzziya Tevfik, *Yeni Osmanlılar*, vol. 1, pp. 233–92; for Namık Kemal, see Ebüzziya Tevfik, *Yeni Osmanlılar*, vol. 2, pp. 5–32.

31. Koçak, 'Osmanlı Türk Siyasi Geleneğinde'; Karpat, *Ottoman Social and Political History*.
32. Koçak, 'Osmanlı Türk Siyasi Geleneğinde', p. 76.
33. Koçak, 'Osmanlı Türk Siyasi Geleneğinde', pp. 76–9.
34. I use the term 'ex-Young Ottomans' since on the return of the movement from European exile, the loose unity between the Young Ottomans was dissolved. For details, see Mardin, *Genesis of Young Ottoman Thought*.
35. See, for example, the travel of Abdülaziz to Egypt, *Tasvir-i Efkar* no. 81 (16 Şevval 1279/5 April 1863) and to Europe, no. 486 (23 Muharrem 1284/27 May 1867) and no. 489 (3 Safer 1284/6 July 1867). For promotions of officials see, for example, no. 5 (15 Muharrem 1279/12 July 1862); regarding fires, no. 45 (7 Cemaziyelahir 1279/30 October 1862); agricultural production, no. 80 (13 Şevval 1279/2 April 1863); damages to harvests, no. 29 (11 Rebiülahir 1279/5 October 1862); import and export taxes, no. 21 (13 Rebiülevvel 1279/7 September 1862).
36. The state was able to control the flow and distribution of news in various ways. Modelled on the French Press Law of 1852, formal censorship began with the passing of the Matbuat Nizamnamesi (Publication Act) in 1864 and became more severe in 1867 with the Ali Kararname (Sublime Decree). For the regulations, see İskit, *Türkiye'de Matbuat İdareleri ve Rejimleri*. When the Porte attempted to apply these press controls to prevent any kind of opposition, however, as happened when many Young Ottomans had to flee to Europe and publish their newspapers *Hürriyet* and *İttihad* as exiles in London and Paris, journalists found ways to circulate their newspapers through underground methods, such as the foreign postal system that functioned in the empire, and the bookstores and tobacco shops that clandestinely sold banned pamphlets, newspapers and books (Ebüzziya Tevfik, *Yeni Osmanlılar*, vol. 1, pp. 208–9).

37. Revisionist media studies question the notions of journalistic objectivity, impartiality, and clear distinctions between opinion and fact in news writing (see Halloran, *Mass Media*, pp. 14–15) and many scholars argue that news reports are either culturally and socially constructed narratives or commodities selected and published with economic motives. For culturalist approaches that consider news 'as a particular kind of symbolic system', see Bird and Dardanne, 'Myth, Chronicle and Story'. For a political economy perspective, see Mosco, *Political Economy of Communication*.
38. Darnton, 'Early Information Society', p. 1. For example, while *Hadika* reported on the protests of navy shipyard workers to the Porte about not being paid wages for eleven months in 1873, the editors of *İbret* chose to skip this news. See 'Tersane Amelesi Ayaklanması', *Hadika* no. 57 (23 Zilkade 1289/23 January 1873); no. 54 (27 Zilkade 1289/27 January 1873). As media scholars and historians argue, news is more than simply information; news is selected 'stories' about what happened. See Boyd-Barrett and Rantanen, 'Globalization of News'. For a similar argument, see also Tuchman, 'Telling Stories', p. 93.
39. See, for example, *Tasvir-i Efkar* no. 2 (5 Muharrem 1279/2 July 1862); no. 25 (27 Rebiülevvel 1279/22 September 1862); no. 421 (3 Cemaziyelevvel 1283/13 September 1866).
40. See also Tuchman, 'Telling Stories', p. 93.
41. *Tasvir-i Efkar* no. 294 (7 Zilhicce 1281/2 May 1865).
42. *Tasvir-i Efkar* no. 125 (23 Rebiülahir 1280/7 October 1863).
43. *İbret* no. 12 (25 Rebiülahir 1289/1 July 1872).
44. *İbret* no. 83 (16 Şevval 1289/17 December 1872).
45. See 'Masraf ve İradımız', *İbret* no. 90 (10 Zilkade 1289/10 January 1873).
46. N. K. [Namık Kemal], 'Mürteni'at', *Hadika* no. 23 (13 Şevval 1289/14 December 1872).
47. Ebüzziya Tevfik, *Yeni Osmanlılar*, vol. 2, p. 166.
48. For editorial articles on Ottoman finance, see Untitled, *İbret* no. 33 (15 Şaban 1289/18 October 1872); N. K. [Namık Kemal], 'İflas', *Hadika* no. 19 (8 Şevval 1289/9 December 1872); 'Devlet-i Aliye Mukrizleri', *İstikbal* no. 45 (11 Ramazan 1292/11 October 1875).
49. The first issue of *İstikbal* was published on 20 Recep 1292/22 August 1875.
50. 'Dünkü Borsa Ahvali', *İstikbal* no. 40 (5 Ramazan 1292/5 October 1875).
51. Ibid.
52. BOA, Meclis-i Vala, 19973 (undated). See Ziyad Ebüzziya, *Şinasi*, p. 193.
53. See 'Mukaddime', *Takvim-i Vekayi* no. 1 (1 November 1831).

54. For example, [lectures of] Salih Efendi, 'Tarih-i Tabii', *Tasvir-i Efkar* no. 77 (1 Şevval 1279/21 March 1863) and no. 98 (17 Zilhicce 1279/4 June 1863); 'Devlet-i Aliyye'nin Devri istilasına Dair Bir Makaledir', *Tasvir-i Efkar* nos 443–51 (6 Şaban 1283–7 Ramazan 1283/13 December 1866–13 January 1867).
55. 'Mukaddime', *Tasvir-i Efkar* no. 1 (18 Rebiülevvel 1279/28 June 1862).
56. Ibid.
57. Ebüzziya Tevfik, *Yeni Osmanlılar*, vol. 1, p. 153.
58. *İbret* no. 1 (7 Rebiülahir 1289/13 June 1872).
59. Ebüzziya Tevfik, *Yeni Osmanlılar*, vol. 2, p. 127.
60. See *Hadika* no. 1 (8 Ramazan 1289/9 November 1872).
61. 'Edep ve ahlaka riayet'. See [Ebüzziya Tevfik], 'İhtar', *Hadika* no. 1 (8 Ramazan 1289/9 November 1872).
62. *İstikbal* no. 1 (20 Recep 1292/22 August 1875).
63. For a report on the trade agreement between France and England, see *Hadika* no. 1 (8 Ramazan 1289/9 November 1872); for a letter explaining the difficulty experienced by the bakery artisans due to the increase in grain prices, 'Varaka', *İstikbal* no. 33 (27 Şaban 1292/28 September 1875); for the unpaid wages of Anatolian railway workers, *İstikbal* no. 72 (16 Şevval 1292/15 November 1875).
64. Despite this, the circulation of *Hadika* reached only 3,000 while that of *İbret* reached 12,000 from the ninth issue of publication. Ebüzziya Tevfik, *Yeni Osmanlılar*, vol. 2, pp. 126–7 (*İbret*), p. 222 (*Hadika*).
65. Herman and Chomsky developed the propaganda model to analyse the function of mass media in societies where free market conditions prevail. 'A Propaganda Model', in Herman and Chomsky, *Manufacturing Consent*, pp. 1–2.
66. For example, 'Varaka', *İstikbal* no. 33 (27 Şaban 1292/28 September 1875); B. M., 'Ziraatimiz', *İbret* no. 61 (25 Ramazan 1289/26 Kasım 1872). For the representation of Ottoman urban workers in *Hadika*, see Gül Karagöz-Kızılca, 'Giving an "Active Voice" to Ottoman Urban Workers'.
67. I adopt the term 'counter-elites' from Fortna, 'Education and Autobiography', p. 2.

Bibliography

Archives

Turkey: Ottoman State Archives, Istanbul (BOA)

Newspapers (all Istanbul)

Tasvir-i Efkar (1862–9)
İbret (1870–3)
Hadika (1872–3)
İstikbal (1875)

Published Works

Alkan, Mehmet Ö., 'Osmanlı İmparatorluğu'nda Eğitim ve Eğitim İstatistikleri (1839–1924)', in Şevket Pamuk (ed.), *Osmanlı Devleti'nde Bilgi ve İstatistik* (Ankara: T. C. Devlet İstatistik Enstitüsü Yayınları, Aralık, 2000) pp. 125–45.

Berkowitz, Daniel Allen, *Social Meanings of News: A Text-Reader* (Thousand Oaks, CA, London and New Delhi: Sage, 1997).

Bird, S. Elizabeth and Robert W. Dardanne, 'Myth, Chronicle and Story: Exploring the Narrative Qualities of News', in J. W. Carey (ed.), *Media, Myths and Narratives: Television and the Press* (London: Sage, 1988), pp. 67–86.

Blaisdell, Donald C., *European Financial Control in the Ottoman Empire: A Study of the Establishment, Activities, and Significance of the Administration of the Ottoman Public Debt* (New York: AMS Press, 1966).

Boyd-Barrett, Oliver and Terhi Rantanen, 'The Globalization of News', in Oliver Boyd-Barrett and Terhi Rantanen (eds), *The Globalization of News* (London: Sage, 1998), pp. 1–14.

Brummett, Palmira, *Image and Imperialism in the Ottoman Revolutionary Press, 1908–1911* (Albany, NY: State University of New York Press, 2000).

Çakır, Hamza, *Osmanlıda Basın İktidar İlişkileri* (Ankara: Siyasal Kitabevi, 2002).

Darnton, Robert, 'An Early Information Society: News and the Media in Eighteenth-Century Paris', *The American Historical Review* 105:1 (2000), pp. 1–31.

Ebüzziya Tevfik, *Yeni Osmanlılar Tarihi*, 3 vols (Istanbul: Kervan Yayınları, 1973).

Eley, Geoff, 'Nations, Publics, and Political Cultures: Placing Habermas in the Nineteenth Century', in Craig Calhoun (ed.), *Habermas and the Public Sphere* (Cambridge, MA: MIT Press, 1992), pp. 289–339.

Fortna, Benjamin, 'Education and Autobiography at the End of the Ottoman Empire', *Die Welt des Islams* 41:1 (2001), pp. 1–31.

Goldfrank, David, *The Origins of the Crimean War* (New York: Longman Publishing, 1994).

Halloran, J. D., *Mass Media and Society* (Leicester: Leicester University Press, 1974).

Herman, Edward S. and Noam Chomsky, *Manufacturing Consent: The Political Economy of the Mass Media* (New York: Pantheon, 1988).
İskit, Server, *Türkiye'de Matbuat İdareleri ve Rejimleri* (Istanbul: Ülkü Matbaası, Mutbuat Umum Müdürlüğü, 1939).
Karagöz-Kızılca, Gül, 'Giving an "Active Voice" to Ottoman Urban Workers: *Hadika* and Forming Public Opinion for Resistance in 1872–1873', in Selim Karahasanoğlu and Deniz Cenk Demir (eds), *History from Below: A Tribute in Memory of Donald Quataert* (Istanbul: Bilgi Üniversitesi Yayınları, 2016), pp. 585–602.
Karagöz-Kızılca, Gül, '"Voicing the Interests of the Public?" Contestation, Negotiation, and the Emergence of Ottoman Language Newspapers during the Financial Crises of the Ottoman Empire, 1862–1875' (PhD dissertation, State University of New York at Binghamton, 2011).
Karpat, Kemal H., *Studies on Ottoman Social and Political History* (Leiden, Boston and Cologne: Brill, 2002).
Karpat, Kemal H., 'The Transformation of the Ottoman State, 1789–1908', *International Journal of the Middle East Studies* 3:3 (1972), pp. 243–81.
Kasaba, Reşat, *The Ottoman Empire and the World Economy: The Nineteenth Century* (Albany, NY: State University of New York Press, 1988).
Keyder, Çağlar, Y. Eyüp Özveren and Donald Quataert, 'Port Cities in the Ottoman Empire: Some Theoretical and Historical Perspectives', *Port-Cities of the Eastern Mediterranean, 1800–1914*, Special Issue, *Review* 16:4 (Fall 1993), pp. 519–58.
Koçak, Cemil, 'Osmanlı Türk Siyasi Geleneğinde Modern Bir Toplum Yaratma Projesi Olarak Anayasanın Keşfi: Yeni Osmanlılar ve Birinci Meşruiyet', in Mehmet Ö. Alkan (ed.), *Modern Türkiye'de Siyasi Düşünce: Cumhuriyet'e Devreden Düşünce Mirası Tanzimat ve Meşrutiyet'in Birikimi*, vol. 1, 4th edn (Istanbul: İletişim, 2002), pp. 72–82.
Koloğlu, Orhan, *Osmanlı'dan Günümüze Türkiye'de Basın* (Istanbul: İletişim, 1992).
Makdisi, Usama, *The Culture of Sectarianism: Community, History, and Violence in Nineteenth-Century Ottoman Lebanon* (Berkeley: University of California Press, 2000).
Mardin, Şerif, *The Genesis of Young Ottoman Thought: A Study in the Modernization of Turkish Political Ideas* (Syracuse, NY: Syracuse University Press, [1962] 2000).
Mardin, Şerif, 'Yeni Osmanlı Düşüncesi', in Mehmet Ö. Alkan (ed.), *Modern Türkiye'de Siyasi Düşünce: Cumhuriyet'e Devreden Düşünce Mirası Tanzimat ve Meşrutiyet'in Birikimi* vol. 1, 4th edn (Istanbul: İletişim, 2002), pp. 42–53.

Mosco, Vincent, *The Political Economy of Communication: Rethinking and Renewal* (London: Sage, 1996).

Okyar, Osman, 'Economic Growth and the Ottoman Empire, 1800–1914', *Asian and African Studies* 21:1 (January 1987), pp. 87–118.

Quataert, Donald, 'Janissaries, Artisans and the Question of Ottoman Decline 1730–1826', in *Workers, Peasants and Economic Change in the Ottoman Empire 1730–1914* (Istanbul: The Isis Press, 1993), pp. 197–203.

Quataert, Donald, *The Ottoman Empire, 1700–1922* (Cambridge: Cambridge University Press, 2000).

Quataert, Donald, 'Rural Unrest in the Ottoman Empire, 1830–1914', in Farhad Kazemi and John Waterbury (eds), *Peasants and Politics in the Modern Middle East* (Miami: Florida International University Press, 1991), pp. 38–49.

Şakul, Kahraman, 'Eastern Question', in Gabor Agoston and Bruce Masters (eds), *Encyclopedia of the Ottoman Empire* (New York: Facts on File, 2009), pp. 191–2.

Sommerville, C. John, *The News Revolution in England* (New York and Oxford: Oxford University Press, 1996).

Tanpınar, Ahmet Hamdi, *19. Asır Türk Edebiyatı*, 7th edn (Istanbul: Çağlayan Kitabevi, 1988).

Tuchman, Gaye, 'Telling Stories', *Journal of Communication Studies* 26:4 (1976), pp. 93–7.

Yerlikaya, İlhan, *XIX Yüzyıl Osmanlı Siyasi Hayatında Basiret Gazetesi* (Van: Yüzüncü Yıl Üniversitesi Fen Edebiyat Fakültesi Yayınları, 1994).

Ziyad Ebüzziya, *Şinasi*, ed. Hüseyin Çelik (Istanbul: İletişim, 1997).

2

Disruptions of the Local, Eruptions of the Feminine: Local Reportage and National Anxieties in Egypt's 1890s

Marilyn Booth

In January 1892, the Cairo newspaper *al-Mu'ayyad* reported that a woman from Minufiyya province – in the delta north of Egypt's capital – had gone to court seeking a divorce. Her husband, with eight years in prison behind him, faced seven more. When the court refused her request, 'she worked out a stratagem to rid herself of boredom and irritation'. The woman baked a delicacy beloved of Egyptians, *fatira*, a rich layered pastry. She awaited her husband along the route by which he would descend the *jabal*, returning to prison from the day's hard labour. He and five work-crew prison mates ate the *fatira*. All became ill and two died – the husband not among them.[1] The *fatira* enveloped poisoned filling.

This woman who tried to poison her husband, remarked *al-Mu'ayyad*, had been sought in marriage by her first cousin. Editorialising about motives (in shedding her husband she wished to shed 'boredom and irritation'), *al-Mu'ayyad* suggested she acted selfishly; it did not broach other possibilities: economic need? social vulnerability? the right to sexual satisfaction as stipulated in Islamic jurisprudence?

In *al-Mu'ayyad*'s local reportage, female subjects in public spaces appeared often as disruptive forces (disprivileged-class adult females) or cherished-but-fragile national commodities (privileged-class schoolgirls, 'public space' a gender-segregated classroom). Terse, dramatic reports of incidents and crimes also sketched females as objects of transaction handled by males: relatives, husbands, state employees. As schoolgirl, the female figure emblematised the state's benevolent modernising energies. As woman on the street – spectacle – she signalled a world out of control.

Such vignettes provided fodder for newspaper commentaries on how gender segregation practices meant to guarantee public morals were breaking down. Representations of women and girls in the Egyptian press were not innocent given the era's fierce debates on present and optimal gendered practices in the context of Egyptians' struggle for independence, and an intensely articulated concern over public order. Representations in *al-Mu'ayyad* of sexed bodies poised along a range of gendered social practices; bodies as points of access to particular political configurations, physical spaces and modes of legitimacy: these were key to crafting competing visions of what modernity meant, how to perform it, and who would have access to it.

Such images may not surface much in front-page headline articles but they do populate back-page reportage of *hawadith* (incidents, events, accidents) and announcements of institutional progress (school openings). These narratives of daily scuffles and mundane triumphs enliven and underwrite front-page editorialising commentary. Such 'incidentals' spoke to broad social and political transactions and highlighted pivots of public responsibility for those who produced and read newspapers, and those (literate or not) who heard them read out loud in cafes or at home. These reports, like other newspaper content, inscribed viewpoints of an emergent nationalist intelligentsia; newspapers attended to non-elite negotiations, but these were voiced through correspondents and editors.

The 1890s witnessed Egyptians' cautious and then fiercer reactions to Egypt's 1882 occupation by Britain, as well as to imperial 'adventures' elsewhere. Debate over appropriate nationalist ideologies in a handful of newspapers comprise the better-known face of this emergent public-political discourse. Scholarship on political dailies has focused on representations of big-picture politics, political constituencies and programmes, analysed for their formative roles in building national community. This privileges front-page material and categorises periodicals by the politics of founder-editors. My focus is not major editorials or leading news items but rather, inside features that mapped the nation's interior. Content, rhetoric and placement of *hawadith* in *al-Mu'ayyad* – Cairo's pre-eminent Egyptian-run independent daily (est. December 1889) – were more than informational: they acted representationally in the politics of nation formation. They echoed, buttressed, critically surveilled and often called for state regulation of space and intervention in the intimate lives of Egyptians.

Dailies were more than conduits of information: they were spaces of communication between state and subjects. Local reporting conveyed demands and pleas – unofficial petitions – from subjects to state, and regulations and warnings from state to subjects. Correspondents were mediators, speaking from and to local communities. One of many examples occurs on 25 January 1891: 'People are complaining of treatment by security personnel at prisons, who deal with them roughly and mercilessly. We entreat the Director of Prisons to direct his attention to this.'[2] Such requests emerged from provincial reports, which became the (narrated, constructed) empirical fact base – and moral grounding – for putative state action.

Studying intersections of legal reform discourse, official interventions and local practices in nineteenth-century Bombay's sex trade, Ashwini Tambe argues that discourses and apparatuses of law – and the circulating texts of reformist-nationalist newspapers and pronouncements of law courts and police stations – were constitutive of a flourishing yet disapproved sector while nourishing competing visions of public good and political authority. Measures to restrict, remove, register or re-socialise prostitutes were not efficacious as law but were highly effective as public rhetoric: 'projects bound to fail', they 'generate[d] corrective discourses and devices of surveillance by members of the populace'. Thus, 'the substance of the law was less an issue than the circuits it established'.[3] I view *al-Mu'ayyad*'s 'incidental reports' similarly. They maintained visibility for a cluster of issues pivotal to imagining a postcolonial Egypt. Through narratives of spectacular dailiness, the respectable female body became a signifier of national possibility and honour, while the opposite – the 'public woman' – was regarded by some as indicating a vernacular moral degeneration, an argument responsive to European-colonial rhetoric of 'Eastern' immorality, deployed as one justification for ongoing colonial rule.[4] But images of women-on-the-street were also responses to changing socio-economic conditions and cultural practices that perhaps *had* brought more women onto Cairo streets, sharpening the salience of female visibility as a political issue, spurring state initiatives and vigorous policing.[5] Of course, women had never been absent from Cairo's lanes. But classed configurations of gendered visibility were shifting, sparking a scare discourse that highlighted 'modernity' as a sexualised concept. Reportage indicated how particular bodies legitimately occupied – or alternatively, were by 'nature' outside of – particular spaces. The normative spatial array of local subjects was mapped onto, and constitutive of, social relations and their concomitant property relations, where issues of kinship and inheritance (and therefore, 'legitimate' reproduction) remained crucial. Hence the discursively archived anxiety over the spatial distribution of gendered and classed bodies, in Egypt as elsewhere.

Al-Mu'ayyad's incidentals designated everyday social actors in their accustomed spaces as proper objects of public discussion, inserting the newspaper into national politics as mediator between state authorities and subjects, appropriating its own surveillance role in an increasingly policed society. *Hawadith* columns were roughly equivalent to the *faits divers* that made nineteenth-century French newspapers (in)famous and possibly inspired editors in Egypt. French culture and media were models for Egypt's nationalist intelligentsia and consuming bourgeoisie.[6] Indeed, the fictional genre that emerged from and spoke to French readers' obsession with *faits divers* was popular in Egypt. Ponson de Terrail's *Les exploits de Rocambole* (1859) and other crime and detective fictions were translated into Arabic early and often. Yet it is likely that no external influence need be implicated: why would a national newspaper *not* report local news? 'Human interest' was as appealing in Cairo as in Paris. But the nature of *faits divers* lends particular force, as will be elaborated below.

Al-Mu'ayyad would have had readers who were familiar with French public culture. But scrutinising *al-Mu'ayyad*'s practices through the lens of *faits divers* does not mean this was wholly a borrowed form. *Faits divers* names a narrative practice that readers might recognise as both vernacular and imported. A 'local' genealogy might be found in the centuries-long presence in Arabic letters of massed *akhbar* (anecdotes, news), a staple structural component of biographical dictionaries, belles-lettres compendia and historical chronicles. Biographical dictionary entries included anecdotes to give literary context or fill out worthy epithets by narrating memorable deeds and encounters, preserved through eye-witness accounts. Annalistic historical chronicles ended each year with a listing of miscellaneous 'events', *hawadith*. Ibn al-Athir's (1160–1233 CE) illustrious world history, *al-Kamil fi al-tarikh*, recorded skirmishes and feuds, famines and epidemics, ceremonies and proclamations, political appointments, and deaths of important individuals, often accompanied by biographical anecdotes.[7] Though evidencing concern with public order, these entries rarely chronicle ordinary individuals but occasionally they offer affecting exempla. The obituary of pious Iraqi Sufi 'Abd al-Razzaq recounted his wife worrying about family disgrace should he die without leaving funds for a burial shroud.[8] Non-elite individuals, unnamed, appeared when their actions had major repercussions, as in one report that reads like a distant ancestor of *al-Mu'ayyad*'s gender-focused reportage. A major Baghdad fire in the summer of 1108 CE is said to have been caused when

> a servant-girl, having fallen in love with a man, arranged for him to spend the night secretly with her in her master's house. She prepared something that he could steal when he left . . . they set fire to the house, but God revealed their guilt and brought swift shame upon them. They were seized and imprisoned.[9]

In nineteenth-century Egypt, as for the earlier Ibn al-Athir, history-writing provided lessons for living and governing, exemplary guidance for behaviour. *Hawadith* were microhistory. In *al-Mu'ayyad* they might act as exempla, the accumulation of small tales composing an ongoing story about the nation's morals and its goings-on – as adduced particularly in the behaviour of women.

Gendered-feminine images were central to *al-Mu'ayyad*'s representation of daily sociality. The newspaper's *faits divers* most often portrayed females as loud and assertive, qualities represented as inappropriate and as linked to transgressions of acceptable morality. Such figures bore contagion, infecting the innocent through their loud-and-lewd presence. The newspaper's overlapping, repetitive images illustrated – and fortified – arguments across the press concerning girls' and women's socio-spatial movements as changing, transformative and nationally dangerous. These representations were attached to the rhetoric of advocacy mentioned above. Correspondents' dispatches often culminated in what were presented as locally generated demands for state intervention to control public and especially female behaviour. Newspaper diction suggests editors and correspondents aspired to construct activist reader-citizens who sought responsive government; and their aspirations registered gender-specific tonalities. These news items along with other texts – editorials, conduct literature, exemplary biography, fiction, satirical poetry – tendered a discourse on the gendering of space that took account of older customary practices, sedimented legal discourses, changing consumption patterns, new educational sites and the emerging political structures of imperial 'oversight'. *Faits divers* in the 1890s Egyptian press comprise a daily indication of how representations of women were linked to nationalist formations of a moral-political constellation of values as defining the good national subject.[10]

Nationalist Journalism

The civic importance of a responsible independent press was a nineteenth-century leitmotif. On the new century's cusp, the monthly *al-Hilal* declared:

> The nineteenth century has ended leaving imprints for future memory. We cannot bid it farewell without mentioning its impact and enumerating its innumerable virtues: consider how Egypt and Ottoman Syria have seen knowledge's banner spread . . . the 'recent knowledge awakening' has five foundations: schools, printing presses, books, newspapers, associations.[11]

By this time – 1901 – magazines could speak confidently of a press-led 'awakening', while the history of press regulation suggested the periodicals sector's exuberant vitality:

> To execute [1881's press law only on natives, *al-wataniyyun*] was, the government recognised, unjust and biased; gradually it was disregarded until a few years ago it was for all practical purposes eliminated. Publications had free rein; people thronged to found presses and newspapers like the hungry swarm toward food. Without permissions or oversight, presses and newspapers skyrocketed and more people entered the profession. Writings – both thin and robust – on myriad topics appeared. It got so bad we found ourselves

lamenting a broadened freedom that generated publications crammed with insults and disgraceful slanders, undermining the order of things.[12]

Publishing 'useful ideas and accurate news', *al-Mu'ayyad* aimed to 'circulate internal incidents [*al-hawadith al-dakhiliyya*] for reflection and warning, diversion and forecast'.[13] From the start, editor 'Ali Yusuf included such items as integral to *al-Mu'ayyad*'s mission of instilling moral rectitude as underpinning national resistance to imperialism.

Inclusion of local news was not unprecedented, nor was its political-regulatory role. Describing 1870s newspapers, press historian Ibrahim 'Abduh observed that

> popular newspapers noted small internal issues, not neglecting to report on an *'umda* or *ma'mur* showing he was not performing duty well and signaling the government to punish him. They paid attention when a bridge collapsed or agricultural land flooded, so that the government would undertake to repair the breach, dam the waters, and compensate owners of the flooded land [citing *al-Watan* 1878]. Correspondents in cities and regions provided such news by telegram or mail. The popular press became a critical observer of small events as it did of big ones.[14]

Al-Mu'ayyad's announcement of purpose – reflection and warning, diversion and forecast – encapsulates the various functions of reportage on local incidents, combining news, distraction and the didactic. These features had made *faits divers* a driver of the popular press in France.

Status of the 'Small Event'

The Petit Robert and Larousse dictionaries define *faits divers* diversely, focusing respectively on events' positioning in a discursive hierarchy and on their material fact – 'the news of little importance in a newspaper' and 'an event without general significance which pertains to daily life'.[15] Gregory Shaya defines the rubric as coverage of 'crimes, accidents and scandals'.[16] Dominique Kalifa characterises it as a genre offering 'a close-up, organised around a limited set of fixed discursive structures – paradoxes of aberrant, unusual or scandalous causality . . . coincidences of repetition or antithesis . . . in effect, stories without bearing or bulk, a sort of small infinity'.[17]

Paradox: the genre is *mundane* yet *extraordinary*, encapsulating (constructing) interruptions of accepted social norms and of social behaviour and quotidian patterns. Diverse yet repetitive, reminding readers of like events from the past (the weird repeatability of happenstance), such texts insist on the novelty of the representative. They propose to relay 'just the facts' (*les faits*) yet they narrativise, evaluate, moralise. Occupying liminal space and marginal status, *faits divers* are overlooked, anonymous, just filling (little) space. This might provide subversive potential, conveying what some preferred not to see; it might act as psychological and political 'safety valve'.[18] A 'useless anecdote that carries one back to the essential',[19] singular and multiple ('a fact' and 'diverse'), its 'very name simultaneously implies and evades patterns of classification'.[20] Presented as life's raw material, it is a challenge to verisimilitude. Circulating as a written text, it partakes of the stuff of hearsay. The scene is ordinary, yet yields a story riveting in its horror, its publicised intimacy:

> In al-Kafaru [Village], a woman was asleep with her husband on the rooftop of their home. She awoke to find the bedlinens over her in flames. She put out the fire and went to 'Abdin police station, claiming her husband had done it after their quarrelling reached boiling point. His aim was to end her life, and thus take the house . . .[21]

> Dumyat, 1 April, from our correspondent (delayed): Last night a disquieting incident here had a grievous impact on the minds of all. Three people, one Greek and the others [Egyptian] Coptic, went to a certain prostitute's residence, finding two women there. They drank and drank. When the alcohol had played with their minds each took a woman (the Greek claims he left then). Later, one drew out a knife, slit the throat of the woman he'd slept with, and fled . . .[22]

From the 1860s, *faits divers* emerged in the relatively new French popular press,[23] helped popularise it, and encouraged public engagement in crime issues. As crime's hold on imaginations seemed to grow, the event as focus gave way to emphasis on processes of justice, turning readers (and journalists) into amateur detectives, fuelling the popular detective-novel industry. From 'the savage and picturesque description of crime' to 'the investigation, presented as methodical and reasoned', the style shifted and the narrative lengthened.[24] Before World War I,

> One would recall briefly the deed ... accumulating concrete information: names, age, profession, address. The paragraph would end with announcement of the arrest or opening of an investigation. Here, the narrative closes, the transgression related never being matter for inquiry or new development.[25]

Over time the genre became sensationalised, emphasising the 'mystery' of investigation over prosaic facts, dwelling on details of décor, weapon and personality. Kalifa emphasises crime narratives; others see *faits divers* as encompassing spectacular or disruptive events such as accidents and catastrophes that drew sympathy from onlooking crowds,[26] or radical and ironic reversals of normality. Kolstrup's simple definition as 'news from the street'[27] highlights *faits divers* as creating spaces for local voices – the newspaper as channel between subjects and state. All of these elements could be found in Egyptian *hawadith*. A variety of newspaper headings bundled *faits divers*, arising from concrete local incidents to which they give narrative shape. Commentary within the reportage builds on incident(s) and aftermath. Simple in language, these short features seem especially accessible to new audiences, whether lone silent readers or listeners clustered in city cafes. Would readers new to the press be particularly attracted to these items with their referentiality, matter-of-fact prose and concision?

That the genre gestures to what is 'unimportant' is important; this 'notion of triviality' may be 'a defensive reaction, a measure of potential to unsettle those categories which define what is significant'.[28] For Baudrillard, this category of sense-making exemplifies the fantasy–desire–everyday violence continuum of the mass-mediatised modern consuming subject.[29] Kalifa emphasises *faits divers* as historical facts, partaking of older forms but malleable to social transformation, deeply expressive of 'social and political mutations'.[30] Eugen Weber emphasises such representations' role in the circulation of French *fin-de-siècle* social anxieties.[31] Similar perturbations were articulated in Egypt; *faits divers* made of these worries stories. *Al-Mu'ayyad* turned them into editorial occasions for querying authorities, intervening in outcomes and deploring the state of the nation. Women (and young men) acted as red lines between indigenous and colonising cultures. The sexed body became a sign demarcating stress in the system, even as that system incorporated, and reshaped itself around, shifting notions of gendered access.[32]

Diverse Acts, Diverting Events

What was news in Egypt, early in January 1894? In Minya, 'these days, crowds of gamblers have become so large that they fill entire cafes and hotels. The whole city is choked with them. We draw the authorities' attention to . . . these corrupt practices that threaten thriving homes with ruin.'[33] Men and women flocked to bars. In Suez, a Greek man knifed an Egyptian man in front of a tavern.[34] In Banha, a Syrian immigrant who managed a hotel was stabbed by another Syrian-origin resident after a drinking bout, possibly over a homoerotic triangle.[35] In al-Ibrahimiyya, complained a correspondent,

> there is a group . . . of those types who have nowhere to go but hashish cafes and no work but grabbing, pillage, and disturbing every passerby. With obscene expressions, they jeer at passing women – regrettable! We must turn the attention of the decision-makers toward these people, hoping they will [be made to] desist from their errors.[36]

In Bani Suwayf, sex workers were moving into 'respectable neighbourhoods'. The Interior Ministry's order to transfer them to sites 'distant from town' had been discarded when no suitable site emerged, and 'they began to settle amidst the homes of respectable secluded ladies. The annoyance they caused grew more intense, vexatious, and harmful.' Townsfolk were demanding that the governor relocate these women 'far away from the residences of the respectable'.[37]

Local reporting covered an enormous range of events. That same January fortnight saw the announcement of an Egyptian manufacturers' exhibition and the opening of a new school in Minuf, important 'especially for children who are not raised properly, left to wander like animals through the streets'. Young men skilled in French and Arabic had formed a society to discuss and practise translation.[38] But more narratives of local encounters concerned disruptions of the normal, or more accurately, of the normative as defined by *al-Mu'ayyad*'s nationalist approach, privileging a heritage of Islamically defined customary norms.

Sex, Drugs and *Faits divers*

> Yesterday the swindler went to the home of a midwife, Zannuba bt. Muhammad Efendi al-Hamshari, in al-Batiniyya within Darb al-Ahmar municipal administrative district [Cairo]. He gave her some grapes, saying, 'The district head sends these to you, requesting two pounds'. Immediately she pounced on him, seizing him with the help of women there with her at home. She took him to the police station.[39]

The report alerted readers to a scam. The fellow had been making the rounds of Cairo neighbourhoods delivering fruit and demanding money for these 'gifts'. The case shows an alert subject and her friends working with the state's security apparatus, thus recognising and helping to consolidate its authority.

This report is unusual in featuring a woman as savvy agent of the public order. More often, women appear as victims or as individuals standing outside accepted gendered behavioural norms, well outside the moral compass the newspaper espouses. Women are more likely to appear entering public space via unacceptable pathways:

> Bulaq, from our correspondent: Amongst deviations from our rules of decency we find bars for purposes of intoxication and hashish cafes opening on women's, not men's, initiative. If only this were all the women did. But no – they imbibe both [substances] along with the men, leading these women into quarrelsome and depraved behaviour; they go out in the streets in a state people find disgusting. We plead with the men of importance and influence to eliminate these abominations that exceed the bounds of moderation.[40]

We may ask what the biggest issue is: women's 'initiative' in business, or women haunting these sites, breaking gender norms of homosociality and behaviour by drinking alcohol and smoking hashish? Or that then they go into the streets? Here, only women are singled out as exhibiting consequences of these 'abominations'; *their* presence in bars and streets, not men's, sparks moral outrage and calls for public aversion (though men are not exempt from criticism in *al-Mu'ayyad*). As the educator, social activist and essayist Malak Hifni Nasif would emphasise a few years later in *al-Jarida*, it was women who most drew the ire of male intellectuals. Women were first to be censured and ridiculed for bad behaviour, social deterioration and what was bemoaned as the nation's generally dire and chaotic state.[41] Repeatedly this was linked to female presences in public space.

An incident at a mosque during the holy month of Ramadan, reported to *al-Mu'ayyad* at indignant length by an Alexandria resident, involved no illicit substances but was similarly concerned with women's visibility and behaviour as spatially transgressive of public morals:

> I sought to attend Friday prayers on 27 Ramadan at the Mosque of Sidi Abu al-Abbas, but this large mosque was jammed with worshipers and I found no space. I resolved to perform my religious duty next to the mosque with a group of worshipers. As the collective prayer began, worshipers could hear nothing but the talk of women who were pressing in on the praying men, giving them headaches with the racket they made. Two women quarrelled; another shushed her children and still another complained to her companion about how bad things were with her husband … No sooner did the prayer end than I saw … about six women surrounding two youths, one a sailor in the Egyptian Navy and the other in civilian clothes. They were all party to this flirtatious exchange, fully in sight of these worshipers at the mosque in their state of piety.
>
> Since this is contrary to right conduct and religious practice, I wanted to address these people but feared my intervention would result in discomfort or set worshipers against them. I left the mosque precinct to fetch a policeman who would thwart this indecent act. I found Sergeant no. 1348 near the mosque entrance … He appeared concerned but reaching the gate his pace slowed. After all, he claimed, the government man flirting with the women at the mosque was also police. His orders did not permit him to call off the man since they were of the same service and rank … I draw the authorities' attention to this sort of thing, unbefitting to public conduct, especially at times of worship. (Name Withheld)[42]

Though men were implicated in this challenge to mosque decorum, it was 'loud' women who disturbed the peace, instigating 'flirtatious exchange' in public (indeed sanctified) space. The report drew lines of normativity as spatialised boundaries that women transgressed. Often in such reports, men appeared as willing but passive targets, indeed sometimes hapless ones.

Discursive anxiety about women in public spaces concerned spaces themselves, ways the articulation of the city was changing, with new, European-style open public spaces – boulevards, parks – surrounding or creating a palimpsest over the older city, and new forms of transportation (and requisite spaces – train stations and tram stops) offering more possibilities for mobility. If women were availing themselves of these open spaces – and what choice did most have, outside of the wealthy elite? – and if reconfigured public space made it more difficult to preserve homosocial boundaries, then perhaps this gave starker visibility to issues about gendered spatial boundaries as assumed guarantors of family honour. Yet it is notable that most of *al-Mu'ayyad*'s notices about women's alleged transgressions were set in older parts of the city or outside of Cairo: the availability of new spaces was not the only issue at stake.

Women transgressing conventional expectations show up with impressive consistency:

> News from Fayyum: A woman who claims to be among the virtuous and chaste who enjoy protection against damage to their purity[43] got in the habit of going into a foreign-owned bar and getting drunk regularly in the evening, for which she became notorious. Word got around; her deeds were on every tongue. The police mounted a watch. They seized her as she came out intoxicated, her judgment gone and her mind lost. They arrested her and prepared the obligatory police report. Thus we anticipated her punishment at the hands of the law, based on the warped behaviour, licentiousness and corrupt morals for which she was infamous. There is no doubt that her presence among respectable women [*al-ahrar*] is something decency must reject, especially since her slyness and cunning have damaged many women who knew nothing [previously] of reprehensible behaviour.[44]

Relying on the stereotype of *kayd al-nisa'* (women's cunning), this report railed against the contaminating effects of women's bad behaviour, linking them to the corrupting commercial presence of foreigners in an entertainment service economy that angered nationalists for allegedly draining national resources and luring nice young Egyptian men and women into costly ruin. *Kayd al-nisa'* invoked a particular legacy of judgement; the term came from the Qur'an itself. In Surat Yusuf, Pharaoh condemns 'women's trickery' collectively upon realising his wife has framed Joseph. This trope runs through a long heritage of orally transmitted and manuscript texts which publishers further circulated. The correspondent drew on a deeply instantiated popular understanding whereby one woman's reported conduct became a gender-wide denunciation. The editorialising targets less the drunken woman than the imagined consequences of her conduct, worrying that 'respectable women' would follow her lead (or already had). If gendering social disruption as a feminine trait also carried classed implications, naturalising *kayd*, with the sacred discourse hovering, damned women of all strata.

Al-Mu'ayyad's very next issue featured a front-page article on France's declining birth rate: 'Research has established the cause of the birthrate scare: giving free rein to young women through the freedom the law establishes, bestowing on them the right to [control] their own purity [*'isma*], adultery grew widespread.' The first nation to legislate women's control of their sexuality, France was 'reaping the fruits of this law' (or the lack thereof).[45] Such scares were rife in the French press, linked to the circulating discourse of 'degeneration' that was a hallmark of the European *fin de siècle*[46] and was reported copiously in the Arabic press.

'Isma was the quality the Fayyum woman in the bar 'claimed' to have. Did readers catch the echoes and worry that this feminine virtue was under threat everywhere, and seeping into Egypt through foreign-owned bars? And then, what did readers think days later, finding the Fayyum woman in *al-Mu'ayyad* again? She was back in the newspaper because she was back in the bar. The police chief's investigation following the first newspaper report 'found what we said to be correct, and he expelled her',[47] confirming the correspondent's usefulness as a monitor of public behaviour. But how useful was this intervention if she was back in the bar? The reporter might relish his role as adjunct to the state's disciplinary system but the outcome suggested the woman's ability to evade it.

Egyptian Women, Foreign Men

Nationalist periodicals might feed anti-foreign sentiment by narrating local incidents and framing them with politically resonant commentary. If unruly females populated these mini-dramas, so did disruptive foreigners. Both situated the reader at a particular viewing threshold, that of the native Egyptian male.

Al-Mu'ayyad's follow-on explanation attached to its opening editorial had set out newspapers' public responsibility by invoking national duty and precedent:

> The deeds of predecessors form the school for successors. There we learn that service to homelands is among the most obligatory duties and imperative commands: shrugging them off condemns one by nature's law to everlasting deprivation and eternal misery. Our aim in publishing *al-Mu'ayyad* is to perform that commanded task . . .[48]

This declaration uses language associated with Muslim believers' obligations (*wajib, fard*). The law of nature is *shari'at al-tabi'a*, superimposing the diction of Islamic right practice. To threaten deprivation and misery echoes the fate of wayward believers, yet the emphasis is national-territorial more than confessional. *Al-Mu'ayyad* focused predominantly on territorially focused nationalism, inflected by Muslim identity but open to others with allegiance to Egypt's national cause.[49] Its title signalled duality: *al-mu'ayyad* suggests the 'well-corroborated' newspaper. The opening asked God's support, using the same linguistic root (*wa an tu'ayyidana bi-'inayatika al-samdaniyya*): one can read *al-mu'ayyad* as 'the [divinely] supported'. Its mission statement privileged the nation while drawing on religiously salient diction:

> to make appear a daily political newspaper adhering to the programme of truth in the presence of the people, calling from the [Muslim/national] community's pulpit [*minbar al-umma*] with the voice of conscience, summoning readers in a clear Arabic tongue as service to the nation's [*watan*] children, undertaking duties for a country [*bilad*] of whose primordial matter we are the surface images.[50]

The newspaper emphasises national unity, declares the precedence of Egyptianness over other identities, and constructs Egyptian history as a continuum, beginning with ancient Egyptians' remarkable engineering of territory and sociality, linking them with contemporary Copts. Articles attacked *nuzala'* (incomers; derogatively, non-Egyptian immigrants) for exploiting sectarian distinctions to break up national unity.

In *hawadith*, Egyptian Muslim males were the unmarked norm while others (including Copts) were (sometimes?) defined by religion and/or ethnicity. This is not surprising, nor is it necessarily meant negatively. But labelling non-Egyptians or non-Muslims by origin or identity sets them up as types and othered beings, and their frequent presence in negative situations casts shadows. As *al-Mu'ayyad*'s front-page editorials attacked foreign activities – whether in furthering commerce, opening schools or intervening in politics – *faits divers* highlighting foreigners' deleterious impact on local gender arrangements added thick description. Occasionally *al-Mu'ayyad* made positive references to 'Western' practices worthy of emulation but these were usually abstract. Foreigners might be lauded if they remained distant or formless, but foreigners in Egypt as represented in *hawadith* and *mukatabat* (correspondence) were usually deleterious presences. Describing behaviours of resident non-Egyptians, these narratives did indicate how intimate the encounters were between individuals of different ethnic origins.

European sex workers, Greek and Lebanese bar owners, British soldiers and Syrian bureaucrats: references to individuals' ethnicities lent nationalist overtones to incidents even if there was nothing overtly political about them. In a Delta town,

> an al-Qadaba native was getting drunk with a group of Greeks in a tavern where they often caroused. When the alcohol diffused through their heads and their good sense vanished, they painted the man's face with methylated spirits and set him on fire. Had his condition not been dealt with immediately, he would have been ashes. His condition remains serious. The incident was handled appropriately with the police informed.[51]

The text did not claim that ethnic or national difference motivated the incident. But to persistently link bars and Greeks (as owners or patrons), and juxtapose them with Egyptians as their financial or physical victims resonated with the newspaper's nationalist rhetoric. Petty local incidents reported nationally linked foreign presence and illicit behaviour. This trope was ubiquitous in satirical vernacular poetry, song and theatre as well as formal nationalist rhetoric,[52] buttressed by contemporaneous production of scientifically oriented conduct works on the dangers of stimulants and narcotics that announced them as foreign imports infecting the local young.[53]

Narration of outrageous events involving foreign men and local women took on allegorical overtones, representing shared colonial powerlessness. A victimised father in Algeria garnered sympathy in Egypt:

> A French military officer in Algeria demanded of a Tlemcen notable that he marry him to his daughter. The man got angry ... and began cursing the French; the police had to arrest him on the allegation that he was stirring up people's ideas. He was imprisoned on 22 Dhu al-hujja 1307. Called for interrogation several times, he related simply what had happened to him and was returned to gaol. He demanded many times that his case be sent to court ... the response was that this would happen when they arrested the rest of the secret gang participating in the incitement. Every time he left prison he encountered that officer, who demanded the marriage ... God ruled that there be communication between the officer and the girl such that she was drawn to him. He played tricks on her that finally allowed him to seize her and put her in his house. Even then, he did not intervene to free the father ... He left ... the girl was with him ... A few days later the father was released, went home and learned the news ... Everyone was very angry. He decided to go to Paris and mount a case. We all hope he obtains justice.[54]

The Algerian is arrested for 'stirring up ideas'; the European gets the daughter. The incarcerated (male) nationalist watches helplessly as the coloniser rapes the (daughter)land. Conjunctures of family, gender and national politics turn private confrontations into explosive public ones. Newspapers circulate the event from one colonised territory to another. A family story from Algeria – politicised by colonial authorities there – resonates in Egypt.

Women were written into newspapers as the most abject victims of foreigners, most vulnerable to imperial privilege in the form of bodily humiliation and pain inflicted by European visitors and residents:

> Alexandria, 17 July: A European was sitting at a '*bira*' [tavern] near the Paradiso Café. The waitress came over and asked him to pay for his drink. Our friend's response was to raise his hand, gripping a cane, and strike her

in the face. The blow hit the poor woman on her brow. She began screaming and crying for help, blood running down to stain her clothes ... an awful sight, leading one to feel astonished at the customs and morals of Europeans. When those sitting in the bar and passersby saw this and everyone heard the woman's wailing, they hurried to her and began binding her wound with whatever they could find. They seized the assailant and delivered him to a policeman, who dragged him to the police station. Hardly did he stand before the senior officer when a companion gave surety so his esteem would not be lowered by detainment. Were he a person of honour and conscience, he would not have done this horrible thing, possible only from someone with a cowardly soul that has sunk low, remote from high-minded mores.⁵⁵

The incident illustrates graphically the bloody encounter of colonised and coloniser: bodily assault on a woman made powerless by her class and gender, coupled with the foreigner's power to circumvent the justice system through connections and money. That the woman is a bar waitress (readers are not told her ethnicity or national origin) and must mix with unrelated men means she is not an impeccable figure of 'honour' herself; onlookers' compassion might then seem particularly generous, in contrast to the European's violence.

In these terse narratives, *al-Mu'ayyad* rarely defines female protagonists ethnically or nationally. Often they were clearly local from name or context, described through relationships to male family members. But for women more than for men as subjects, these narrated incidents occasioned generalised commentary. What began as a singular incident comes to embrace women as a category. This is the forte of the *fait divers*. Its specificity expands categorically.

Sex Work: Blurring Gender Boundaries of Social Stability

In *al-Mu'ayyad*'s third issue, a correspondent complained that in Alexandria,

a person cannot walk down the street without seeing an establishment for prostitutes, especially in the vicinity of 'Attarin [traditionally the perfumers' quarter]. One can no longer distinguish their houses from those of respectable women [*al-ahrar*, the free] for [the houses] conceal what they are. As for the public [legal] ones, they are everywhere.⁵⁶

Al-Mu'ayyad manifested early and consistent concern about sex work, partly via the ambiguous juxtaposition of public visibility and dangerous invisibility it offered. One news item after another represented prostitutes collectively as a contagious roving body threatening the nation's social fabric. Meanwhile, often on the same pages, anonymous female subjects – and lone bodies – interrupted this public monologue of outrage with their inexplicable, silent but reported acts: *a girl has thrown herself into the Mahmudiyya Canal.*[57] Spatial proximity (the page) linked the suicidal female to the roving sex workers. Female bodies were everywhere in national space, puncturing the social-moral order.

Anxiety about the morals of youth, public discipline, spatial order and national economic health condensed around narratives about sex work: its sites, its (female) agents and its invasive infections, physical and moral. In Zaqaziq, 'people are complaining about prostitutes who go about city streets with faces uncovered, speaking words that breach moral bounds. We direct the authorities' attention to such matters.'[58] In the Fayyum oasis, sex workers

> have so multiplied and pervaded the town that one can hardly walk through the streets without seeing a great many around him. They compete to exchange words with him; if he is a man of upright and honourable nature who makes no response, they pelt him with the stones of foul language . . . It is astounding that some have procured sites alongside [those of] respectable people on the pretext that they are women of chastity and protected honour, innocent of all that is attributed to them. If a neighbour remonstrates against them for the immoral ways they conduct themselves, they shower him with curses . . . if he goes looking for help from a policeman he finds none nearby . . . Everyone knows the harms that come to good folk when such women are left to do as they please: most are afflicted with syphilis, whose outcome cannot be other than bodily destruction, weak bones, and corrupted reproduction . . . We hoped to see a law prescribing a boundary where they would halt, in the name of protecting the sanctity of morals. But this hope is lost at the gate of the freedom they enjoy . . . On the public's behalf we demand from the authorities a law on these women, these prostitutes, as we also request them urgently to supply sufficient police strength here to confront these incidents that transgress honour and religion.[59]

The language of spatial boundaries actively breached is notable. The newspaper narrated sex workers as not just *signs* but *agents* of urban spatial chaos and national moral decay. But they were not the only targets of journalistic anxiety. Reports suggested that other women ('mistresses of the household') were complicit in allowing these women to invade, inhabit and infect the national threshold:

> Women who make a pretense of purity and well-protected morals [*'isma, siyana*] have grown plentiful near homes of the respectable [*al-ahrar*]. On a daily basis we hear of their acts and ugly aims: to beget reprehensible behaviour and transgress honour and decency. How many a mistress of the household has brought in a girl from the riffraff who seduces one man and leads another on, until those of weak mind fall into corrupt practices and bring about moral death.
>
> It is not news to anyone that those female tricksters [*muhtalat*] pretty up their words and practice flattery and fawning, attaching themselves to the eminent and the great among those of family and lineage. Using this trap, one of the ugliest there can be, they amass money. The tricks by which they perpetrate reprehensible deeds have proliferated to where we now expect the greatest evils of this sort. Most of these women are afflicted with infectious and enervating diseases; yet no one examines them, and no inhibition or check impedes them. How excellent it would be if the authorities [or police: *rijal al-zabt*] concerned themselves with those women; if they were punished with the heaviest punishments so they would not return to these corrupt practices.
>
> I am indeed astonished to find such situations [continuing] when all local newspapers have undertaken to criticise and name it as abhorrent, demanding from those in charge that they restrict it, to restore souls, put natures in order, and preserve decency and honour. It is not an issue requiring hard [thinking] ... We place strong hope in the authorities. It is not difficult for them to maintain surveillance over those little houses to curtail their inhabitants. They will reap gratitude.[60]

Men were presented as blameless victims of venereal disease-ridden women who had the gracelessness to insinuate their 'houses' into respectable neighbourhoods of civil servants, if they did not enter bourgeois homes themselves.

Such texts exhibit a pattern of imagery foregrounding 'weak' masculinity, unable to withstand these women's skills: the ultimate female trickster persona, echoing the venerable social and literary topos of 'women's wiles'. Constructing prostitutes as agents removed responsibility from customers, pimps or socioeconomic circumstances that might draw women to brothels. Clear class assignments were represented here: girls 'from the riffraff' seduced, and siphoned money from, the nation's 'eminent' families.

Al-Mu'ayyad's rhetoric on sex workers echoed state policy. Spatial restrictions had long regulated sex work. An 1834 law banned sex workers from Cairo; authorities monitored them via a name registry.[61] Though public hostility may have been a factor, Khaled Fahmy argues that 'concerns about the health and discipline of the troops and students of his newly founded army and schools . . . prompted the Pasha [Muhammad Ali] to ban prostitution' from areas where troops and military schools were concentrated.[62] '[H]ad the ban been caused by concerns about public morals and common decency, it would have been more thoroughly applied throughout Egypt.'[63] Threats to public order engendered by prostitutes carrying liquor, rather than their presence per se, apparently engendered official action, while spectres of venereal disease motivated government action.[64] These concerns surfaced regularly in the press, where women were consistently blamed for spreading the disease. In *al-Mu'ayyad*, one hears echoes of Muhammad 'Ali's head army physician, French doctor Clot Bey, writing half a century before: 'these women . . . have no sense of propriety in shamelessly practising prostitution and adultery'.[65]

If the dominant concern was regulating sex work to minimise threats to men's health, which meant focusing on spaces of prostitution – the brothel more than the prostitute's body, as Fahmy says – it makes sense that newspaper stories conveyed anxiety about urban neighbourhoods as spaces to be 'protected' against prostitutes. These stories echoed petitions and responded to police reports. The dispatch from Bani Suwayf quoted earlier responds to an 1893 Interior Ministry directive saying prostitutes were to be barred 'from taking up residence among the dwellings of *al-ahrar*'.[66] But the state did not provide alternatives. Sex workers continued to settle in these neighbourhoods, and newspapers continued to report and complain.

Commenting on Foucault's elaboration of *faits divers* as a genre with disciplinary implications, Ann Miller notes:

from the nineteenth century onwards [the *fait divers*] has offered newspaper readers a constant reminder of the menacing presence of criminals in their midst, thereby performing the important function of marking the boundary which separates delinquents from their poor but honest fellow-members of the working class.[67]

As in cases of criminality, repeated reminders of prostitutes in society's midst could – to follow Foucault's argument summarised by Miller – 'justify the apparatus of surveillance and control to which all members of the public must be subjected'.[68] Yet such narratives accepted and underwrote a social differentiation: economic standing, social status and gender mark out striated positions in the emerging nation's hierarchised diagram of its national public. As authorities were called upon to rescue Egypt's young elite males from corruption and disease by removing from their sight the infecting female presence of the sex worker, all readers were reminded that these women effaced red lines of respectability. They required constant watching – as did 'respectable women' who appeared so vulnerable to infection. And yet, did such texts not only 'justify' disciplinary action but call its efficacy into question? Textual repetition of such incidents, and the tone of exasperation accompanying them, could cast doubt on the state's authority through the very necessity of repetition. Narratives of anxiety about the tainting proximity of prostitutes came not only from Alexandria, Zaqaziq and Fayyum but also from Bani Suwayf, Port Said, Qena, Dumyat, Tanta ... and the peril lay not simply in their presence but in their acts of 'wily' concealment, pretending to be 'honourable women', infecting the social body from within the neighbourhood:

> Secret houses of prostitutes concealed by the garb of chasteness and protection [*al-'ahirat al-mukhtafiyyat bi-zayy al-'iffa wa al-sawn*] have become numerous. The existence of these houses amidst homes of respectable women [*al-ahrar*] indubitably creates a channel of infection geared to sow corruption, eliminate the formalities of decency and end human taboos. We turn the attention of our government to deflecting these corrupt women [*al-fajirat*] from conveying reprehensible practices. Moreover, often youths [spending time] among them are stricken with venereal disease – indeed it is a rare one who is not afflicted by these women. This [neighbourhood] Kafrat Iskarus is the grandest example of such reprehensible practices, even

if it does contain many houses occupied by government bureaucrats and respected people ... no neighbour can speak to this dissolute mistress of the house [*rabbat al-manzil al-fajira*] because she is as obscene/whorish [*mufhisha*] in words as in deeds.⁶⁹

Such concerns were not unique to Egypt, nor were anxieties about 'contamination' of good neighbourhoods, with their classed or colonial implications. In eighteenth-century Damascus, judges had sex workers removed from neighbourhoods when residents complained.⁷⁰ As Deborah Epstein Nord comments about nineteenth-century Britain and France: 'The narratives of prostitutes' lives that began to appear in certain mid-century treatises and investigations encouraged the idea that the woman of the streets was not wholly separable from the respectable bourgeois home.'⁷¹ Considering prostitution in Britain's Southeast Asian colonies, Philippa Levine notes colonial officials' alarm over prostitutes' visibility and yet their anxiety over concealed prostitution, for 'the public/private dichotomy of the metropole broke apart easily in the unstable and dangerous colonial environment'.⁷² Colonial officials worked to separate brothels from residential districts 'not only to sharpen the distinction between respectable and unrespectable but to separate the business of sex from the place of feminine domesticity'.⁷³ Scandal erupted in 1890s Rangoon when brothels opened 'in respectable parts of the Town', as a contemporary notice announced.⁷⁴ In colonial Bombay, an increasingly concentrated red-light district vigorously policed by the colonial state was partly the result of demographic pressures with increased migration to cities, and complaints from 'respectable' areas; symbiotic relationships between police and brothel keepers yielded 'coercive protection' for sex workers, easier to control in designated city spaces.⁷⁵ In 1890s Cairo, colonial officials were concerned with regulating sex work,⁷⁶ but in the nationalist press this was a discourse of the *indigenous* male intelligentsia, shaped partly by publicised views of French and British officials on the 'essentially sexualised nature of "orientals"'.⁷⁷

As noted, sex workers' nationalities were rarely mentioned, particularly as they appeared as anonymous aggregates.⁷⁸ Perhaps readers understood complaints in the context of anxieties about non-Egyptians in Egypt, especially when coupled with polemics on such presences tainting young Egyptians

– women by giving them seductive examples in their own neighbourhoods, men by drawing their custom, taking their money and being infected with syphilis. Readers may have understood 'riffraff' (as in the earlier quote) as signifying a European-origin underclass circulating through Mediterranean ports. Yet *al-Mu'ayyad*'s Alexandria correspondent warned against automatically blaming foreigners as he noted widespread complaints about prostitutes (so abundant, he said, that city folk were moving to less appealing areas further from their workplaces). He criticised those who placed blame on 'some foreign tramps, men and women . . . spreading like locusts'; Egyptians were equally culpable.[79]

Narratives of 'respectable' women allegedly drawn into prostitution did occasionally implicate local women; detachment from a local moral community was the scandal. Amidst front-page essays on divorce and rights of children born of relationships outside marriage, *al-Mu'ayyad* reported an honour crime near Shabas wa'l-Safiya. A true *fait divers* – a crime and its consequences – moved from local reporting to front-page news:

> Near Qaranshu lives a man named al-Hajj 'Ali al-'Antabli with a married daughter. But it got around that she was violating the purity of her reputation and selling her honour in prostitution. When anger goaded her family, her brothers devised a ruse, pouring poison into a bottle containing medicine she took daily. When signs of poisoning appeared on her and the village elders heard, they informed the police who brought the doctor. His examination determined she had been poisoned. Further investigation revealed poison in that bottle. Though what happened was officially known, her brothers showed up [again] with a vessel of poison and poured it for her, saying it was medicine. She took it and died instantly. The affair reached the police who informed the public prosecutor's office. There was an investigation; the judge attended along with the prosecutor's representative and doctor. They arrested those upon whom the accusation focused.[80]

Older patterns of justice that might exonerate brothers on the argument of protecting family honour (and the hint that the brothers, bringing more poison after their ruse was uncovered, were confident of this) give way to intervention by the state's local representatives.[81] Local young women – and not only in cities – were acting in ways that led family members to accuse them of prostitution, yielding family quarrels that got into the newspaper and circulated within ongoing representation of disruptive subjects. The acts might not be new but their labelling, and new status as national events once reported in a national/ist newspaper, were novel. One could argue that women appeared in these features because they were exceptional, not ordinary; because women in bars and villagers turned alleged prostitutes were rarities. Yet the repeated worry that 'respectable women' were following such examples suggests these representations were more than curiosities with entertainment value.

How new were such concerns? The spatial management of gendered bodies had long been recognised in Islamic law as crucial to the management of the community of believers. Issues of gender mixing percolated through earlier Muslim jurists' writings, though this concerned not a public–private divide nor a fixed sense of gendered spaces and places. Islamic law did address gender-spatial segregation

> on the principle that space was and should be gendered, that a cardinal principle of social organization was that of gender segregation spatially constructed. Such segregation was directly and consciously linked, not to a philosophy of separate spheres, but rather to the problem of human sexuality and the power of sexual attraction to disrupt society and threaten the unity and stability of Muslim communities . . . Muslim jurists engaged the issue of space as an issue of male and female interaction: space was gendered in the sense that they thought some social boundaries between men and women should be maintained, and male–female interaction should be carefully regulated.[82]

The principle that women should stay at home featured in later jurisprudence. Re-voicing such principles in the press conveyed them to a larger public. Concern with the contaminating potential of women who moved freely through city neighbourhoods – and in and out of bars – suggests these principles and the vision of social organisation shaping them not only remained strongly salient but were all the more important given increasing numbers of European residents, new types of social spaces and new possibilities for feminine mobility. 'News from the street' was read within a related continuum, an incessant commentary on the perceived emergence of more women into public spaces. If the spatial distribution of sex work and its contamination effects were at issue, the visibility of female bodies and the bleeding of this visibility from sex workers to 'free women' haunted press reports. For earlier jurists, '*fitna* or disorder arising from uncontrolled lust and illicit sexual interactions does not originate with women per se, but rather is attributed to some disreputable men, even if it is a problem to be solved by restricting women's movements'.[83] In these press reports though, blame passed to women. Women in open carriages, women walking the streets: represented as 'invasions' of public space, they suggest generalised anxiety. Decades earlier the sex worker's body and workplace perhaps generated concern more about security than morality. But by the mid-1890s, representation of sex work took on synechdochal resonance in warning against women's visibility and mobility across social strata. Images framed in warnings articulated a sense that policing women's activities was part of what it meant to be a modern state, its international image dependent on the reputation of 'its women'.

In this context, notices about sex workers' visibility were not unconnected to polemics on women's other activities. A report from Port Said complained of women's funeral rites:

> I intended to furnish you with an explanation of the reprehensible custom women employ behind funeral processions. They wail, faces uncovered, hands and garb dyed, all the while screaming and moaning. Your Samanud correspondent spared me the trouble. Just let me say I share his outlook, raising a plea to the authorities to investigate this ugly custom with a perceptive eye and to issue severe orders to prevent it, in order to preserve public decency, safeguard honour and fortify the *shari'a*.[84]

That the women wailed 'faces uncovered', making themselves a *spectacle*, seemed as disturbing as the sound of women's voices, whether to conservative critics arguing that women's voices were *'awra*, impermissibly revealed private parts, or to nationalist men who supported a more visible social role for women (of their own strata) but sought an orderly, quiet public street and orderly, quiet women as emblems of Egypt's capacity for self-rule. Women's public mourning had long been a loudly bemoaned target of reformers (as manifesting women's adherence to 'superstitious' practices); Khedive Isma'il had banned the practice of women following funeral corteges.[85]

In *al-Mu'ayyad*, this report of public spectacle immediately followed one from Port Said on another procession through city streets:

> Late yesterday afternoon there formed the opening procession [of the annual Sufi celebration of the Prophet's birthday], according to customary practice. It moved through the streets of the port city with utter orderliness, preceded by the men of the police under the leadership of the fine and energetic Muhammad Efendi Subhi, senior officer of al-'Arab precinct.[86]

This male-populated event enjoyed the cooperation, indeed leadership, of the state in the form of its participating officers, who in turn enjoyed the bounty of a religious aura in celebrating the Prophet's birthday. The orthodox establishment did not always look kindly on Sufi activities but this respectable version received its blessing. Variants of the related terms *'ada, mu'tada* (custom, customary) describe both processions. But only in the case of the women is 'custom' modified by *qabiha* (ugly, reprehensible).

Thus, consistently voiced concern about women in public focused on females as vocal and visible: voices and faces uncovered, moving bodies. An 'apparatus of surveillance and control', in Levine's words, was repeatedly invoked not only to curtail sex workers but to keep other visible women from infecting women in general by their example:

> Many who love the nation's/community's honour [*karamat al-umma*] and preserve its morals have asked us to solicit from our government a restriction on women riding in open carriages, showing off their adornment and flashy finery. They circulate among the ranks of men's carriages, in places of public promenade. This act transgresses decency and lowers the value of the country's honour. If these women are prostitutes, the system of public order requires they not be present in these public places which are not devoid of the people or upper classes, not to mention modest secluded women from well-known families in their closed carriages. If there is among those showy women anyone who is not a prostitute, it is incumbent on her like not to ride in an uncovered carriage, exposing herself to accusations and suspicion. This matter is entirely within the expertise and duties of the Diwan al-Muhafaza, which should scrutinise it.[87]

Good Women in Print

Al-Mu'ayyad did not report all instances of 'visible' females negatively. Not long after this notice, the newspaper reported approvingly on the new Ottoman policy of granting medical licences to female physicians. This would make possible the unfettered physical examination of female patients.[88] Nor were women the only disturbers of the peace: recall the correspondent from al-Ibrahimiyya who complained about loud, obscene, pillaging male hashish-den customers. Also countering the trope of women as unacceptably 'public' was the appearance of *al-Mu'ayyad*'s first female bylines. Egyptian poet 'A'isha Taymur sent an encomium to the Khedive;[89] the newspaper announced publication of her treatise *Mir'at al-ta'ammul fi al-umur*. It published an essay by Sara Nawfal on dangers of restrictive clothing,[90] and several by Zaynab Fawwaz.[91] There were approving notices of girls' school openings and graduations where female students recited poems, making everyone proud. *Faits divers* that narrated disturbances to the social fabric – and the reweaving of that fabric through family and state interventions – were interleaved with references to progress and deficiency in the nation's educational infrastructure for girls and boys.

But the outcome of these positive examples of female 'visibility' confirmed the opposite. Licensed female physicians assured that female patients remained secluded from unrelated men. Women who wrote at home and published in the press were a reassuring indication that one could be modern without challenging the physical separation of genders. Girls' schools carried a similar message. The opposite image of the woman in the bar or the loud, unveiled woman in the open carriage was the elite schoolgirl, precious burden borne between home and school in her family's closed carriage. She was not as frequent an inhabitant of newspaper pages as the sex worker; she was less visible, less vocal except inside the school walls – a quiet sign of shifting understandings:

> The girls' school run by Mrs. Kastaniyoli, located in Qasurat Bughus, celebrated handing diplomas to entitled students. This took place the day before yesterday in the presence of many senior civil servants, literary lights, and notables. [The girl students] acted a lovely play in French; the actresses did very well. This was followed by recitation in Arabic, ending with a

dialogue; those present laughed at its fine meanings. Prizes went to deserving recipients . . . invitees departed thanking the esteemed school director and praising her fine efforts.[92]

Gender politics saturated *al-Mu'ayyad*, from articles on how gendered practices defined the nation to announcing publication of a novel focusing on coerced marriage, to articles on the importance of the family. But 'news from the street' invaded with stark reminders that the preferred gender arrangements of modern nationalists with their cautious, reform-minded debates were not spaces inhabited by all. These local columns are rich with stories, lives and local issues, but day after day women appear as personae who are lewd, loud and obnoxiously visible, if they are not dead – victims of crime, medical mishaps or economic want.

National Mediators and Active Readers

In its opening article, *al-Mu'ayyad*'s editor explicated how newspapers carry out their duty:

> As long as everyone needs a share in things, they cannot do without exchange of ideas and knowledge of news . . . People are either one man or the other: ruler, ruled [*al-nas rajulan: hakimun wa-mahkumun*]. Between the two are reciprocal demands and commensurate rights . . . The function of truthful national newspapers is to explain the two sides' demands and translate their ideas . . . *Al-Mu'ayyad* is a national/ist newspaper aiming to be emissary of the good, a postal channel [*al-barid*] for claims. It explains sentiments of the ruled body [*al-hay'a al-mahkuma*], striving to air concealed needs, putting these into the hands of the ruling body [*al-hay'a al-hakima*], even if the latter is more knowledgeable, has more accurate information, is more powerful to act, more aware of symptoms or harbingers of the times and more knowing of where needs are situated. Likewise, it will clarify to the community [*al-umma*] [every] demand it thinks right and appropriate . . .
>
> And so here for you, sons of Egypt [*ya bani Misr*] is a newspaper formed in the cradle of sincere fidelity . . .[93]

Invoking an audience, the newspaper's terms of address were gendered. While *bani Misr*, drawing on a kinship metaphor (sons/tribe of Egypt), is reasonably seen as gender-inclusive, implied readership was more forthrightly gendered through the plural *abna'* (sons) and *rajul/rijal* (man/men). Readers were exhorted to recognise 'present conditions, demanding you do your duty, making you men who compete with men'.[94] Each (male) corporate group was addressed, beginning with the *fallah* (peasant), exhorting him to 'cooperate through devout duty, not in crime and aggression'. Second-person address interpolated male peasants as readers.

As noted earlier, *al-Mu'ayyad*'s deictics constructed three-way discursive relationships – local residents, correspondents communicating residents' demands to authorities, and the newspaper as a forum disseminating this news to locales nationwide. The local correspondent spoke for residents; as reader he read and responded to other correspondents' words; as first-person narrator he engaged in events; as a local person of some authority he communicated to local governmental authorities and reported it ('They believed what I said and arrested him'). As examples have shown, correspondents – usually residents of towns or regions from which they reported – editorialised, urging official action, implying official inaction. The newspaper's rhetoric authorised it as spokesperson for local constituencies: 'We draw the attention of the authorities . . .' Local reportage thus combined event reporting and political advocacy – in John Hartley's terms, active readership.[95] Use of first person made the correspondent part of the scene, dramatising and personalising reports, and set up a 'we/them' dichotomy putting newspaper and correspondent/reader/consumer in contestation but also conversation with the state, as canny collective questioner of authorities. Announcing events to local constituencies, correspondents might affirm met needs, if through tragedy:

> Shirbin, 31 December 1892, from our correspondent: Into God's mercy passed the wife of Mr. Mustafa al-Hishi. The cause of her death was this: with her time of delivery at hand, she spent four days with the fetus in her womb though it had died. When it proved difficult to extract the fetus, her soul left her. May God have the vastest mercy on her and give her family patience and condolences.
>
> We seize the opportunity of this ill-omened event to inform guardians of families that a physician has been appointed to our town to catch such

incidents. Otherwise we could not but hear daily news of pregnant women, rending one's insides from grief, sending hearts into despair.[96]

The paper's rhetorical self-situating as agent of national/ist development gave *faits divers* an interventionary role: correspondents' clever praise of officials applied pressure – and readers across the nation were listening:

> Port Said 22 August, from our correspondent: We have written before on the police in incidents that contravene justice. We begged the police to investigate.
>
> This morning, a policeman came and took possession of a [public] spigot ... and barred the public from it. He prevented a poor woman wanting to fill her jug but she would not stay away so he hit her to get her to retreat, and tore her tattered clothes. A civil servant from the Interior Ministry was passing by and was seized by sympathy for this poor woman so he pushed the policeman away from her. The policeman grabbed him, meaning to drag him to the senior officer at Hayy al-Gharb [district station]. A crowd gathered. A detachment from the police [station] came and extracted the civil servant from the policeman. The problem was dispelled.
>
> When I requested the police officers to look into this matter, they gave us no ear. This time, with the tongue of your *Mu'ayyad* I entreat His Honour the Governor to investigate, well known as he is for love of reform and [caring about] the comfort of the populace.[97]

'With the tongue of your *Mu'ayyad*': the correspondent worked for the newspaper, wrote as local resident. Unsigned, he was the newspaper's presence in the town and the town's presence in the newspaper. He addressed local officials, provincial governors and central government. Can it be said that in Egypt, as in France, the reporter felt 'rival to the police, equal of the magistrate, the conscience of politics'?[98] I think so. As Tambe elaborates for Bombay and Liat Kozma for earlier nineteenth-century Egypt, newspapers, official reports and court records were more than informational reportage: on these terrains, workings of the modern state were announced, debated, contested, even formed.[99] Tambe notes the importance of the vernacular press in Bombay, through which a rising middle-class intelligentsia 'railed against the government, since they were unable to get a hearing in official debates'.¹⁰⁰ In Cairo, as Bombay, discursive spaces with material consequences put women's bodies and men's acts at the forefront of political representations.

And in Paris. It is important to consider coeval discourses and to think about what that means for communications amongst newspapers and intelligentsias; I can only gesture to that here. The 1890s press in France was saturated with stories of catastrophe, scandal and human creepiness, fuelling a discourse about public insecurity, a perceived rise in urban crime rates, articulations of anger at incompetence or inaction by authorities. This textually marked-out increase in crime – thus, in fear of it – was not borne out by statistics. It seems a product of increased competition for circulation, a response to what editors and *fait-diversiers* figured readers wanted. In Egypt, increasingly fierce nationalist discourse about public order – particularly young women's and young men's public behaviour – was fuelled by *hawadith*. Repeated narratives about sex workers and 'respectable matrons' might invoke fears of blurred spatial and social boundaries through a blurred journalistic genre, simultaneously *faits divers* and petition.

Conclusion

Recent work on the nineteenth-century emergence of the modern Egyptian state emphasises it as an outcome of negotiations between subjects and state representatives in local venues.¹⁰¹ Representation of such daily negotiations proliferated in back-page news of Egyptians' occupation of spaces. These figures appear as simultaneously undisciplined and unevenly subject to constraining forces of journalist-citizens seeking state intervention to discipline their use of public and 'neighbourly' space.

Barthes's notion of 'immanence' in *faits divers* centres on reported events' lack of concrete external political context; they escape the realm of 'partial' meaning, requiring an external referent.¹⁰² *Faits divers* are whole unto themselves:

> Al-Rahaniyya: A woman washing her clothes at the river fell into the water and drowned. Her corpse was pulled out. Police were informed. After examination of her corpse and signing [the report], the order to hold her burial was given.¹⁰³

This terse narrative – the sense of which does not depend on the reader's familiarity with an individual or family – holds meaning that in a different sense makes it 'partial'. It shows the state at work, the orderly progression of events after an everyday tragedy, the presence of authorities, the family's recognition of the state's claims to participation. Beyond its immediate circuit of reference the *fait divers* participates in a larger system of meaning-making, a circulation of ideas about social norms and boundaries, and appropriate institutional interventions in individual lives.

None of this material found its way into *al-Mu'ayyad*'s annual volume of selected articles. This was not the visible, up-front stuff of nationalist dailies.[104] Yet, to focus on anonymous women whose presence in public space was deemed disruptive resonated with core contestations of public politics. For nationalists espousing divergent programmes, a coherent or at least shared nationalist perspective was coalescing, imagining the 'good' woman and/as the nation versus the representationally disruptive and disobedient woman claiming public space. Good females in public space rode in closed carriages, were silent, went to girls' schools and directly home afterwards. A few women were shown as pursuing rights through courts. But loud reported clamour of 'public' women as disruptions of national fabric was a consistent presence on the represented street, spilling over to 'infect' representation of all women. As Tambe notes, 'It is a commonplace of feminist theory that the cultural denigration of sexually promiscuous women assists in disciplining women in general.'[105] These press vignettes, targeting 'a' gender, use sexualised and violent images of gendered social positions to delineate a notion of modernly proper and properly modern spatial and social organisation. Pressures forming an activist Egyptian nationalism as a vocal response to colonial rule – an observer and shaper of new social understandings whose validity was contested through representing (and disciplining) women – murmured quietly but insistently through *faits divers* as they reverberated loudly through the newspaper's more prominent front-page features.

Notes

1. 'Mukatabat', *al-Mu'ayyad* 3:595 (17 January 1892), p. 3. Another woman poisoning her husband appears, 3:604 (27 January 1892), p. 2. The woman

seeking divorce/annulment would not have received it; Hanafi jurisprudence did not allow this concerning husbands' prison sentences, until 1920 and 1929 personal status law modifications (communication from Ken Cuno). All translations (Arabic and French) are mine. This paper was delivered at the Mediterranean Research Meeting, Robert Schumann Centre of the European University, Montecatini Terme, March 2008 and revised soon afterwards; referencing some newer research, I have not reworked the chapter in the long interval between original revision and publication.

2. 'Hawadith mahalliyya', *al-Mu'ayyad* 2:341 (25 January 1891), p. 3.
3. Tambe, *[codes of misconduct]*, pp. 19, 20, 27.
4. See also ibid., pp. 80, 102–3.
5. Kozma, *Policing Egyptian Women*. Police records and the 1880 Police Act she relies on correlate with what I had already found in newspaper vignettes of this later period.
6. Local French-language media were perhaps models.
7. For example, Ibn al-Athir, *Chronicle*.
8. Ibid., p. 33.
9. Ibid., p. 134.
10. When I wrote this chapter little attention had been given to this for the nineteenth century, more to the twentieth, especially the 1920s as key years for formation of an Egyptian moral modernity. For instance, highlighting crime reporting, Shaun Lopez argued it was the 'major media sensation' sparked by the 1921 trials of sisters Raya and Sakina for multiple murder that led 'commentators . . . [to] formulate[ ] an Egyptian cultural identity based on a unitary, national notion of moral behavior . . . Examples of immorality . . . became symbolic of the negative impact of Europe on Egyptian society, and of the need to formulate a modernity that respected the cultural practices of the Egyptian nation.' Lopez dismisses earlier crime coverage as insignificant in scope and readership but the process he describes was well under way a quarter-century before. Perhaps coverage of the trial was resonant *because* it built upon well-established tropes in the national/ist press. Lopez, 'Madams, Murders, and the Media', pp. 372, 377.
11. 'Bab al-maqalat: tarikh al-nahda al-'ilmiyya al-akhira fi misr wa al-sham', *al-Hilal* 9:7 (1 January 1901), p. 201.
12. 'Bab al-maqalat: tarikh al-nahda al-'ilmiyya al-akhira fi misr wa al-sham: IV: al-tiba'a fi Misr', *al-Hilal* 9:11 (1 March 1901), pp. 319–23. On the press law, see pp. 321–3; quote on p. 323.

13. 'Maqasid *al-Mu'ayyad*', *al-Mu'ayyad* 1:1 (1 December 1889), p. 1; also in *Muntakhabat al-Mu'ayyad*, pp. 2–3. On newspaper and proprietor, see Salih, *al-Shaykh 'Ali Yusuf*.
14. 'Abduh, *Tatawwur al-sihafa al-misriyya 1798–1951*, p. 100; called the 'third printing', it carries the story to 1951 and so is an updated edition.
15. Walker, *Outrage*, p. 1.
16. Shaya, 'The *Flâneur*'.
17. Kalifa, *L'encre*, p. 28.
18. Walker, *Outrage*, p. 2.
19. Monestier, *Le fait divers*, p. 56, quoted in Walker, *Outrage*, p. 18.
20. Walker, *Outrage*, p. 18.
21. 'Hawadith mahalliyya', *al-Mu'ayyad* 4:1040 (26 August 1893), p. 3.
22. 'Mukatabatuna', *al-Mu'ayyad* 4:954 (4 April 1893), p. 2.
23. Polydore Michaud's *Le Petit Journal* (1863) is deemed the epitome and engine of *faits divers*, derived from earlier event reporting in broadsheets. This and other journals instituted illustrated supplements with text and photogravure focused on *faits divers*. Kalifa dates 'the era of the *fait divers*' to 1869, via 'l'affaire Troppmann'. Kalifa, *L'encre*, p. 11.
24. Kalifa, *L'encre*, p. 53.
25. Ibid., p. 54.
26. Shaya, 'The *Flâneur*'; Kolstrup, 'Les fonctions du fait divers', pp. 146–59.
27. Kolstrup, 'Les fonction du fait divers', p. 148.
28. Walker, *Outrage*, p. 1.
29. Baudrillard, *La société de consommation*.
30. Kalifa, *L'encre*, pp. 9–10.
31. Weber, *France, Fin de siècle*.
32. For a fine exploration of this, see Chandra, *Sexual Life of English*.
33. 'Mukatabat: Minya', *al-Mu'ayyad* 5:1177 (7 January 1894), p. 3.
34. 'Mukatabat', *al-Mu'ayyad* 5:1173 (2 January 1894), p. 3.
35. 'Mukatabat', *al-Mu'ayyad* 5:1174 (3 January 1894), p. 2.
36. 'Hawadith mahalliyya: al-Ibrahimiyya', *al-Mu'ayyad* 5:1183 (15 January 1894), p. 2. *Khatf*: grabbing things or people, kidnapping, or rape; here, probably purse-snatching or groping.
37. 'Hawadith mahalliyya: Bani Suwayf', *al-Mu'ayyad* 5:1186 (18 January 1894), p. 2.
38. *Al-Mu'ayyad* 5:1182 (14 January 1894), p. 1; 5:1183 (15 January 1894), p. 2; 5:1183 (15 January 1894), p. 3.

39. 'Hawadith', *al-Mu'ayyad* 2:519 (8 September 1891), p. 3.
40. *Al-Mu'ayyad* 1:12 (25 Rabi' II/18 December 1889), p. 3.
41. Nasif, *al-Nisa'iyyat*.
42. *Al-Mu'ayyad* 1:141 (24 May 1890), p. 1.
43. *'isma wa-siyana*: *'isma* connotes (for women) virtuousness, particularly imperviousness to sexual transgressions or temptations, implying sexual 'purity'. *Siyana* means 'preservation', safe-guarding', having male protection against sexual transgression; the passive participle *masuna*, 'well-protected', is an epithet for virtuous women and can carry class connotations – a woman well enough off that she need not go into public. Both invoke sexual purity's importance to family reputation. Mere suggestion of women in bars demolishes *'isma wa-siyana*; 'well-protected' means isolated from such sites. A woman in a bar is already 'damaged goods', hence lacking *siyana*.
44. 'Min akhbar al-Fayyum', *al-Mu'ayyad* 2:313 (23 December 1890), p. 2.
45. 'Al-Dhuriyya fi Faransa', *al-Mu'ayyad* 2:314 (24 December 1890), p. 1. Reports from the French press on out-of-wedlock births, abortions and female suicides during the Third Republic appear in other journals, such as *al-Nil* and *al-Ahram*.
46. Weber, *France, Fin de siècle*, pp. 12–13, 23.
47. 'Al-Fayyum', *al-Mu'ayyad* 2:316 (27 December 1890), p. 2.
48. 'Maqasid *al-Mu'ayyad*', *al-Mu'ayyad* 1:1 (1 December 1889), p. 1; also in *Muntakhabat al-Mu'ayyad*, pp. 2–3; quote on p. 2.
49. This is complicated by the politics of alliance locally and vis-à-vis the Ottoman Sultan, including shifting relationships between the Khedive and 'Ali Yusuf, in the colonial context – too vast to broach here.
50. 'al-Fatiha', *al-Mu'ayyad* 1:1 (1 December 1889), p. 1; also in *Muntakhabat al-Mu'ayyad*, p. 1.
51. 'Mukatabat: Shabas wa al-Safiya', *al-Mu'ayyad* 2:408 (15 April 1891), p. 2.
52. *Al-Mu'ayyad* claimed a *Times* article advised Egypt's government to grant licences for importing hashish, 'saying it was as necessary to Egyptians as opium to Indians – what a piece of advice the English rulers and political writers give us! . . . They know the spread of hashish in Egyptian territory corrupts morals and comportment and kills a person's honorable sensibilities and will.' *Al-Mu'ayyad* 5:1176 (6 January 1894), p. 2.
53. For example, a treatise published by an Ottoman military man, Rashid Ghazi b. Abi 'Ubayd Ahmad b. Sulayman al-Sayrafi, *Kitab kashf al-niqab 'an anwa' al-sharab* ([1887] 1306). Fierce about medical ramifications of alcohol,

hashish, coffee and tea, it invokes Islamic injunctions but recognises human frailties.
54. Ahad fudala' Tlimsin, 'Al-Zawaj al-qahri fi al-Jaza'ir', *al-Mu'ayyad* 2:417 (26 April 1891), p. 1.
55. 'Al-Iskandariyya', *al-Mu'ayyad* 3:741 (19 July 1892), p. 2.
56. 'Al-Iskandariyya', *al-Mu'ayyad* 1:3 (15 Rabi' II/8 December 1889), p. 2.
57. Ibid., p. 3.
58. *Al-Mu'ayyad* 5:1225 (5 March 1894), p. 2.
59. *Al-Mu'ayyad* 3:556 (2 December 1891), p. 2.
60. 'Mukatabat: al-Fayyum', *al-Mu'ayyad* 2:521 (10 September 1891), p. 2.
61. Fahmy, 'Prostitution', pp. 78–9.
62. Ibid., pp. 81–2. On sex work and the state, see Booth, 'Un/safe/ly at Home'; Booth, 'Between Harem and Houseboat'; Tucker, *Women in Nineteenth-Century Egypt*; Hilal, *Al-Baghaya fi Misr*.
63. Fahmy, 'Prostitution', p. 82.
64. Ibid., pp. 83–4.
65. Egyptian National Archives (Dar al-Watha'iq al-Qawmiyya), *Diwan al-Jihadiyya*, Register 437, Doc. 143, p. 169, 7 Jumada II 1263/23 May 1847, in English translation in Fahmy, 'Prostitution', p. 86.
66. An 1892 petition from a Cairo neighbourhood and the 1893 Interior Ministry directive, quoted in Fahmy, 'Prostitution', pp. 88–9.
67. Miller, 'Teulé's Gens de France', p. 320.
68. Ibid., p. 320.
69. 'Mukatabat: Tanta', *al-Mu'ayyad* 2:428 (14 May 1891), p. 2.
70. Rafeq, 'Public Morality in 18th-Century Ottoman Damascus', pp. 181–3, quoted in Tucker, *Women, Family, and Gender*, p. 198.
71. Nord, *Walking the Victorian Streets*, p. 10.
72. Levine, 'Cordon Sanitaire', p. 52.
73. Ibid., p. 55.
74. Ibid., p. 55.
75. Tambe, *[codes of misconduct]*, pp. 59–66, 100–1.
76. Booth, 'Un/safe/ly at Home'; Booth, 'Between Harem and Houseboat'; Fahmy, 'Prostitution'.
77. Fahmy, 'Prostitution', p. 85.
78. We find occasional references to 'female prostitutes foreign and national', as in a report from Alexandria on the Municipal Council's decision to open an inspection bureau. See *al-Mu'ayyad* 3:557 (3 December 1891), p. 2.

79. 'Al-Iskandariyya', *al-Mu'ayyad* 4:1075 (6 September 1893), p. 2.
80. 'Mukatabat: Shabas wa al-Safiya', *al-Mu'ayyad* 2:408 (15 April 1891), p. 2.
81. In another case, where brothers are arrested, tried and sentenced, *al-Mu'ayyad* calls the punishment unfair because – unlike husbands – brothers are part of the 'dishonourable' woman's birth family and can never disassociate themselves.
82. Tucker, *Women, Family, and Gender*, p. 177.
83. Ibid., p. 179.
84. 'Al-Wajh al-bahri', *al-Mu'ayyad* 4:1082 (14 September 1893), p. 2.
85. Thanks to Ken Cuno.
86. 'Al-Wajh al-bahri', *al-Mu'ayyad* 4:1082 (14 September 1893), p. 2.
87. 'Hawadith mahalliyya', *al-Mu'ayyad* 4:1119 (30 October 1893), p. 3.
88. 'Al-Tabibat fi al-mamalik al-shahaniyya', *al-Mu'ayyad* 5:1179 (9 January 1894), p. 1.
89. 'A'isha al-Taymuriyya, [Untitled poem], *al-Mu'ayyad* 1:269 (1 November 1890), p. 3; 'Mirat al-ta'ammul fi al-umur', *al-Mu'ayyad* 4:944 (23 March 1893), p. 3.
90. Sara Nawfal, 'Al-sihha afdal aw al-zayy', *al-Mu'ayyad* 3:652 (23 March 1893), p. 2. From *al-Ahram*.
91. Zaynab Fawwaz, 'Laysat al-sa'ada bi-kathrat al-mal', *al-Mu'ayyad* 667 (10 April 1892), p. 1.
92. *Al-Mu'ayyad* 2:527 (14 September 1891), p. 3.
93. 'Maqasad *al-Mu'ayyad*', *al-Mu'ayyad* 1:1 (1 December 1889), p. 1.
94. 'Ya bani Misr', *al-Mu'ayyad* 1:2 (4 December 1889), p. 1; also in *Muntakhabat al-Mu'ayyad*, pp. 7–11. On periodicals' rhetoric of address, see Booth, 'Woman in Islam'.
95. Hartley, *Popular Reality*.
96. *Al-Mu'ayyad* 4:875 (1 January 1893), p. 2.
97. 'Mukatabat', *al-Mu'ayyad* 3:767 (24 August 1892), p. 1.
98. Kalifa, *L'encre*, p. 69.
99. Tambe, *[codes of misconduct]*; Kozma, *Policing Egyptian Women*.
100. Tambe, *[codes of misconduct]*, pp. 47–8.
101. For example, Kozma, *Policing Egyptian Women*; El Shakry, *Great Social Laboratory*.
102. Barthes, 'Structure of the *Fait-Divers*'.
103. 'Mukatabat', *al-Mu'ayyad* 5:1287 (26 May 1894), p. 2.

104. *Muntakhabat al-Mu'ayyad.*
105. Tambe, *[codes of misconduct]*, p. 23.

Bibliography

'Abduh, Ibrahim, *Tatawwur al-sihafa al-misriyya 1798–1951* (Cairo: Maktabat al-adab, 1951).

Barthes, Roland, 'Structure of the *Fait-Divers*' (1962), in *Critical Essays*, trans. Richard Howard (Evanston, IL: Northwestern University Press, 1972), pp. 185–95.

Baudrillard, Jean, *La société de consommation* (Paris: Gallimard, 1970).

Booth, Marilyn, 'Between Harem and Houseboat: "Fallenness," Gendered Spaces and the Female National Subject in 1920s Egypt', in Marilyn Booth (ed.), *Harem Histories: Envisioning Places and Living Spaces* (Durham, NC: Duke University Press, 2011), pp. 342–73.

Booth, Marilyn, 'Un/safe/ly at Home: Narratives of Sexual Coercion in 1920s Egypt', *Gender and History* 16:3 (November 2004), pp. 744–68.

Booth, Marilyn, '*Woman in Islam*: Men and the "Women's Press" in Turn-of-the-20th-Century Egypt', *International Journal of Middle East Studies* 33:2 (May 2001), pp. 171–201.

Chandra, Shefali, *The Sexual Life of English: Languages of Caste and Desire in Colonial India* (Durham, NC: Duke University Press, 2012).

El Shakry, Omnia, *The Great Social Laboratory: Subjects of Knowledge in Colonial and Postcolonial Egypt* (Stanford: Stanford University Press, 2007).

Fahmy, Khaled, 'Prostitution in Egypt in the Nineteenth Century', in Eugene Rogan (ed.), *Outside In: On the Margins of the Modern Middle East* (London: I. B. Tauris, 2002), pp. 77–103.

Fawwaz, Zaynab, 'Laysat al-sa'ada bi-kathrat al-mal', *al-Mu'ayyad* 667 (10 April 1892), p. 1.

Hartley, John, *Popular Reality: Journalism, Modernity, Popular Culture* (London: Arnold, 1996).

Hilal, 'Imad, *Al-Baghaya fi Misr: Dirasa tarikhiyya ijtima'iyya (min 1834–1949)* (Cairo: al-'Arabi lil-nashr wa al-tawzi', 2001).

Ibn al-Athir, *The Chronicle of Ibn al-Kathir for the Crusading Period from* al-Kamil fi al-tarikh, *I: The Years 491–541/1097–1146: The Coming of the Franks and the Muslim Response*, trans. D. S. Richards (London: Ashgate, 2006).

Kalifa, Dominique, *L'encre et le sang: Récits de crimes et société à la Belle Époque* (Paris: Fayard, 1995).

Kolstrup, Søren, 'Les fonctions du fait divers dans la presse danoise (1850–1875)', *Les cahiers du Journalisme* 17 (Summer 2007), pp. 146–59.

Kozma, Liat, *Policing Egyptian Women: Sex, Law and Medicine in Khedivial Egypt* (Syracuse, NY: Syracuse University Press, 2011).

Levine, Philippa, 'The Cordon Sanitaire: Mobility and Space in the Regulation of Colonial Prostitution', in Sonita Sarker and Esha Niyogi De (eds), *Trans-Status Subjects: Gender in the Globalization of South and Southeast Asia* (Durham, NC: Duke University Press, 2002), pp. 51–66.

Lopez, Shaun T., 'Madams, Murders, and the Media: *Akhbar al-hawadith* and the Emergence of a Mass Culture in 1920s Egypt', in Arthur Goldschmidt, Amy J. Johnson and Barak A. Salmoni (eds), *Re-envisioning Egypt 1919–1952* (Cairo: American University in Cairo Press, 2005), pp. 371–97.

Miller, Ann, 'Teulé's Gens de France: Retelling the Fait Divers and Reframing the Evidence', *French Cultural Studies* 12 (2001), pp. 319–32.

Monestier, Alain (ed.), *Le fait divers* (Paris: Éditions de la Réunion des musées nationaux, 1982).

Muntakhabat al-Mu'ayyad: al-Sana al-ula 1890 (Cairo: Matba'at al-Mu'ayyad, 1324 AH).

Nasif, Malak Hifni, *al-Nisa'iyyat: Majmu'at maqalat nushirat fi* al-Jarida *fi mawdu' al-mar'a al-misriyya*, I–II (Cairo: Matba'at al-taqaddum, n.d.).

Nawfal, Sara, 'Al-sihha afdal aw al-zayy', *al-Mu'ayyad* 3:652 (23 March 1893), p. 2.

Nord, Deborah Epstein, *Walking the Victorian Streets: Women, Representation, and the City* (Ithaca, NY: Cornell University Press, 1995).

Salih, Sulayman, *al-Shaykh 'Ali Yusuf wa-jaridat* al-Mu'ayyad: *Tarikh al-haraka al-wataniyya fi rub' qarn* (Cairo: al-Hay'a al-'amma lil-kitab, 1990).

al-Sayrafi, Rashid Ghazi b. Abi 'Ubayd Ahmad b. Sulayman, *Kitab kashf al-niqab 'an anwa' al-sharab* (Beirut: al-Matba'a al-adabiyya, 1306 AH).

Shaya, Gregory, 'The *Flâneur*, the *Badaud*, and the Making of a Mass Public in France, circa 1860–1910', *American Historical Review* 109:1 (2004), pp. 41–77.

Tambe, Ashwini, *[codes of misconduct]: Regulating Prostitution in Late Colonial Bombay* (New Delhi: Zubaan, 2009).

al-Taymuriyya, 'A'isha, [Untitled poem], *al-Mu'ayyad* 1:269 (1 November 1890), p. 3.

Tucker, Judith E., *Women, Family, and Gender in Islamic Law* (Cambridge: Cambridge University Press, 2008).

Tucker, Judith, *Women in Nineteenth-Century Egypt* (Cambridge: Cambridge University Press, 1984).

Walker, David H., *Outrage and Insight: Modern French Writers and the 'Faits Divers'* (Oxford: Berg, 1995).

Weber, Eugen, *France, Fin de siècle* (Cambridge, MA: Belknap/Harvard University Press, 1986).

3

The Arabic Palestinian Press between the Two World Wars

Mustafa Kabha

The appearance of Arabic newspapers and journalistic discourse on the Palestinian political, social and cultural stage during the Mandate period shaped the social and cultural awareness of the readers to a great degree. Newspapers reflected the various opinions prevalent among the different sectors of readers and expressed the readers' social and cultural expectations. This occurred not only in the political sphere. Various social classes perceived the newspapers and the journalistic discourse as a suitable platform for expressing themselves and presenting demands, desires and criticism in a Palestine confronting the Zionist project under the British rule.

Global Dimensions of the Palestinian Press

Palestinian society gave rise to a dynamic and diverse press with different kinds of periodicals (dailies, weeklies, monthlies, reviews) that were a central element in the political expression of different trends and outlooks. Some newspapers gave voice to the causes of these sectors as practical fulfilment of their role as an informative instrument shaping and influencing public opinion. The newspaper *al-Karmil*, for example, side by side with years of political activity, also dedicated a great deal of attention to the rural classes and to topics of land and agriculture. It often addressed the peasants and guided them on issues such as modern methods of cultivation, desirable crops, circumventing the dominance and the control of the wealthy families who owned the large agricultural assets, or fighting the phenomenon of the sale of land and speculation, which had become very prevalent.

Najib Nassar, the editor of *al-Karmil*, in contrast to the various Palestinian political organisations and institutions such as the Arab Executive Committee and the Higher Muslim Council, believed that words alone were not sufficient. He often visited distant villages and Bedouin encampments, in particular in the north and in the Valley of Bisan. In his travels he tried to organise alternatives to the traditional institutions that would be capable of assisting the peasants with their problems so that they would be able to resist the proposals of agents and speculators.

This activity is attested to in letters sent by readers from the villages visited by Nassar. They expressed thanks to the editor for his actions as well as raising questions relating to agricultural work and desirable crops or how to avoid paying commissions and to bypass the marketing monopoly of the urban notable families who owned the most significant agricultural assets.[1]

Despite the responses and reactions of the readers, Nassar constantly complained of being poorly compensated for supporting the cause of the peasants and other underrepresented groups. From time to time he addressed rural subscribers and demanded that they pay their dues, and when general appeals proved of no avail he began citing names, criticising those who liked to read the paper but did not want to pay for it.

Other influential newspapers controlled by the rich urban families did not dwell much on these issues, and their reporters in the rural sector were apparently also discouraged from doing so. Thus they avoided harming the interests of newspaper owners who had accumulated their fortunes from profits made in the agricultural sector (the al-'Isa family, for example, who owned the newspaper *Filastin*, reaped profits from their involvement in the citrus industry, and some of these profits were invested in the newspaper).[2] Newspapers owned by these families usually expressed conservative views, claiming that Palestinian society had been debilitated by the pervasion of foreign ideologies, particularly communism, amongst the new Palestinian intelligentsia. The newspaper editors and journalists affiliated with these traditional camps claimed that communist ideology was very harmful to the working class targeted by the communists. They were apprehensive at the increasing power of the workers' unions in the early 1930s, when the workers began their struggle for higher wages and shorter working days, and they conducted an extensive campaign against communism and against strikes in general.[3] The newspaper *Filastin*, for example, objected to the use of strikes as a means of achieving goals.[4] In contrast, *al-Karmil* attacked this view and stated that it was based on the concerns of employers and merchants who sought to protect their own interests.[5]

Filastin and other newspapers owned by rich urban families were not able to convince the readers of their conflicting views on the most important issues occupying the Palestinians at this time, namely the matter of the sale of lands and the accelerated process of urbanisation that brought thousands of destitute villagers to search for work in the rapidly developing coastal cities (mainly Haifa and Jaffa). These two processes were interrelated. Following the sale of extensive agricultural lands to the Jewish Agency in the first half of the 1930s, thousands of tenants and peasants lost their main source of livelihood and began arriving in the cities en masse in search of work. Since they could not return home at the end of the working day, they built tin huts and shacks near their workplaces. In time many slums were formed and these became fertile ground for the vigorous activities of religious activists (such as Shaykh 'Iz al-Din al-Qassam and Shaykh Yusuf al-Zibawi) or communist activists (such as Bulus Farah), who tried to organise the masses of poor and exploited workers in groups and organisations to improve their miserable conditions. The religious activists saw Britain and the Jewish settlement as the target of their protests and struggle, conducting at times violent underground activities to achieve their political and social goals. Communist activists, on the other hand, claimed that the Palestinian upper class was equally responsible for the existing situation and believed that the class struggle should be led by the unions. The Palestinian newspapers, most of whose owners belonged to the new intelligentsia, tended to accept the version of the religious activists and even cooperate with them (a phenomenon facilitated by the death of Shaykh al-Qassam in November 1935, who was later recognised as a national hero and a symbol of the Palestinian struggle). These newspapers rejected the platform of the communist activists, and even fought against them.

The newspaper owners, editors and kindred members of the rich families benefited a great deal from both processes – the sale of lands and urbanisation – and were not interested in ending them. With regard to the sale of lands, for example, some newspaper editors received money from the Jewish Agency in return for publishing articles that attempted to moderate the enraged reactions against those engaged in such dealings, or at least did not report such reactions.[6] Concerning the cheap labour arriving in the cities from the villages, some newspaper owners, such as the al-'Isa family, owned businesses that employed rural workers for many hours a day in return for very low wages. These people were not interested in changing the situation or in allowing workers' unions to use their newspapers for the purpose of organising opposition to land sales.

Initially, certain newspaper owners who did not belong to the urban notability attempted to attack the more senior newspapers on the issue of land sales; however, in time they came to cooperate with the policies of the established press. The newspaper *al-Difa'* represents a good example from this group. Owned by the rural al-Shanti family from Qalqilya who moved to Jaffa at the beginning of the Mandate period, *al-Difa'* was founded in April 1934 by Ibrahim al-Shanti with expatriate Syrian journalists like Khayr al-Din al-Zirikli and Sami al-Sarraj. At first the newspaper criticised its rival *Filastin* for representing the wealthy urban stratum, which was mainly Christian. *Al-Difa'* presented views objecting to the Christian dominance of the national press and of institutions like the Arab Executive Committee. In this way it sought to win the approval of both villagers and Muslims.[7] In time, however, when the al-Shanti family took over full control of the newspaper and some of its members became involved in deals related to the sale of lands and in the citrus industry, thus acquiring different interests from those of the villagers they supposedly represented earlier, the newspaper's policy changed.[8] This trend was also true of the newspaper *al-Sirat al-Mustaqim* (The Straight Road) and its owner, 'Abdullah al-Qalqili, who had moved from Qalqilya to Jaffa, where he was known for his opposition to the Mufti and the Mufti's relatively moderate attitude towards the Mandate authorities and the Jewish settlement.[9]

During the Great Strike (16 April–13 October 1936) and the revolt of 1936–9 which broke out against the British Mandate and the Zionist activities, the peasants' cause acquired greater respect, and the newspapers that expressed the views of the urban notable families, headed by *Filastin*, were compelled to become more flexible in their attitude towards the villagers. The armed bands founded at the time were comprised of peasants, and their struggle encompassed elements of the class struggle. The leaders of these bands, such as 'Abd al-Rahim al-Haj Muhammad, 'Arif 'Abd al-Raziq, Yusuf Abu Durra and Hassan Salame, initiated a new social order (between the Urbans and the Villagers) during the years of revolt (in the cities as well as the rural areas). The residents of the cities, who did not approve of this course, and some of their leaders preferred to leave the country rather than submit to the dictates of the peasants. 'Isa al-'Isa, editor of *Filastin*, and 'Isa al-Bandak, editor of *Sawt al-Sha'b*, fled the country in 1938. This stemmed among other things from their objection to the band leaders' demand that all city residents wear a *kufiyya* and *'iqal* (the rural head covering) instead of the fez, in order to make it more difficult for the British authorities to identify members of the armed bands.[10]

Newspaper Publication Patterns

During the Mandate period thirty-eight new newspapers were published: eleven dailies, fourteen weeklies, four biweeklies and nine monthlies. Weeklies and monthlies had first appeared twenty years before; however, the innovation of the period was the emergence and establishment of daily newspapers.[11] Daily newspapers appeared in response to the many decisive political developments concerning the struggle for Palestine, that is, the struggle for land against the plan for a Jewish homeland. Until the establishment of the radio station (under British supervision) in 1936, the press was the only medium providing the public with news concerning the Palestinian issue and other global issues. The weeklies could not keep up with the pace of developments and were unable to provide prompt reports. This led to the appearance of daily newspapers, such as *Filastin*, which in October 1929 was the first newspaper to establish itself successfully as a daily.[12] Another veteran newspaper, *al-Karmil*, promised its readers repeatedly to appear in a daily edition but never succeeded in doing so. While for a time it appeared twice a week, even this frequency was a burden on its financial resources, and finally it resumed its weekly appearance. When its financial difficulties grew during World War II it ceased publication.[13]

The status of *Filastin* as a daily newspaper and the rise in its circulation were supported by the large financial resources provided by 'Isa al-'Isa, the newspaper's owner. His businesses and properties enabled him to manage the newspaper as a commercial enterprise. The newspaper was a type of family business, and many of the al-'Isa family members worked for it and helped in its distribution. Ibrahim al-Shanti, the founder of *al-Difa'*, learned from *Filastin* and raised the necessary funding to support the newspaper by selling citrus groves belonging to the family and investing the returns in the newspaper,[14] and securing favourable credit terms from the Arab Bank where he had been employed.[15]

The support of political organisations and institutions for newspapers affiliated with or belonging to them also contributed to their stability. When this support ended, however, once the political organisation ceased to exist or weakened, the newspaper stopped appearing or appeared less frequently. This is what happened to *al-Jami'a al-'Arabiyya* and *al-Yarmuk*, newspapers that had supported the Husayni camp (and specifically the Executive Committee and the Higher Muslim Council) but ceased publication when these institutions lost influence. A similar fate befell *al-'Arab*, voice of the al-Istiqlal Party, a Pan-Arabist party established at the beginning of the thirties.

Most daily newspapers were printed on eight pages in a large format, although some were sixteen pages in a smaller format. Often the layout was determined by the financial situation of the time or by the quantity of newsprint available in the country, and was not the result of decisions taken by the newspapers themselves. In October 1936, for example, *Filastin* appeared in a small format and informed its readers that this was the result of a lack of newsprint available. It added that in the event of a long-term shortage it would be forced to reduce the number of pages of the newspaper even further and even cease publication, as it had only a limited stock of paper.[16] Three days later the newspaper reported to its readers that the newsprint had arrived in a shipment from Europe, and that the newspaper would resume its previous format.[17] In 1937 the newspaper held a poll asking its readers which format they preferred. The results 'surprised' the editors, who reported that a large majority of the readers who sent letters preferred the smaller format as it was easier to read.[18]

Until *al-Difa'* began appearing in 1934 the Palestinian press suffered from poor professional quality in the arrangement and presentation of the journalistic material. Most of the journalistic material was comprised of news, which was strewn throughout the pages, usually with no thematic or logical order. In many cases sentences were mistakenly omitted, or the editor did not refer readers to the continuation of items appearing on the first page, and in some cases the continuation was missing. At the time there were almost no editorials, aside from *al-Karmil*, *Filastin* and later *al-Jami'a al-Islamiyya*, whose owners wrote short leads in almost every issue.[19] The appearance of *al-'Arab* and *al-Jami'a al-Islamiyya* in 1932, produced by the best contemporary journalists and intellectuals, raised the professional level of the press but the publication of *al-Difa'* in April 1934 was the most important event in the history of the Palestinian press during the British Mandate period. This newspaper succeeded in attracting skilled and professional journalists with much experience in journalism from various Arab countries, such as the Syrian Khayr al-Din al-Zirikli and Sami al-Sarraj, in addition to the newspaper's owner and editor-in-chief, Ibrahim al-Shanti, who wrote the editorials, which he signed 'Ibrahim'. At the time when Sami al-Sarraj served as acting editor of the newspaper and wrote the editorial, Ibrahim al-Shanti had two regular columns: one was 'al-Naqqada'[20] (The Critic) and the other appeared under the title 'Ahadith 'ala al-shabab'[21] (Words to the Young). *Al-Difa'* often used pictures from all over the world and had a wide network of reporters in the capitals of major countries, specifically in Cairo, Beirut, London, Baghdad and Berlin. A month after first appearing, *al-Difa'* boasted of its innovative contributions and improvements in the newspaper industry. It even bragged of its superiority over other newspapers and said:

> The greatness of *al-Difa'* is in its ability to print fresh news 24 hours before other newspapers. This proves beyond a doubt its advantage in eliciting firsthand news ... Our newspaper is always first and thus throws salt in the eyes of the jealous.[22]

Well aware of the successes of *al-Difa'*, the staff of *Filastin* responded with their own improvements in news presentation. The acting editor, Yusuf Hanna, began writing editorials entitled 'Masa'il al-yawm' (Current Matters). He often apologised to the readers for mistakes in the presentation of the journalistic material (mistakes in spelling and language or the finishing shape of the text) due to the newspaper's difficulties caused by the British authorities and the censor, and promised that the newspaper would do everything it could to correct these mistakes as soon as possible.[23]

Once the necessary improvements had been implemented, the staff of *Filastin* challenged *al-Difa'* and published statements from readers concerning the quality and merits of the newspaper. In one of these statements, a truck driver named 'Umar 'Abdullah from the village of 'Arabeh near Jenin said:

> I am a driver from the village of 'Arabeh. Reading the newspaper *Filastin* gives me special pleasure. I would be unwilling to read any other newspaper, as this is the only newspaper whose news and articles can be understood by any person, and I think that its news items are always one hundred percent true.[24]

This testimony was part of the strong rivalry between the two largest daily newspapers, *Filastin* and *al-Difa'*. During this period *al-Difa'* expanded its distribution among the rural population in particular and among the Muslim population in general, which construed it as a counterbalance to the Christian *Filastin*.

Filastin intentionally sought to be representative of the rural sector and the Muslim population to extol its merits in order to prove that it had readers in these sectors. The newspaper wished to show that it served the whole nation and that even the uneducated (such as truck drivers) could understand it. This implied a certain criticism of *al-Difa'*, which employed intellectuals who usually wrote in a high-level language style that was difficult for common people to understand. During the events of 1936–9 newspapers tended in general to use more 'popular' words and even colloquial expressions. This was true of *Filastin, al-Difa'* and even *al-Jami'a al-Islamiyya*, whose editor, Shaykh al-Faruqi, was known for his figurative style. Even al-Faruqi endeavoured to use colloquial expressions and sayings in order to appeal to the working class. In an article speaking of the conscience of European politicians, al-Faruqi said that this conscience was made of rubber. He explained the nature of rubber to the readers, saying: 'Rubber is a material that does not break and can withstand pressure and blows, but when the pressure rises it tears and cannot be mended whether hot or cold, as car drivers say.'[25] Elsewhere the editor employed a saying used by peasants, when he spoke of the British laws restricting Jewish immigration as a 'rope made of grass' (*habl min hashish*),[26] that is, a soft rope that is unable to restrain even the lightest object.[27] *Al-Difa'*, whose reporters previously used a traditional and figurative style, also switched to more colloquial popular expressions.[28] *Al-Zumur*, published in Acre, for its part used a rhyming style and colloquial language to express harsh social and political criticism.[29]

The tendency to write in a popular style and in simple colloquial language intensified during 1935–6 and reached its zenith on the eve of World War II. This probably stemmed from the wish of the press to win over a large percentage of readers, especially among the popular classes, for whom figurative literary language was often 'too difficult'. In addition, the intelligentsia, who were at first the only potential readers of the press, had a clear conception of political reality. These people were by now used to reading certain newspapers (according to their political, factional and even religious affiliation) and would not willingly change their habits. Subscribers of the newspaper *al-Liwa'*, the journal of the Husaynis and the Arab Palestinian Party, were at first party members drawn from the urban intelligentsia and notable classes. This newspaper was perceived as the newspaper of the social elite (*effendiyya*) and was mostly distributed in the large cities. In December 1935 it sold an average of 200 copies in Jerusalem, 160 in Jaffa and 200 in Haifa, while in the rural centres few copies were sold (7 in Qalqilya, 5 in Safed).[30] In its first week 1,147 copies were sold and in its fourth week 1,272; however, sales had dropped to 643 by the eighth week.[31] In a letter to the owner, Jamal al-Husayni, the newspaper's agent in Haifa said that in his opinion the drop in sales stemmed from the newspaper's difficult language and its ignorance of matters concerning the common people.[32]

A look at the newspaper's subscribers in Haifa shows that this was indeed a newspaper for the *effendiyya*.[33] The sixty subscribers in this city included senior clerics, such as Shaykh Yunis al-Khatib,[34] Shaykh Subhi Khizran, attorneys such as Muhammad al-Madi,[35] writers and journalists such as Ahmad al-Imam,[36] and business and property owners such as Imil Butaji and Tahir Qaraman.

The readiness of the press to use more popular language was apparently also related to the rising power of the peasants during the second stage of the revolt when the centre of military activities removed to the villages, particularly after the senior urban leadership was exiled in October 1937. Newspaper editors, aware of the power of the new masters and knowing that they had mostly only a lower, shallow and poor education, tried to write in a language that would be understood by leaders of the armed bands.[37] The editor of *al-Karmil* discussed the mutual relations between the press and the people in November 1939:

> On the one hand we are aware of the influence of the press on the popular classes, who have started to express interest in newspapers, after previously scorning them and their facilities. However this influence is not expressed by appreciation of the journalists and their efforts to produce newspapers. They try to obtain newspapers from their friends or to read them in the cafes, and thus cheat the newspaper owners out of their meagre profits that do not equal half the money a person pays, for example, for shining his shoes.[38]

Nassar added that 'the Palestinian journalist would prefer to be a beggar in Italy and Switzerland than a journalist in his own country'.[39] This can be understood to mean that although the public began expressing much interest in the press, they did not appreciate the work and efforts of the journalists on behalf of their people. At the time that Nassar wrote this his newspaper was in a difficult financial situation, causing him to lay off all employees and employ members of his family in their stead. These travails can be felt in Nassar's agitated appeal to overdue subscribers, saying that he could no longer pay the rent or even feed his sons.[40] It was also possible, as Nassar said, to receive the newspaper from friends or to read it in cafes, which usually had copies of the various newspapers. Newspapers were even read out loud in the cafes for the benefit of the illiterate.

Another problem encountered by Nassar and the editors of other weeklies was the inability to compete with the large daily newspapers, in particular *Filastin* and *al-Difaʿ*. These were able to provide the readers with current news every day, while the weeklies had to search for special topics that would attract the readers. They also competed with weeklies from neighbouring Arab countries, such as the Egyptian *al-Hilal* and *al-Musawwar*, which were of much better quality than the local weeklies.

In February 1937 *al-Karmil* announced to its readers that it would soon be published on daily basis once certain technical and professional arrangements pertaining to printing the newspaper and the wages of the editors were made.[41] It explained the need to appear daily and said:

> Had we wished to make commercial profits from our newspaper, we would have turned it into a daily newspaper long ago. However the homeland and our principles are more precious than money, profits, influence and well-being. We would never have thought of turning the newspaper into a daily if we had not been implored to do so by some dear friends, and if we did not know, from our extensive experience, that people tend to read news more than they tend to read about principles and ideals. Due to these two factors we are compelled to overcome all the difficulties and make every effort to obtain the daily news while maintaining our national principles.[42]

In fact, the newspaper never did appear as a daily and in 1942 it was overcome by financial hardships and ceased publication. *Al-Karmil* was not the only weekly that tried to compete with the daily newspapers, but it could not withstand the competition and ultimately was compelled to close down. It was preceded by *al-'Arab*, voice of the al-Istiqlal Party, which had opened with great excitement but closed quietly and without fanfare.

Monthly periodicals in Palestine were almost insignificant. Most were Christian religious journals or school and college journals that appeared irregularly, and the topics they discussed had very little to do with the critical issues on the Palestinian public agenda.

Symbols and Slogans in the Press

The names chosen by newspaper owners for their publications and the symbols and slogans that appeared on their title pages were aimed at stressing certain ideological trends or political or social views. These were anchored in the historical context of each newspaper's establishment. The names of newspapers established towards the end of the Ottoman period usually expressed the emphasis given by the owners and editors (mostly Orthodox Christians) to local national sentiments. The names *Filastin* and *al-Karmil*, given in this period, are unique Palestinian names.

After World War I and the establishment of the Mandate, newspapers carried titles that expressed political views prevalent among Palestinian society. For example, the newspaper *Suriyya al-Janubiyya* (Southern Syria) expressed the ideal of Greater Syria with Palestine as its southern part, while *Mir'at al-Sharq* (Mirror of the West) promoted the idea of pan-Eastern unity based on the belief of one political entity in the Middle East with all the ethnic and religious elements. In 1924 the Pan-Islamist *al-Sirat al-Mustaqim* (The Straight Path) was founded, and in 1927 the Pan-Arabist *al-Jami'a al-'Arabiyya* launched. In 1932 the Pan-Islam inclined *al-Jami'a al-Islamiyya* was founded (which believed in the idea of the construction of a Pan-Arab entity in Greater Syrian territory).

Some newspaper names were also derived from Islamic tradition, although they were not necessarily Islamically inclined, such as *al-Yarmuk* (named after the Yarmouk river, the site of the decisive battle in 636 CE between Muslims and Byzantines) or *al-Zumur* (named after a sura in the Quran). Some newspapers were named after famous newspapers in other Arab countries, such as *al-Liwa'* (The Flag), the nationalist newspaper founded by Mustafa Kamil in Egypt in 1900.

Among the symbols and slogans, it is very interesting to mention the characterisations noted below the name of each newspaper. *Mir'at al-Sharq*, for example, defined itself as a newspaper dealing with political, social, economic and educational matters.[43] The newspaper *al-'Arab* defined its fields of interest as political, educational, historical and cultural.[44] The newspaper *al-Khamis*, published in Jaffa in 1935, outdid itself by delineating seven fields of interest: political, critical, comic, literary, social, artistic and cartoons.[45] Other newspapers sought to emphasise their character through their titles: *Al-'Arab*, for example, expressed its Pan-Arab tendencies by defining itself as a 'newspaper that discusses matters of the Arab and Islamic world'.[46] The backdrop of the title was a map of the Arab world, including the countries of the Fertile Crescent, the Arabian Peninsula, Egypt and North Africa.[47] *Al-Jami'a al-'Arabiyya* also chose a map of the Arab world, coloured a vivid red, as the backdrop for its name.[48] The slogan written below this backdrop, 'If the Arabs are humiliated Islam will be humiliated', appears to see Islam and Arabism as twins impossible to separate. *Al-Difa'* chose to emphasise on its title page a verse by the Syrian poet Khayr al-Din al-Zirikli, one of its owners, saying: 'If you can't mount a crushing attack, you had better maintain a preventive policy of defence.'[49] The name of the newspaper, *al-Difaʿ* (The Defence), was derived from a verse of this poem.[50]

Most of the newspapers felt that their work was intended, first and foremost, for the benefit of the homeland and its interests. The words 'homeland' (*watan*) and 'nationalism' (*wataniyya*) were commonly found in slogans coined by the newspapers for their title pages or quoted in their editorials. Almost all the newspapers presented their appearance as the most important event of Arab or Palestinian nationalism. *Al-ʿArab* defined itself, saying: 'The newspaper *al-ʿArab* is the postman, the messenger, the mouth and the platform of every Arab in the Arab homeland.'[51] *Al-Shabab* described itself as a newspaper serving the young and edited by a group of 'free people bearing the flag of the national ideal'.[52] The title page of *al-Lahab* carried the slogan: 'One homeland, one people and one leader.'[53] It expressed the newspaper's support of Haj Amin al-Husayni (the Grand Mufti of Jerusalem and the president of the Higher Muslim Council, and the most dominant leader of the Palestinian national movement in the Mandate period), in face of the British refusal to acknowledge him as the representative of Palestinian Arabs in a convention they were planning to hold in London in early 1939. In the editorial of its first issue it announced:

> In the name of God and in the name of the homeland, we hereby open the first issue of this newspaper. Its publication is intended to serve this country and to fight for its interests in a special way. We support the general interests and we are aware of all the plots aimed at the Arab homeland in these dark times.[54]

The one leader mentioned by the newspaper together with the homeland and the people was the Mufti, who after his exile in 1937 became a symbol whom the newspapers competed at praising and extolling. This was even true of newspapers known for their extreme hostility towards the Mufti, such as *al-Jamiʿa al-Islamiyya* and *al-Sirat al-Mustaqim*, the editors of which thought that they were better nominees for the Mufti's post.

The Journalists: A Profile

During the British Mandate period approximately 253 Arab journalists were employed in Palestine, amongst them 233 Palestinians, 8 Syrians,

5 Lebanese, 4 Egyptians 2 Iraqis, and one from both Jordan and India. With regard to sectarian distribution, there were 187 Muslims (including 4 Druze)[55] and 65 Christians.[56] With regard to geographical distribution, most of the journalists came from urban families or were sons of rural families who migrated to the cities. They originated mainly from the three major Palestinian cities: Jerusalem, Jaffa and Haifa. In the early 1930s journalists from smaller centres – such as Nablus, Gaza, Ramle, Acre and Bethlehem – and even from provincial towns such as Tulkarm, Qalqilya and Majdal also began appearing on the journalistic stage. The distribution of Palestinian journalists by urban origin is shown in Table 3.1.

The Educational Background of Journalists

Before the 1930s most newspaper owners, editors and journalists had received only elementary or at best secondary education, with only very few holding higher education qualifications, such as 'Isa al-'Isa who studied at the

Table 3.1 City of origin of Palestinian journalists

City[a]	Number of journalists
Jaffa	85
Jerusalem	75
Haifa	30
Nablus	10
Gaza	6
Acre	4
Nazareth	4
Ramle	4
Bethlehem	3
Qalqilya	3
Ramallah	3
Tulkarm	3
Jenin	1
Majdal	1
Safed	1
Total	233

[a] This distribution includes towns on the outskirts of these cities or included in their jurisdiction. The table indicates that the main centres of journalistic activity were in Jaffa, Jerusalem and Haifa; however, the dominance of these cities in the 1920s gradually declined in the 1930s and 1940s. During these years, Jaffa replaced Jerusalem as the major location of journalists and newspapers after it became the main centre of the Palestinian economy and culture.

American University of Beirut,[57] and Bulus Shihada who graduated from the English College of Jerusalem.[58] Some journalists had graduated from religious colleges such as the al-Azhar College, where Shaykh 'Abdullah al-Qalqili[59] and Shaykh Sulayman al-Taji al-Faruqi studied.[60]

In the early 1930s a group of young university graduates from Lebanese and Egyptian universities began working as journalists in Palestine. Some of these were sons of notable families although not necessarily from the large cities, and others were sons of wealthy rural families who migrated to the large cities but maintained their property, lands and relationships with their original villages. The former included Akram Zu'aytir, son of 'Umar Zu'aytir, Mayor of Nablus at the turn of the twentieth century. He began his studies at the American University of Beirut but was compelled to interrupt them and return to Palestine due to his political activities and his pursuit by the French authorities. In Palestine he was appointed as a teacher in Nablus and Acre, studied law in Jerusalem and was certified as an attorney.[61] Ibrahim al-Shanti belonged to the second group, having completed a bachelor's degree in economics and political science at the American University of Beirut. His family was a wealthy rural one from Qalqilya, some of whose sons moved to Jaffa where they dealt, among other things, in books, newspapers and printing houses.[62]

In the mid-1930s the field was augmented by young people who had studied journalism in Western universities. The two most significant figures in this category were Emil al-Ghuri, who completed his studies in 1933 at the University of Cincinnati in the United States and upon his return to Palestine worked for newspapers that supported the Husayni camp,[63] and Ya'qub Saba, who completed his bachelor's degree at the American University of Beirut and his master's degree in Britain.[64]

Most of these young graduates worked as journalists for larger newspapers such as *Filastin*, *al-Difa'* and *al-Liwa'*, which had sufficient financial support and could pay their salaries. Editors of other newspapers were either not paid or were only reimbursed for their expenses. The best example is Akram Zu'aytir: when working as editor of the newspaper *Mir'at al-Sharq* he was aware of the newspaper's difficult situation and did not care ask its owner, Bulus Shihada, for payment in return for editing the newspaper. He recalled:

I began working for the newspaper and I didn't want to discuss financial matters with the owner. I knew from my predecessor, Ahmad al-Shuqayri, that he would not pay me a thing for my work. It was sufficient that the newspaper served as a platform from which I could serve my nation'.⁶⁵

Not all journalists were as committed as Zu'aytir, however, in particular those whose journalism work was their only source of support. This group included the journalists from neighbouring Arab countries who came to Palestine as political refugees or as professional journalists and sought to support themselves by their journalism. Most of them had much experience in journalism and some of them, such as Khayr al-Din al-Zirakli and Sami al-Sarraj (both of Syrian background) and 'Ajaj Nuwayhid (of Lebanese descent) were renowned as journalists and first-rate authors in their countries of origin. Al-Zirikli and al-Sarraj worked for *al-Jami'a al-Islamiyya* and later took part in the establishment of *al-Difa'*. In addition, the Egyptians Yusuf Hanna and 'Ali Mansur and the Syrians Kamil 'Abbas and Muhammad Chirqas worked in Palestine for lengthy periods. Yusuf Hanna worked as editor of *Filastin* from the mid-1920s until 1948, while the other three worked for almost all the significant Arabic newspapers in Palestine at one time or another.

Journalists and their Political Connections

Almost all the newspaper owners in the 1920s were politically active in the Palestinian national movement. 'Isa al-'Isa, Bulus Shihada and Shaykh al-Faruqi were members of the Arab Executive Committee, the first Palestinian national body that was active from 1920 to 1934. Al-Faruqi, 'Omar al-Barguthi and Najib Nassar were also active at the beginning of the Mandate in establishing the Liberal Arab Party (1924–7) and the National Arab Party (1925–8), parties formed under the inspiration of the British authorities.⁶⁶

Through their support of the British, these journalists hoped to reduce the power and the influence of the two large blocs in the Palestinian national movement: the Majlisiyyun (the Husaynis and their allies) and the Mu'aridun (the Nashashibis and their allies), who had in turn their own newspapers to voice their concerns and protect their views. When the large blocs in the Palestinian movement won the sympathy of the Palestinian public through displays of hostility towards the British, however, those who had supported the British, headed by al-Faruqi and Nassar, became very critical, and sometimes even hostile, towards the Mandate authorities. Their newspapers, *al-Jami'a al-Islamiyya* and *al-Karmil*, led the criticism against the developing relationship between the British authorities and the Jewish Settlement.

Frequent shifts in the political views of the newspapers were also evident amongst journalists. Three political groups were active amongst the journalists, although there were frequent and sometimes sharp transitions between the various groups. These were as follows:

1. Journalists who supported the Palestinian representative institutions, that is, the Executive Committee, the High Muslim Council and the Arab Higher Committee. They included Munif al-Husayni, Jamal al-Husayni and Emil al-Ghuri, all involved in the publication and editing of all the newspapers known for their support of the Husaynis.
2. Journalists who opposed these representative institutions and the Husaynis during this period and were affiliated with the Nashashibi camp, such as Hasan Sidqi al-Dajani, 'Abdullah al-Qalqili and As'ad al-Shuqayri.
3. Journalists who vacillated between the two camps, usually according to changing interests and circumstances. This represented the largest group and included senior newspaper editors 'Isa al-'Isa, Najib Nassar and Bulus Shihada, and supporters of the Istiqlal Party and the Pan-Arab ideology, such as Ibrahim al-Shanti, Akram Zu'aytir and 'Ajaj Nuwayhid.

During this period the first two groups were very well defined with almost no defections from one to the other. This may have been a result of the financial support received from the organisations with which they were affiliated (the Executive Committee and the Muslim Council in the case of the Husaynis and the local municipalities in the case of the Nashashibis).

The frequent defections of members of the third group to the first or second group stemmed from two main reasons: the first reason was based on interests, that is, as long as they received financial support from the Husayni institutions, they supported the Husaynis; and when they received more support from the Nashashibis, they did not hesitate to support them. The second reason was based on ideology and the positions stated by the leaders of the two camps. These journalists were mostly supporters of al-Istiqlal, the organisation that supposedly displayed a neutral attitude towards the Husayni–Nashashibi struggle. Their support of either camp depended on the affinity of this camp with their ideological views, in particular with the Pan-Arab ideal.[67]

News of possible desertions from the two first groups was often mentioned in the 'Arab Office News' documents of the Jewish Agency. Eliyahu Sasson reported in May 1935 that Emil al-Ghuri, who was one of the most active journalists in the Husayni camp, came to Fakhri al-Nashashibi and told him that he had had enough of politics and if he had 500 Palestinian pounds, he would leave for America. He asked al-Nashashibi for this sum but al-Nashashibi requested him to publish a statement describing 'the deeds of the Mufti' before he left. Eventually the deal did not materialise as al-Ghuri did not reply to al-Nashashibi and in any case al-Nashashibi was unwilling to pay him more than 50 Palestinian pounds.[68] Al-Ghuri's appeal to the Nashashibis must have reflected his difficult financial situation. One month after the failed deal with Fakhri al-Nashashibi, he sold a significant part of his printing house to the owners of the newspaper *al-Difa'*.[69]

Of the 233 working Palestinian journalists of the time, 187 were politically active, that is, were members of political parties.[70] The proportion of journalists among contemporary political activists is presented in Table 3.2.

These findings clearly indicate that the activists of the al-Istiqlal Party were the most active in the field of journalism, as this was a party of the intelligentsia that objected to the traditional clan division and most of their activity was expressed by writing in newspapers or speaking at demonstrations. This party had almost no popular base, unlike the other parties, and

Table 3.2 Political affiliation of Palestinian journalists. (Source: al-Hut, *Al-Qiyadat*, p. 688)

Political party or organisation	Percentage who were journalists
The Christian Islamic Societies	5
The Youth Congress	18.5
The al-Istiqlal Party	36.5
The Defence Party (Nashashibi)	31
The Arab Party (Husayni)	7
The Reform Party	29
The Popular Committees	19

particularly the Husayni Arab Party, whose leaders (aside from Jamal and Munif al-Husayni) devoted themselves to political organisation and delegated the journalism work to hired journalists, particularly from neighbouring Arab countries.

Readership and Circulation

Table 3.3 shows the circulation of newspapers during 1929–39 by number of copies.

The circulation data do not necessarily indicate the actual number of readers; indeed, it can be assumed that this number was significantly higher than the number of copies printed. Each copy served entire families and even villages. Thus the content of the newspapers reached the illiterate through the custom of reading the newspaper in groups at home, in cafes, in village *madafas* and in factories with 'reading newspaper breaks'.[71] For example, a newspaper (usually *al-Difa'*) would reach distant villages once a week. It was delivered to the house of the Mukhtar, who would invite the few literate people in the village, and sometimes from neighbouring villages, to read the newspaper to the people in his *madafa*.[72] For this reason the literate were considered influential people, and in the long winter nights or on the nights during Ramadan they played the renowned part of storyteller (*hakawati*).[73]

Table 3.3 Circulation of Arabic Palestinian newspapers, 1929–39. (Sources: Ayalon, *Press in the Arab Middle East*, pp. 148–51; CO 733/207; DEC P/986/03093)

	1929–32	1935–6	1937–9
Filastin	2,500–3,000	4,000–6,000[a]	2,000–4,000
al-Jami'a al-'Arabiyya	1,500–2,000	2,000	–
al-Hayat	1,500	–	–
al-Karmil	1,000–1,500	1,500–2,000	1,000
Sawt al-Sha'b	1,000	up to 1,000	up to 1,000
Mir'at al-Sharq	1,000	up to 1,000	up to 1,000
al-Aqdam	800	–	–
al-Jami'a al-Islamiyya	–	1,200–2,000	1,000
al-Difa'	–	4,000–6,000[b]	2,000–4,000
al-Liwa'	–	3,000–4,000	2,000–3,000

[a] During the 1936 strike and when its rival *al-Difa'* did not appear, circulation reached 8,000 copies.
[b] During the 1936 strike and when its rival *Filastin* did not appear, circulation reached 8,000–10,000 copies.

The villagers who came to town would return with the newspapers, especially in periods of tension and conflict, when newspapers were considered an important and necessary commodity even in the villages.[74]

Villages near the main roads (especially the Jaffa–Haifa road, which originally passed through Tulkarm and Jenin) received newspapers from the vehicle that transported them from Jaffa to Haifa and vice versa, which stopped near the villages and distributed a certain number of issues. This led to a larger circulation of newspapers and to greater involvement of the rural population in journalistic and political activities in general.[75]

In addition, in the villages there were people who specialised in reading and went from place to place telling people the recent news. In Nablus, for example, as historian Ihsan al-Nimr relates, there were two such people – Raghib Shahin, nicknamed 'Reuter' (after the famous news agency) and Salih Bishara, nicknamed 'Hawwasa' – who went from place to place, from shop to shop and from meeting to meeting in order to collect news for circulation, while also relating the news that they had read in the various newspapers.[76]

Distribution of Readers by Sex, Age and Community

In this period there were many more literate men than women and it seems that men were also more interested in the contents of the newspapers (which were mostly political).[77] We can assume, however, that Palestinian women, especially in the cities and among the higher classes, read Palestinian newspapers and newspapers from other Arab countries (*al-Ahram* or *al-Musawwar* from Egypt). This assumption is strengthened by letters written by women to the editorial offices of newspapers and their participation in the discussion on matters of women's status and women's contribution to society.[78] Women also actively participated in fundraising campaigns held by the newspapers in support of Palestinian national activities.

The assumption of a female readership is also reinforced by commercial advertisements that addressed the female public by advertising women's products (perfumes, hygiene products, jewellery, hats and other apparel).[79] Towards the end of this period, special sections for women began appearing in the newspapers, with most material taken from the Egyptian press, particularly the magazine *al-Musawwar*, or translated from the Western press.[80]

In terms of the age of the readership, it may be assumed that the majority of the literate people were members of the younger generation who had studied in the educational system established in Palestine by the Mandate authorities. The proportion of schoolchildren among the readers was very high. Although the British authorities did not permit unrestricted newspaper reading in times of tension, as Akram Zu'aytir relates, this did not prevent children and youth from being exposed to the press.[81] Indeed, many teachers passed on the newspapers' messages to their pupils, recommended certain newspapers and even read important articles to their classes.[82]

Conclusion

During the Mandate period the press served as an influential and important factor in the process of both shaping and reflecting political, social and cultural changes in Palestinian society. The major contribution of journalism was the creation of a cultural discourse among a new generation of intelligentsia. The press also contributed a great deal to enriching the cultural life of this generation by advertising plays, films and other cultural activities. It served as a window to the wide world and as a powerful instrument for spreading human culture and increasing awareness. In the context of British rule, it thus became a key tool in the production and the dissemination of different nationalist agendas when the threat of the confrontation with the Zionist project was becoming critical.

Notes

1. See, for example, *al-Karmil* 12 August 1933.
2. Interview with Ahmad al-Shanti, Jerusalem, 4 June 1994.
3. Information on the increasing power of the workers' unions in the early 1930s from interview with Bulus Farah, Haifa, 27 December 1992.
4. *Filastin* 17 June 1933.
5. *Al-Karmil* 19 August 1933.
6. For example, Bulus Shihada, editor of the Jerusalem newspaper *Mir'at al-Sharq*. For further on this, see CZA, S25/3303, 15 June 1935.
7. Interview with Ahmad al-Shanti, Jerusalem, 5 September 2005.
8. On the activities of some of the members of this family, see CZA, S25/2798.
9. For al-Qalqili's meetings with Jewish Agency representatives, see CZA, S25/3303.

10. On the British suppression of the Arab Revolt and the reactions of the armed bands to the British measures, see Eyal, *Ha'intifada Harishona*.
11. The statistical data regarding newspapers in this chapter, including circulation, editors and dates of publication, is derived mainly from the following sources: *al-Mawsu'a al-filastiniyya*, vol. 2, pp. 438–43; Khuri, *al-Sihafa al-'arabiyya*, pp. 53–108; al-'Aqqad, *al-Sihafa al-'arabiyya*, pp. 90–215; Yehoshuwa, *Tarikh al-sihafa al-filastiniyya*, pp. 7–50.
12. There were a number of attempts to publish daily newspapers before 1929 but all were short-lived due to the difficulties involved.
13. Khuri, *al-Sihafa al-'arabiyya*, p. 14.
14. Interview with Fawzi al-Shanti, Jerusalem, 5 September 2005.
15. Shimoni, *'Arviyei*, p. 406.
16. *Filastin* 9 October 1936.
17. *Filastin* 12 October 1936.
18. *Filastin* 17 February 1937; the number of letters received was not stated.
19. *Al-Karmil* did not carry an editorial as such but usually addressed the public on the first page or gave advice to the Mandate government and Arab countries on the preferred manner of action with regard to the Palestinian issue.
20. See, for example, *al-Difa'* 4 May 1934.
21. *al-Difa'* 19 August 1934.
22. *al-Difa'* 4 May 1934.
23. *Filastin* 7 January 1937.
24. *Filastin* 7 May 1937.
25. *Al-Jami'a al-Islamiyya* 25 June 1939.
26. A grass rope was used by peasants to tie sheaves of wheat and could easily be removed when necessary.
27. *Al-Jami'a al-Islamiyya* 28 July 1939.
28. *Al-Difa'* 23 April 1934.
29. See, for example, *al-Zumur* 12 May 1932.
30. DEC P/350/167.
31. Ibid.
32. Ibid.
33. This list is among the documents of Yosef Vashitz in the Yad Ya'ari Archives, 4.35–95(5).
34. Yunis al-Khatib represented Haifa on the High Muslim Council and was one of the city's senior clerics. He was considered to be affiliated with the Majlisiyyun.
35. Muhammad al-Madi came from the village of Ijzim in the Haifa district. His

family was the dominant family in the village and influential even beyond it. He engaged in advocacy in addition to agriculture. Politically he belonged to the Muʻaridun camp, despite the inclination of the family's more senior leader (Muʻin al-Madi) towards the Majlisiyyun camp. See Vashitz documents, Yad Yaʻari Archives, 14.35–95(3).

36. Secretary of the Muslim Society of Haifa for many years, Ahmad al-Imam was the Haifa representative on the Arab Executive Committee. He was also an official of the High Muslim Council and represented the Mufti in Haifa and the north. He was involved in the establishment of the newspaper *al-Yarmuk* and often wrote for it. During the events of 1936–9 he was in touch with members of the armed bands and in particular with Yusuf Abu Durra. When the senior leadership was exiled in 1937 he became one of the most prominent second-level leaders; for more details, see CZA, S25/3045.
37. For more details, see Zuʻaytir, *Wathaʼiq*, pp. 540–55.
38. *Al-Karmil* 11 November 1939.
39. Ibid.
40. *Al-Karmil* 30 September 1939.
41. *Al-Karmil* 13 February 1937.
42. Ibid.
43. *Al-Waqaʼiʻ al-filastiniyya* no. 361 (5 November 1933), p. 692.
44. Ibid., pp. 692–3.
45. Ibid., p. 546; *Al-Waqaʼiʻ al-filastiniyya* Appendix 2 (24 October 1935), p. 1409.
46. *Al-ʻArab* 27 August 1932.
47. Ibid.
48. See, for example, *Al-Jamiʻa al-ʻArabiyya* 14 January 1933.
49. *Al-Difaʻ* 20 April 1934.
50. There is no connection between the Nashashibi Defence Party and the newspaper *al-Difaʻ*, which was the voice of the al-Istiqlal Party, although some researchers have mistakenly connected the two. See al-ʻAbbasi, *Tatawwur al-riwaya*, p. 74.
51. *Al-ʻArab* 27 August 1932.
52. *Al-Shabab* 11 June 1934.
53. *Al-Lahab* 12 February 1938.
54. Ibid.
55. The four Druze are included in the Muslim category since they perceived themselves as Muslim and were even members of representative Muslim organisations.

They included 'Ajaj Nuwayhid, a member and an official of the High Muslim Council, and Hani Abi Muslih, vice-chairman of the Muslim Youth Society in Haifa.

56. These data are derived mainly from the following: al-'Aqqad, *al-Sihafa al-'arabiyya*; Yehoshuwa, Khuri, *al-Sihafa al-'arabiyya*; Zu'aytir, *al-Haraka al-wataniyya al-filastiniyya*; Yehoshuwa, *Tarikh al-sihafa al-filastiniyya*; Shimoni, *'Arviyei*; *al-Waqa'i' al-filastiniyya*, years 1933–40; al-'Udat, *A'lam al-fikr*; Abu Hammad, *A'lam min ard al-salam*.
57. al-'Udat, *A'lam al-fikr*, p. 477.
58. Ibid., pp. 302–3.
59. Yehoshuwa, *Tarikh al-sihafa al-filastiniyya*, p. 103.
60. al-'Udat, *A'lam al-fikr*, pp. 501–3.
61. On Zu'aytir's studies, see Zu'aytir, *Bawakir al-Nidal*, pp. 8–10.
62. The al-Shanti family included five senior journalists, of whom two (Ibrahim and Muhammad Farid) were also newspaper editors. This family served as a counterbalance to the Christian al-'Isa family that published the newspaper *Filastin*. Interview with Fawzi al-Shanti, Jerusalem, 5 September 2005.
63. Yehoshuwa, *Tarikh al-sihafa al-filastiniyya*, p. 33.
64. al-'Udat, *A'lam al- fikr*, pp. 254–5.
65. Zu'aytir, *Bawakir al-Nidal*, p. 104.
66. See Khalla, *Filastin*, pp. 125–8.
67. See Zu'aytir, *Bawakir al-Nidal*, pp. 412–15.
68. Arab Office News, 23 May 1935, CZA, S25/22224.
69. Ibid., 25 June 1935.
70. al-Hut, *Al-Qiyadat*, p. 686.
71. Interviews with Bulus Farah and 'Ali 'Ashur, Haifa, 5 December 2004.
72. This is related by Muhammad Hijaz (an educated man of the period from the village 'Inibta near Tulkarm) in his memoirs maintained in a private collection.
73. Ibid.
74. Ibid.
75. Interview with Atiyya Nayif Ghazala, Mukhtar of the village Labad, Tulkarm, 31 March 2000. As a boy, Atiyya Nayif Ghazala would bring the newspaper from the main road to the house of his father, the Mukhtar.
76. al-Nimr, *Tarikh Jabal Nablus*, vol. 4, p. 19.
77. Interview with Salma al-Husayni, an educated woman of the period who had a women's parlour, Jerusalem, 5 July 2002.
78. See, for example, *Sawt al-Sha'b* November–December 1939.

79. See, for example, the newspapers *Filastin* and *al-Difa'* during the Great Strike of April–October 1936.
80. *Al-Karmil* 9 July 1939.
81. Akram Zu'aytir was himself a high school teacher in Acre in 1929, while volunteering as a journalist for the Haifa newspaper *al-Yarmuk*. He was dismissed from his government position because of his articles in that newspaper, which contained materials against the policy of the Mandate government and against the Jewish Yishuv. See Kabha, *Palestinian Press*, pp. 27–42.
82. This is related by Muhammad Hijaz, a teacher in a number of schools. Despite restrictions imposed by authorities, he continued to inform his pupils of messages transmitted in the press (memoirs maintained in a private collection).

Bibliography

Archives

United Kingdom: The National Archives, London
Colonial Office (CO)
Foreign Office (FO)
Israel: Central Zionist Archives, Jerusalem (CZA)
Israel State Archives, Jerusalem
Documents of the Palestinian Executive Committee (DEC)
Yad Ya'ari Archives, Givat Haviva

Interviews

Ahmad al-Shanti, Jerusalem, 4 June 1994
Ahmad al-Shanti, Jerusalem, 5 September 2005
'Ali 'Ashur, Haifa, 5 December 2004
'Atiyya Nayif Ghazala, Tulkarm, 31 March 2000
Bulus Farah, Haifa, 5 December 1992
Bulus Farah, Haifa, 27 December 1992
Fawzi al-Shanti, Jerusalem, 5 September 2005
Salma al-Husayni, Jerusalem, 5 July 2002

Newspapers

Al-'Arab (Jerusalem), 1932–4
al-Difa' (Jaffa), 1934–48
Filastin (Jaffa), 1911–48

Al-Jami'a al-Islamiyya (Jaffa), 1933–9
Al-Karmil (Haifa), 1908–42
Al-Lahab (Jerusalem), 1942
Mir'at al-Sharq (Jerusalem), 1919–39
Sawt al-Sha'b (Bethlehem), 1939
Al-Shabab (Jerusalem), 1934
al-Waqa'i' al-Filastiniyya (Jerusalem), 1933–40
al-Yarmuk (Haifa), 1929–32
al-Zumur (Acre), 1932–6

Published Works

al-'Abbasi, Mahmud, *Tatawwur al-riwaya wa al-qissa al-qasira fi al-adab al-'arabi fi Isra'il, 1948–1976* (Shafa'amre: Dar al-Mashriq, 1998).
Abu Hammad, 'Irfan, *A'lam min ard al-salam* (Haifa: Haifa University, 1979).
al-'Aqqad, Ahmad Khalil, *al-Sihafa al-'arabiyya fi filastin* (Damascus: Dar al-'uruba lil-nashr, 1967).
Ayalon, Ami, *The Press in the Arab Middle East: A History* (New York: Oxford University Press, 1995).
Eyal, Yigal, *Ha'intifada harishona: dikuy hamered ha'arvi biydei hashiltonot habritiyim* (Tel Aviv: Ma'rachot, 1998).
al-Hut, Bayan Nuwayhid, *Al-Qiyadat wa al-mu'assasat al-siyasiyya fi filastin, 1918–1948* (Acre: Dar al-huda, 1986).
Kabha, Mustafa, *The Palestinian Press as Shaper of Public Opinion 1929–1939: Writing Up a Storm* (London and Portland, OR: Vallentine Mitchell, 2007).
Khallah, Muhammad Kamil, *Filastin wa al-intidab al-baritani, 1922–1939* (Beirut: Mu'assasat dirasat filastin, 1974).
Khuri, Yusuf, *al-Sihafa al-'arabiyya fi filastin, 1867–1948* (Beirut: Mu'assasat dirasat filastin, 1976).
al-Mawsu'a al-filastiniyya, vol. 2 (Damascus: Hay'at al-mawsu'a al-filastiniyya, 1984).
al-Nimr, Ihsan, *Tarikh Jabal Nablus wa al-Balqa*, 4 vols (Nablus: Jam'iyyat 'ummal al- matabi' atta'awuniyyin, 1995).
Shimoni, Ya'qov, *'Arviyei Eretz Yisrael* (Tel Aviv: Sifriyat Po'aleem, 1947).
al-'Udat, Ya'qub, *A'lam al-fikr wa al-adab fi filastin* (Jerusalem: Dar al-asra', 1992).
Yehoshuwa, Ya'qov, *Tarikh al-sihafa al-filastiniyya fi 'ahd al-intidab al-baritani 'ala Filastin, 1930–1948* (Jerusalem: Matba'at al-Ma'arif, 1983).
Zu'aytir, Akram, *al-Haraka al-wataniyya al-filastiniyya, 1935–1939* (Beirut: Mu'assasat dirasat Filastin, 1994).

Zu'aytir, Akram, *Min mudhakkirat Akram Zu'aytir*, vol. 1: *Bawakir al-nidal* (Beirut: al-Mu'assasa al-'arabiyya lil-dirasat wa al-nashr, 1994).

Zu'aytir, Akram, *Watha'iq al-haraka al-wataniyya al-filastiniyya, 1918–1939* (Beirut: Mu'assasat dirasat Filastin, 1979).

4

Falastin: An Experiment in Promoting Palestinian Nationalism through the English-language Press

Fred H. Lawson

On 16 September 1929, the influential Jaffa newspaper *Filastin*, which had resumed publication in March 1921 under the supervision of 'Isa Da'ud al-'Isa,[1] started to publish a weekly English-language edition. The editors pointed out in the inaugural issue that such a publication would play a vital role in advancing the Palestinian national cause, since

> our political opponents possess and run one of the most elaborate systems of propaganda the world has ever known . . . In almost every European and American Capital, especially in England, they either publish or subsidise newspapers and other periodicals which speak for them and persistently propagate their unlawful and unjustifiable greedy political ambitions in our country.[2]

More important, the time was now ripe for the appearance of an English-language edition of *Filastin*: a month earlier, large-scale popular disorders had broken out, called by the Palestinians the al-Buraq Revolution (*Thawra al-Buraq*) and more commonly known as the Wailing Wall riots.[3] 'During the recent disturbances,' the new paper's editors observed,

> we met several English correspondents. Their first Question to us, separately, was composed almost of the same words[:] 'So far all the news we

have been reading are from Jewish sources. Our source of information is unilateral. For Heaven's sake give us your point of view.'[4]

As soon as a modicum of order had been restored, the British government set up a formal committee of inquiry, known as the Shaw Commission, to look into the causes of the unrest.[5] In the words of Tamir Sorek, the appointment of the Shaw Commission 'created the impression that the destiny of Palestine was at stake and would be determined in the very near future'.[6] It therefore seemed evident to the editors of *Filastin* that 'the fact that we are on the eve of the arrival of the Enquiry Commission to this country [made September 1929] the very right moment for the publication of such a paper',[7] which adopted the slightly modified title *Falastin*.

In order to disseminate its message as widely as possible, the editors of *Falastin* announced: 'we intend to send gratis hundreds of copies to all the leading newspapers, the political centres, and all the distinguished politicians of the world so that they may hear our voice and give it their full attention and consideration'.[8] The chief editor of the English-language edition – the 26-year-old, American University of Beirut-educated 'Azmi al-Nashashibi – added 'A Word of Apology and Explanation' at the bottom of the front page of the first issue:

> The stringent conditions under which Palestine exists in the present moment precipitated the publication of this paper. The suddenness with which the recent events overtook us left us with a very short period of time for adequate preparations . . . But in our opinion the opportunity is great and must be seized at all costs. So we beg our readers to overlook any shortcoming which they might come across in the first few numbers of this paper and to have full trust and confidence in us and be sure that we shall not fail to try our very utmost to attain a progressive improvement and to bring up their newspaper to the standard they wish.[9]

Structure and Contents of *Falastin*

At the outset, each issue of *Falastin* ran to four pages in length. The inaugural issue printed on its front page two proclamations that the British High Commissioner for Palestine, Sir John Chancellor, had issued in the aftermath of the August 1929 disorders; the second page included a pair of lengthy anti-Zionist manifestos; three shorter polemics made up the third page; and the last page consisted of a response to the High Commissioner's proclamations from a group of 'Arab lawyers'.[10] This basic structure was repeated in subsequent issues. The front page of the second issue printed two open entreaties to the British authorities to rescind the Balfour Declaration of 1917 and take steps to block the spread of Zionist influence throughout the country; the second page consisted of a critique of the composition and operating assumptions of the Shaw Commission; a letter from a British political activist who vigorously supported Arab rights anchored the third page; and the last page (very atypically) featured a lengthy French-language protest against ongoing Zionist activities.[11] The front page of the third issue consisted of a sustained critique of the British administration that had been set up under the auspices of the League of Nations Mandate.[12]

With the third issue, a section entitled 'Miscellaneous' started to appear on page three of the newspaper.[13] This section at first consisted of short commentaries on local affairs, but in the next few issues dealt primarily with international and British matters, rather than with events in Palestine. The section returned its attention to Palestinian developments in the sixth issue, with the announcement of a forthcoming general strike and the listing of a half dozen resolutions that had been drafted by the 'Arab Advocates of Palestine' to protest infringements against the civil rights of Palestinians who had been arrested during the August disorders.[14]

By late October, coverage of local events in the 'Miscellaneous' section became more detailed. Most notable was a report of the proceedings of the first Palestine Arab Women's Congress in Jerusalem. 'It is gratifying', the account began,

> to be able to inform the West and Westerners that an end is being put to their misconception of the Arab Woman and her alleged slavish status. The Arab woman is not, as most Westerners think, a veiled creature hidden behind screens in voluptuous Hareems of wealthy Pashas and Beys. She is an enlightened and free citizen enjoying equal rights and privileges as her mate, and participating in his political activities.[15]

The story went on to list the six major resolutions that had been adopted by the congress, and to name the ten women who had been elected to posts on the Women's Arab Executive. Similar coverage was accorded the first All Palestine Arab Villagers' Congress that convened in Jaffa on 9 November 1929. Once again, the paper listed the resolutions that were passed – for instance, that the government should take steps to liquidate farmers' outstanding debts, set up an agricultural bank and 'employ more villagers in its public works'.[16]

News stories about events in Palestine displaced editorials on the front page of the paper in mid-November. The front page of one issue featured an account of the visit of the Shaw Commission to the district around Jaffa,[17] while the next issue printed on its opening page a summary of the proceedings of the first Arab Economic Congress in Haifa.[18] The major story on page one on 7 December 1929 was an account of a tour of Palestine undertaken by a British military officer, Captain R. G. Canning, which was continued on the front page of the following issue. The trend towards highlighting local news reached a zenith on 21 December, with the inclusion of a section entitled 'Notes of the Week' on the front page that included brief commentaries on a half dozen recent events.

As 1930 opened, the paper reverted to its original structure. The first and second pages started once more to consist entirely of editorials and other sorts of polemical material, while news stories about local events got relegated to page three. Nevertheless, news reporting continued on occasion to be carried out in considerable detail. In early April, for example, the paper published an account of the proceedings of 'The Farmers' Conference':

> A conference of the farmers was held in Ajur, which is situated at a distance of 47 kilometers from Hebron on the North-Eastern side. About 1,000 farmers attended the conference which was held under tents. The most important resolutions were the demand of the abolition of tithes, abolition of 50 per cent of the [extraordinary house and building tax] which was doubled during the war as a war measure, protection of Agricultural products, abolition of [the] Camel-tax as the camels are used for Irrigation purpose, permission of tobacco cultivation like other products.[19]

The story ended with a brief but pithy editorial remark:

> That such a conference was required is indisputable. Whether the time was convenient seems to be doubtful as a great deal depended on the future

Land Policy of the Government which will be framed on the recommendations of the Commission of Enquiry.[20]

Equally careful attention was paid to the organisational meeting of the All Palestine Arab Labourers' Congress.[21]

In the spring of 1930, *Falastin* began to cover major developments in surrounding countries, as well as Palestinian affairs. The 29 March 1930 issue included comments on current events in Syria, Lebanon, Najd, Iraq and Turkey. Similar regional notes appeared on 26 April and 3 May; on 10 and 17 May, news from India was added to the mix. Many of these comments seem superficial: a paragraph concerning developments in Syria read simply:

> The latest news do [sic] not clear the position very much. There is too great a movement of high personages between Beirut and Damascus and there is too little news to show. Political prophets are making hay, while the dark outlook lasts.[22]

Other notes, however, were considerably more substantial. The descriptions of the ongoing constitutional crisis in Egypt provided particularly meticulous summaries of the machinations of the Egyptian nationalist leadership and its struggle against the British administration in Cairo.[23] Thorough coverage was also accorded to the controversial Anglo-Iraqi Treaty of 1930.[24]

News of the Jewish community in Palestine tended to get reported in a much more sporadic fashion, although the few stories that did appear proved to be comparatively substantial. A lengthy editorial poked fun at a public lecture delivered by the Revisionist Zionist leader Vladimir Jabotinsky, particularly his affirmation that 'Running after peace does not bring peace.' 'To him,' the editors remark, 'peace is evidently feminine. The best thing is to disregard peace and to go counter to it so that peace may be had.'[25] A great deal of attention was paid to an apparently unprovoked attack on a prominent eye doctor in Jerusalem, who had gone out of his way to care for poorer members of the city's Arab community.[26] At the same time, the paper offered details of the arms smuggling that was being carried out by Zionist agents, as well as a report on a wildcat strike by Jewish butchers in Tel Aviv that sharply diminished the supply of kosher meat to that city's inhabitants.[27] A follow-up story on arms smuggling appeared on 22 March 1930, and the

14 June 1930 issue reported that a general strike that had been called by the Zionist leadership to protest continued restrictions on Jewish immigration had ended up being aborted.

By the spring of 1930, *Falastin* was devoting sustained attention to trends in local agriculture. A sharp downturn in the local orange crop was first reported in early April, and a detailed description of the persistent problems that plagued the orange industry appeared at the end of the month.[28] A front-page editorial highlighted the difficulties facing agricultural labourers ('the fellaheen'), accompanied by a long essay on 'Co-operative Societies and the Palestinian Peasant'.[29] The next issue opened with a full-page explanation for the drop in orange exports, written by the British administration's Chief Horticultural Officer, Mr A. G. Turner.[30] A week later, the second page contained an editorial that asserted the importance of creating a state agricultural bank instead of relying on cooperative societies to provide funding for the activities of local farmers, while the third page consisted of a lengthy critique of the policies and practices of the British-run department of agriculture.[31]

Criticisms of government agencies continued throughout the autumn of 1930. A page one editorial castigated the department of education;[32] a similar condemnation of the public works department took up the first page of the next issue.[33] The newspaper also argued in favour of making deep cuts in the state budget, along the lines that were taking place in Germany and Syria.[34] But it was matters associated with agriculture that the editors chose to spotlight in their summation of the accomplishments of the English-language edition at the end of its first year of publication:

> Conscious of the important problem of development confronting Palestine, this paper, with all the limitations of size, has not restricted itself to fight the lies and the half-lies of Zionism but devoted a substantial space to the greatest problem of all: The Palestine Peasant. It is the simple truth [the editors affirmed] that this paper has contributed more than any other to [illuminating] this problem.[35]

As *Falastin*'s second year of publication opened, the amount of space devoted to local news shrank dramatically. In its place appeared stories about current developments throughout the wider Muslim world. A violent uprising on the part of initiates of an Anatolian Sufi order against the secularist regime of Mustafa Kemal Atatürk elicited detailed coverage.[36] The death of the prominent South Asian religious and political figure Maulana Mohamed Ali, who had championed the revival of the office of Successor to the Prophet (*khalifa*) and the interests of Muslims in British India, received equally prominent treatment.[37] The visit to Egypt and Palestine of Mohamed Ali's successor, his older brother Maulana Shaukat Ali, prompted not only a lengthy page three description but also a front-page editorial that heralded the immanent rise of 'Neo Pan-Islamism' as a concomitant of Shaukat Ali's international tour.[38] A subsequent issue contained both a front-page editorial that demanded a formal inquiry into Italian military operations in Libya and a page two rebuttal from the Italian Consul General regarding reports of widespread atrocities there, which was supplemented by probing questions from the editors of *Falastin*.[39]

Pan-Islamism rose to greater prominence in the pages of the newspaper as 1931 went by, and preparations moved ahead for the proposed General Islamic Conference in Jerusalem.[40] The editors explicitly endorsed the principles of the Pan-Islamist movement, and enumerated the shortcomings of its earlier incarnation, which had inadvertently alienated the Arabs from the Turks.[41] A front-page interview with Shaukat Ali was accompanied by his photograph – the first photograph to appear in the pages of *Falastin*, aside from a memorial portrait of Mohamed Ali.[42] Interviews with Egypt's Makram 'Ubayd and India's Mahatma Gandhi, both illustrated with photographs, were featured in the next issue.[43] An interview with King Faysal bin al-Husayn was printed two weeks later, along with a photograph of the Iraqi monarch,[44] and one with Mohamed Ali's most influential ally, Muhammad Iqbal (accompanied by a photograph), appeared at the end of the year.[45] Two stories describing the activities of the Indian nationalist movement took up all of page three of the 9 January 1932 issue, while page four of the following issue was given over to a detailed summary of the perilous political situation that confronted India's Muslim community.[46] The fourth page of the 14 May 1932 issue featured an account of the wedding of Shaukat Ali, and the 28 May issue reported the creation of an Indian branch of the World Muslim Congress.

Complementing the emphasis on international affairs in general and Pan-Islamism in particular was a turn towards heightened attention to communist activity in Palestine.⁴⁷ The tenor of the reporting that one finds in 1931 contrasts markedly with the treatment of communism that one sees in the initial issues of *Falastin*: in its first year of publication, the newspaper reprinted an anti-Zionist essay written by none other than Karl Kautsky, which had originally appeared in the radical German journal *Vorwärts*.⁴⁸ An early front-page editorial expressed indignation that British officials had described Arab nationalist activity as communist in nature.⁴⁹ By the spring of 1930, however, the paper had changed its tune, publishing a short article under the headline 'Bolshevism' that read as follows:

> Three facts stand out prominently during this week. Communistic literature was distributed in the area of the Haram. Mr. Jacob Shifman has been arrested in Kfar Hassidim, being suspected with distributing Communistic literature there. Twenty arrests have been made in Jerusalem in a case where one hundred Communists had a clash with the Police. We recommend the Government to make an effective campaign against these mischievous agents as, considering the present economic condition of the rural population, such propaganda is more dangerous than usual. At the same time we want to know how such Bolshevic [sic] Agents found entry into Palestine? Is this the way to prove that the quality and character of every immigrant is rigorously scrutinised? Those who gave these [immigration] certificates are directly responsible. As far as the Arabs are concerned they will help the Government wholeheartedly in deleting from Palestinian Political life this new weapon of subversion.⁵⁰

Communism from this point on would be presented in a consistently unfavourable light, and linked explicitly to the Zionist movement. No more essays by Kautsky.

Articles that offered news of communist organisations appeared with greater frequency during the second year of *Falastin*'s existence. A front-page editorial warned of the continuing circulation of a leaflet that had been issued by the central committee of the Communist Party of Palestine, which appealed directly to displaced farmers and the Bedouin of Wadi al-Hawarith.⁵¹ Four months later, the paper printed an editorial on the front page claiming that the marked rise in both crime and communist influence was a direct result of the spread of Zionism into impoverished agricultural districts.[52] The 30 April 1932 issue featured not only a page two commentary lambasting communist governments around the world but also an inflammatory story that was headlined 'Communist Propaganda'. The story included the complete translation of a leaflet that was said to have been 'distributed recently by Communists' operating in the countryside around Jerusalem:

> To the inhabitants of Ain Karim and suburbs and to all the farmers and labourers of Palestine, who participate in Nebi Musa's festival:[53]
>
> The bad conditions in Palestine have reached their climax. Poverty and drought prevail and are constantly increasing. The season this year is sure to be very bad, therefore the farmer is hungry and angry, too, and the time is near when he shall say his word to settle his account with those who were the cause of his misery.
>
> At this time and in these conditions what do we behold? The High Commissioner presides [over] the Zionist's [sic] athletic games and opens their Levant Fair in Tel-Aviv; the Government helps the usurpers of Arab lands, in their aggressive deeds against the inhabitants of the country; it permits the Zionists and encourages them to carry out demonstrations in which they cry asking for Arab's [sic] lands and right of labour. It aids the Zionists, which is apparent by many proofs. The Government shows by these actions her clear enmity toward the Arabs. This enmity appeared lately when the Government sent and warned the Arabs forbidding them from walking under their emblems and banners in the coming festivals while their friends, the foreign Zionists, walk under their banners singing their aggressive songs to the people of the country within the hearing of the Government.[54]
>
> What does this mean? It means that the Government wants to crush the Arabs and the spirit of their revolutionary union. It also means that the Governmentt [sic] fears the Arabs' violence because it feels the revolting spirit which is dominant amongst the Arab masses and which if it explodes will be effectively strong to send the colonists to where they came from. Therefore the Government fears Arabs' revolt and is doing its utmost to crush them, but the Arabs will know how to resist and return its attacks with their unity and steadfastness.

And let us now see what did the so-called Arab leaders do towards these deeds? They were silent, and they will remain silent because they are allied to the colonists in order to exploit the Arab masses. This is only natural since they cannot take any other position. Why? Because these effendi leaders are in the first place Government Officials; secondly, they are rich and do not care in the least if the farmer lives or dies; thirdly they themselves are the farmers' robbers etc. Therefore you cannot, ye farmers, but depend on yourself and on yourself only.

People of Ain Karem [sic] and suburbs!

We must know by now how to answer the Government (for her forbidding us from walking under our banners). We must walk under our banners notwithstanding the Government's warning and threatening, for if we walk in unity we shall form a strong force that will oppose any other force.

Long live the Arab masses' unity under the revolutionary banners. Let us demonstrate and oppose the mandate and occupation of lands and against taxes and debts.[55]

Presenting this manifesto to readers in its entirety was no doubt intended to underscore the self-evident threat that untamed radical forces posed to public order, if cooler heads did not prevail. To drive home the subversive and alien nature of communism, the next issue of the newspaper featured a roster of Jews who held senior posts in the Soviet Union, under the eye-catching headline 'Bolshevism is Jewish'.[55]

Alongside greater coverage of communist agitation, *Falastin* during its third year of publication began to feature detailed statistical reports concerning an assortment of trends in Palestinian affairs. One table showed the annual totals of loans and cash advances made by the Central Bank of Co-operative Institutions in Palestine;[57] another traced fluctuations in government revenue derived from import duties.[58] The 19 March 1932 issue printed two pages of such tables: one showing the size of the local police force, along with tables indicating the composition and value of imports for 1931 (page three) and ones for postal revenues and the amount of postal traffic for 1930–1 (page four). The paper then published a table of statistics measuring the incidence of 'serious crimes' from 1928 to 1931,[59] and estimates of output of various agricultural products for 1932 and of total egg production.[60] Such tables steadily pushed aside the printed text, leaving little room for anything else except editorials and a small but growing number of commercial advertisements.

Throughout 1929–32, *Falastin* engaged in a running battle with *The Palestine Bulletin*, an English-language daily published in Jerusalem by the Jewish-owned Palestine Telegraphic Agency.[61] As early as the fourth issue of the paper, *Falastin*'s editors observed, 'Soon after the publication of our first number, *The Palestine Bulletin* promised its readers "To double its size and add new features to its contents."'[62] Three weeks later, *Falastin* printed a critique of a pro-Mandate essay that had appeared in the *Bulletin*.[63] Statements made by the *Bulletin*'s editors served as the subject of lengthy editorials during the winter of 1929–30.[64] A shorter comment was published the next spring under the headline 'A Disappointment': '"The Palestine Bulletin" is read with a microscopic eye by the Hebrew and Arabic press says that daily. May be but even with the metaphorical use of this instrument we have not been able to see a speck of sense.'[65]

By May 1930, *Falastin* was devoting a significant amount of space to its rivalry with *The Palestine Bulletin*. Page two of the 31 May issue featured a detailed refutation of an article on land issues that had appeared in summary form in the *Bulletin*. *Falastin* offered a point-by-point analysis of a half dozen claims that had been advanced in the article, along with statistics on working capital, cultivable land, land prices and the 'excess of expenses over income' that characterised eighteen Jewish agricultural settlements.[66] The story ended with an admission that much remained to be investigated about Arab and Jewish farming practices in Palestine, but urged readers to question pervasive Zionist reports that touted the success of Jewish agrarian enterprises.

Among the very few literary items to be printed in the pages of *Falastin* was a poem composed by Anwar bin Zaki Effendi Nusaibah of Jerusalem. The poem, entitled 'A Translation of an Arabian Song', had originally been published in the *Perse School Magazine* of Cambridge, where the author was studying. In the words of the editors, it represented 'a juvenile exhibition of patriotism [which] is published [here] because it is a very fair sample of what the Arab youth are thinking even when [they are] away from the country'.[67] The poem opened as follows:

May God preserve thee, Country dear
Against the forces of thy foes.
How often drops my eye a tear,
To see thy nursery's epoch close.

It ended with a rousing call to action:

'O, tell me where is Saladin
To help me if no friend would tend?
Does in my lair survive no kin
Of heroes who should have no end?'
'No!' I replied, ''tis not so much
These people's deeds recall the past,
And we the sons of heroes such
Shall do what will for ever last.'⁶⁸

Falastin and *Filastin*

'Isa Da'ud al-'Isa's English-language newspaper differed in several important respects from its older, better-known Arabic-language sister. In the first place, *Falastin* consistently overlooked the deep-seated political and familial fissures that characterised the Palestinian national movement during the 1930s.⁶⁹ Such divisions are generally considered to have had a major impact on journalistic practice in the country, and to have shaped the tone and content of most major newspapers.⁷⁰ Mustafa Kabha asserts that 'in the period immediately preceding the [uprising of 1936] the *Mu'aridhun* [opposition] newspapers, led by *Filastin*, regularly attacked the Jerusalem leadership [the Higher Muslim Council and Arab High Committee alike] in their writings'.⁷¹ The publisher himself would often use the pages of the Arabic-language edition to attack the members of the High Committee, or to implore them to take a more vigorous part in leading the national movement. *Falastin*, by contrast, made no mention of divisions inside the nationalist camp, and raised no criticisms of the movement's leading figures. The focus of the English-language edition's editorials remained firmly fixed on the British administration and the Zionist adversary, giving readers no hint that deep-seated rivalry and dissension might be present among the Palestinians.

Second, the Arabic-language paper frequently deployed religious idioms and symbols in its campaign to mobilise popular resistance against foreign intrusion. During the course of the 1936 general strike, for example, *Filastin* proclaimed that 'the nation is fighting a jihad. Do not take advantage of the jihad for your own benefit, and do not try to harm the morale of the nation through complacency or hesitation.'[72] Similarly, *Filastin* referred to the activists who took part in the strike as mujahidin, and asserted that all of those individuals who had perished while taking part in the protest had 'written their names in the heavens with their magnificent sacrifice'.[73] *Falastin*, on the other hand, scrupulously avoided using religiously charged language. Its appeals were consistently framed in terms of modernist notions of nationalism and progress. Palestinians were urged to fight against their adversaries in order to win the status and prerogatives that were enjoyed by other nations in the contemporary world, not in order to preserve the faith.

Even with regard to issues directly related to morality, the English-language edition adopted a posture that emphasised the ways in which immoral behaviour hurt the capacity of the Palestinian people to flourish, rather than such behaviour's inherent sinfulness. In one instance, *Falastin* ran a story under the headline 'Social Evils and the Jaffa Police'. The article began: 'It was a pleasure to learn that our remarks about the undesirability of some dancing saloons coincided with the determination of the Police to reduce this evil to a minimum . . . Unless drastically treated,' it continued, 'the evil will not be appreciably reduced. Some of these places must be closed and the licenses withdrawn.'[74] But why should the authorities make a concerted effort to crack down on such questionable establishments? The newspaper offers a pragmatic, almost utilitarian answer: 'These places are ruining the health and money of the youth and we would welcome any steps taken by the Government to arm the superior officers of the Police with special powers to deal with this cancer.'[75]

Third, *Filastin* persistently campaigned to promote the creation of a fully autonomous Palestinian national economy, and even manipulated its paid advertising in such a way as to demonstrate how the products and services that were on display might contribute to the expansion of local industry, trade, skills and employment.[76] *Falastin*, by contrast, published entirely different sorts of advertisements. The great majority of ads were pitched directly to European residents and tourists, with hotels featured most frequently and prominently. Cigarettes made up the largest part of the remaining advertisements in the English-language edition; all of the cigarette ads featured prizes that were available to anyone who purchased a sufficient quantity of the brand. The prizes consisted of jewellery, clothing accessories, cigarette cases and other smoking paraphernalia of a distinctly modern, European variety. Office supplies and sewing machines made up the remainder of the goods that were regularly advertised.

Fourth, the Arabic-language edition made it a point of principle to avoid all kinds of 'collaboration with either the British Mandate government or the Jewish Agency . . . especially [with regard to] the question of selling land'.[77] According to Kabha, *Filastin* 'vigorously protested against collaboration and land sales and even made threats against those involves [sic] in these activities'.[78] The English-language edition, by contrast, praised the Jaffa police force for its campaign to shut down the city's dance halls, despite its being an instrument of the British administration. Somewhat later, the paper associated itself with the workings of the Mandate's judicial apparatus as well, by running this notice:

> Notice From the Court of the Magistrate of Nablus to The defendant, Shibli bin Yusuf of Rafidiah residence unknown: Your presence is required in this court as a defendant in a suit filed in by Selim Yusuf Alkhuri of Rafidiah, demanding his share of the house shared between you and others of Rafidiah, on Monday the 24th, August, 1931 at 8 a.m. In case of your absence the necessary legal steps will be taken.[79]

Falastin therefore provided a channel whereby official announcements from the British authorities were transmitted to the country's English-speaking populace.

More remarkably, *Falastin* printed periodic notices of public auctions of real estate that had been ordered by the courts. One such notice listed several parcels of land that were to be sold off from the estate of Francis Daoud Aljiaar in order to pay the outstanding taxes owed by his widow, on the orders of the 'Execution Office Bethlehem'.[80] Such announcements described the properties involved in considerable detail, including the overall quality of the soil, whether or not the land was irrigated and what type of crop was presently being cultivated. It is hard to imagine that these announcements would, or even could, have attracted the attention of prospective buyers from the local Arab community. This implies that the auction notices were most likely directed at the very non-Arab purchasers who were roundly castigated in the Arabic-language edition.

Falastin's Appeal

It quickly becomes obvious to the reader that the English-language edition targeted an audience that had little direct contact with, and knew very little about, the land of Palestine. The newspaper's editorials consistently described the problems that confronted the local inhabitants using language that outside readers could easily understand, even if this meant appropriating images and terminology drawn from British society and politics. To this end, the editors frequently reprinted summaries of anti-Zionist editorials that had originally been published in British and, increasingly as time went by, American newspapers and periodicals. Thus the front page of the 5 October 1929 issue featured summaries of anti-Zionist editorials culled from the American press, while page four highlighted a letter to the editor of *The Times* of London that lambasted Zionist initiatives in Palestine. The next issue contained five similar letters, including one from a writer in Florida.

Whenever possible, *Falastin* used material written by Europeans and Americans to drive home a major point. One issue printed on its front page a manifesto against Zionism that had been formulated by a collection of German Jews, and reprinted on page two a pamphlet that had been composed by a British cleric demanding that the government in London immediately rescind the Balfour Declaration.[81] The text of a public address given by the visiting Captain Canning took up most of the front page of the 30 November 1929 issue, followed a week later by Kautsky's essay from *Vorwärts*. Page two of the 27 March 1932 issue featured an article on 'My Impressions' of the Palestine problem that was composed by Professor Peter Dughman of the University of Cincinnati.

As the paper shifted in a Pan-Islamist direction, scarce column space was handed over to writers hailing from other parts of the Muslim world. The 23 January 1932 issue reprinted a pamphlet from South Africa entitled 'Organised Jewry and Islam in Palestine', which charged that Jews dominated the Mandate administration and dictated government policy along pro-Zionist lines. A month later, the paper published a letter to the editor from a group of South Asian students who, having 'devoted themselves to a study of the situation in Palestine', offered a relatively straightforward solution to the conflict between the Zionists and the Arab population.[82] The month after that, page two reprinted an interview on the dangers of Zionism that had been given by Maulana Shaukat Ali to *The Jewish Advocate* newspaper of Bombay.[83]

Relying on foreign voices to articulate the demands of the Palestinian people ran the risk of violating one of the founding principles of the English-language edition. The editors had argued in the inaugural issue of *Falastin* that 'for the last ten years we have been complaining, protesting and laying open our case to the world in our own language only. The result was we wrote the stuff and we read it.'[84] Rather than writing the story of the Palestinians in English themselves, however, they came to look increasingly to sympathetic outsiders to get the message across. Nevertheless, the editors also recognised the importance of publishing items that could resonate with policymakers and public opinion in Europe and North America, and seem to have been willing to make use of whatever material might contribute to that larger cause.

Providing a forum for anti-Zionist essays written by Europeans, Americans and South Asians came at a substantial cost. The editors pointed out at the end of the first year of publication:

> we can boast of having aroused an interest, based on a just curiosity, in the [sic] Arab affairs. Indian papers have translated it. European papers of all countries have quoted it. American libraries have demanded it and one of the members of the Permanent Mandates Commission has asked questions based on the information derived through this paper. [Yet] all this has not been easy to achieve. The paper was not supported as the papers of [the] rival community are. The result was a certain financial loss. The lack of [an] English-reading public amongst the Arabs and the limited number of non-Arab English speaking public in Palestine limited the subscribers.[85]

When expenses continued to mount during the second year, *Falastin* announced that 'in compliance with the demand of oversea [sic] readers it is proposed to keep a special space in our columns for the news of the week as well as ample space for news of Arab and Eastern countries'.[86] In fact, the paper exhibited an overall reduction in news reporting during its third year of publication, and a particularly marked diminution in the coverage of events taking place in other Arab countries.

Falastin as Historical Source

Social historians of the Mandate period in Palestine can find useful information in the pages of *Falastin*, and students of the rhetoric and imagery of Palestinian nationalism will no doubt be able to mine fruitful ore from the editorials and commentaries that dominate each issue of the newspaper. Articles concerning a number of important congresses and public gatherings, particularly during the newspaper's second year of publication, provide details of the proceedings and personalities involved in an accessible and trustworthy fashion. Such reports complement Arabic-language sources to good effect, particularly with regard to topics that the editors of the English-language edition thought might be of significance to foreign readers. Ellen Fleischmann demonstrates just how helpful *Falastin* can be for understanding the political mobilisation of Palestinian women.[87]

Of particular interest to anyone interested in cultural studies is the attention that the newspaper paid to the production of local oranges. The state of the orange crop was used as a key indicator of developments in Palestinian agriculture as a whole, and when the editors decided to highlight the steady deterioration of local farming,[88] it was this particular product that they opted to chronicle. The initial page-long analysis of the downturn in orange output was juxtaposed against both the account of the farmers' meeting at 'Ajjur and a commentary that urged the authorities to protect the domestic market by imposing higher tariffs on imports of agricultural products.[89] By far the most detailed piece of original reporting that was published during the paper's first year in operation was a meticulous description of the various problems that faced the orange industry, both at that time and in the immediate future.[90]

By emphasising trends in orange production, *Falastin* reflected the nationalist movement's use of this particular fruit as the primary symbol of the Palestinian national economy.[91] The year before the English-language edition set its sights on developments in the orange industry, the Arabic-language edition had generated a heated public debate over the flag that the Palestinian national movement might best adopt.⁹² The newspaper itself proposed two alternative designs: one consisting of the four colours associated with the revolt of Faysal bin al-Husayn against the Ottomans (red, white, black and green) and another that placed these same four colours around a central diamond of orange. The former design enjoyed a fabled history in both nationalist and popular circles, despite the fact that it had been introduced by non-Palestinians.⁹³ Nevertheless, many individuals responded favourably to the inclusion of a distinctively local component, namely the colour orange, to the venerable foursome. One reader 'even proposed drawing an [actual] orange on the flag'.⁹⁴

It may well be that those who championed the addition of an orange field to the Palestinian flag intended to underscore Palestine's political autonomy from the surrounding Arab states.⁹⁵ In any event, charting the rise and fall of orange production served as a symbolic way to trace the trajectory of the local economy as a whole, while at the same time acquainting European readers with the severe threat that Zionism posed to the one export item that was most closely identified with the country.

Finally, a careful perusal of *Falastin* opens the door to further exploration of the connections that existed between the nationalist movement in Palestine and political developments in South Asia. The prominence that was accorded to articles about Shaukat Ali and the Muslims of the Indian subcontinent throughout the third year of the newspaper's publication indicates that at least one influential group of Palestinian nationalists kept up with news from South Asia, and did its best to forge links between the two regions. That the attempt to conjoin these two parts of the Islamic world was carried out in the English language comes as little surprise. That it was undertaken in full view of an international readership that no doubt included agents of the British administration is a bit more startling. Just who was it that the editors of *Falastin* expected to care about the details of Shaukat Ali's wedding? And who was supposed to take seriously the South Asian students' simplistic plan to resolve the escalating conflict between the Zionists and the Palestinian Arabs? It is questions like these that arise most forcefully out of a careful reading of this exceptional example of the Middle Eastern press in the era before independence.

Notes

1. Khalidi, 'Anti-Zionism, Arabism and Palestinian Identity'; Ayalon, *Press in the Arab Middle East*, p. 96.
2. *Falastin* 16 September 1929.
3. Sela, 'The "Wailing Wall" Riots (1929)'; Lundsten, 'Wall Politics'; Segev, *One Palestine*, ch. 13; Winder, 'The "Western Wall" Riots of 1929'.
4. *Falastin* 16 September 1929.
5. Segev, *One Palestine*, pp. 332–3; Ofer, 'The Commission on the Palestine Disturbances of August 1929'.
6. Sorek, 'The Orange and the "Cross in the Crescent"', p. 269.
7. *Falastin* 16 September 1929.
8. Ibid. Free copies of *Filastin* had been distributed to village headmen throughout Palestine from the beginning. Khalidi, *Palestinian Identity*, p. 57.
9. *Falastin* 16 September 1929. While acting as editor of *Falastin*, al-Nashashibi pursued coursework in journalism and political science at the University of London. See Hadi, *Palestinian Personalities*, s.v. Azmi al-Nashashibi.
10. *Falastin* 16 September 1929.
11. *Falastin* 23 September 1929.
12. *Falastin* 28 September 1929.
13. Ibid.
14. *Falastin* 19 October 1929.
15. *Falastin* 26 October 1929.
16. *Falastin* 16 November 1929.
17. Ibid.
18. *Falastin* 23 November 1929.
19. *Falastin* 5 April 1930.
20. Ibid. *Falastin*'s coverage of the congress ignored the pro-Zionist overtones of the meeting, along with those of the farmers' parties more generally. See Cohen, *Army of Shadows*, pp. 23–4.
21. *Falastin* 17 January 1930.
22. *Falastin* 3 May 1930.
23. *Falastin* 28 June and 5 July 1930.
24. *Falastin* 5 July 1930.
25. *Falastin* 4 January 1930 (erroneously dated 4 January 1929). For coverage of Jabotinsky's activities in the Arabic-language edition, see Khalaf, '*Falastin* versus the British Mandate and Zionism', pp. 19–22.

26. *Falastin* 16 November 1929.
27. Ibid.
28. *Falastin* 5 and 26 April 1930.
29. *Falastin* 16 August 1930.
30. *Falastin* 23 August 1930.
31. *Falastin* 30 August 1930.
32. *Falastin* 4 October 1930.
33. *Falastin* 11 October 1930.
34. Ibid.
35. *Falastin* 6 September 1930.
36. *Falastin* 10 January 1931. On the so-called Menemen incident, see Azak, 'A Reaction to Authoritarian Modernization'.
37. *Falastin* 24 January 1931. On Mohamed Ali, see Hasan, *Mohamed Ali*; Jalal, *Self and Sovereignty*.
38. *Falastin* 14 February 1931.
39. *Falastin* 25 April 1931.
40. Matthews, *Confronting an Empire*, pp. 105–10.
41. *Falastin* 30 May 1931.
42. *Falastin* 5 September 1931.
43. *Falastin* 12 September 1931.
44. *Falastin* 26 September 1931.
45. *Falastin* 19 December 1931.
46. *Falastin* 16 January 1932.
47. See Budeiri, *Palestine Communist Party*; Franzen, 'Communism versus Zionism'.
48. *Falastin* 7 December 1929.
49. *Falastin* 14 December 1929.
50. *Falastin* 19 April 1930.
51. *Falastin* 17 January 1931. See Matthews, *Confronting an Empire*, pp. 188–93.
52. *Falastin* 23 May 1931.
53. On the role of the Nabi Musa festival in Palestinian nationalism, see Halabi, 'The Nabi Musa Festival'; Halabi, 'Symbols of Hegemony'; Halabi, 'Islamic Ritual'.
54. During the Nabi Musa festivals of both 1931 and 1932, the Mandate authorities blocked the residents of 'Ain Karim from taking part in the proceedings while carrying banners of their own, which would have constituted a challenge to Palestinian elites and British officials alike. See Halabi, 'Symbols of Hegemony', pp. 73–5. Uniformed groups of Jewish militants, by contrast, had marched

towards the Haram al-Sharif on several occasions in the weeks prior to the 1932 celebration. See Segev, *One Palestine*, p. 316.
55. *Falastin* 30 April 1932.
56. *Falastin* 7 May 1932.
57. *Falastin* 23 January 1932.
58. *Falastin* 12 March 1932.
59. *Falastin* 27 March 1932.
60. *Falastin* 3 April 1932.
61. *The Palestine Bulletin* first appeared on 12 January 1924 and was incorporated into *The Palestine Post* in December 1932, which in April 1950 transformed into *The Jerusalem Post*.
62. *Falastin* 5 October 1929.
63. *Falastin* 26 October 1929.
64. *Falastin* 28 December 1929.
65. *Falastin* 12 April 1930
66. *Falastin* 31 May 1930.
67. *Falastin* 3 May 1930.
68. Ibid.
69. See Hassassian, *Palestine*.
70. See, for example, Sulayman, *Tarikh al-sihafa al-filastiniyya*, pp. 117–18; Ayalon, *Press in the Arab Middle East*, pp. 97–8, 100; Najjar, 'The Arabic Press and Nationalism', pp. 77–8.
71. Kabha, 'The Palestinian Press', p. 172.
72. *Filastin* 5 May 1936, quoted in Kabha, 'Palestinian Press', p. 177.
73. *Filastin* 27 July 1936, quoted in Kabha, 'Palestinian Press', pp. 179–80.
74. *Falastin* 7 June 1930.
75. Ibid.
76. Kabha, 'Palestinian Press', pp. 182–3.
77. Ibid., p. 186.
78. Ibid., p. 186; Khalidi, 'Anti-Zionism, Arabism and Palestinian Identity', p. 92.
79. *Falastin* 4 July 1931.
80. *Falastin* 31 May 1930.
81. *Falastin* 26 October 1929.
82. *Falastin* 27 February 1932.
83. *Falastin* 27 March 1932.
84. *Falastin* 16 September 1929.
85. *Falastin* 6 September 1930.

86. *Falastin* 29 August 1931.
87. Fleischmann, *Jerusalem Women's Organizations*.
88. Agriculture in Palestine suffered from a sobering list of maladies around the time that *Falastin* appeared in print, including 'a cattle pestilence in 1926; some degree of drought in 1927, 1928 and 1931–1933; infection of 80% of the local dairy herds in 1930; four consecutive years of locust plague from 1928 through 1931; [and] field mice depredations in 1928, 1930 and 1931–33'. Stein, 'Palestine's Rural Economy', p. 40.
89. *Falastin* 5 April 1930.
90. *Falastin* 26 April 1930.
91. It may also reflect, as Mustafa Kabha points out in his contribution to this volume, the al-'Isa family's extensive holdings of orange groves.
92. Sorek, 'The Orange and the "Cross in the Crescent"', p. 270.
93. Ibid., p. 275.
94. Ibid., p. 278.
95. Ibid., pp. 280–1.

Bibliography

Ayalon, Ami, *The Press in the Arab Middle East: A History* (New York: Oxford University Press, 1995).

Azak, Umut, 'A Reaction to Authoritarian Modernization in Turkey: The Menemen Incident and the Creation and Contestation of a Myth, 1930–31', in Touraj Atabaki (ed.), *The State and the Subaltern* (London: I. B. Tauris, 2007), pp. 143–58.

Budeiri, Musa, *The Palestine Communist Party, 1919–1948* (London: Ithaca Press, 1979).

Cohen, Hillel, *Army of Shadows* (Berkeley: University of California Press, 2008).

Fleischmann, Ellen, *Jerusalem Women's Organizations during the British Mandate, 1920s–1930s* (Jerusalem: Palestinian Academic Society for the Study of International Affairs, 1995).

Franzen, Johan, 'Communism versus Zionism: The Comintern, Yishuvism and the Palestine Communist Party', *Journal of Palestine Studies* 36 (Winter 2007), pp. 6–24.

Hadi, Mahdi Abdul (ed.), *Palestinian Personalities*, 2nd edn (Jerusalem: Palestinian Academic Society for the Study of International Affairs, 2006).

Halabi, Awad, 'Islamic Ritual and Palestinian Nationalism: al-Hajj Amin and the Prophet Moses Festival in Jerusalem, 1921 to 1936', in Lena Jayyusi (ed.), *Jerusalem Interrupted* (Northampton, MA: Olive Branch Press, 2013), pp. 139–52.

Halabi, Awad, 'The Nabi Musa Festival under British-Ruled Palestine', *ISIM Newsletter* 10 (2002), p. 27.

Halabi, Awad, 'Symbols of Hegemony and Resistance: Banners and Flags in British-Ruled Palestine', *Jerusalem Quarterly* 36 (Winter 2009), pp. 66–78.

Hasan, Mushirul, *Mohamed Ali: Ideology and Politics* (Delhi: Manhar, 1981).

Hassassian, Manuel S., *Palestine: Factionalism in the National Movement (1919–1939)* (Jerusalem: Palestinian Academic Society for the Study of International Affairs, 1990).

Jalal, Ayesha, *Self and Sovereignty: Individual and Community in South Asian Islam since 1850* (London: Routledge, 2000).

Kabha, Mustafa, 'The Palestinian Press and the General Strike, April–October 1936: Filastin as a Case Study', *Middle Eastern Studies* 39 (July 2003), pp. 169–89.

Khalaf, Noha Tadros, 'Falastin versus the British Mandate and Zionism (1921–1931)', *Jerusalem Quarterly* 45 (Spring 2011), pp. 6–24.

Khalidi, Rashid I., 'Anti-Zionism, Arabism and Palestinian Identity: 'Isa al-'Isa and Filastin', in Samir M. Seikaly (ed.), *Configuring Identity in the Modern Arab East* (Beirut: American University of Beirut Press, 2009), pp. 83–96.

Khalidi, Rashid I., *Palestinian Identity* (New York: Columbia University Press, 1997).

Lundsten, Mary Ellen, 'Wall Politics: Zionist and Palestinian Strategies in Jerusalem, 1928', *Journal of Palestine Studies* 8 (Autumn 1978), pp. 3–27.

Matthews, Weldon C., *Confronting an Empire, Constructing a Nation: Arab Nationalists and Popular Politics in Mandate Palestine* (London: I. B. Tauris, 2006).

Najjar, Aida Ali, 'The Arabic Press and Nationalism in Palestine 1920–1948' (PhD dissertation, Syracuse University, December 1975).

Ofer, Pinhas, 'The Commission on the Palestine Disturbances of August 1929: Appointment, Terms of Reference, Procedure and Report', *Middle Eastern Studies* 21 (July 1985), pp. 349–61.

Segev, Tom, *One Palestine, Complete* (New York: Metropolitan Books, 2000).

Sela, Avraham, 'The "Wailing Wall" Riots (1929) as a Watershed in the Palestine Conflict', *The Muslim World* 84 (January–April 1994), pp. 60–94.

Sorek, Tamir, 'The Orange and the "Cross in the Crescent": Imagining Palestine in 1929', *Nations and Nationalism* 10 (July 2004), pp. 269–91.

Stein, Kenneth W., 'Palestine's Rural Economy, 1917–1939', *Studies in Zionism* 8 (1987), pp. 25–49.

Sulayman, Muhammad, *Tarikh al-sihafa al-filastiniyya 1876–1918* (Nicosia: Mu'assasat Bisan, 1987).

Winder, Alex, 'The "Western Wall" Riots of 1929: Religious Boundaries and Communal Violence', *Journal of Palestine Studies* 42 (Autumn 2012), pp. 6–23.

PART II
THE RISE OF THE JOURNALIST

5

Press Propaganda and Subaltern Agents of Pan-Islamic Networks in the Muslim Mediterranean World prior to World War I

Odile Moreau

The Muslim Mediterranean is considered as a relevant framework to analyse interrelated connections on its shores.[1] Here, I follow Julia Clancy-Smith's conceptualisation of 'the idea of a "central Mediterranean corridor", which can be imagined as a series of linked, intersecting borderland regions'.[2] This chapter on press propaganda and subaltern agents of Pan-Islamic networks in the Muslim Mediterranean, dealing with movements and circulations around the Mediterranean, will be particularly concerned with the interface of these two Mediterranean spaces: Middle East (Egypt, Ottoman Empire) and North Africa (Morocco). It is devoted to the study of the external component of resistance movements in North Africa, dealing especially with press propaganda, contributing to the emerging field of the Mediterranean history. Morocco is viewed as a case study of the extent to which movements of resistance sought external allies as a way of compensating for their weaknesses.[3]

The approach developed in this chapter has two sources of inspiration, the micro-historians and the Subaltern school of Asian historians. Following the micro-historical approach, the attention is focused on individuals, with an actor-centred perspective.[4] Subaltern historians focused on non-elite subalterns as agents of political and social change in the context of the British

Empire. More recently, the subaltern in the Middle East has become a source of interest.[5] Subaltern history is very useful to shed light on events or people not well known, belonging to non-elite circles. Both approaches promote a new historical object, history from below, which is much more concerned with the base levels of society than the elite. In this respect, I try to reconstruct micro-histories, or at least part of individuals' lives and trajectories. Agents of press propaganda, and especially Aref Taher Bey, were not known. Taher Bey conducted subversive activities and travelled widely all around the Mediterranean and had contacts with large networks, such as Pan-Islamic networks. As a modern military officer, he had difficulties finding a place between core and periphery and his position could be viewed as belonging to marginality. In fact, if he could be considered as a member of the elite in his native homeland, he had to migrate and lost his social status, then belonging to the marginal, or subaltern. His activities as a journalist and press propaganda agitator were unexpected. He was certainly an activist, but could perhaps also be considered as belonging to a 'subaltern group', doing underground networking. In this chapter, I will explore how a secret society called al-Ittihad al-Maghribi (The Maghrabi Union), based in Egypt, and its members, a very active group of individuals, used the press as an arena for political contest in Morocco.

Political Situation in North Africa at the End of the Nineteenth Century

Like most of the states in the Middle East in the nineteenth century, Morocco faced huge external and internal challenges. France occupied Algeria from 1830, which created serious tensions in North Africa. In the 1880s, France promulgated a protectorate in Tunisia in 1881 and Egypt was under British control from 1882. At the end of the nineteenth century, however, Libya was still an Ottoman province and Morocco an independent sultanate. The year 1830, when the French invaded Algeria, was a watershed for Morocco. Then, after the French victory at the battle of Isly in 1844 over the Moroccan army, the Makhzan recognised the inferiority of its army and aimed at reform by creating a modern and reliable army and administration. Then the Moroccan sultan had recourse to European expertise.[6] Morocco also faced a considerably difficult financial situation worsened by the war indemnity it had to pay to Spain (after the Tetouan War). In addition, the treaty of commerce of 1856 with England opened up the Moroccan market to Europe and gave many privileges to the Western countries. With all these new constraints, the Moroccan Treasury began its indebtedness to European bankers.

The political situation in Morocco in the early twentieth century was very difficult and foreign observers labelled it the 'Moroccan Crisis' or the 'Moroccan Question'. Moroccan officials played upon the dissensions between European powers;[7] however, Germany had begun to play an important commercial role in Southern Morocco. After the surprise visit of Kaiser Wilhelm II to Tangiers in 1905, Germany seemed to play the role of Morocco's protector against invading enemies. A year later, at the Algeciras Conference, in 1906, the decisions gave France a free hand to follow its own interests. Nevertheless, the Franco-German rivalry over Morocco extended until the Agadir Crisis in July 1911 when an agreement on the Moroccan Question was reached whereby Germany, in return for obtaining a part of the Congo and a strip around the edge of Cameroon in West Africa, allowed France to pursue its Moroccan 'colonial agenda'.

The Situation of the Press in Morocco

From very early in the nineteenth century, foreign-language newspapers were published in Morocco. The port city of Tangiers, where a lot of foreigners lived, was especially the theatre of the mushrooming press. Due to its geographical position and its mixed cosmopolitan and multicultural population, Tangiers played an avant-garde role in the history of the press in Morocco before the establishment of the protectorate. Even a long time before the French-Spanish Protectorate settled in 1912, Tangiers was an attractive place for foreigners and also a special place exciting international rivalry.[8]

The first attempt at a newspaper took place in 1870 and was led by two Jewish publishers under the auspices of the Alliance Israélite Universelle (AIU) from Paris.[9] Later on, other publishing houses and newspapers opened in order to satisfy the growing European community of Tangiers. Appearing in 1883, *Le réveil du Maroc* presented itself as the first French-language newspaper in Morocco.[10] Generally, these newspapers led press campaigns against the Makhzan and its civil servants.[11] Among these newspapers, *Le réveil du Maroc* was perhaps the most pugnacious and at the forefront of the press campaigns.[12] The situation was so tense in 1886 that the Moroccan government tried to close all the foreign newspapers published in Tangiers. Due to their legal status, however, the owners of the newspapers – being either foreigners or protected by foreign powers – escaped the control of the Moroccan government, enjoying freedom of the press in Tangiers. After this incident, the newspapers moderated their criticism but again in January 1887, the Makhzan sought in vain to close down the Moroccan press in Tangiers. This became a recursive process in the following years.[13] The lack of legal status of the press prevented an effective control on the newspapers in Tangiers. Afterwards, in addition to *Le réveil du Maroc*, three other French-language newspapers opened before the end of the nineteenth century.[14] The press printed in Morocco in the last quarter of the nineteenth century was almost a propaganda tool directed towards European public opinion and the governors of the metropolis.[15]

Later on, the first Arabic-language newspaper in Morocco, *al-Maghrib*, was published in Marrakesh by two Syrian-Lebanese in 1889 but disappeared quickly. Except for a few pages in Arabic written in Western newspapers aiming at propaganda, Morocco then had no effective Arabic press until 1904, when the French authorities founded the Arabic-language newspaper *al-Sa'ada*, financed by the Légation de France.[16] *Lisan al-Maghrib*, a Tangiers-based Arabic weekly newspaper, is considered as the first national Moroccan newspaper.[17] Opposing the French propaganda disseminated by *al-Sa'ada*, *Lisan al-Maghrib* reflected the views of the Palace.[18] It seems that *Lisan al-Maghrib* was supported by the Committee for Union and Progress in Istanbul – or at least was in contact with it – and that Germany encouraged it in order to create a Moroccan opposition to the French authorities.[19] A few weeks after the arrival of Mawlay 'Abd al-Hafidh in Fez, *Lisan al-Maghrib* published articles dealing with constitutionalism.[20] Afterwards, Syrian journalists began to return home.[21] The same year, in 1908, the first 'newspaper' directed by a Moroccan, *al-Ta'un* (The Pestilence), was launched by Sharif Muhammad al-Kattani in Fez with very modest means and very small-scale production.[22] This short-lived news journal perhaps looked more like a leaflet. That same year, Wadi Karam, a Lebanese, published *al-Sabah* in Tangiers.[23]

Al-Fajr appeared for the first time in Tangiers in July 1908, edited and written by a Christian from Syria: Ni'met Allah Dahdah. After seven issues, the Makhzan suppressed it because of its Hafidhian tendencies.[24] The years

1907–8, in fact, were a very turbulent time of civil war in Morocco when Mawlay 'Abd al-'Aziz and his half-brother and the sultan's viceroy, Mawlay 'Abd al-Hafidh, divided the kingdom's forces.²⁵ In 1909, *al-Sabah* was transformed into a bi-monthly journal when *al-Fajr*, the official organ of the Moroccan government, appeared in Fez. General news was relayed from the European Press and from *al-Mu'ayyad* (1889–1915) concerning the Islamic issues.²⁶ As in Egypt, at the beginning, journalism in Arabic language was led by Syrians in Morocco. The prominence of Lebanese and Syrians in the field was due to their bilingualism in Arabic and French.²⁷

The Moroccan local press being not so important, this gave more importance to the foreign newspapers entering Morocco. Rather little information is available on the circulation of newspapers in Morocco prior to the establishment of the Protectorate but it seems that the circulation was quite limited at this time.²⁸ The Egyptian newspaper *al-Mu'ayyad* played an important role in information about the Middle East in Morocco.²⁹ Therefore, initially the press propaganda directed against French imperialism was organised, at least in part, from outside with the support of the newspaper *al-Mu'ayyad*.

The Network's Egyptian Actors

During this period of political effervescence in Egypt, *al-Mu'ayyad* was the Islamic community's voice of protest. Its editor was Shaykh 'Ali Yusuf (1863–1913), a member of the entourage of the Khedive 'Abbas Hilmi Pasha (1874–1944),³⁰ and someone who had strong contacts in Istanbul. At the same time, Shaykh 'Ali Yusuf was in close contact with Aref Taher. *Al-Mu'ayyad*, one of the leading Egyptian newspapers, was perhaps also one of the most popular. It was one of the principal journals in the Arabic language, publishing famous names such as Qasim Amin, Mustafa Kamil and Sa'd Zaghlul, and was read from Tangiers to India and from Turkey to Zanzibar.³¹

The pro-Khedivial *al-Mu'ayyad*, founded in 1889, supported the Pan-Islamic anti-British position of Shaykh 'Ali Yusuf and promoted later the political goals of his party, Hizb al-Islah al-Dusturi (Constitutional Reform Party) after its founding in 1907, under Palace control.³² Shaykh 'Ali Yusuf remained the Khedive's ally even when others broke with him after Sir Eldon Gorst became Consul General in Egypt, and the Khedive became more conciliatory towards the British.³³ He was also a close confidant of the Khedive

'Abbas Hilmi Pasha.[34] The Khedive needed an ally such as Shaykh 'Ali Yusuf, giving a religious legitimacy to his rule. If the Khedive was a Europeanised man, at the same time we can notice in his memoirs a pious man.[35] In his writings, the Khedive acknowledges that he played a double game and encouraged two discordant national trends: the conservative party under the leadership of Shaykh 'Ali Yusuf, and the extremist nationalist party led by Mustafa Kamil.[36] Shaykh 'Ali Yusuf came from the village of Balasfura in Upper Egypt and was raised in a clerical environment. He studied at al-Azhar and was active as a nationalist and a journalist.[37] His policies were based on the prestige of the caliph and he sometimes styled himself as the defender of Islam. According to 'Abbas Hilmi Pasha in his memoirs, Shaykh 'Ali Yusuf's policies were never particularly Turkish or Muslim, but concerned with nationalism.[38] He considered that Shaykh 'Ali Yusuf had never been Turkey's man and if he supported the caliphate, it was to encourage his position as the Commander of Islam and his approach had much in common with Pan-Arabism.[39] We can consider that Shaykh 'Ali Yusuf and his newspaper encouraged Islamic unity (*al-Ittihad al-Islam*) and played a great role in promoting the idea.

Aref Taher Bey: From the Military to Journalism

Born in the European Ottoman province of Albania in the 1880s, Aref Taher Bey was a captain of the operations staff in the Ottoman army. In fact, in the initial stage of his career he could be considered to have been a member of the modern military elite. After the Young Turk Revolution of 1908, and more precisely after the Counter Revolution of April 1909 (31 Mart vakaası), he left Istanbul and served in different regions of the Muslim Mediterranean. It seems that he was tried by court martial in Istanbul because of *casusluk* (spy activities) before the Young Turk Revolution of 1908, and consequently cashiered from the Ottoman army.[40] In such a situation, he appears to have been, at least at that time, an opponent to the Committee for Union and Progress (CUP). He left for Egypt, where he stayed six months.

At the same time, the Khedive 'Abbas Hilmi Pasha and prominent Egyptian nationalists obtained financial support from Istanbul against the English colonial power. Clandestine activities sponsored by Pan-Islamic circles connected with the Ottoman government added to this official support.

These Egyptian secret societies were especially involved in the opposition to the French presence in the two main non-colonised regions of North Africa, namely Morocco and Libya.[41] It seems that Ottoman officers, who were exiled in Egypt in 1909, came through an invitation of Muhammad Pasha al-Shara'i.[42]

After arriving in Egypt, Aref Taher Bey was in contact with the secret Cairo-based al-Ittihad al-Maghribi. He accepted the offer made through the Khedive to be recruited in Morocco.[43] In fact, when Aref Taher Bey arrived in Morocco, he had a single recommendation letter written by Muhammad Pasha al-Shara'i to be given to El Hadj Hammed el-Mokri.[44] In later years, a veteran of this military mission would reveal yet another motive of greater personal importance: the Unity of Islam (*Ittihad-i Islam*). *Ittihad-i Islam* was also labelled Pan-Islamism and tried to utilise the links within the Muslim community, the *umma*, the community of the faithful. The intellectual content of Pan-Islamism was the Brotherhood of all Muslims.[45]

So in 1909, Aref Taher Bey travelled to Morocco to meet his fellow officers who had gone there via Tripoli on the Barbary Coast. As senior officer, he led the non-official Turkish Military Mission to Morocco until 1910, describing himself on his visiting card as 'A. Tahir, Etat-major, chef de la Mission Turque'.[46] As head of the military mission, he also spoke French and German as well as Turkish (but no Arabic, at least at first). In his opinion, the Moroccan army owed its order and discipline to the intervention of the Ottoman officers, who tried to instruct and educate the soldiers and train them in modern weaponry. At the same time, Aref Taher Bey wrote articles in Ottoman newspapers discussing Morocco's precarious situation regarding the imperial views of the Great Powers, especially France.

In September 1910, Aref Taher Bey wrote in *Yeni Gazete* an article entitled 'Is Mawlay Hafidh a tyrant or not?' in which he supported the Moroccan sultan's action.[47] In response, the Ottoman War Minister published an article in the same newspaper, on 11 September 1910, declaring that the former captain was no longer a member of the Ottoman army and consequently any views he expressed were his own and did not reflect those of the Ottoman army.[48] He and his fellow officers were then publicly disowned by the Ottoman government.

That same day, the *Tasvir-i Efkar* published an article with a mocking title: 'Those Who Serve the Constitution'.⁴⁹ It was written that ten former students at the military school in Istanbul had escaped from the military gaol after being struck off the roll, and left for Egypt and then for Morocco. While serving in the Moroccan army they were dismissed for being at odds with the French officers. Once expelled, they left for Paris where at that time they served Sherif Pasha,⁵⁰ the former Ottoman ambassador in Stockholm. After having long talks, they agreed to distribute the free *Meşrutiyet*, a newspaper published in three languages – Ottoman, French and English – by Sherif Pasha.⁵¹ The local Egyptian press dealt several times with the presence of these officers in Cairo and related their past. For example, both of the above-mentioned articles published in Istanbul's press were commented on.⁵² After the recall of the Turkish Military Mission in March 1910, only informal contacts continued between Morocco and the Middle East, mainly via the Egyptian Arabic press.⁵³

In November 1910, after the removal of the Turkish Military Mission and upon his return to Fez, Aref Taher Bey introduced himself as a correspondent to the Egyptian newspaper *al-Mu'ayyad*. It served perhaps as camouflage; however, he did the job and worked as a political journalist all the same. The newspaper paid him twenty Egyptian pounds a month for the information he collected, which represented a rather good salary at that time. Aref Taher Bey's articles, which gave him the opportunity to freely express his ideas, increasingly turned into outright anti-French propaganda. He published a number of articles vehemently attacking French interventions in Morocco and presence in North Africa.⁵⁴ This attracted the anger of the French authorities, which responded by prohibiting him from entering Moroccan territory.

To name but one example, Aref Taher Bey set out the case of Turkey, which, thanks to support from Germany and Austria-Hungary, managed to shake off the menace of a financial yoke imposed by France by granting loans to the Ottoman Empire. According to Aref Taher Bey, Morocco ought to have followed the Turkish example and allied itself with its 'true friends', Germany in particular. In another article published in *al-Mu'ayyad* on 29 January 1911, he criticised the French Military Mission to Morocco, saying: 'Moroccans ignore the ambitions of their enemies and at the same time are so unconscious that they entrust the Moroccan army organisation to

French officers.'⁵⁵ He warned that the Moroccan authorities should not give a predominant position to the French military instructors, paving the way for Morocco's French Protectorate. He meant that the French were Morocco's enemy and that the Moroccan sultan should turn to Germany.

It seems that Aref Taher Bey did not write these articles himself in Arabic. According to a French report, Muhammad Belghiti, a former secretary of the Dar al-Niyaba in Tangiers, helped him, at least as a translator.⁵⁶ In fact, Muhammad Belghiti was dismissed from his office at the time of the Turkish Military Mission, accused of being the writer of several anti-French articles published in the newspaper *al-Mu'ayyad* and signed by the head of the Turkish Military Mission, Aref Taher Bey. Afterwards, Muhammad Belghiti collaborated again with another newspaper in Tangiers, *al-Haqq*, with a strong involvement in anti-French propaganda, and he was also connected to the secret society al-Ittihad al-Maghribi.⁵⁷

Pan-Islamic Press Propaganda

We can distinguish two periods of time in press propaganda dealing with Morocco and organised by the network of the secret society al-Ittihad al-Maghribi. Al-Ittihad al-Maghribi, one among several secret societies in Egypt, whose objects included propaganda beyond Egyptian territory, was designed on Pan-Islamic lines with its goal being to unite the North African States (Algeria, Tunisia, Morocco and Tripolitania).⁵⁸ It dreamed of a Maghribi Union and of the restoration of a large Muslim Empire in North Africa under the auspices of Germany. Founded in Cairo by Muhammad Pasha al-Shara'i of Moroccan origin, it was also in contact with the Egyptian Khedive 'Abbas Hilmi II.

Initially, articles were written in the Egyptian newspaper *al-Mu'ayyad*, which was sent to Morocco. We can notice that not so many foreign newspapers entered Morocco at that time. Among these were the Egyptian *al-Mu'ayyad* (pro-Khedive), *al-Liwa'* (Pan-Islamic),⁵⁹ *al-Ahram* (pro-French), *al-Muqattam* (pro-British) and *al-Manar* (the journal of Muslim reformism).⁶⁰ In *al-Mu'ayyad*, news reports on the Moroccan situation were written by an anonymous 'A.T.', possibly Aref Taher Bey, the ex-Ottoman officer representing al-Ittihad al-Maghribi. According to Aref Taher Bey, a thousand copies of *al-Mu'ayyad* were sent in early 1911 to Morocco to be distributed among the various regions of the country.⁶¹ This newspaper could also be found in the Moroccan mosques. It seems that this estimate was an exaggeration, however; according to Edmund Burke, there were some fifty regular subscribers of the Pan-Islamic *al-Mu'ayyad* in Fez alone in 1911, including Muhammad al-Muqri, the Foreign Minister, and other important officials.⁶² Sultan 'Abd al-Hafidh and the Moroccan elite read *al-Mu'ayyad*, as did the Makhzan. 'Abd al-Hafidh and his Grand Vizier Madani al-Glawi were both known to be readers of the Near Eastern and European Press.⁶³ In 1909, the Ottoman government had banned the distribution of *al-Mu'ayyad* within Turkey as it was considered to be the organ of monarchist Egyptians, and its editor and proprietor, Shaykh 'Ali Yusuf, was believed to be in close contact with 'Arab' Izzet Pasha, Sultan 'Abd al-Hamid II's former Chamberlain who managed his household.

Later in 1911, the secret society al-Ittihad al-Maghribi planned to open a German–Arabic-language newspaper with an anti-French editorial line, which would address the urban elite in Morocco.⁶⁴ The principal actors involved in this project were Muhammad Pasha al-Shara'i, Aref Taher Bey and Shaykh 'Ali Yusuf. In 1910, they had begun negotiations with German intermediaries in Morocco, among them the Mannesmann brothers. Aref Taher Bey had several meetings with the Minister of Germany in Egypt and Mr Singer, the Director of the Deutsche Orient Bank,⁶⁵ which was a very active centre spreading anti-French propaganda and ideas of *Ittihad-i Islam*.⁶⁶ Singer also had a very good relationship with the German Diplomatic Agency in Cairo (*Agence diplomatique d'Allemagne au Caire*),⁶⁷ and was in contact in Cairo with Baron Max Freiherr von Oppenheim, the famous German scholar, archaeologist and traveller who spent decades of his life in the Middle East.⁶⁸ German interests in North Africa were openly in competition with those of France in Morocco until France and Germany reached an agreement after the Agadir Crisis in July 1911. Franco-German rivalry was violent and used the press as a tool of propaganda. The German intervention in Morocco slowed the French process of control of the country, although it was unable to stop it. At the same time, the Germans used their military involvement in Morocco to support the local resistance. In May 1911, some members of al-Ittihad al-Maghribi established contact with Mawlay Zayn al-'Abidin, a pretender to the Moroccan throne. They intended to provide him with military advice and monetary backing, financed by the Cairo-based Maghribi Union; however, they never accomplished their goals, being arrested by the French in June 1911.[69]

This planned local Moroccan newspaper was to be published in Arabic, French and German with the support of the German Diplomatic Agency in Cairo. The correspondent of the *Gazette de Cologne* was to be in charge of the pages in French and German. 'Abd al-Azim Ahmad Rif'at, an Egyptian who had arrived in Tangiers about a year earlier, also joined the efforts of this group to promote this new publication. The provisional title of the newspaper was *Nahdat al-Maghrib* (Maghrib's Revival). Below the title was a verse: 'Unissez-vous tous en Dieu et ne vous désunissez pas' (All of you unite in God and do not divide) and also the description: 'Political, Literary and Economic Newspaper for the Progress of the Maghreb'. In spite of the long consultation process between al-Ittihad al-Maghribi and German officials, the newspaper was never published. In June 1911, when Aref Taher Bey went to Tangiers to found the newspaper, he was arrested by the French authorities and expelled, taking refuge in Spain.[70]

French Protectorate officials took very seriously the political danger represented by Pan-Islamic and German propaganda in Morocco. This Pan-Islamic propaganda benefited from the Spanish authorities benevolence and sometimes from the help of some of their agents.[71] Political Pan-Islam used various tactics to organise resistance activities against the French colonial power to encourage unrest by distributing leaflets, press propaganda and infiltration by trained guerrilla fighters.

In fact, the Arabic-language newspaper *al-Haqq* founded and published in Tangiers in 1912, a newspaper sponsored by the Spanish Legation, seems to have been supported by the secret society al-Ittihad al-Magaribi. This second editorial attempt succeeded thanks to the Spanish Legation's help.[72] 'Abd al-Azim Ahmad Rif'at,[73] an Egyptian, was the director of *al-Haqq*, which had an anti-French editorial line and employed correspondents in Algeria, Tunisia and Tripolitania. Most of the articles published in *al-Haqq* criticised the French politics across North Africa, in Morocco, Algeria, Tunisia and Tripolitania. For example, articles compared the Arab resistance supported by Ottoman officers in Trablusgarb (Tripoli in Barbary) and Benghazi and the Moroccan resistance to the French troops in order to encourage it.[74]

In addition, this newspaper was an important element of the 1912 plot of the Pan-Islamic group al-Ittihad al-Maghribi. On many occasions, Middle Eastern Arabic newspapers – and also opponent newspapers against the French colonial power – had been banned by the Protectorate authorities in order to avoid uprisings against the colonial authorities.[75]

Aref Taher Bey was also one of the leaders of the 'al-Ittihad al-Maghribi conspiracy' in 1912 in Morocco. During World War I, while based at the Ottoman Embassy in Madrid, he became involved in the common programme – at least, a German-Ottoman programme – called by the Germans 'Morokko Aktion'. He was the second of the Turkish Military Mission to organise clandestine operations in Morocco. As Ottoman advisor, he joined German agents in the Moroccan field under the banner of what was at that time called 'Pan-Islam'. In the summer of 1918, Aref Taher Bey returned to Istanbul where he was called to become aide-de-camp to Sultan Vahiddetin.[76]

Conclusion

The resistance movement in Morocco in the early twentieth century was strongly influenced by Middle Eastern currents of thought, including Pan-Islamism, Islamic reformism and Ottoman constitutionalism.[77] The press served as a very useful vehicle to spread propaganda and the Middle Eastern press was especially rich. A translocal network within the Muslim Mediterranean based in Cairo was very active and Morocco represented a fight arena against imperialism. These translocal connections between the Middle East and North Africa were supported by the secret society al-Ittihad al-Maghribi, involving Ottomans, Egyptians and North Africans. These translocal spaces represented sites through which many cultures travelled,[78] and the various actors spread these cultures and propagandist ideas throughout the Mediterranean (Egypt, the Ottoman Empire, Morocco, Algeria, Tunisia and Tripolitania). There is evidence of the circulation of this propaganda to be found throughout the press.

Uniquely, one of the main actors in this network dealing with press propaganda, Aref Taher Bey, was not just a non-professional journalist but also a military officer from the Ottoman origin. It was very rare that Ottoman officers were involved in journalism and especially in non-military newspapers. Aref Taher Bey was in a marginal position from the point of view of the Ottoman army. He also had a subaltern position in the network of the secret society al-Ittihad al-Maghribi. After the failure of military training in Morocco at the time of the Turkish Military Mission to Morocco in 1909, press propaganda became a major activity involving Aref Taher Bey.

The different press campaigns created an emerging public space between North Africa and the Middle East. The local Moroccan press was in its infancy. In a first phase, press propaganda was introduced secretly from abroad by way of the Egyptian newspaper *al-Mu'ayyad*, avoiding French censorship. In a second phase, the secret society al-Ittihad al-Maghribi tried to open a local German-Arabic newspaper, *Nahdat al-Maghrib*, with an anti-French editorial line in Morocco in 1911. But the French authorities arrested Aref Taher Bey in June 1911 and the newspaper project never materialised. The project of al-Ittihad al-Maghribi to unite the North African states (Algeria, Tunisia, Morocco and Tripolitania) failed after the signature of the Franco-German Convention of 4 November 1911.[79] However, al-Ittihad al-Maghribi succeeded in publishing an Arabic-language newspaper in Tangiers, *al-Haqq*, under the protection of the Spanish Legation in 1912. These anti-French press campaigns show that the Ottoman–Egyptian–Moroccan network interacted closely with Germany, and they demonstrate the important place Morocco held, both in the Muslim Mediterranean and in German political concerns.

Notes

1. See Clancy-Smith, *Mediterraneans*, who places Tunisia within a larger framework and demonstrates interrelationships between the varied peoples who settled on the shores of the Mediterranean and finally joined the French colonial enterprise. David Abulafia in his works *Mediterranean in History* and *The Great Sea: A Human History of the Mediterranean* has established the Mediterranean sea as relevant area for study.
2. Clancy-Smith, *Mediterraneans*, p. 11.
3. See Burke, 'Moroccan Resistance', p. 436.
4. Carlo Ginzburg's best-known book is *The Cheese and the Worms*. See also Levi, *Inheriting Power*.
5. Burke and Yaghoubian, *Struggle and Survival*; Cronin, *Subalterns and Social Protest*. Both collected editions deal with subalterns in the Middle East and North Africa as actors involved in social protest at the very bottom of the society.

6. This defensive modernisation paved the way for reforms for the first time along Ottoman and Egyptian lines; however, after the Tétouan War (1859–60) between Morocco and Spain, a minor power in Europe, the Moroccan elite recognised the need for more extensive reforms in order to give a new impetus to the Moroccan army. Under the reign of Mawlay al-Hasan I (1873–94), the new armed forces were directed by European military advisors from England, France, Spain, Italy and Germany.
7. The situation changed with the diplomatic agreement known as the Entente Cordiale in 1904 when France conceded British control over Egypt in exchange for a free hand in Morocco. Spain recognised France's predominance in Morocco and signed a parallel agreement with France confirming its own zone of influence in Northern Morocco. From the turn of the century, Morocco became a new priority on France's colonial agenda.
8. In fact, between 1820 and 1880, several newspapers in Spanish appeared in Morocco, followed by a number of English and French newspapers. In 1870, there were already nearly a thousand foreigners living in Tangiers. In addition, Tangiers was the diplomatic capital of Morocco where the diplomatic missions lived until the Treaty of Fez in 1912, when the French authorities selected Rabat as the new administrative capital of Morocco.
9. Baida, *La presse marocaine*, pp. 34–40. After the Madrid Conference in 1880, a Gibraltarian, Gregorio Trinidad Abrines, opened the Abrines printing house, which produced a great many publications (books, brochures, circulars and posters). First in Spanish then in English, Abrines also published the weekly newspaper *al-Maghrib al-Aqsa* (The Far Occident), the oldest Tangerian newspaper, with the exception of a Jewish newspaper published in 1870.
10. Published by Levy Abraham Cohen, the first issue of this weekly appeared on 14 July 1883, the anniversary of the French Revolution, denoting its pro-French orientation.
11. These press campaigns criticised and denigrated the Makhzan and the Moroccan elite, pointing out the weaknesses of Moroccan power. Journalists reported on the abuses and systematic extortion by government officials at all levels. Not even the Moroccan sultan was spared. The articles advocated for reforms and Morocco's opening to European commerce, for example. Such hostile remarks and critics shocked local religious feelings. An official Press Centre (*Bureau de presse*) founded during the time of Mawlay Hasan I (1874–94) kept the Moroccan sultan informed of the publications dealing with him, whether published in the country or abroad. This *Bureau de presse* was still

functioning under Sultans ʿAbd al-ʿAziz (1894–1908) and ʿAbd al-Hafidh (1908–12).
12. Baida, *La presse marocaine*, p. 45.
13. Ibid., pp. 50–1.
14. *Le commerce du Maroc* was founded in March 1886 under German patronage. The other two titles, *Le Maroc* (1893) and *Le Maroc commercial* (1895), were both launched by V. A. Serph. Baida, *La presse marocaine*, p. 55.
15. French-language newspapers promoted the ideas of the enlightenment through reforms and advocated French peaceful penetration ('pénétration pacifique'), insisting on all its positive aspects. Slowly, these press campaigns accustomed French public opinion to the idea of a future French colonial occupation of Morocco. The French-language press was used as a prelude or a tool for colonial penetration and then for military occupation. It wrote for the foreigners in Morocco but was also read outside the country. Because the local readership was very small, the interest in Moroccan public opinion came later. Baida, *La presse marocaine*, p. 35.
16. *Al-Saʿada* continued as a tool of the peaceful penetration ('pénétration pacifique') in Morocco for more than half a century (from 1904 until 1913 in Tangiers and from 1913 until 1956 in Rabat). *Al-Saʿada* was read in the milieu of the Makhzan. Laroui, *Les origines sociales*, p. 397. Its editor was an Algerian, Moulay Idris Ben Mohammed al-Khabzaoui al-Jazairi. Bensoussan, *Il était une fois le Maroc*, p. 183.
17. *Lisan al-Maghrib* was founded on 28 February 1907 by the brothers Farajallah and Arthur Nammur, Lebanese Maronites who came to Tangiers from Jaffa. The Makhzan had in fact engaged a number of Arab intellectuals from various Arab countries. For example, ʿAbd-al-Karim at-Tunusi had been recruited as legal advisor to the Makhzan and the Nammur brothers themselves were engaged to promote counter-propaganda against *al-Saʿada*. See Kably, *Histoire du Maroc*, p. 530.
18. *Lisan al-Maghrib* was supported by the Makhzan. Ibid., p. 530.
19. Hanna Elias, *La presse arabe*, p. 67.
20. In four successive articles that appeared in October and November 1908, *Lisan al-Maghrib* published a constitution proposal, the first in Morocco. The consequence was the breaking off of relations between Mawlay ʿAbd al-Hafidh and the *Lisan al-Maghrib* group. Laroui, *Les origines sociales*, p. 403.
21. In fact, the brothers Nammur received no more subsides from Mawlay ʿAbd al-Hafidh and began to have a more critical attitude towards him. Having

the impression of being threatened, they placed themselves under the protection of the French Legation. Then, they sold all their printing equipment to Mawlay 'Abd al-Hafidh who lost no time in closing the newspaper. Ibid., p. 405.

22. According to Mercier, al-Kattani organised meetings at his home where scribes copied articles he dictated to them in notebooks. It is also well known that al-Kattani and his family had already been using the technology of printing. See Bazzaz, *Forgotten Saints*, p. 119.
23. *Al-Sabah* directed by a Syrian, Wadi Karam appeared in Tangiers in August 1908 and had a scientific, economic, political, and literary programme, with the motto 'Au matin les hommes louent l'Être mystérieux'.
24. At the time of the dynastic war in Morocco, Ni'met Allah Dahdah was on the side of Mawlay 'Abd al-Hafidh, half-brother and an opponent of Sultan Mawlay 'Abd al-'Aziz.
25. After the proclamation of Mawlay 'Abd al-Hafidh as sultan in 1908, *al-Fajr* reopened but for only a short time. Two issues were published in Fez in December 1908 by Vaffier-Pollet and Ni'met Allah Dahdah, but the newspaper was closed under pressure from the ulama. See Mercier, 'La presse arabe au Maroc', p. 381.
26. Mercier, 'La presse arabe au Maroc', pp. 131–2.
27. We can observe a similar situation in Tunisia.
28. Bazzaz, *Forgotten Saints*, p. 123n.31.
29. The local newspapers *al-Sa'ada* and *Lisan al-Maghrib* had close ties with the Middle Eastern press and especially with *al-Mu'ayyad*, a leading Egyptian newspaper of the Pan-Islamic line, whose news they carried.
30. In 1892, Khedive 'Abbas Hilmi Pasha II ascended the throne when his father Khedive Tawfiq died suddenly. When he tried during his first years to oppose Cromer, he was immediately threatened with deposition. This led him to encourage secretly the nationalist movement. For example, the Khedive financed Kamil to go to France to get a law degree and to carry out a press campaign to swing European public opinion against the British occupation of Egypt. Al-Sayyid Marsot, *History of Egypt*, p. 92. See also foreword by Afaf Lutfi al-Sayyid Marsot to Sonbol, *Last Khedive of Egypt*, pp. ix–x.
31. Sonbol, *Last Khedive of Egypt*, p. 133.
32. Goldschmidt, *Modern Egypt*, p. 61; cf. Pollard, *Nurturing the Nation*, p. 141.
33. Mustafa Kamil, Muhammad Farid and Shaykh 'Abd al-'Aziz Shawish adopted an uncompromising position regarding Great Britain.

34. 'Abbas Hilmi Pasha supported Shaykh 'Ali Yusuf, including over the crisis he went through because of his marriage to Safiya al-Sadat. Sonbol, *Last Khedive of Egypt*, p. 126.
35. Ibid., p. 17.
36. Ibid., p. 125.
37. Shaykh 'Ali Yusuf began his journalistic career as a reporter for *al-Qahira al-Hurra* and afterwards published *Majalat al-Adab*. He later became founder and editor of *al-Mu'ayyad*. Ibid., pp. 125–6.
38. Ibid., p. 132.
39. Ibid., pp. 133–4.
40. This information was given by the Ottoman War Minister in an article in *Yeni Gazete* 11 September 1910.
41. Burke, 'Pan-Islam and Moroccan Resistance', p. 102.
42. Deny, 'Instructeurs militaires turcs'. This is the translation and commentary of an article written by a former officer of the Turkish Military Mission, published in the newspaper *Vakit* in 1926 in Istanbul.
43. Ahmed Bedevi (Kuran), in exile in Egypt at that time, writes in his memoirs that the Khedive 'Abbas Hilmi Pasha proposed to this group of officers to join the Moroccan army and arranged everything with the Moroccan ambassador in Paris, al-Muqri. Then, a part of this group decided to go to Morocco and 'Abbas Hilmi Pasha paid all the travel expenses. A first group led by a captain of the operations staff, Aref Taher Bey, arrived in Morocco in November 1909. Upon their arrival in Morocco, they represented themselves as adventurers seeking employment. In Fez, the Turkish officers were received by al-Muqri and introduced to the Sultan's Court. At any rate, the mission was the cause of much discontent. Since February 1909, the French Military Mission to Morocco had been the head of all the European foreign military missions appointed in Morocco and was in a predominant position. Despite the protests of the French Military Mission, the officers were attached to the Makhzan army as advisors and soon began accompanying the troops on manoeuvres against dissident tribes to the north of Fez. They continued acting until March 2010, when they were compelled to leave as a result of French diplomatic pressure; however, they did not leave Moroccan territory until the month of August 1910. Kuran, *Inkilap Tarihimiz ve Jön Türkler*, pp. 348–51.
44. MAE (French Ministry of Foreign Affairs, Paris), NS 277, Maroc, Défense Nationale, VI, 2 December 1909, p. 196.
45. Burke, 'Pan-Islam and Moroccan Resistance', p. 99.

46. FO 371/931 confidential, no. 1, Mr White to Sir Edward Grey, Tangiers, 10 July 1910, p. 271.
47. This article was published in *Yeni Gazete* no. 732 (25 Agustos 1326/7 September 1910).
48. The Minister of War presented a very pejorative image of Aref Taher Bey, explaining that he was a former whistle blower who had denounced a number of his comrades.
49. *Tasvir-i Efkar* 11 September 1910.
50. An opponent of the Committee for Union and Progress, Sherif Pasha founded the Ottoman Radical Party in Paris in November 1909.
51. *Tasvir-i Efkar* 11 September 1910; cf. NS 279, Maroc, Défense nationale, VIII, ambassade de France près la Porte ottomane, dir. aff. Pol. et co., no. 364, Thérapia, le 16 septembre 1910, ambassadeur de France à M. le ministre des Affaires étrangères, pp. 74–5.
52. MAE, NS 279, Maroc, Défense nationale, VIII, dir. aff. Pol. et co., Charles-Roux, chargé d'affaires de l'agence et du consulat général de France au Caire à M. Pichon, ministre des Affaires étrangères, no. 322, p. 81.
53. Burke, 'Pan-Islam and Moroccan Resistance', pp. 109–10.
54. Examples of Aref Taher Bey's articles in *al-Mu'ayyad* include: 'Morocco's Situation in 1911' on 11 April 1911, where he was advocating in favour of Sultan 'Abd al-Hafidh. He explained how French politics became stronger in 1910. There was a popular upheaval in Marrakesh because the population did not accept the French interference in Moroccan affairs; however, according to him, 'Abd al-Hafidh would never voluntarily renounce Morocco's independence. He asked the rebels to lay down their arms and to work with the sultan. On 4 April 1911, he wrote an article titled 'Great Britain and France Set Up an Arrangement to Manoeuvre an Exchange of Muslim Countries, Egypt and Morocco'; and on 11 April 1911, he denounced the Anglo-French collaboration on the expense of both Egyptians and Moroccans. It seems that Aref Taher wrote at least an article per month for *al-Mu'ayyad* in 1911, a very tense year of French–German rivalry in Morocco.
55. CADN, DAI, 220, vol. II, p. 103.
56. The *Dar al-Niyaba* was an institution established by the Makhzan in the middle of the nineteenth century, directed by a *na'ib* who represented the sultan in communications with the foreign legations. The office was abolished with the establishment of the Protectorate. See Kably, *Histoire du Maroc*, p. 782.
57. CADN, DAI, 220, vol. I, p. 11.

58. This secret society is described in the memorandum entitled 'Report Respecting Secret Societies' issued in June 1911 by the Secret Service Bureau, which was formed in the Egyptian Ministry of the Interior in late 1910 after the murder of Egyptian Prime Minister Butrus Ghali by Wardani. In fact, twenty-six secret societies were operating in Egypt at that time. The report indicates that No. 7, Jam'iyyat al-Ittihad al-Maghribi's meeting place was the president's house (Muhammad Pasha al-Sharai Pasha) at Izbat al-Zaytun, near Cairo. 'This society is worked on Pan-Islamic lines and has agents amongst the Azharian Maghribis who propagate its principles amongst Maghribis returning to their country.' See FO Kitchener Papers 30/57, vol. 36, quoted in Tauber, 'Egyptian Secret Societies, 1911', pp. 603–23.
59. Kamil launched his journal *al-Liwa'* in 1900, which later served as an organ for his political party, al-Hizb al-Watani.
60. *Al-Manar* was founded by the famous Rashid Rida in March 1898 in Cairo.
61. MAE, Maroc, Défense nationale, IX; M. Defrance, chargé of the Agence and the General Consulate of France in Cairo to M. Cruppi, 7 June 1911, no. 297, annex.
62. Burke, 'Pan-Islam and Moroccan Resistance', p. 104.
63. Sultan 'Abd al-Hafidh read the local and international press assiduously, with *al-Mu'ayyad* among his Arabic-language subscriptions. He also employed local and foreign translators to translate the foreign press. Kably, *Histoire du Maroc*, p. 541.
64. CADN, Tanger 469, M. Defrance à M. Poincaré, Président du Conseil, ministre des Affaires étrangères, no. 202, Cairo, 8 May 1912.
65. CADN, DAI 220, vol. I, pp. 103–4.
66. German Middle Eastern policy gave priority first to the Turkish heartland, then countries under British or French influence (Greater Syria), then the other French-influenced territories such as Algeria and Morocco, and finally the Central Asian Muslim lands. See Schwanitz, 'German Middle Eastern Policy', p. 18.
67. CADN, DAI 220, vol. I, p. 102, Letter of Mr Defrance, chargé of the Agence and the General Consulate of France in Cairo to Mr Pichon, Minister of Foreign Affairs, 6 February 1911.
68. Von Oppenheim had very deep connections and interactions in the Middle East. According to his memoirs, he had close contacts with Arab notables and intellectuals, among them Khedive 'Abbas Hilmi, who stood for the idea of Pan-Islamism, and Shaykh 'Ali Yusuf. He also enjoyed good relations with

Muhammad 'Abduh, a passionate advocate for Muslim revival and modernisation. See Marchand, *German Orientalism*, p. 440.
69. Burke, *Prelude to Protectorate*, p. 161.
70. Aref Taher Bey was arrested on 11 June 1911. CADN, DAI, 220, vol. II, p. 104.
71. CADN, Tanger 469, M. Cambon, French Ambassador to London to M. Poincaré, Minister of Foreign Affairs, no. 416, 3 October 1912.
72. Burke, 'Pan Islam and Moroccan Resistance', pp. 111–12.
73. 'Abd al-Azim Ahmad Rif'at, an Egyptian Muslim, had studied in Great Britain and spent time in Beirut. When he arrived in Tangiers, the Legation of Spain was looking for an editor to found an Arabic-language newspaper. Rif'at was appointed director of this newspaper and also held the position of Arabic-language teacher at the Spanish school. CADN, Tanger 469, Résident Général, Rabat, no. 97, 3 August 1912.
74. CADN, Tanger 469, Résident Général, Rabat, no. 97, 3 August 1912.
75. Burke, 'Moroccan Resistance', p. 455.
76. On November 1922, Aref Taher Bey escaped to Europe with the ex-Ottoman Sultan Vahidettin and thereafter he was not authorised to return to Turkey. In fact, his name was in the sixth position on the list of the 150 persons forbidden from returning to Turkey as a member of Vahidettin's retinue (*Yaverandan Erkan-ı Harp Miralay Tahir*). He remained in San Remo in Italy with the ex-Sultan Vahidettin until the latter's death, then moved to France, and finally settled in Albania where he became a general during Zogo's reign.
77. Burke, 'Moroccan Resistance', p. 437.
78. Mandaville, *Transnational Muslim Politics*, p. 85.
79. Despite this agreement, the mutiny in Fez and the promulgation of the French Protectorate in 1912 provoked several activities of al-Ittihad al-Maghribi's network. During World War I, the German–Ottoman cooperation created a new framework to organise uprisings.

Bibliography

Archives

United Kingdom: The National Archives, London
Foreign Office (FO)
France: Centre des Archives diplomatiques de Nantes, Nantes (CADN)
Direction des Affaires indigènes (DAI)
Ministère des Affaires étrangères, Paris (MAE)

Published Works

Abulafia, David, *The Great Sea: A Human History of the Mediterranean* (Oxford: Oxford University Press, 2012).

Abulafia, David (ed.), *The Mediterranean in History* (Los Angeles: J. Paul Getty Museum, 2011).

Baida, Jamaâ, *La presse marocaine d'expression française, des origines à 1956* (Rabat: Faculté des Lettres et des Sciences Humaines de Rabat, 1996).

Bazzaz, Sahar, *Forgotten Saints: History, Power and Politics in the Making of Modern Morocco* (Cambridge, MA: Harvard Center for Middle Eastern Studies, 2010).

Bensoussan, David, *Il était une fois le Maroc: Témoignages du passé judéo-marocain* (Montréal: Éditions du Lys, 2010).

Burke III, Edmund, 'Moroccan Resistance, Pan-Islam and German War Strategy, 1914–1918', *Francia* 3 (1975), pp. 434–64.

Burke III, Edmund, 'Pan-Islam and Moroccan Resistance to French Colonial Penetration, 1900–1912', *Journal of African History* 13:1 (1972), pp. 97–118.

Burke III, Edmund, *Prelude to Protectorate in Morocco: Precolonial Protest and Resistance, 1860–1912* (Chicago: University of Chicago Press, 1976).

Burke III, Edmund and David Yaghoubian (eds), *Struggle and Survival in the Modern Middle East*, 2nd edn (Berkeley: University of California Press, 2005).

Clancy-Smith, Julia, *Mediterraneans: North Africa and Europe in the Age of Migration, c. 1800–1900* (Berkeley: University of California Press, 2011).

Cronin, Stephanie (ed.), *Subalterns and Social Protest: History from below in the Middle East and North Africa* (London: Routledge, 2008).

Deny, Jean, 'Instructeurs militaires turcs au Maroc sous Mawlay Hafidh', in *Mémorial Henri Basset: Nouvelles études nord-africaines et orientales* (Paris: Paul Geuthner, 1928), pp. 219–27.

Goldschmidt, Arthur, *Modern Egypt: The Formation of a Nation State* (Boulder, CO: Westview Press, 2004).

Ginzburg, Carlo, *The Cheese and the Worms: The Cosmos of a Sixteenth-Century Miller*, trans. John Tedeschi and Anne Tedeschi (Baltimore: Johns Hopkins University Press, 1980).

Hanioğlu, M. Şükrü, *Preparation for a Revolution: The Young Turks 1902–1908* (Oxford: Oxford University Press, 2001).

Hanna Elias, Elias, *La presse arabe* (Paris: Maisonneuve et Larose, 1993).

Kably, Mohammed (ed.), *Histoire du Maroc: Réactualisation et synthèse* (Rabat:

Publications de l'Institut Royal pour la Recherche sur l'Histoire du Maroc, 2012).

Kansu, Aykut, *Politics in Post-Revolutionary Turkey, 1908–1913* (Leiden: Brill, 2000).

Kelidar, Abbas Rashid, 'The Political Press in Egypt, 1882–1914', in Charles Tripp (ed.), *Contemporary Egypt through Egyptian Eyes: Essays in Honour of Professor P. J. Vatikiotis* (London: Routledge, 1993), pp. 1–21.

Kuran, Ahmed Bedevi, *Inkılap Tarihimiz ve Ittihad ve Terakki* (Istanbul: Tan Matbaası, 1948).

Kuran, Ahmed Bedevi, *Inkilap Tarihimiz ve Jön Türkler*, 2nd edn (Istanbul: Kaynak Yayınları, 1945).

Kuran, Ahmed Bedevi, *Osmanlı Imparatorluğunda Inkılap Hareketleri ve Milli Mücadele* (Istanbul: Baha Matbaası, 1956).

Landau, Jacob, *The Politics of Pan-Islam, Ideology and Organization*, 2nd edn (Oxford: Clarendon Press, 1992).

Laroui, Abdallah, *Les origines sociales et culturelles du nationalisme marocain* (Paris: Maspéro, 1977).

Levi, Giovanni, *Inheriting Power: The Story of an Exorcist*, trans. Lydia G. Cochrane (Chicago: University of Chicago Press, 1985).

Mandaville, Peter, *Transnational Muslim Politics: Reimagining the Umma* (London: Routledge, 2001).

al-Manuni, Muhammad, *Al-Masadir al-'arabiyya li-tarikh al-maghrib: al-fatra al-mu'asira (1790–1930)*, 2 vols (Rabat: Université Mohammed V, Faculté des Lettres et des Sciences Humaines, 1989).

al-Manuni, Muhammad, *Mazahir yaqazat al-maghrib al-hadith*, 2 vols (Beirut and Casablanca: Dar al-gharb al-islami/al-madaris, 1999).

Marchand, Suzanne L., *German Orientalism in the Age of Empire: Religion, Race, and Scholarship* (Cambridge: Cambridge University Press, 2009).

Mercier, Louis, 'La presse arabe au Maroc', *Revue du Monde Musulman* 7:1–2 (1909), pp. 128–33.

Miège, Jean-Louis, 'Journaux et journalistes à Tanger au 19e siècle', *Hespéris, Archives berbères et bulletin de l'Institut des hautes études marocaines* 41 (1954), pp. 191–228.

Moreau, Odile, *L'Empire ottoman à l'âge des réformes: Les hommes et les idées du 'Nouvel Ordre' militaire, 1826–1914* (Paris: Maisonneuve et Larose-IFEA, 2007).

Moreau, Odile, 'Une "mission militaire" ottomane au Maroc au début du 20e siècle', *The Maghreb Review* 30:2–4 (2005), pp. 209–24.

Pollard, Lisa, *Nurturing the Nation: The Family Politics of Modernizing, Colonizing, and Liberalizing Egypt, 1805–1923* (Berkeley: University of California Press, 2005).

Rollman, Wilfrid, 'The "New Order" in a Pre-colonial Muslim Society: Military Reform in Morocco, 1844–1904', 2 vols (PhD thesis, University of Michigan, 1983).

al-Sayyid Marsot, Afaf Lutfi, *A History of Egypt: From the Arab Conquest to the Present*, 2nd edn (Cambridge: Cambridge University Press, 2007).

Schwanitz, Wolfgang G., 'The German Middle Eastern Policy, 1871–1945', in Wolfgang G. Schwanitz (ed.), *Germany and the Middle East, 1871–1945* (Princeton, NJ: Markus Wiener Publishers, 2004), pp. 1–24.

Sonbol, Amira (ed.), *The Last Khedive of Egypt: Memoirs of Abbas Hilmi II* (Cairo: American University in Cairo Press, 2006).

Strauss, Johann, *The Egyptian Connection in Nineteenth-Century Ottoman Literary and Intellectual History* (Beirut: Orient-Institut der Deutschen Morgenländischen, 2000).

Tauber, Eliezer, 'Egyptian Secret Societies, 1911', *Middle Eastern Studies* 42:4 (2006), pp. 603–62.

6

The Publicist and his Newspaper in Syria in the Era of the Young Turk Revolution, between Reformist Commitment and Political Pressures: Muhammad Kurd 'Ali and *al-Muqtabas* (1908–17)

Kaïs Ezzerelli

The daily newspaper *al-Muqtabas*[1] was founded on 17 December 1908 in Damascus by the Syrian publicist Muhammad Kurd 'Ali (1876–1953). Kurd 'Ali was newly returned from exile in Cairo where he had gained a solid grounding in journalism and where, in 1906, he had already established a literary and scientific review of the same name (*al-Muqtabas*).[2] Thanks in no small part to the fact that they owned their own printing house, Matba'at al-Muqtabas, and helped along by the climate of liberalisation brought about by the Young Turk Revolution of July 1908, Muhammad Kurd 'Ali and his brothers Ahmad and 'Adil found themselves at the head of a press enterprise whose workings – from editing right down to sales – were under their sole control. With the assistance of a team of casual editors, one of whom was the famous representative for Damascus in the Ottoman parliament, Shukri al-'Asali (1878–1916), they embarked on a pioneering enterprise in the years leading up to World War I that secured *al-Muqtabas*'s status as a cultural phenomenon and an artefact of Syria's newly introduced press technology.[3] *Al-Muqtabas* thus became a vehicle for specific norms and values that we may refer to as 'reformist' and, in so doing, had a significant impact on the Damascene society of the time.

The political context of the era was conducive to the success of the brothers' enterprise since the re-establishment of the Constitution in 1908 proclaimed freedom of expression (and thus freedom of the press) as a fundamental principle of the new regime. Between 1908 and 1914, around forty newspapers and reviews were set up in the city of Damascus alone.[4] The link between these press organs and Arabist organisations (or Arab reformists) is well known and *al-Muqtabas* was a case in point because a great many of its editors, the most notable amongst them being Muhammad Kurd 'Ali himself, were members of the Society for Arab Renaissance which had been founded at the end of 1906 by Muhibb al-Din al-Khatib (1886–1969).[5] These close ties were to see *al-Muqtabas* take on the role of advocate for Arab demands in the Ottoman Empire and, in particular, those concerning the preservation of Arabic language and culture within the empire. United with the Young Turks by their shared experience of past struggle against the despotic regime of 'Abd al-Hamid II, Muhammad Kurd 'Ali and his friends were engaged as actors as well as critical observers in the cut and thrust of public debate and political life.

The rapidly changing political situation in the Ottoman Empire and the resulting upheaval within regional and international power structures that came about in the first years of the new regime all forced the reformist Arab press within Syria (and especially the *al-Muqtabas* newspaper) to define its stance and its pro-reform commitments, as well as its relationship with the Ottoman administration and the colonial powers active in the region. Was *al-Muqtabas* able to assume its oppositional role and challenge the established order as fully as it had intended and, if so, on what basis? Was the paper able to preserve its independence under the weight of political pressure and, if so, to what extent? What was the role of the *al-Muqtabas* newspaper and its editors in the tripartite game being played in Syria amongst Arab reformists, the Young Turk regime and the principal external powers of France, Great Britain and Germany?

The primary sources when dealing with the above questions are of course the *al-Muqtabas* newspaper and review. Published between 1906 and 1917, the *al-Muqtabas* review is available to consult in any of the main libraries specialising in Middle Eastern studies. There are nine volumes of the review, with the ninth containing only two issues. An index of this review (organised by title, author and subject) that was published as a posthumous homage to Muhammad Kurd 'Ali in 1977 by the Arabic Academy of Damascus to mark the centenary of his birth makes the volumes easier to consult.[6] Published between 1908 and 1928, the *al-Muqtabas* newspaper is only available in selected libraries in microfilm.[7] The series of microfilms is, however, incomplete. In any case, study of the *al-Muqtabas* newspaper requires the use of other sources, including other newspapers from the period, diplomatic archives and personal accounts in the form of the contemporary witnesses' memoirs, all of which contain traces of the *al-Muqtabas* newspaper – be they reproductions or commentaries on its articles, or mere allusions to the newspaper or its editor.

After highlighting the success of *al-Muqtabas* and the explanations given by Muhammad Kurd 'Ali for it, this chapter will explore the question of the newspaper's commitments. The recurrent themes used by Muhammad Kurd 'Ali in the *al-Muqtabas* newspaper and review will be examined thematically and considered within the context of their formulation. This examination of the sequence of events connecting Muhammad Kurd 'Ali and his current of thought (as presented through his newspaper) on the one hand, as well as that of the Young Turks and the colonial powers on the other hand, will be clarified according to the political situation of the Arab provinces of the Ottoman Empire and, in particular, to what was perceived as a new 'Syrian question'.

Al-Muqtabas: Muhammad Kurd 'Ali's Successful Venture

According to dispatches sent by Paul Ottavi, France's consul in Damascus and a keen observer of local political life from 1909 to 1914, *al-Muqtabas* was 'by far the most famous newspaper in Damascus and the only one to hold powerful and far-reaching sway over the opinions of its Muslim population'.[8] As early as May 1909, his predecessor Collomb had noted *al-Muqtabas*'s 'large readership in Damascus' and in February 1914 Ottavi pointed out it was 'the most widely-read newspaper from Aleppo to Mecca and from Damascus to Baghdad, not only amongst reformists but even amongst [the] others'.[9] Such popularity, as confirmed by his contemporaries, was a testament to Muhammad Kurd 'Ali's professionalism and the fruit of a decade's experience in journalism.[10]

Al-Muqtabas as the Culmination of a Firm Grounding in Journalism

According to his memoirs, Muhammad Kurd 'Ali took his first steps in journalism at the age of sixteen, in around 1892.[11] It was then that he is thought to have started to occasionally subedit the Arabic-language section of the official daily paper called *Suriyya* (Syria), which appeared in 1865.[12] Around 1897, he worked translating dispatches published in French and Turkish into Arabic and quickly became the editor-in-chief of the semi-official Ottoman newspaper *al-Sham*. Founded in 1896, *al-Sham* was run by Mustafa Wasif, who also ran the Vilayet's printing house and was the fire chief in Damascus.[13] It was then that Kurd 'Ali learned to write under the constraints of censorship and showed the first signs of his resilient personality and spirit of independence when he refused to accept an award that the editor of his newspaper had asked the Hamidian authorities to bestow upon him.[14] In 1900, he left his post with *al-Sham* and published his first article, entitled 'Asl al-Wahhabiyya' (On the Origins of Wahhabism), in the prestigious review *al-Muqtataf*. This was largely thanks to his friend Shakib Arslan (1869–1946) who recommended him to one of the newspaper's editors (Ya'qub Sarruf or Faris Nimr).[15] Up until 1905, he was to write a total of seventeen articles for *al-Muqtataf*, one of which – a long article from 1901–2 called 'Umran Dimashq' (Architecture in Damascus)[16] – was serialised. Another of his articles from 1904 about the railroad in the Hijaz region, 'Sikkat al-Hijaz', earned him praise from Shaykh Muhammad 'Abduh.[17]

Between 1901 and 1902, Muhammad Kurd 'Ali made his first trip to Egypt where, at the same time as his articles were being published in *al-Muqtataf*, he was working at *al-Ra'id al-Misri* (The Egyptian Scout), which was founded in 1896 and run by Nicolas Shihada from Zahle in Lebanon. Kurd 'Ali was introduced to Shihada by his friend Rashid Rida (1865–1935) and contributed to *al-Manar*, which was founded in 1898 by Rida.[18] In a 1901 article entitled 'al-Ittikal wa-l-Istiqlal' (Submission and Independence), Kurd 'Ali launched into a severe criticism of what he saw as the decadence that prevailed in Arab countries and called on his compatriots to awaken from their state of dependency.[19]

During his second stay in Cairo (1905–8), Kurd 'Ali was preparing his review, *al-Muqtabas*, for publication whilst working at the same time for Egyptian newspapers. He worked for *al-Mu'ayyad*, founded in 1889 by Shaykh 'Ali Yusuf – who still ran the newspaper that vied for position with Mustafa Kamil's *al-Liwa'* – and contributed to *al-Zahir*, founded in 1895 and run by Muhammad Abu Shadi. Kurd 'Ali was able to meet Abu Shadi (thanks to his friend Sami Qasiri) who soon brought him in as editor-in-chief to replace Mahmud Wasif. He also translated two novels for a newspaper founded in 1904 and run by Khalil Sadiq called *Musamarat al-Sha'b*, finally becoming the head editor at *al-Mu'ayyad* in 1907. From that point onwards, he became involved in Egyptian political life and earnt some notoriety both in Egypt and in Syria. *Al-Muqtabas*, launched on 25 February 1906, gained recognition amongst literary circles following praise by 'Ali Yusuf in *al-Mu'ayyad*, by Jurji Zaydan in *al-Hilal* and from European orientalists like Alfred Le Chatelier who wrote that 'the excellent literary, scientific and sociological Arab review that Mr. Mohammed Kurd Ali publishes in Cairo . . . associates sciences of the West with purely Eastern studies and, by the wise choice of its articles, endeavours to satisfy all readers'.[20]

Although *al-Muqtabas* was written entirely in Arabic, its cover was bilingual (in French and Arabic) from its sixth edition onwards. Its subtitle attested to its eclectic nature: 'Pédagogie, sociologie, économie, politique, littérature, histoire, archéologie, philologie, ménagerie, hygiène, bibliographie, civilisation arabe et occidentale'. The publication's annual subscription fee was set at two and a half riyals in Damascus and at thirteen francs elsewhere.

The Newspaper's Founding and its Rapid Rise to Success

At the end of 1908 the Kurd 'Ali brothers set up their printing house (Matba'at al-Muqtabas) in the upstairs of the Khan al-Muradiyya in the Bab al-Barid area located at the end of the Suq al-Hamidiyya in Damascus's old town. The site soon took on a double role, functioning both as a professional space dedicated to the production of the newspaper and review and as a meeting place where the reformist intellectuals who contributed to *al-Muqtabas* could meet.[21] In March 1909 it relocated to the new city centre built around the Sérail square (the present Merjeh Square), facing the new Sérail (Dar al-Hukuma) and near the office of the postal services and telecommunications.[22]

Al-Muqtabas first appeared as a four-page daily newspaper, formatted in four columns and carrying the subtitle 'a political, economic and social daily newspaper'. The paper's subscription price was displayed on the right-hand side of its banner and this price was reduced for those who also had a subscription to the *al-Muqtabas* review. On the left-hand side, readers were informed that any letters, advertisements or ideas for articles should be written legibly and addressed to the editor, Muhammad Kurd 'Ali. The price of advertisements or announcements for the paper's back page was set at two qirsh (piastres). On a streamer underneath it stated Damascus as the place of publication, as well as the day's date according to the Muslim, Gregorian and Oriental calendars. From number 358 (1 May 1910), Ahmad Kurd 'Ali was credited as 'director of publications' alongside his brother, who kept his titles of 'owner' and 'editor-in-chief'. *Al-Muqtabas*'s relationship with the Ottoman administration meant that these roles were to be subject to change, with Muhammad Kurd 'Ali using his brother and then Shukri al-'Asali as cover during run-ins with the local authorities. *Al-Muqtabas* was generally comprised of an editorial followed by an article or two on national or international affairs, then a series of brief news items concerning 'internal matters', with advertisements and classifieds on the back page. Its circulation, estimated at around 1,500 copies, was relatively small. This figure was misleading, however, since it was a widespread practice of communal or collective reading that many would read the same copy of any publication, or one person would read the newspaper for those gathered around him, in private circles and in Damascus's many cafes. This effectively increased its readership tenfold.[23]

The success of the Kurd 'Ali brothers' enterprise was confirmed in the dispatches of foreign consuls in Damascus, who themselves relied on translated articles from *al-Muqtabas* when writing reports on the local political situation. Kurd 'Ali recalled this popularity in his memoirs:

> *Al-Muqtabas* acquired a notoriety that no other newspaper in Arabic enjoyed in the Ottoman Empire because it was written with a great freedom of tone, to such a point that it was often taken for an Egyptian newspaper of the time of Lord Cromer, under the administration of which Egypt knew a freedom somewhat similar to that of England. In Syria, the tyrannical leaders discouraged the petty functionaries that they mistreated to go and complain to *al-Muqtabas*, which means that the newspaper had become a forum, whose growing influence frightened the walis, who had to return reports to their superiors.[24]

Later on an amused Muhammad Kurd 'Ali recounted how the *wali* of Syria, Nazim Pasha – whose failing administration was the constant target of criticism for *al-Muqtabas* – had resorted to hiding from his constituents and taking elaborate detours to avoid them when moving around.

In his *Reisebriefe aus Syrien*, Martin Hartmann reports having met Muhammad Kurd 'Ali in March 1913 at the office of *al-Muqtabas*, affirming that the newspaper and the review outstripped other Arabic publications in influence by far and that, in his view, only the 'Christian' reviews *al-Muqtataf* and *al-Hilal* were capable of competing with it.[25]

Factors behind the Success of al-Muqtabas

Amongst the many factors explaining such exceptional success, aside from the personal qualities of Muhammad Kurd 'Ali (whose tenacity and keenness of wit were widely recognised by his contemporaries), were the liberal press climate, the paper's financial independence, the richness of its content and the liberal tone that pervaded *al-Muqtabas*, thanks to its editors and an editorial team at the forefront of Syria's Arabist movement.

In an article on the Ottoman press published in 1909, Muhammad Kurd 'Ali himself established the link between the quality of the press of any given society and that society's state of development, before making a comparison between the Arab and Turkish press in which the latter came out on top. Turning his attention to the Arab provinces, he noted the ground covered by Egypt in this respect, remarking that reviews published there often belonged to Syrians who were judged more tenacious than Egyptians in achieving their ends. He also praised the Syrian press (not forgetting his own *al-Muqtabas*) for its quality and style, concluding with a wish that the development of the press would continue in the Arab provinces of the Ottoman Empire.[26] Later developments were to see his dream become reality, since the period from 1908 to 1914 proved to be one of the most prosperous in the history of the Syrian press when more than a hundred new titles were published whose liberal tone was unprecedented. Noteworthy amongst these were *al-Mishkat*, *al-Muhajir* and *al-Qabas* in Damascus, *al-Mufid*, *al-Ittihad al-'Uthmani* and *Ababil* in Beirut and *Kashkul* in Aleppo.[27] This proliferation of new titles was made possible by the relative ease of obtaining permission to publish compared with the Hamidian era. Further, the new liberal legislation brought about a mass influx of Syrian men of letters who had been forced to seek exile in Egypt, where they not only benefited from greater freedom of expression but also from a more established press infrastructure, greater opportunities to raise capital and a larger readership. Such publications included *al-Ahram*, *al-Hilal*, *al-Manar* and *al-Muqtataf*.[28]

The editorial team of *al-Muqtabas* was quite exceptional, if we consider the number and standing of its contributors. One of the first dailies to be founded in the aftermath of the Revolution of July 1908, *al-Muqtabas* already benefited from the good reputation of its sister publication, the *al-Muqtabas* review (itself advertised on the back page of the newspaper), which accounts for the draw it had on Syrian men of letters. Furthermore, we must not discount the close ties between Muhammad Kurd 'Ali and the majority of those who wrote for his paper. Essentially, these bonds were forged through contact with the reformist Shaykh Tahir al-Jaza'iri (1851–1920) who had assembled study circles (*halaqat*) attended by many past and present pupils of Ottoman schools in Damascus, such as Maktab Anbar.[29] Of *al-Muqtabas*'s editors known to have frequented the first generation (*al-halaqa al-kabira*) were Shukri al-'Asali (1878–1916), 'Abd al-Wahhab al-Inglizi (1878–1916), 'Abd al-Rahman Shahbandar (1882–1940), Faris al-Khuri (1877–1962) and Rafiq al-'Azm (1867–1925), and from the second generation (*al-halaqa al-saghira*), Muhibb al-Din al-Khatib (1886–1969), Salah al-Din al-Qasimi (1887–1916) and Lutfi al-Haffar (1885–1968).[30] Later, other editors achieved recognition amongst Syrians exiled in Egypt or within the Society for Arab Renaissance (*Jam'iyyat al-nahda al-'arabiyya*), such as Haqqi al-'Azm (1864–1955), 'Adil Arslan (1887–1954) and Jamil Mardam Bik (1894–1960). Rushdi al-Sham'a (1865–1916), representative for Damascus with al-'Asali, was an occasional editor at *al-Muqtabas*, as were Khayr al-Din al-Zirikli (1893–1976) and Fakhri al-Barudi (1887–1966). Put simply, *al-Muqtabas*, at that time can be considered as the meeting place and as the common denominator uniting Damascus's men of letters (*adib*, pl. *udaba'* in Arabic) with liberal (*ahrar*) and reformist (*islahiyyun*) leanings with Kurd 'Ali as the link between them. Some of those who survived the repression of Djemal Pasha during the war were destined for distinguished political and literary careers.[31]

In addition, *al-Muqtabas* benefited from a valuable network of informants within the Ottoman administration. Muhammad Kurd 'Ali underlined the essential role these young Syrians (graduates of Constantinople's *mülkiyye*) who, before being named *qa'im maqam*s, found themselves on the Vilayet's governing bodies.[32] As Ottoman patriots committed to the defence of their language and culture, they were driven by the desire for reform and helped the Kurd 'Ali brothers obtain reliable information about cases of corruption that they would expose in their paper.[33]

In his memoirs Muhammad Kurd 'Ali stated that the key factor in the success of his newspaper was that it was entirely financially self-sufficient through subscriptions, over-the-counter sales and advertising revenues. The start-up capital came from loans secured against the mortgage of certain family lands. He also unequivocally stated that he received no subsidies whatsoever and the newspaper's freedom was a direct result of its financial independence.[34] Kurd 'Ali dwelt on this point because in times of trouble he was accused of accepting kickbacks from representatives of colonial powers.

The preceding explains how *al-Muqtabas* was able to deliver its readers quality, well-informed articles on a daily basis written in the most classical of styles and with content in keeping with the reformist ideals of its editors. The reputation for integrity that the newspaper and the Kurd 'Ali brothers had, the denunciation of corruption of the local Syrian administration and the defence of Arab interests throughout the Ottoman Empire were all key ingredients to its popularity. Kurd 'Ali would later sum up his paper's editorial line in five points: to champion reform, expose corrupt civil servants, encourage Arabs into meaningful work and successful enterprise, call for the sending of delegations for study abroad and to harness existing skills as well as educational outreach to the poorest in society.[35]

Committed to Reform: *Al-Muqtabas* as Observer and Participant in the Syrian Political Life

An examination of the content in the *al-Muqtabas* newspaper and review allows us to identify its recurrent themes which were to form the basis of the new media's identity within nascent Syrian public opinion. These embodied the reformist agenda of the Kurd 'Ali brothers as well as the common concept of a politically committed press.

The Constant Struggle against Corruption, Political Stagnation and Religious Conservatism

Muhammad Kurd 'Ali was very much influenced by the teachings of his mentors – Shaykhs Tahir al-Jaza'ir in Damascus and Muhammad 'Abduh in Cairo – both of whom were figureheads in the Islamic reformist current. Criticism of the religious decadence prevalent in Muslim countries thus constitutes one of the leitmotifs of Kurd 'Ali's work. In an article entitled 'The Ancient and the Modern', he threw his weight behind the reformists when he touched on the ignorance of the official ulama, which he saw as the result of their hereditary structure of power and the ossification of their traditional teaching. For Kurd 'Ali, this traditional teaching was an instrument to maintain control over the masses. That said, he believed that a kind of syncretism (*tawfiqiyya*) between the ancient and the modern was necessary. He took France as an example, stating his opinion that the country's decline was a result of its detachment from its Christian roots. Kurd 'Ali held that, contrary to the French approach, the survival of a nation depended on its ability to achieve a synthesis of tradition and modernity.[36]

The idea of an educational mission lay at the very heart of Kurd 'Ali's approach; he wanted to develop authentic public opinion in his country and, in doing so, develop an audience for his paper. He held that the press should play a wider role in society and not simply limit itself to its primary function as a source of information. There can be no doubt that there was a great call for such an approach at that time, since the majority of the population was still illiterate and reading remained an elitist practice. When publishing his newspaper in Damascus, Kurd 'Ali was no doubt aware he was addressing a readership that was very restricted. Publishing a newspaper in the Syria of 1908 was, then, an act of faith in the country's future, and concern for the education of the masses was one of the features of the reformist philosophy of Kurd 'Ali, who himself had grown up around the peasant population in the Ghuta (the oasis surrounding Damascus) and illustrated his attachment to it in his writings.[37]

The role of whistle blower taken on by Muhammad Kurd 'Ali in *al-Muqtabas* was to lead him into a great many difficulties. Indeed, he claims in his memoirs to have brought about the dismissal of tens of civil servants, including a *wali*, two *mutasarrifs* and several *qa'im maqam*s, district governors and judges. He recounted one particular anecdote of a court case in which all involved were apparently dismissed at the same time, following the paper's revelation of a corruption scandal.[38] Hermann can rightly claim that:

> Muhammad Kurd 'Ali introduced a new set of norms to the fields of political and literary journalism. Writing in Damascus, he was better able to shed light on the causes of the Ottoman Empire's decadence and on the reforms needed than he could from Cairo.[39]

Ottomanism, Pan-Islamism and Arabism: al-Muqtabas at the Political Crossroads

At the end of 1912, Muhammad Kurd 'Ali published a blistering attack in response to a declaration made in the senate by Premier Raymond Poincaré, in which the latter proclaimed the primacy of French interests in Syria:

> Intriguers benefited from the trouble that the war with the Balkan states causes Turkey in order to invent stories about Syria and to make believe that there exists a Syrian question which touches closely on a European power [France] and which this power would only allow the solution so as to guarantee the interests that it has there . . . If therefore it is said that there is a Syrian question that means: Syria for the Syrians and not for the French . . . Syria is first an Ottoman country then Arab that will not allow a grain of its ground to be trampled underfoot by a foreigner . . . There is no doubt that the majority of the Syrian people are attached to Ottomanism first, then to their nationality, and opposed to all change.[40]

These lines perfectly reflect the double commitment (Arab and Ottoman) of Syrian reformists at a time when the Ottoman Empire was at war on several fronts – in the Balkans and Tripolitania. Poincaré's declaration, which came following diplomatic exchanges with Great Britain that had clarified the latter's intentions in the region, once again posed the question of the future of Arab provinces. In this climate of confusion, Kurd 'Ali affirmed that the solidarity of Syrian reformists lay with the Ottoman government, then controlled by the Liberty and Entente Party. In accordance with this party's programme, he considered that the defence of Arab demands for decentralisation (and so for administrative autonomy of the Arab provinces) was a means to strengthen the Ottoman Empire and save it from collapse.

As the regime moved towards increased centralisation as well as an unofficial programme of Turkification in education, justice, administration and – after the elections of April 1912 – even in the parliament, Arabist demands increasingly came into conflict with the Young Turks' unionist current. Like other Arab reformist entities, *al-Muqtabas* found itself opposed to the members of the Committee of Union and Progress (CUP). Indeed, in his memoirs, Kurd 'Ali made clear his commitment to the preservation of the Arabic language in schools and the judiciary and, more generally, as the second official language of the Ottoman Empire, and he presented the persecution he suffered at the hands of unionist authorities as retribution for his championing of Arab rights.[41]

In addition to its Ottomanist and Arabist ties, among the identifying features of *al-Muqtabas* was a religious element which cannot be discounted. It should be noted that despite the city's minority Christian, Jewish and Shi'i communities, Damascus, at that time, was considered the regional capital for Sunni Muslims. Despite the regime's apparent secularism, Kurd 'Ali was unable to abandon Pan-Islamic discourse in *al-Muqtabas* for fear of dismaying part of his readership. So in the name of religious solidarity and brotherhood he took up the defence of the Algerians who were victims of colonial oppression at that time. In fact, during the years 1909–13 he criticised the decision of the French administration in both Algeria and Tunisia to ban indigenous Muslims from going on pilgrimage to Mecca on 'sanitary' grounds – a highly polemical decision in the Muslim world.[42] Kurd 'Ali was accused by French consuls in Damascus of attacking French policy in North Africa and sullying its image in the Middle East as a result. In his notes containing 'information about Muslim notabilities in Damascus', Collomb went so far as to describe him as 'a fanatic with xenophobic tendencies who is imbued with ideas of pan-Islamism'.[43] In fact, in his articles Kurd 'Ali sometimes displayed a tendency to group all Ottomans as Muslims:

> It is necessary to re-examine history without indulgence to deal with the relations between the Ottoman Empire and Europe. The Muslim conquerors should not have allowed the natives to keep their faith, as was the case

in Andalusia ... Europe does not hide [the fact] that it wants to drive out the Muslims or the Ottomans, assimilated to Asian people ... The consequence of the principle of interference is to drive out the Ottomans from the countries where the Muslims do not constitute the majority.[44]

Taking the plight of Muslims in Macedonia at the hands of (Christian) Greek, Serbian and Bulgarian militias during the Balkan wars as an example, he denounced the so-called civilised states for supporting these militias in their crimes. Such discourse, however, though described as 'Pan-Islamic' by Western chancelleries, can also be considered as a response to the imperialist politics of European powers as well as an expression of solidarity with Muslim peoples. It is interesting to highlight such manifestations of politico-religious belonging in the writing of an author generally considered 'secular'.[45]

Al-Muqtabas's *Anti-imperialism and Openness to the West*

In both his daily newspaper and review, the relationship between Eastern and Western civilisations was one of Muhammad Kurd 'Ali's favourite themes. His motivations in exploiting this theme were twofold: at once pleading for openness to the West and the adoption of the expertise and mindset that had been its making, while not missing the opportunity to denounce the imperialist designs of European powers (particularly in Syria and the rest of the Ottoman Empire).

The influence that orientalist scholars had on Muhammad Kurd 'Ali can be seen clearly in his articles and critical reviews of the works on the subject of Arab civilisation published in the West.[46] Indeed, Kurd 'Ali would often refer to the studies of French Orientalists (whose language he understood and whose works he could read in the original) to develop his own reflections on questions relating to civilisation. Some of these scholars include Gustave Le Bon (author of *La civilisation des Arabes*), Charles Seignobos (whose *Histoire de la civilisation* was translated by Kurd 'Ali in 1908) and Edmond Demolins (author of *A quoi tient la supériorité des Anglo-Saxons*, translated into Arabic by Ahmad Fathi Zaghlul). Muhammad Kurd 'Ali, in fact, did not hide his admiration for Western achievements in many different fields of knowledge. This can be seen in the series of articles he wrote during his travels in Europe (in 1909–10 and 1913–14), published as *Ghara'ib al-gharb* (The Wonders of the West), in which he enumerated the great achievements of universities, scientific academies and orientalist institutions in Europe.[47] Beyond his description of the scientific basis of European power, Muhammad Kurd 'Ali touched on the West's superiority over the East, before moving on to stress the necessity for the East to borrow from the knowledge of the West and to recognise the benefits of the cultural policy of the colonial powers in Syria.

In a seemingly contradictory way, some of Kurd 'Ali's articles in *al-Muqtabas* violently criticise the Western imperialist designs and point out referenced orientalist scholars as agents of the colonial powers. In a May 1909 dispatch addressed to the French ambassador in Istanbul, the French consul in Damascus, Collomb, flagged *al-Muqtabas*'s reporting of a speech by Fakhreddine Bey – then political director of the CUP in the Vilayet of Damascus – in which Fakhreddine was very critical of French policy towards Muslims in North Africa.[48] In another article, Kurd 'Ali took a strong denunciatory tone, condemning imperialism and the plundering of the wealth of countries in the Orient. Oriental nations in turn – with the notable exception of Japan – were judged as being inert and like 'slaves before their masters'. Kurd 'Ali also denounced the Western policy of dividing the Ottoman Empire, which broke with the traditional policy of maintaining its integrity.[49]

The themes taken up by Muhammad Kurd 'Ali in *al-Muqtabas* newspaper and review – and that we may associate with his political commitments – may seem to be filled with contradictory statements. This is particularly true when we consider the plurality of Kurd 'Ali's political affiliations (Ottomanist, Arabist and Pan-Islamic) as well as his constant alternation between praise and criticism for the policies of the great powers in the Ottoman Empire. Though we may be able to assimilate the concomitance (or superposition) of complex identities in the individual, translating them into coherent political discourse proves problematic at a time when individuals were compelled to choose sides.

From Independence to Instrumentalisation: *Al-Muqtabas* and the Powers

If we now consider the political opinions contained in *al-Muqtabas* in their context, we notice that to a certain extent they mirror the power plays amongst political figures in the Syrian provinces of the Ottoman Empire, and in Damascus more specifically. These figures can be divided into three distinct groups: Syrian notables divided on reformist and conservative lines,[50] the Young Turk authorities who were essentially unionist (apart from the six-month period when supporters of the Entente Party assumed control), and finally the French, German and British colonial powers represented locally by their consuls who vied for control of the region. Once over their initial astonishment at the phenomenon that was the emergence of a free press in Damascus, Ottoman and colonial powers not only realised how much of a threat it could pose to their interests but also how much there was to be gained from a media allied to their 'cause'. This assessment sparked a series of diplomatic pressures and games in which the stakes were *al-Muqtabas* and Muhammad Kurd 'Ali. The newspaper's continued loyalty to its principles of independence was to be increasingly tested until the outbreak of World War I, which was to change the face of the Arab press.

Al-Muqtabas *and the CUP: From Alliance to Separation (1908–9)*

In little over a year, relations between *al-Muqtabas*, its editor and its reformist allies on the one hand, and the Young Turk authorities of the CUP on the other, gradually soured.[51] While in May 1909 the French consul in Damascus (Collomb) still described *al-Muqtabas* as an 'organe jeune turc, très lu à Damas [an organ of the Young Turks, much read in Damascus]', then in July 1909 as a 'liberal' Ottoman publication whose avid readers included the *wali* himself,[52] in fact Muhammad Kurd 'Ali and the *wali* Nazim Pasha were soon at war when, on 16 September 1909, *al-Muqtabas* was suspended for the first time. Apparently, this was for having published a speech by Shaykh al-Islam in which he denied the sultan's caliphal legitimacy (claiming that only the first four of the Prophet Muhammad's successors could claim such). In this speech, unionists saw confirmation of their suspicions that Arab reformists would support the establishment of an Arab caliphate. Threatened with imprisonment, Kurd 'Ali was forced to flee to Lebanon and then to Europe. Awaiting the return of his brother, Ahmad Kurd 'Ali took over from 4 December 1909, registering the newspaper under a new name, *Al-Umma* (The Nation), which was published until 5 March 1910.

In actual fact, the authorities' decision appears to have been chiefly motivated by *al-Muqtabas*'s repeated attacks against the local administration's incompetence and corruption and those that Kurd 'Ali called 'emirs and pashas', great landowners specialising in the spoliation of peasant lands. Moreover, the political context had changed: the revolutionary euphoria and brotherly atmosphere between Young Turk and Arab reformists had been replaced by a fear of new conservative uprisings, following the near success of the Muhammadist movement in staging a counter-coup in Istanbul in the name of 'Abd al-Hamid II in April 1909. In Damascus Arab reformists remained a minority group when faced with this movement (headed notably by Salah al-Din al-Tunisi), as evidenced by the violent protests against Rashid Rida following his sermon at the Umayyad Mosque on 23 October 1908.[33] It is probable that the Young Turk authorities judged it wiser to win over this movement and 'drop' their old allies by suspending *al-Muqtabas* and banning the activities of the Arab Renaissance Society, whose Damascus branch had been set up as early as 1907 at the instigation of Muhibb al-Din al-Khatib, aided by Salah al-Din al-Qasimi and Lutfi al-Haffar.[54]

The ties linking the newspaper and the Arab Renaissance Society are manifest. Indeed, the Kurd 'Ali brothers had been close to Muhibb al-Din al-Khatib ever since they were regulars at the gatherings of Tahir al-Jaza'iri's intellectual circle and they became Society members when they returned to Damascus, as attested by a photo taken in 1908. From the start, they regularly made space for its members in the pages of *al-Muqtabas*. Such exchanges could only be strengthened by the proximity of the *al-Muqtabas* printing house (located in Khan al-Muradiyya) to one of the Society's meeting places (in Khan al-Jumruk) where Muhammad Kurd 'Ali gave a few lectures. The headquarters of *al-Muqtabas* was moved to the new city centre from March 1909, however, at exactly the same time that the Arab Renaissance Society came under the scrutiny of the Young Turk authorities. The Society failed to obtain accreditation from the Young Turk authorities, who insisted that it change its name. Its founder (Muhibb al-Din al-Khatib) was forced to flee Damascus following the publication of a satirical paper called *Tar al-khurj* which caused a great sensation, in particular because it exposed a sex case concerning the *wali* Nazim Pasha. Since al-Khatib had used the *al-Muqtabas* printing house to produce this paper (apparently without the Kurd 'Ali brothers knowing), the newspaper and those in charge of it logically came under suspicion too.[55]

Changing Alliances, Pressure and Repression (1909–14)

On his return from Europe in early 1910, following the calming of suspicions surrounding the Arab Renaissance Society and the transfer of the *wali* Nazim Pasha to Beirut, Muhammad Kurd 'Ali made a stop in Constantinople, where he gave a patriotic lecture to an audience largely made up of students at the Arab Club (subsequently reprinted in *al-Muqtabas*).[56] On 7 March 1910 he again was able to publish his newspaper under the name of *al-Muqtabas*, and the following two years seem to have passed without major incident, although Kurd 'Ali noted the constant harassment by the authorities in his memoirs.[57]

Unhappy with the regime's tendency towards Turkification, Arab reformists in Damascus moved closer to the Liberty and Entente Party, which had been founded in November 1911 and brought together the CUP's opponents in defence of the principle of administrative decentralisation against the latter's centralist agenda. When, during the general election, *al-Muqtabas* threw its weight behind Liberty and Entente candidates – which included two of its editors (Rushdi al-Sham'a and Shukri al-'Asali) – it was again suspended on 17 April 1912 and its owner forced to flee a second time – this time to Egypt – to evade the police. Ahmad Kurd 'Ali is believed to have been placed under house arrest for two weeks before being sent to Istanbul, where he was held for a further fifty days. The motive behind this suspension remains unclear. According to the French consul in Damascus, it came as a result of *al-Muqtabas*'s reprinting of a satirical poem from a Baghdadi newspaper, whilst other sources attribute it to an article entitled 'Tatrik' (Turkification).[58] Muhammad Kurd 'Ali asserts the cause was a poem about the sultan written by the Damascene Shaykh Ibrahim al-Uskubi who was sent to prison with his brother Ahmad later on.[59] Following the results of the rigged elections, the majority of Arab representatives (as well the other opponents of the CUP) were ousted from the Ottoman parliament, which became even more 'Turkified' as a result.[60]

According to the French consul in Damascus, Muhammad Kurd 'Ali took advantage of his stay in Egypt to contact 'Anglo-Egyptian agents' and draw up plans to unify Syria and Egypt under British control. These suspicions, though unproven, were indicative of the interest French diplomatic agents started to take in the activities of Syrian reformists who were liable to play a key role in the aftermath of any collapse of the Ottoman Empire. The Arab press, in particular, was judged capable of strongly influencing public opinion in the event of a resurgence of the Syrian question.[61]

Kurd 'Ali returned to Damascus after the Entente Party took power on 10 July 1912 and received what he termed a hero's welcome from the people.[62] His printing house had been sold in his absence, so he had his review and his newspaper printed by the publishing firm Dar al-Taraqqi, located in the Qaymariyya district of Damascus's old town. Now aligned with the new regime, his publications quickly resumed with boxed articles accounting for the newspaper's silence and for the review's delayed delivery to subscribers. They also singled out the *wali* Nazim Pasha, in no uncertain terms, as the 'cause of [their] misfortunes'.[63]

Muhammad Kurd 'Ali, along with his friends Shukri al-'Asali, 'Abd al-Wahhab al-Inglizi, Rushdi and Ahmad Pasha al-Sham'a, soon came to be regarded by the French consul as the leaders of the Entente Party in Damascus[64] and when Kurd 'Ali gave a patriotic lecture (reprinted in *al-Muqtabas* review), it was at the party's headquarters. Once again he took up his anti-imperialist ideology and used the occasion to criticise the interference of the colonial powers in Ottoman internal affairs and even France's religious and cultural policy in the Orient, citing the expansion of French schools and the protection of Christians as 'a prelude to colonisation'.[65]

After the coup of 23 January 1913 and the establishment of a quasi-dictatorship of the triumvirate of Enver, Djemal and Talaat, Syrian reformists (now avowed opponents of the CUP and without firm allies in the Ottoman Empire) sought fresh support from European colonial powers. Whilst Shukri al-'Asali requested the protection of France's consul in Damascus, Paul Ottavi, as early as 25 January, a more prudent Muhammad Kurd 'Ali waited until 27 March before approaching him. According to the consul, Kurd 'Ali's visit marked his 'return to neutrality' towards French policy in Syria. Thereafter, the two men communicated much more frequently and Ottavi was to prove tenacious in requesting funds from the Ministry of Foreign Affairs to organise a 'campaign to defend French interests' in the Syrian press.

By doing so, Ottavi hoped to get *al-Muqtabas* on side by subsidising it, as had been the case for a number of Egyptian newspapers. In June 1913 the sum of 1,500 francs was allocated to Ottavi to this end. We cannot be sure, however, whether the money was received.[66] In his subsequent request for funding for *al-Muqtabas* that he made the following year, Ottavi was to argue that:

> Mohamed Effendi Kurd Ali seems to me to have the qualities that are necessary to lend us the help that we need in an intelligent way . . . Moreover, he has been accused of selling out to us since he stopped attacking us, before even he had started from time to time to address some kind allusions towards us, and that it continues to be done all the while knowing that there is nothing in it, one would not immediately suspect the special relations which would be suddenly established between him and the Consulate . . . It would be difficult to offer less than 300 francs per month to Mohamed Efendi Kurd Ali for the services that we would ask from him after those which he has already rendered to us spontaneously in recent times.[67]

In response to the consul's moral, if not financial, support for Syrian reformists and that provided by the French government to Arab reformists more generally on the occasion of the Arab Syrian Congress (held in Paris in June 1913), the articles in *al-Muqtabas* portrayed France's actions in Syria more favourably. In his memoirs, however, Kurd 'Ali categorically denied having accepted any financial support from the French government, and even claimed he had fended off attempts by an unnamed figure from the Ministry of Foreign Affairs to make *al-Muqtabas* a puppet publication designed to further French interests.[68]

This connection became more pronounced as the net around Syrian reformists tightened. In September 1913 Ahmad Kurd 'Ali was assaulted by a group of CUP members for having republished an article in *al-Muqtabas* on 14 September written by the head of the Arab reformists in Basra, Sayyid Talib al-Naqib, which had first appeared in *al-Dustur* newspaper. In the article, al-Naqib responded to accusations of his working for Basra's independence from the Sublime Porte.[69] On 25 September 1913 *al-Muqtabas* was suspended for a third time, with Ahmad Kurd 'Ali being sentenced to a month in prison and fined five pounds.[70] Though the sentence was never applied, the newspaper itself had nonetheless to be replaced by *al-Qabas* from late September onwards. The paper was now officially owned and directed by Shukri al-'Asali but it was Muhammad Kurd 'Ali who remained at its helm. Nothing of its form or spirit had changed and it could once again resume publication as *al-Muqtabas* on 31 January 1914. Meanwhile, Kurd 'Ali went to stay a second time in Europe (first in Italy, then in Switzerland and finally back in France). It was then that he wrote a new series of articles in the style of a reportage, one of which (sent from Paris), extolled France's linguistic policy in the Orient and urged those living in the region to recognise its virtues.[71]

This mutual support, which successfully served the convergent interests of the French government and the Syrian reformists for a time, allowed the latter to push through some of their decentralist reforms. It also allowed some of the movement's leaders to rise to high office, such as 'Abd al-Hamid al-Zuhrawi, who became a senator, as well as Shukri al-'Asali and 'Abd al-Wahab al-Inglizi, who became government inspectors (*qa'im maqam*). In February 1914 Kurd 'Ali met up with some of his reformist friends in Constantinople to lend his support to their pleas for reform (and perhaps to seek a position in turn, as alleged by the French consul).[72] The issue of nominations and of the naming of foreign counsellors wanted by the Lebanese to ensure reform was implemented divided the movement, however, and saw it peter out in the months that followed.

The unionist government capitalised on the situation and suspended *al-Muqtabas* for a fourth time on 16 April 1914. This suspension, which came about as a result of its publication of information relating to a group of feminists in Constantinople opposed to wearing the veil, was to be long-lasting. Paul Ottavi sent word of this suspension to his superiors, and the French Minister for Foreign Affairs at the time, Gaston Doumergue, offered to intervene in Muhammad Kurd 'Ali's favour and plead his case to the Ottoman authorities. It would appear, however, that a then embittered Kurd 'Ali was so disheartened as to seriously consider turning his back on journalism altogether.[73]

In his memoirs, Muhammad Kurd 'Ali wrote that he had to face a great many dangers during these tense years – a statement confirmed in diplomatic dispatches – and that he successfully negotiated them with a mixture of cunning and tenacity. He also claimed to have been graced with good luck, since he never saw the inside of a prison cell and was never fined a single piastre. In addition, a Palestinian judge appointed as presiding judge for Damascus had Kurd 'Ali's many trials combined into one and found him innocent of the defamation charges brought against him. During an attempt at reconciliation with the *wali* Nazim Pasha, Kurd 'Ali had a chance to set out his line of conduct:

> We are writing to submit our point of view, and to indicate to you the misdeeds which occur in your administration. Our objective is noble so I believe; it is the reform of the administration which the new officials have not changed anything in spirit. We do not deviate from the freedom which the Constitution grants to us.[74]

He further clarified that he always made a point of avoiding personal attacks. Of the number of factors that allowed Muhammad Kurd 'Ali to escape his enemies' clutches, we should also mention the backing he had within the Ottoman administration, and particularly that of Shakib Arslan, which proved of inestimable value in the opening stages of World War I.

Al-Muqtabas as a Mouthpiece for German and Ottoman War Propaganda (1915–17)

By July 1914, increasing pressure was mounting on Arab reformists with no foreign consulate to turn to for help except for that of Germany (which oversaw war propaganda in the region's Arab press). It would appear, then, that Muhammad Kurd 'Ali had no other option but to rally to the regime. With the Ottoman Empire on the point of joining the war alongside Germany and Austria-Hungary, he was summoned by the *wali* Khulusi Bik for interrogation about his past relationship with the French consul. He was cleared of the suspicions of treason hanging over him after the French consulates' archives in Damascus and Beirut were searched. For the whole of World War I, he nonetheless remained subject to the whims of both the *wali* and then of the commander in chief, Ahmad Djemal Pasha. Because of this, he was obliged to remain at the authorities' disposal during that period.[75]

While their German allies were setting up a press agency in Istanbul called *die Nachrichtenstelle für den Orient*, designed to cover the entire Ottoman Empire with the help of relay stations, the Young Turks – apparently at the suggestion of the German consul, Loytved Hardegg[76] – were contemplating using *al-Muqtabas* as a propaganda tool. Kurd 'Ali later wrote that he could not have stopped this move since he would have been accused of rebelling against the regime, had he tried. He then asked for the sum of 2,000 pounds in order to pay debts resulting from the closure of his newspaper and the loss his printing house made when sold.[77] As a recognised Ottoman patriot, he received 1,000 pounds during a meeting with Djemal Pasha, who urged him to relaunch his publication as soon as possible.[78]

Al-Muqtabas made its reappearance on 2 January 1915, losing, at a stroke, both the critical independence that had once been its founding principle and a good deal of its credibility. In his first editorial, Kurd 'Ali was able to allude to the paper's republication as being 'forced' by political circumstances.[79] The logic of his cooperation with Djemal Pasha coupled with his fear of sharing the fate of a number of his reformist friends (such as Shukri al-'Asali, 'Abd al-Wahhab al-Inglizi and Rushdi al-Sham'a, who were found guilty at the Aley trials and executed in May 1916), led him to go one step further and contribute alongside Shakib Arslan to *al-Sharq*, another propagandist newspaper founded in Damascus in May 1916, initially run by Taj al-Din al-Hasani.[80] Having asked him to head up this paper, Djemal Pasha requested that Kurd 'Ali leave the running of *al-Muqtabas* to his brother Ahmad. In 1916 alone, Muhammad Kurd 'Ali published two travel books in praise of the regime and its leaders, Enver and Djemal.[81] When, in the autumn of 1916, he obtained permission to resume publication of his review, he opened with the following:

> This review appears again after an interruption which deprived its readers of it over two whole years, because of the world war by which the relations between nations also stopped, the language of the press and the pen having left the place to that of the gun and the sabre . . . But when we had to accept the situation which affects other reviews of the West and the East, God delivered a man to us who is unique among the greats of this world by his spirit of initiative in the cultural and scientific fields, we wish to speak about the champion of the Ottomans, the Minister for the Navy Ahmad Jemal Pasha, commander of the IVth army. Indeed, it is he – may God preserve success for him – who wanted us to resume our publication and who helped us to overcome the difficulties.[82]

Conclusion

Press freedom, though guaranteed by the Ottoman constitution re-established in 1908, was far from a foregone conclusion in Syria. Preserving it proved a most difficult exercise for the editor of *al-Muqtabas*, who had to muster all of his great skill to uphold the reputation for integrity of his newspaper and review. According to Kurd 'Ali's memoirs, it was almost a miracle that the newspaper should have survived at all. In actual fact, however, we have seen that *al-Muqtabas* held some major trump cards, in particular an editorial team bound by longstanding friendships forged in the days of Hamidian despotism. Both Ottoman patriots and Arab reformists, some of them maintained ties with the Ottoman administration. When relations with the unionist authorities were at their most tense, *al-Muqtabas* and its editors chose to ally themselves with the Entente Party. This move cost them dearly when it was ousted from government in January 1913.

Having then sought support from European powers (principally France, which had sponsored the first Arab Congress in Paris in June 1913), they achieved some success in their demands for decentralisation of the administration and the preservation of the Arabic language; however, the division within the movement as well as the commitment of the Young Turks to the German side during World War I were to prove fatal to the independence of *al-Muqtabas* as well as the wider current of Arabism emerging in Syria. The political context of the era has allowed us to shed light upon the apparent contradictions in the opinions held in an *al-Muqtabas* torn between Ottomanism, Arabism and Pan-Islamism on the one hand, and openness to the West and the denunciation of imperialism on the other. What we can say with little fear of contradiction, however, is that both the review and especially the daily newspaper contributed towards a permanent shift in the Syrian media landscape by forming the beginnings of a genuine readership and cultivation of public opinion, as well as setting the standard for a quality, politically engaged press.

Al-Muqtabas was granted a new lease of life at the end of World War I, thanks to Muhammad Kurd 'Ali's return to grace. Allowed by Prince Faysal to return to Damascus, he resumed publication of the newspaper, which would survive a further ten years. It appeared intermittently during the

French Mandate and again faced censorship when it positioned itself close to the People's Party during the Great Syrian Revolt of 1925–7. It was then that *al-Muqtabas* rediscovered its culture of political engagement, a culture now shared by numerous other newspapers and reviews. Ahmad Kurd 'Ali ran *al-Muqtabas* until his death in 1927 and was succeeded by Najib al-Rayyis until 1928, the year that Muhammad Kurd 'Ali – then the Minister for Education in Shaykh Taj al-Din's government (1928–31) – decided to close it finally. He explained his reasons: unbeknownst to Kurd 'Ali, al-Rayyis had grown too close to 'the parties' (in this case the National Bloc) and had caused outrage by his excessive criticisms of Kurd 'Ali's ministerial colleagues.[83] Following the dismissal of al-Rayyis, Muhammad Kurd 'Ali apparently offered the post to one of the newspaper's editorialists, Nassuh Babil, who appears to have turned it down out of respect for his friend and colleague, al-Rayyis.[84] Najib al-Rayyis then joined forces with 'Adil Kurd 'Ali, a younger brother of Muhammad Kurd 'Ali, to found a new newspaper that took the old name of *al-Qabas*.[85] This new publication would, in its own way, fulfil the same critical role in its relationship with the French mandatory authorities as *al-Muqtabas* had with the Young Turk authorities from 1909 to 1914.

Notes

1. In Arabic *muqtabas* (passive participle of *iqtabas*) means 'to make a literary loan, to imitate, to quote'. *Al-Muqtabas* can therefore be translated as 'The Borrowing', which corresponds better with the spirit of the journal and the Nahda movement in which it participated, meaning to borrow from both Classical Arab heritage and Western modernity. I would like to dedicate this chapter to all honest Arabic journalists who have died while accomplishing their duty of informing the public and to those who are threatened in their careers or in their lives by political repression, states of war and foreign occupation. My thoughts are particularly directed to the Palestinian journalists who died during the Israeli assault on Gaza in 2014 and to the Syrian journalists, victims like their fellow countrymen in a planned destruction of their country since 2011. I would also like to thank Professor Nadine Picaudou as well as Didier Monciaud and Anthony Gorman for their remarks on the earlier drafts of this text. I alone remain responsible for the contents and any errors. [This chapter has been translated from a French original. *Eds*]
2. Among the works dedicated to Muhammad Kurd 'Ali, see Al-Alusi, *Muhammad Kurd 'Ali*; *Muhammad Kurd 'Ali: Mu'assis al-majma' al-'ilmi al-'arabi*; Dahhan,

'Mohammed Kurd Ali (1876–1953)', pp. 379–94; Hermann, *Kulturkrise*. On the review *al-Muqtabas*, see Seikaly, 'Damascene Intellectual Life' and Shukri Faysal, 'Muhammad Kurd 'Ali min khilal al-Muqtabas', in *Muhammad Kurd 'Ali: mu'assis al-majma' al-'ilmi al-'arabi*, p. 115–41.

3. The term 'Syria' is used here in the sense of the time, namely Bilad al-Sham, which comprised the Vilayets of Syria (centred on Damascus), Aleppo and Beirut (including the semi-autonomous sanjak of Mount Lebanon) as well as the sanjak of Jerusalem.
4. de Tarrazi, *Tarikh al-Sihafa*, pp. 43, 129.
5. Tauber, *Emergence of the Arab Movements*, pp. 43–50; Tauber, 'The Press and the Journalist'. The principal source in Arabic is al-Khatib, *Hayatuhu bi-qalamihi*.
6. Murad, *Faharis*.
7. Among these are the Hafiz al-Asad National Library in Damascus, University of Amman Library, Jaffet Library of American University in Beirut and the Library of the University of Chicago.
8. MAE – NS Turquie 120, pp. 147–9 (dispatch, 7 April 1913).
9. CADN, Damas (consulat), A 18/25, no. 7 (dispatch, 10 May 1909); MAE – NS Turquie 124, pp. 34–40 (dispatch, 19 February 1914).
10. See, in particular, Fakhri al-Barudi in his memoirs, *Mudhakkirat al-Barudi*, pp. 79–80.
11. Kurd 'Ali, 'al-Ishtighal bi-l-sihafa', in *al-Mudhakkirat*, vol. 1, pp. 50–5.
12. Hermann, *Kulturkrise*, p. 95.
13. Al-Malluhi, *Mu'jam*, p. 14; Khoury, Ibish and Yasushi, *Mudawwina*, p. 96.
14. Kurd 'Ali, 'al-Ishtighal bi-l-sihafa', in *al-Mudhakkirat*, vol. 1, pp. 50–5.
15. Kenny, 'East versus West in *al-Muqtataf*'.
16. Kurd 'Ali, 'Uran Dimashq', in *al-Muqtataf*, vol. 26 (1901), pp. 338–47, 497–505, 691–8, 793–9, 881–7, 977–83, 1069–80; vol. 27 (1902), pp. 9–16, 235–46.
17. Kurd 'Ali, 'al-Ishtighal bi-l-sihafa', in *al-Mudhakkirat*, vol. 1, pp. 50–5. See also Kurd 'Ali, *al-Mu'asirun*, pp. 359–60.
18. Ezzerelli, 'Muhammad 'Abduh', pp. 85–93.
19. Kurd 'Ali, 'al-Ittikal wa-l-Istiqlal', in *al-Qadim wa-l-hadith*, pp. 231–42.
20. *Revue du Monde Musulman* 3 (January 1907), pp. 440–1. In addition, Le Chatelier would cover the first issues of *al-Muqtabas* and publish a photo of Muhammad Kurd 'Ali, whom he described as 'un des hommes les plus en vue du journalisme arabe en général, de celui du Caire en particulier' (*Revue du Monde Musulman* 7 (May 1907), p. 417), an assessment repeated by Hartmann, *Der Islamische Orient*, p. 588.

21. Hartmann, *Reisebriefe*, pp. 14–15; al-Barudi, *Mudhakkirat al-Barudi*, p. 79.
22. al-Shihabi, *Sahat al-Marja*; Weber, 'L'aménagement urbain'.
23. Deguilhem, 'Les cafés à Damas'.
24. Kurd 'Ali, 'Nazim Basha wa *al-Muqtabas*', in *al-Mudhakkirat*, vol. 1, pp. 64–8.
25. Hartmann, *Reisebriefe*, p. 13.
26. 'al-Sihafa al-'uthmaniyya', *al-Muqtabas* 4 (1909), pp. 410–13.
27. Al-Malluhi, *Mu'jam*, pp. 15–44; Buheiry, *Intellectual Life*; Khalidi, 'The Press as a Source'.
28. Elias, *La presse arabe*, pp. 33–43, 49–57.
29. Escovitz, 'He was the Muhammad 'Abduh of Syria'.
30. Commins, 'Religious Reformers'.
31. Dakhli, *Une génération d'intellectuels arabes*.
32. The *mülkiyye* was the high school for civil servants (as opposed to the *harbiyye*, which prepared students for military careers).
33. Kurd 'Ali, 'Nazim Basha wa *al-Muqtabas*', in *al-Mudhakkirat*, vol. 1, pp. 64–8.
34. Kurd 'Ali, 'al-Sihafa aydan', in *al-Mudhakkirat*, vol. 1, pp. 56–63.
35. Ibid.
36. 'al-Qadim wa al-hadith', *al-Muqtabas* 4:1 (1909), pp. 30–4. We should recall that the law of separation between church and state, adopted a few years before the publication of this article (on 9 December 1905), remained controversial in France at this time. This text testifies also to the echoes of this debate in the Middle East.
37. Muhammad Kurd 'Ali, 'Dhikrayat al-tufula' in *Al-Mudhakkirat*, vol. 1, pp. 10–20.
38. Kurd 'Ali, 'al-Sihafa aydan', in *al-Mudhakkirat*, vol. 1, pp. 56–63.
39. Hermann, *Kulturkrise*, p. 120.
40. Translation of article in *al-Muqtabas*, 'La Syrie au gouvernement ottoman', attached to dispatch of Consul Paul Ottavi, 24 December 1912, Archives MAE – NS Turquie 118, pp. 129–32.
41. Kurd 'Ali, 'Shabakun Najawtu minhu wa Najawtu bihi', in *al-Mudhakkirat*, vol. 1, pp. 99–102.
42. Ezzerelli, 'Le pèlerinage à La Mecque'.
43. MAE – NS Turquie 112, pp. 120–3 (25 June 1909).
44. 'Nahnu wa-Urubba', *al-Muqtabas* 7 (1913), pp. 728–47.
45. Sharabi, *Arab Intellectuals and the West*, p. 88; Yared, *Secularism and the Arab World*.
46. Among these articles are 'Nahnu wa Urubba', *al-Muqtabas* 7 (1913), pp. 728–47;

'Nahnu wa al-Urubbiyyun', *al-Muqtabas* no. 1269 (14 August 1913); 'Masalih Faransa fi Suriya', *al-Qabas* no. 1303-3 (2 October 1913); 'Nahnu wa Faransa', *al-Muqtabas* no. 1417 (19 February 1914); 'Taqarub al-shu'ub', *al-Muqtabas* no. 1454 (4 April 1914).

47. Kurd 'Ali, *Ghara'ib al-gharb*.
48. CADN, Damas (consulat), A 18/25, report of Collomb, 'Au sujet d'un discours contenant des excitations contre la France', 10 May 1909.
49. 'al-Tarbiya al-urubiyya', *al-Muqtabas* 5:2 (1910), pp. 121–41, which is the transcription of the text of a conference held at the Literary Club of Arab Students of Constantinople. See also 'Junun al-isti'mar', *al-Muqtabas* 7:1 (1912), pp. 60–5.
50. On the notables of Damascus and the development of their political allegiances, see Khoury, *Urban Notables and Arab Nationalism*; Commins, *Islamic Reform*.
51. For a detailed study of the relations between Arab reformists and Young Turks at this time, see Kayali, *Arabs and Young Turks*.
52. CADN, Damas (consulat), A 18/25, Reports of Collomb, no. 7 (10 May 1909) and no. 22 (27 July 1909).
53. Hermann, *Kulturkrise*, pp. 105–6.
54. Tauber, *The Emergence of the Arab Movements*, pp. 47–8.
55. al-Khatib, *Hayatuhu bi-qalamihi*, pp. 46–51; al-Kuzbari, *Lutfi al-Haffar*, pp. 21–38. A photograph of the Society for Arab Renaissance is reproduced in the latter work, pp. 64–5.
56. Kurd 'Ali, 'al-Tarbiya al-urubiyya'.
57. Kurd 'Ali, *Al-Mudhakkirat*, vol. 1, pp. 61–8.
58. MAE – NS Turquie 124, Ottavi to Doumergue (27 April 1914); Tauber, 'The Press and the Journalist', p. 173.
59. Kurd 'Ali, *Khitat al-Sham*, p. 339.
60. On these elections and the role played by the Arab reformist press, see Khalidi, 'The 1912 Election Campaign'; Kayali, *Arabs and Young Turks*, pp. 116–23.
61. For a fuller discussion, see Ezzerelli, *Diplomatie occidentale et dissidence arabe*; Ezzerelli, 'Les arabistes syriens'.
62. Kurd 'Ali, *Khitat al-Sham*, p. 339.
63. 'Sudur al-Muqtabas', *al-Muqtabas* 959 (8 August 1912); *al-Muqtabas* 7 (1912–13), p. 959.
64. MAE – NS Turquie 117, pp. 125–9 (dispatch, 23 November 1912).
65. 'Nahnu wa-Urubba', *al-Muqtabas* 7 (1913), pp. 728–47.
66. MAE – NS Turquie 122, note 3 June 1913.

67. MAE – NS Turquie 124, pp. 62–7, Dispatch, Ottavi to Doumergue, 'Mesures à prendre contre les attaques de la presse arabe', 20 March 1914.
68. Kurd 'Ali, 'Shabakun Najawtu minhu wa Najawtu bihi', *al-Mudhakkirat*, vol. 1, pp. 99–102.
69. 'Al-Nahda al-'arabiyya: Za'im al-'Iraq yukadhibu ma yaftarihi al-muftarun', *al-Muqtabas* no. 1291 (14 September 1913), p. 1.
70. CADN, Damas (consulat) no. 65, Ottavi to Bompard (30 October 1913). Tauber believes that the publication of a rumour concerning the nomination of the Egyptian prince 'Umar Tusun as *wali* of Damascus was the origin of this aggression. Tauber, 'The Press and the Journalist', p. 174.
71. 'Nahnu fi al-bilad al-faransawiyya', *al-Muqtabas* no. 1416 (18 February 1914), translated into French and reproduced in French Consul's dispatch dated 19 February 1914, Damascus. MAE – NS Turquie 124, pp. 34–40. See Ezzerelli, 'Les arabistes syriens', pp. 107–10.
72. MAE – NS Turquie 124, Ottavi to Doumergue (19 February 1914), pp. 39–40.
73. MAE – NS Turquie 124, pp. 98–102 (dispatch, 27 April 1914).
74. Kurd 'Ali, 'Nazim Basha wa *al-Muqtabas*', *al-Mudhakkirat*, vol. 1, pp. 64–8.
75. 'Wali Suriya Khulusi Bik', *al-Mudhakkirat*, vol. 1, pp. 103–6.
76. Farah, *Die Deutsche Pressepolitik*, pp. 235–82.
77. 'Wali Suriya Khulusi Bik', *al-Mudhakkirat*, vol. 1, pp. 103–6.
78. 'Jamal Basha wa *al-Muqtabas*', *al-Mudhakkirat*, vol. 1, p. 107.
79. 'Sudur al-Muqtabas', *al-Muqtabas* no. 1465 (2 January 1915), p. 1.
80. al-Malluhi, *Mu'jam* p. 46; Khoury, Ibish and Yasushi, p. 99.
81. Kurd 'Ali, *al-Ba'tha al-'Ilmiyya*; Kurd 'Ali, *al-Rihla al-Anwariyya*.
82. '*Al-Muqtabas* ba'da hawlayn', *al-Muqtabas* 8:7 (1914–16), p. 481. Only seven supplementary issues appeared up to 1917; volume 9 was interrupted after only two issues.
83. Kurd 'Ali, 'al-Sihafa aydan', *al-Mudhakkirat*, vol. 1, pp. 56–63.
84. Babil, *Sihafa wa siyasa suriyya*.
85. Al-Malluhi, *Mu'jam*, pp. 104–5; Khoury, Ibish and Yasushi, *Mudawwina*, pp. 142–4.

Bibliography

Archives

France: Centre des Archives diplomatiques de Nantes, Nantes (CADN)
Ministère des Affaires étrangères, Paris (MAE)

Published Works

al-Alusi, Jamal al-Din, *Muhammad Kurd 'Ali* (Baghdad: Dar al-shu'un al-thaqafiyya al-amma, 1986).

Babil, Nassuh, *Sihafa wa siyasa suriyya fi al-qarn al-'ishrin* (Beirut: Riad al-Rayyes, 1987).

al-Barudi, Fakhri, *Mudhakkirat al-Barudi: sittuna sana tatakallam*, vol. 1 (Damascus: Matabi' dar al-hayat, 1951).

Commins, David Dean, *Islamic Reform: Politics and Social Change in Late Ottoman Syria* (New York: Oxford University Press, 1990).

Commins, David, 'Religious Reformers and Arabists in Damascus, 1885–1914', *International Journal of Middle East Studies* 18:4 (1986), pp. 405–25.

Dahhan, Sami, 'Mohammed Kurd Ali (1876–1953). Notice biographique', in *Mélanges Louis Massignon*, vol. 1 (Damascus: Institut Français d'Études arabes de Damas, 1956).

Dakhli, Leyla, *Une génération d'intellectuels arabes: Syrie et Liban (1908–1940)* (Paris: IISMM-Karthala, 2009).

Deguilhem, Randi, 'Les cafés à Damas (XIXe–XXe siècles)', in Hélène Desmet-Gregoire and François Georgeon (eds), *Cafés d'Orient revisités* (Paris: CNRS Éditions, 1997), pp. 127–39.

de Tarrazi, Filip, *Tarikh al-sihafa al-'arabiyya*, vol. 4 (Beirut: Matba'at al-adabiyya, 1933).

Escovitz, Joseph, '"He was the Muhammad Abduh of Syria." A Study of Tahir al-Jaza'iri and his Influence', *International Journal of Middle East Studies* 18:3 (1986), pp. 293–310.

Elias, Elias Hanna, *La presse arabe* (Paris: Maisonneuve et Larose, 1993).

Ezzerelli, Kaïs, *Diplomatie occidentale et dissidence arabe: La France coloniale et le mouvement arabiste en Syrie ottomane (1912–1914)* (Tunis: Dar al-Wasla, 2014).

Ezzerelli, Kaïs, 'Muḥammad 'Abduh et les réformistes syro-libanais: influence, image, postérité', in Maher Al-Charif et Sabrina Mervin (eds), *Modernités islamiques* (Damascus: IFPO, 2006), pp. 79–105.

Ezzerelli, Kaïs, 'Le pèlerinage à La Mecque au temps du chemin de fer du Hedjaz (1908–1914)', in Sylvia Chiffoleau and Anna Madoeuf (eds), *Les pèlerinages au Maghreb et au Moyen-Orient: Espaces publics, espaces du public* (Beirut: IFPO, 2005), pp. 167–91.

Ezzerelli, Kaïs, 'Les arabistes syriens et la France de la révolution jeune-turque à la Première Guerre mondiale (1908–1914): L'exemple de Muhammad Kurd 'Ali', *Bulletin d'Études Orientales* 55 (2004), pp. 83–110.

Farah, Irmgard, *Die Deutsche Pressepolitik und Propagandatätigkeit im Osmanischen Reich von 1908–1918 unter besonderer Berücksichtung des 'Osmanischen Lloyd'*, Beiruter Texte und Studien, Band 50 (Beirut: Orient Institut, 1993).

Hartmann, Martin, *Der Islamische Orient*, vol. 2, *Die Arabische Frage, mit einem Versuche der Archäologie Jemens* (Amsterdam: APA–Oriental Press, 1909).

Hartmann, Martin, *Reisebriefe aus Syrien* (Berlin: Dietrich Reimer, 1913).

Hermann, Rainer, *Kulturkrise und konservative Erneuerung: Muhammad Kurd Ali (1876–1953) und das geistige Leben in Damaskus zu Beginn des 20. Jahrhunderts* (Frankfurt: Heidelberg Orientalische Studien, 1990).

Kayali, Hasan, *Arabs and Young Turks: Ottomanism, Arabism and Islamism in the Ottoman Empire, 1908–1918* (Berkeley and Los Angeles: University of California Press, 1997).

Kenny, L. M., 'East versus West in *Al-Muqtataf*, 1875–1900. Image and Self-Image', in Donald P. Little (ed.), *Essays on Islamic Civilization* (Leiden: Brill, 1976), pp. 140–54.

Khalidi, Rashid Ismail, 'The 1912 Election Campaign in the Cities of Bilad al-Sham', *International Journal of Middle East Studies* 16:4 (November 1984), pp. 461–74.

Khalidi, Rashid Ismail, 'The Press as a Source for Modern Arab Political History: 'Abd al-Ghani al-'Uraysi and *Al-Mufid*', *Arab Studies Quarterly* 3: 1 (Winter 1981), pp. 22–42.

al-Khatib, Muhibb al-Din (al-Hasani al-Dimashqi), *Hayatuhu bi-qalamihi tarwi ahdath 'asr wa-hadara* (Damascus: Matba'at jam'iyyat al-tamaddun al-islami, 1979).

Khoury, Philip S., *Urban Notables and Arab Nationalism: The Politics of Damascus (1860–1920)* (New York: Cambridge Middle East Library, 1983).

Khoury, Yusuf Q., Yusuf H. Ibish, and Kosugi Yasushi, *Mudawwina sahafa suriyya* (Kyoto: University of Kyoto, 2004).

Kurd 'Ali, Muhammad, *al-Ba'tha al-'ilmiyya ila dar al-khilafa al-'uthmaniyya* (Beirut: al-Matba'a al-'ilmiyya, 1916).

Kurd 'Ali, Muhammad, *Ghara'ib al-gharb*, 2 vols (Cairo: al-Matba'a al-rahmaniyya, 1923) [1st edn in 1910 for vol. 1].

Kurd 'Ali, Muhammad, *Khitat al-Sham*, vol. 6, 3rd edn (Damascus: Maktabat al-Nuri, 1983).

Kurd 'Ali, Muhammad, *al-Mudhakkirat* (Damascus: Matba at al-Taraqqi, 1948–51).

Kurd 'Ali, Muhammad, *al-Mu'asirun*, ed. Muhammad al-Masri (Damascus: Matba'at majma' al-lugha al-'arabiyya bi-Dimashq, 1980).

Kurd 'Ali, Muhammad, *al-Qadim wa-l-hadith* (Cairo: al-Matba'a al-rahmaniyya, 1925).

Kurd 'Ali, Muhammad, *al-Rihla al-anwariyya ila al-asqa' al-hijaziyya* (Beirut: al-Matba'a al-'ilmiyya, 1916).

al-Kuzbari, Salma al-Haffar, *Lutfi al-Haffar (1885–1968): Mudhakkiratuhu, hayatuhu wa-'asruhu* (London and Beirut: Riad el-Rayyes, 1997).

al-Malluhi, Mihyar A., *Mu'jam al-jara'id al-suriyya, 1865–1965* (Damascus: al-Ula, 2002).

Muhammad Kurd 'Ali: Mu'assis al-majma' al-'ilmi al-'arabi (Damascus: Matba'at al-Hijaz, 1977).

Murad, Riyad 'Abd al-Hamid, *Faharis al-Muqtabas* (Damascus: Matba'at majma' al-lugha al-'arabiyya, 1977).

Seikaly, Samir, 'Shukri al-Asali: A Case Study of a Political Activist', in Rashid Khalidi (ed.), *The Origins of Arab Nationalism* (New York: Columbia University Press, 1991), pp. 73–96.

Seikaly, Samir M., 'Damascene Intellectual Life in the Opening Years of the 20th Century: Muhammad Kurd Ali and *al-Muqtabas*', in Marwan R. Buheiry (ed.), *Intellectual Life in the Arab East (1890–1939)* (Beirut: American University of Beirut Press, 1981), pp. 125–53.

Sharabi, Hisham, *Arab Intellectuals and the West: The Formative Years, 1875–1914* (Baltimore: Johns Hopkins University Press, 1970).

al-Shihabi, Qutayba, *Sahat al-Marja wa-mujawiratuha bayna al-amsi wa al-yawm* (Damascus: Arab Capital of Culture, 2008).

Tauber, Eliezer, *The Emergence of the Arab Movements* (London: Frank Cass, 1993).

Tauber, Eliezer, 'The Press and the Journalist as a Vehicle in Spreading National Ideas in Syria in the Late Ottoman Period', *Die Welt des Islams* 30 (1990), pp. 163–77.

Weber, Stefan, 'L'aménagement urbain entre régulations ottomanes, intérêts privés et participation politique: La municipalité de Damas à la fin de l'époque ottomane (1864–1918)', in Nora Lafi (ed.), *Municipalités méditerranéennes: Les réformes urbaines ottomanes au miroir d'une histoire comparée (Moyen-Orient, Maghreb, Europe méridionale)* (Berlin: ZMO-Studien 21, Klaus Schwartz Verlag, 2005), pp. 173–222.

Yared, Nazik Saba, *Secularism and the Arab World (1850–1939)* (London: Saqi Books, 2002).

7

From Intellectual to Professional: The Move from 'Contributor' to 'Journalist' at *Ruz al-Yusuf* in the 1920s and 1930s

Sonia Temimi

In the press history of Egypt, exceptions to the rule have long held the attention of researchers keen to confirm a mythicised vision of the journalistic profession. In setting out to study the editors who contributed to *Ruz al-Yusuf* between 1925 and 1937, and in the belief that an understanding of the publication's development is impossible without an acquaintance with those who 'made' it, I favoured the collective approach by retaining from individuals' careers only that which might serve to highlight common features in the cultural surroundings of the two generations as well as in the changing perception of the role of the press and of the professional practice of journalism. In order to do this, my approach was to compile information about those who signed the articles, irrespective of the number of times they wrote and of the nature of the text.

Methodologically, such an investigation is impeded by a number of constraints. The more notoriety *Ruz al-Yusuf* gained, the less often its articles were signed. Even some of its most significant editors, such as Mustafa Amin and Muhammad 'Ali Gharib, are only known to have contributed to the newspaper because they are mentioned in other sources and mainly in journalists' memoirs. These editors signed none of their writings. There are, in addition, great disparities in the information available on these editors. Some of the most regular collaborators have nonetheless fallen into obscurity because, their name aside, little or no information exists about them. In short, articles written anonymously, those signed off with a pseudonym or those with no signature whatsoever make up the majority of those to be found in the newspaper.[2] Beyond these methodological constraints – and in the light of available evidence – I first sought to study the ways in which those from ostensibly opposite cultural world(s) as well as different careers met and interacted in a way that allowed for debate amongst editors as to the ultimate function of the 'newspaper'. While for some the newspaper represented a means to participate in public debate, others saw it as 'a product' to be commercialised. This was to change the theory and practice of professional journalism, thereby not only affecting the newspaper as a commercial product but also contributing to the establishment of a distinct and independent press sector. This latter development will provide the focus for the second part of this contribution.

The Key Figures and their Cultural World(s): Two Bilingual Generations

The authors covered in this chapter were, for the most part, educated within the modern Egyptian education system, except for Gharib, who was a graduate of the prestigious al-Azhar University, and Kamil al-Shinnawi, who started but did not complete his studies there. It is notable that many editors went abroad to finish their studies, whether as recipients of a scholarship funded by one of the (then numerous) Egyptian ministries or as self-financing students. This fact, certainly in part, accounts for the astonishing abundance of Western cultural references in their texts and caricatures, that is, any allusions to Western literature and history as well as any expression directly translated from a foreign language which then became an integral part of journalistic and satirical vocabulary. Indeed, close examination of the editors' cultural world(s) reveals their total mastery of a foreign language, mainly English or French. Total mastery and bilingualism are here considered synonymous, the term referring to people able to express themselves as fluently in a foreign language as in their mother tongue (Arabic). So recurrent was this phenomenon that it spurred me to investigate further and to systematically isolate such translations whilst also studying the changing way in which such terms were used.

Until the end of the 1920s, *Ruz al-Yusuf* regularly contained a section entitled 'Short Story of the Week' (*Qissat al-usbu'*) or simply 'Short Story' (*Qissat*), which was devoted to the publication of short stories. (This section was removed in 1929 but reinstated in 1934.) Limiting myself to the study of the writings in this particular section[3] and to those articles which bear a signature, I set out to establish which of the short stories were translated as well as to determine the source language of each. In doing this, I either went by the notice at the start or end of the short story ('translated from English' or 'translated from the work of . . .') or by the fact that the atmosphere depicted in the story and the characters' names suggested that it was a translation, even if this was not explicitly stated. The results of this study show that amongst these largely anonymous authors, there was a significant number who – while not necessarily bilingual – had sufficient command of a foreign language to be able to translate it into their native tongue. From the latter part of the 1930s, however, translations of foreign literature in *Ruz al-Yusuf* became rarer, a symptom less of a dwindling knowledge of second languages than of the concretisation of efforts undertaken in the 1920s towards the emergence of an Egyptian literary tradition. Such a reading would seem to be confirmed by the fact that the majority of short stories published during this period were penned by Egyptian authors. That fact that the trend of 'Western cultural references' in the texts did not decline (in fact, quite the contrary) also confirms this reading. What is more, even though foreign expressions were as prevalent as ever in texts about political life during the entire period from 1925 to 1937, their translation and explanation for readers became less common in the 1930s.

Without wishing to create an exhaustive list, I shall cite a few examples in order to demonstrate the extent of this phenomenon. Casting aside common expressions referring to 'Romeo and Juliet', 'Don Juan', 'to throw down the gauntlet' to designate a challenge, 'crocodile tears' for hypocrisy and 'after the good morning and how do you do' to convey the idea of a greeting (written in Arabic script and with no explanation for the reader), we come across phrases like 'Rome is not big enough for Octavius and Anthony' when speaking about the difference of opinion between a *mudir* and his subordinate,[4] or 'the lamp of Diogenes' that the members of *al-Sha'b* should use in their search for a Wafdist yet to sign up to their party,[5] and 'he is transfer-proof' (*naql-bruf*)[6] when referring to a civil servant who managed to cling on to his post. When talking about an Egyptian politician, the writer observed that he considered himself the 'government's Clemenceau', going on to explain: 'that is, the man who brings down governments'.[7] In another text, 'A. F. Yahya rejected the label given to him by his party's newspaper that compared him to Gaston Doumergue who saved France – just as Yahya had saved Egypt – preferring instead to be called "Richelieu Yahya pacha".'[8] These last two references were never explained for readers.

The sheer abundance of such Western cultural references is striking and close study of one particular issue (no. 352, 11 November 1934) yields the following results: A. Ziwar was reported to have said, 'How can I leave the house *mon chéri* (*munshiri*)? At every turn I am confronted with a "méchant" journalist' (in Latin script and with no explanation) (p. 3); 'the three musketeers' are invoked with an accompanying drawing (p. 6); an individual declared to Z. al-Ibrashi that 'it was better than playing at being Nero and singing while Rome was in flames' (p. 8); 'these days, politics is a game of "chance"' (in Latin script, followed by an explanation for readers) 'bakht'; 'ô chéri' (in Arabic script) (p. 8); and one article is entitled '*Ruz al-Yusuf* Throws Down the Gauntlet' (p. 10), an expression repeated a few pages later (p. 17). When referring to Hasan Sabri, 'It is necessary to render unto Caesar what is Caesar's and what is God's to Caesar as well' (p. 13); A. Ziwar exclaims, 'Voilà' (in Arabic script) and the editor clarifies: 'meaning, "I've found it"' (p. 17); a woman received the second 'coup' (*al-ku*) (strike) (p. 19) and another was said to 'take herself for the daughter of general Wellington or the descendant of Napoleon' (p. 21); 'his office was in a room where the sun never set . . . exactly like the British Empire' (p. 27); 'he greeted the pupil with a "bonjour" (*bunjur*) who replied with a "good morning" (*gud murning*)' (p. 28). We also find reference to 'The school Romeos' with the explanation that 'Romeos is plural for Romeo and is Juliet's male equivalent' (p. 29); 'the three musketeers: Zaki Athos *effendi*, Yusuf Porthos and Ishaq Aramis' (p. 29); 'Cupid, the friend of youth' (p. 33), 'the final whim, o beloved' ('*akhir kabris ya chiri*)' (p. 40); 'she went to get herself ready (lit. adjust her toilette) (*islah al-twalit*)' (p. 41); and 'he took supper (*al*-souper)' (in Latin script with no translation) (p. 42). This is not to mention all the European words found in the same issue which had made their way into Egyptian dialect and adapted to Arabic script: 'bravo', 'carnet' (address book), 'ascenseur' (elevator), 'bonbon', 'jockey', 'chic', 'redingote' (riding coat), 'étiquette' (etiquette), and theatre and film vocabulary such as 'entracte' (intermission), 'artiste' and 'Prima Donna'. This trend continued with European words mentioned in the *zagal-s* of the 1930s written in both Arabic and Latin scripts, something rarely seen prior to this period.[9]

These different developments shed light on the context of journalistic production at the time when we learn of the fluency of editors in at least one foreign language, and with the reception of a public which – while composed of Arabic speakers – was becoming more familiar with foreign cultures, if not foreign languages. Furthermore, one of the pieces of advice many of these authors gave to future generations was to learn foreign languages in order to prevent cultural isolation, an idea to which Fikri Abaza,[10] Hilmi Halim[11] and 'Abbas Mahmud al-'Aqqad returned repeatedly. In 1962, the last was to deplore students' knowledge of both Arabic and foreign languages:

> The greatest authors of the previous generation did their studies in English but their [mastery of] Arabic was formidable . . . When we were children, . . . we read the English reviews which were distributed at the same time to English students in Great Britain.[12]

These two generations of writers (the oldest editor was born in 1879 and the youngest in 1919) were easily able to access Western artistic, literary, philosophical and press production. As Lutfi Jum'a testified, 'The English language gave to me the greatest of services because I had, through [this means], access to books, reviews and the newspapers published in Europe.'[13] Indeed, some of the teaching in public schools was delivered in English at that time, which promoted further learning of English amongst those who had already acquired its fundamentals.[14]

Such details surrounding the cultural background of the editors and the public's reception of their writings call into question certain 'received ideas' about the period most notably popularised by the work of Jankowski and Gershoni.[15] These account for the proliferation of writings about the Prophet and about Islam's most important leaders (commonly known as *islamiyyat*) from the middle of the 1930s by the fact that certain authors – who had previously been known for their attachment to the Western ideals of the

Enlightenment and to the concept of a nation based on the references to Egypt's pharaonic past and the ideals of citizenship – were apparently driven to an about-turn in order to gain favour with a new mass readership produced by the expansion of the educational system.

This reductive framework is open to challenge on at least two fronts.[16] While references to Egypt's Arab and Muslim identities became more frequent during the 1930s, by no means were they absent in the 1920s, nor did references to Egypt's pharaonic era disappeared in the 1930s. Neither does it mean that this change was due to the influence of a totally Arabic-speaking readership. *Ruz al-Yusuf* indeed did contain more references to Egypt as belonging to an 'Arab Muslim world', but references to a world divided into 'colonisers' and 'the colonised' were more numerous still.[17]

Three *Ruz al-Yusuf* authors wrote *islamiyyats*: 'Abbas Mahmud al-'Aqqad,[18] Muhammad Lutfi Jum'a[19] and Muhammad Shawkat al-Tuni.[20] Al-Tuni's motivations are unclear but al-'Aqqad had been irritated, as long ago as 1914, by the way that many scholars presented the history of Islamic civilisation. His *'Abqariyyat Muhammad* appeared in 1942 and was followed by numerous like-minded publications.[21] The same can be said of Muhammad Lutfi Jum'a, who repeatedly challenged received ideas about Islam and the Orient more generally. His memoirs abound with references to his readings[22] and whilst he recognised the efforts of some scholars to rectify the Europeans' erroneous image of the Orient and of Islam, he for the most part contests the content of their writings.[23] It was with this sole purpose in mind that he wrote the first instalment of his work on the Prophet in 1939.[24]

As these examples demonstrate, al-'Aqqad, Jum'a and the *islamiyyats* were more a rejection of the image of 'the self' imposed by 'the Other' than they were an answer to the demands of a specific audience. Revisiting their collective past also allowed these two authors to prove that, contrary to colonial discourse, past Arab and Muslim societies had achieved a great deal and that progress was not the sole preserve of any one civilisation or culture. For this reason the view of Jankowski and Gershoni is flawed in overlooking the importance of the era's political realities and the more deeply rooted motives of the *islamiyyat* as well as in assuming that the Egyptian political sphere functioned independently of the British presence after the introduction of the constitutional regime. They analysed the views expressed in these writings without factoring in the conditions under which they were produced.

Accordingly, I propose a division which would shift their chronological boundaries by a few years to around 1933–5, when all hope in democratic institutions was lost in the shadow of the colonial presence and when the political class of the time contributed to the radicalisation of the nationalist movement. Newspapers such as *Ruz al-Yusuf* concentrated much less on a common or shared culture with other Arab nations and much more on an Egypt under colonial rule. In a section called *Fi al-aqtar al-shaqiqa* (In Fellow Nations),[25] expressly devoted to the countries of the Orient (understood in its widest sense that included India,[26] China and Iran), almost half of the articles (nineteen out of a total of forty-one) refer to either French or British colonial policies. The fictional character of Abu Qasim Za'tar Effendi (the Syrian-Lebanese equivalent of al-Misri Effendi) was dreamt up. Speaking in his own dialect, he would join his Egyptian counterpart in casting a wry glance over political life and the sham democracy that was played out in the shadow of the French colonial regime.

The idea that the parliamentary regime and the colonial presence were incompatible was one to which Fikri Abaza, for example, would frequently return in his autobiographical novel. In it, he states that 'the parliamentary regime and the popular government (*al-hukm al-sha'bi*) are a mere morphine injection when coupled with colonisation'[27] and 'the representation (*niyaba*) of the nation in the shadow of colonisation was a comedy and a mockery'.[28] Though *Ruz al-Yusuf* was to repeat the broad criticisms that Abaza's Watani party levelled when the constitutional regime was established – a regime it alleged would end up dividing the nation through internal partisan squabbling instead of uniting it in communal struggle against its occupiers – it is nonetheless true that the newspaper developed a more trenchant critical tone as time went on. Accordingly, the increasing attention paid to other Arab countries was more likely the product of the realisation of their common destiny under colonialism.

A Newspaper against Colonialist Discourse

The second significant trend that emerges from the comparison of editors is their experience of the colonial presence. We find constant references to this theme where editors left biographical accounts, gave interviews retracing their careers shortly before retiring or were sufficiently well known that some of those closest to them could be found to speak about them after their deaths. While only a few of these editors found themselves in direct confrontation with the colonial administration, the majority found themselves at the receiving end of its contemptuous and reductive view of natives, either during their school years or later in adult life. The case of *Ruz al-Yusuf*'s editor-in-chief from 1925 to 1934 alone is telling: Muhammad al-Tabi'i, like a whole generation of educated youth, found himself torn between admiration for Europe's advances and his pain at its presence in his homeland.[29] The great tragedy of this period is that the West's reappropriation of modernity relied on colonialism, which gave rise to the waves of stigmatisation, stereotyping, as well as 'civilising' and 'modernising' discourse that colonists used to justify their presence in the country. To question this colonialist model was thus to take up arms against its binary world view, in which Europe defined itself as the better half of such dichotomous pairings as superior/inferior, modern/traditional and advanced/backward. A good number of al-Tabi'i's articles contain references to the way Egypt and Egyptians were described in the European press, in travel books and in the memoirs of European politicians who had spent time in the country. *Ruz al-Yusuf* regularly commented on these writings. Several recurring features within the works were to prove a source of indignation for the newspaper, namely the 'false truths' to be found in the memoirs of European former civil servants and journalists as well as travellers' relentless pursuit of the exotic – a pursuit which resulted in such a distorted picture of the country that it ended up justifying the colonial presence in European public opinion.

This colonial presence and the colonial discourse that came with it therefore contributed to forging an image of the Other, as well as a certain view of the self, against which a generation that grew up under occupation and witnessed the signing of Egypt's independence (and so the re-emergence of hope) was to take up arms. This rebellion was made all the more possible by that generation's mastery of what it considered the very strength of the West: its ability to mobilise the opinion of a politicised public through modern means. For some this meant a new, self-proclaimed 'Egyptian' and 'modern' literary strain (novels and plays), while for others it meant a press on its way to becoming democratised, especially in the satirical and humoristic content that made the public laugh. The press became the principal vehicle for everything that authors, journalists and intellectuals admired in Europe and everything they wanted to reproduce in Egypt: humanist culture, civic virtues and democracy.

Dispensing with False Antagonisms

The opposition editors exhibited to colonialism does not, however, mean they were opposed to Western civilisation and less still to the modernity necessary to reform traditions, habits, ways of life as well as common and shared perceptions. What they instead sought to do was question the version of modernity colonial powers tried to impose on them and the forced distancing from their collective history that it involved. For example, Ibrahim 'Abd al-Qadir al-Mazini stopped contributing to the newspaper of the Muslim Brotherhood when he judged its call to burn all English scientific books as an act of 'fanaticism' (*ta'assub*) – a fanaticism with which he could not hold.[30] The same is true of al-'Aqqad, whose anticolonialist stance did not stop him becoming a most fervent advocate of Anglo-Saxon culture – as the debate that erupted between him and Taha Husayn (a staunch defender of Mediterranean culture) showed.[31] It is necessary to understand the situation's many 'paradoxes'. The very same generations who fought against Eurocentrism and who longed for Egypt's cultural development were also those who were the most imbued with the ideals of Western modernism: a rethink of education, openness to the whole range of Western cultural production, grants for studying abroad and a society based on a new set of protocols governing behaviour. The history of the period was no longer viewed through the lens of political struggle which, in binary nationalistic and European accounts, established a clear barrier between East and West. Instead, a cultural overview revealed that these lines were somewhat blurred and that areas of common consensus were starting to form and were less conflicting than they at first appeared. Largely thanks to their ability to access European press and literature in the original, the expertise of these new generations in exploiting various means of artistic expression outstripped that of preceding generations and made them increasingly able to develop new styles and to venture into new forms of expression. They tried to bring the two cultures closer together by the sheer amount of borrowing, translating and adapting of existing genres to Egyptian audiences that they did. To take an example from the press, when – in 1927 – Muhammad al-Tabi'i decided to turn *Ruz al-Yusuf* into a satirical newspaper featuring caricatures, his favourite magazine was none other than the English publication *Punch*,[32] as well as French satirical newspapers *Le Rire* and *Le Sourire*, both of which he quoted abundantly. Taking his inspiration from *Punch*, he was to produce a newspaper whose originality stemmed from its ability to condense all things popular at the time and which so represented the 'spirit' of the 1920s that it is still indelibly linked to the epoch. The secret of its success lay less in its creation of new genres and more in its adaptation and systematic exploitation of tried and tested formulas for the enjoyment of a wider readership. The satirical cartoon, which had featured from the late nineteenth century onwards, became a pillar of its success, as did its new journalistic language, which bridged the divide between colloquial and high Arabic. Al-Tabi'i's biggest contribution was to have used his total fluency in English to permanently rid journalistic language of any remaining pretensions to overwrought expression. This was an especially important contribution to the language and vocabulary of the satirical press. As a journalist in the critical press, he was primarily concerned with communicating ideas to the greatest possible number of readers in colourful language meant at once to draw their attention and to entertain them. To achieve this, he used straightforward language, unburdened by overly complicated words and scattered with local dialect or even with European terms that frequently featured in spoken language. He focused on the newspaper's content and adapted its look according to the zeitgeist. When Salama Musa speaks of al-Tabi'i, it is as the father of a 'popular' press language whose style attracted people to reading and, close as it was to spoken language, nevertheless avoided becoming overly colloquial.[33]

It is thus undeniable that cultural common ground was opening up but we must not ignore areas of conflict in which Egyptian identity was being unilaterally defined according to the agenda of the Other. A 'modern' culture, that is, one that used relatively new forms of expression (theatre, novels, short stories and the press), had to be built up as a matter of great urgency. Not only that, but this culture had to be 'non-Western' and to take account of the country's cultural uniqueness. The aim was to call into question the European aesthetic, cultural and social norms that had been held up as universally valid for all societies – and especially for societies which had been 'colonised'. For the authors we have examined, Egypt's collective identity should take shape in opposition to the societal and cultural model propagated by the West at that time. Whatever their individual area of expertise (some were more or less working in journalism, some in the theatre or in literary production, whilst others frequented the same literary or professional circles), these intellectuals certainly knew each other and frequently mixed, for the crossover between their respective cultural domains was considerable. At the peak of this movement for cultural renewal in the 1920s, the not yet fully specialised press functioned as a medium for all these types of publications and also served to bring these intellectuals together.

The New Profession of Journalism

Another thing many editors have in common is that they resigned from the civil service (H. 'Abd al-'Aziz, al-'Aqqad, al-Mazini, al-Tabi'i, A. Adham and Ahmad Amin). With increased access to university education for the public, the state was finding it increasingly difficult to provide jobs for the ever increasing number of graduates. As Jum'a explained, this situation was also irksome for the colonial administration, which wanted to limit the number of Egyptians recruited to the bare minimum necessary for the service to function normally, whilst simultaneously cherry-picking the best jobs for its own nationals.[34] For certain members of this first generation working for the civil service became synonymous with submission and abandonment of the cause that was intimately connected to the freedom of thought, speech and action. In the 1930s, *Ruz al-Yusuf* would devote two columns to deciphering the dim view these editors took of the civil service. The first, 'Maslahiyyat! Li-mandubina al-mutagawwil fi lazughli! . . .'[35] (The Administration! From our on-site correspondent in Lazughli! . . .) sought to reveal what really went on behind the scenes of the administration within different ministries and focused particularly on the role the English played in the service. The title of the second continued on the same theme by featuring a popular expression about the pull the civil service exerted on new graduates as a career destination: 'in fatak al-miri, itmarragh fi-trabu'[36] (if you can't get into the civil service by the front door, go in by the back door). The column shed light on the clientelism and nepotism which characterised entry to the service,[37] in which 'the most important qualifications are letters of recommendation from senior civil servants'[38] and in which student bursaries that were normally reserved for the needy were doled out by civil servants to their own family members.[39] The column also underlined the preferential treatment in pay and job responsibility given to British civil servants over their Egyptian counterparts, stating that there was a glass ceiling beyond which Egyptians could not hope to progress.[40] By blowing the whistle on the unfairness endemic within the administration's hidden workings, did the newspaper implicitly encourage new graduates to turn their backs on the civil service and seek employment elsewhere?

With the setting up of new political institutions calling for the development of ever growing public opinion came new possibilities for generations of graduates. While in the past the most important jobs had been the preserve of a certain 'caste', work within the new institutions in representational politics, its parties and committees (as well as in professions like journalism) offered new opportunities. A number of *Ruz al-Yusuf*'s editors resigned from their posts in the civil service in order to become full-time journalists. It was then that journalism took an appreciable leap towards professionalism and those in the field went from the status of freelance writers to that of paid employees. The effect wrought by this change is best seen when comparing the make-up of *Ruz al-Yusuf*'s editorial team at its beginnings, as an artistic and literary newspaper between 1925 and 1927, with the team that headed it up in the 1930s and contributed to the phenomenal success of what was now a political and satirical newspaper.

Towards Autonomy: The Building of a Profession and the Honing of a Craft

Before undertaking a study of the editors of *Ruz al-Yusuf* in the 1920s, it was first necessary to identify those who signed off their articles to provide a vital sociological insight into the make-up of the journalistic field. This is particularly important in examining periods when notions of professional identity remained vague, despite growing signs of collective realisation of journalists of a common praxis and shared interests. As far back as the 1910s, journalists had tried to set up their own union[41] and had formed a kind of informal club. They would have to wait until 1941, however, for journalism to assimilate into the corporate sphere and start to find its place as a profession.

The earliest 'contributors' to *Ruz al-Yusuf* (1925–7) dealing with literature and the arts were uncomfortable with any restrictive definition of journalism because of its very subject matter.[42] Most articles that were signed pertained to literature or the theatre and – unless specifically requested by the editing team from an author of some renown – were largely unsolicited contributions sent in by their respective authors. The literary press helped to forge reputations and introduce writers to the general public and, as such, did not lend itself well to authorial anonymity. Christophe Charles stated that French journalism 'was most often practised alongside other related activities... [It] was first and foremost a springboard to another career.'[43] If his statement can be partially applied to Egyptian journalists, then so can Laurent Martin's contention that 'the press industry was at once too poor to pay professional contributors a full-time wage and still too unsure of its unique selling point to attract corporate interest in its activities'.[44] Contributors indulged in press writing as a kind of hobby on top of the day jobs they needed to put food on the table.

The principal common trait shared by the majority of *Ruz al-Yusuf*'s contributors was that they were not professional journalists making a living as press writers. As members of the new, educated elite, being mainly graduates, future teachers, lawyers, civil servants or already working in the professions, almost all of them had another job. They were also mainly from Cairo and Alexandria, since these cities were most affected by the blossoming press and cultural industries, and most were not paid for their work, which means we can be all the more certain of their social and professional position. They were not 'journalists supplementing their income with a second job to "make ends meet"'[45] but rather people for whom press writing was a means of escaping their everyday lives. Budding writers and intellectuals keen to declare their literary allegiance flocked to these new publications to offer their services as critics of every genre, be it literature, art, theatre or the nascent cinema. Some contributors had already made their name in the press industry and would split their time between work for various publications but these were very few in number in comparison because professional journalists generally required payment. This was much easier said than done for cash-strapped newspapers. The world of journalism thus remained accessible to people from many different walks of life, with different backgrounds and views on the ultimate role of the newspaper. The press provided a forum for anyone wishing to participate, regularly or occasionally, in public debate as well as for anyone venturing into literary production. Such conditions meant that any single overarching definition of what constituted the journalist craft remained elusive and, as such, vague. Fatima al-Yusuf described those who collaborated with *Ruz al-Yusuf* in 1928 as 'intellectuals' or 'men of letters' (*adib*), adding that 'every true journalist must fall into that category'.[46] Later, those who mainly earned a living by writing for the press were to be referred to as *suhufi* (journalist). This shift in status from 'freelance amateur' to 'contracted professional'[47] was to have a considerable effect on *Ruz al-Yusuf* in the 1930s.

One Newspaper Born of Team Effort

> Although the press of this time was a press of individuals, a newspaper remained attached to the name of its owner or to its 'first pen' which ensured its distribution, it was not the case for the Wafdist press. Only the partisan membership of this press was the criterion of the success of a newspaper and of its diffusion to the readers, without consideration of the name of its journalists. The proof is that as soon as a newspaper separated from the Wafd, its circulation fell and its financial position worsened because of the little interest which the readers gave it . . . *Ruz Al-Yusuf* also suffered after its separation from the Wafd, which obliged the owner to sell some personal effects to pay off her debts. The membership of the newspaper to the Wafd was thus the basis for its good circulation and not the fact that al-'Aqqad, Hamza or Diyab took part in its writing.[48]

This observation by the specialist of the Wafdist press, Najwa Kamil, warrants qualification inasmuch as it mistakenly relies on a purely political reading of the journalistic field. Following Muhammad Mahmud's term in government (June 1928–October 1929) that consolidated the newspaper's renowned partisan stance, there were indeed fewer signed satirical articles in *Ruz al-Yusuf*. This was not, however, a phenomenon peculiar to the pro-Wafd press, for signed articles in a satirical daily newspapers like *al-Kashkul* were rare.

Under the effect of the transformation of the press (such as the move towards opening culture to the masses) professional practices forced change but stopped short of eradicating old standards completely. Articles signed off with pen names continued to sell and newspapers continued to inform readers of their input in the editing process. Muhammad al-Tabi'i himself only rarely signed off his articles. Nonetheless, a permanent boxed article located in the paper's main political column informed readers that he 'works on the editing team'. When he had to temporarily cease working at the paper in 1932, the editors gave readers a full explanation why and later hastened to announce his return. Contrary to his own custom, al-Tabi'i signed off the first subsequent article he wrote to mark his return. But what else did he write besides that one column? The constantly changing practices of certain editors make it impossible for us to be certain. When the political column and brainchild of al-Tabi'i, 'Khitabat maftuha ila al-'uzama' wa al-sa'alik' (Open Letters to Men both Great and Wretched), found its way back onto the pages of the newspaper after a five-year absence,[49] we learn only through accounts in journalists' memoirs that the column was taken over by Muhammad 'Ali Gharib.[50]

How, then, did readers choose which publication to buy? Political leanings certainly played a part in the choice of newspapers but what differentiated like publications was the 'end product' of the editing process. When, for example, a publishing ban was slapped on *Ruz al-Yusuf* and it was forced to assume different names (the last of which, *al-Sarkha*, lasted almost a year), the newspaper's cover proclaimed until its very last issue that the 'editors are Ruz al-Yusuf, Muhammad al-Tabi'i and Muhammad 'Ali Hammad';[51] however, no articles were signed. More than anything else, therefore, the absence of signatures (even if the inclusion of the names of a selected few helped further sales) was symptomatic of the merging together of separate individuals to form a team focused on creating a product. The newspaper was showcased as a 'finished product', changing the reading experience at a stroke. The only category of journalist that remained something of an exception to the rule was the press illustrator, though Sarukhan, who was reputed to be the paper's only illustrator between 1928 and 1934, chose not to sign each and every one of his illustrations. Contrary to what Nagwa Kamil claims, this was a practice commonly observed across the whole spectrum of the political press at the time.

This result was the product of a small but significant change of direction in professional practice. Corporate connections in many cases got the better of partisan divisions. Having been drafted to replace the then imprisoned Muhammad al-Tabi'i, Fikri Abaza, a member of the Watani Party, wrote for the Wafdist *Ruz al-Yusuf* in 1933. The former approved of the idea and wrote a letter to Fatima al-Yusuf to that effect, even suggesting that Abaza be given responsibility for the newspaper's feature column 'in a way that does not betray the principles of either the Watani Party or the newspaper's Wafdist principles'. He also asked the newspaper's founder to halt *Ruz al-Yusuf*'s campaign against Hafiz Ramadan 'out of respect' and so as not to 'embarrass' Abaza.[52] The same went for other parties as well. The Constitutional Liberals would oftentimes recruit journalists from the other side of the political divide.[53] Moreover, a closer look at these budding journalists reveals that what brought them through *Ruz al-Yusuf*'s doors was not so much the newspaper's political allegiance as the chance to learn 'trade secrets'. Fatima al-Yusuf reiterated that 'Like every successful publication, *Ruz al-Yusuf* started to attract a great many young people with dreams of a bright future in the press industry.'[54] With the exception of Sa'id 'Abduh, every member of *Ruz al-Yusuf*'s first generation would eventually sever ties with the Wafd.

The process of constructing a culture and a collective identity was facilitated by the appearance of the sort of social infrastructure that corporate journalism needed to thrive. Ideological division amongst individual journalists became secondary to the unity felt between colleagues. From then on, all journalists – whatever their politics or whatever paper they worked for – had their own private meeting places in the centre of Cairo. Locations differed according to the 'types' of journalist that frequented them: 'reporters' (*mukhbirun*) would for the most part meet at the buffet of Cairo's train station;, art correspondents met at the Ramses Café (better known as the *qahwat al-Fann* or Art Café) on the Rue 'Imad al-Din; ministerial correspondents gathered at a small cafe next to the Ministry of the Interior. Finally, there was also the Press Club (*Nadi al-sihafa*), which was open to all types of journalists and founded in 1933 next to the Ministry of Wafqs. The Club had replaced the al-Liwa' Bar, which was located near the offices of *al-Ahram* newspaper and had, up until then, served as an informal club for journalists.[55] The latter venue appears to have been the favourite of the journalists at *Ruz al-Yusuf* since it is referred to more than any other in the newspaper.

An examination of the journalistic field (and even its partisan elements) gains relevance when no longer 'blinkered' by a purely political reading of the press. Leaving aside the political leanings of a newspaper that declared itself as Wafdist and which mocked newspapers and journalists of any other persuasion, we begin to recognise the characteristics that define today's modern press, such as the emergence of teams substituting individual work to collectively create a 'product' as well as processes that ushered in the arrival of a unifying social infrastructure for journalists. As well as giving an idea of the success of specific publications, increased staff turnover across the whole industry during this period indicates that the passing on of professional know-how characterised by 'objectivity' became more important than the 'distinctiveness of individual newspapers'. This development was to have a lasting impact on the press, with many contributors working short stints at one newspaper before leaving for another, only to return later. What, then, of the staff at *Ruz al-Yusuf* in the 1930s?

An Overview of the Staff at *Ruz Al-Yusuf*

In the absence of administrative records, compiling a complete overview of the newspaper staff is impossible. That said, in comparing the different memories and memoirs of the protagonists of the time, it would appear that in addition to the casual contributors drafted in on short-term contracts to write articles and feature columns, a 'hard core' of editors was formed. In the 1930s, this hard core consisted of Muhammad al-Tabi'i, Sarukhan, Mustafa and 'Ali Amin, Muhammad 'Ali Hammad, Sa'id 'Abduh, 'Abd al-Rahman Nasr and Ahmad Hasan who would later become editor-in-chief. They were joined on a more or less permanent basis by Muhammad 'Ali Gharib, Galal al-Din al-Hamamsi, Karim Thabit and the al-Shinnawi brothers. Just as in the 1920s, sources are almost totally lacking for the 1930s on how the editors of *Ruz al-Yusuf* managed its financial affairs, and we must settle for the incomplete, imprecise and even contradictory information that is available. Nevertheless, there was a noticeable development as journalists worked under contract with regular salaries (Mustafa Amin had to do unpaid work for almost three years before receiving his first wage).

Fatima al-Yusuf stated that the salaries of editors were between four and eight Egyptian pounds (LE) per month and 'were without doubt high when you consider how strong the currency was at the time . . . Then, a pound got you five times as much as it does today.'[56] These wages seem relatively low, however, when compared with those of the people employed in the newspaper's technical department. According to Muhammad al-Tabi'i, unskilled workers in the printing press were being paid between 12 and 15 piastres per day (LE3.6–4.5 per month) with a foreman receiving almost twice that amount (25 piastres per day or LE7.5 per month).[57] The monthly rent for the newspaper's office (a large, six-room apartment on the Rue al-Amir Qadadar, in the centre of Cairo) was also LE6.[58] Al-Tabi'i concluded by adding that at that time, 'everything was so cheap'. Six pounds was, therefore, a relatively small amount – a fact confirmed when *Ruz al-Yusuf* published a list of the media's highest-paid journalists in 1926. The list included journalists at such newspapers as *al-Ahram*, *al-Siyasa*, *al-Balagh* and *Kawkab al-Sharq*, whose wages ranged from LE12 to LE25 per month.[59] Though readers were reminded that the amounts stated were approximate, and editors were invited to correct any mistakes, these wages remain high compared with those of the star contributors at *Ruz al-Yusuf* (with Sarukhan on LE15 per month and Sa'id 'Abduh on LE20 per month).

Strictly speaking, the money Muhammad al-Tabi'i received from *Ruz al-Yusuf*'s founder, Fatima al-Yusuf, was not a salary per se but an equal share of the newspaper's profits with her. Though more realistic than the LE500 per month Gharib suggested the former was paid from 1933 to 1934, a wage of LE100–150 still seems low until we consider that Fatima al-Yusuf took over the responsibility for al-Tabi'i's household running costs (such as rent and the payment of servants) while he was in Europe between March and June 1934, and would send him the remaining money. Taking all these factors into account, al-Tabi'i probably made about LE87 per month.[60] This roughly corresponds to the amount put forward by the newspaper's founder and appears plausible at a time when advertising revenues and sales figures were dropping. The figure still appears somewhat low, however, since according to our best (though admittedly incomplete) industry-wide wage comparisons, al-Tabi'i would have been making only slightly more than the average successful editor. When Fatima al-Yusuf was coordinating the launch of a new newspaper in 1935, its editor-in-chief Mahmud 'Azmi was given a monthly wage of LE60 as well as a commission on each paper sold, and al-'Aqqad left his post with *al-Jihad* where he was paid LE70 per month to join this new team for an increased salary of LE80 per month.

Differences in wages aside, contemporary accounts reveal two major transformations within *Ruz al-Yusuf*: the status of its press illustrator Sarukhan from a secondary to a key figure in the editing team (as evidenced by the fact that al-Tabi'i paid him 'the highest wage') as well as the increased importance of 'reporters' or journalists sent out to hunt for news. The role of reporter was filled at the time by Mustafa Amin and Karim Thabit. Fatima al-Yusuf said of the former that he had an 'innate predisposition to be a reporter' (*mukhbir bil-saliqa*)[61] and of the latter that he 'would come [to the newspaper] to give the information he had collected to al-Tabi'i and then leave again'.[62]

Judging by the changing composition of *Ruz al-Yusuf*'s editorial team, the 1930s was a decade that saw professional journalism become more organised. The dwindling number of paid and unpaid 'freelancers' compared with contracted employees was a sign of the times. Salaries for initiates to the profession were unattractive, however, and so required them, at least at first, to be motivated by more than material gain. As well as joining an editing team at *Ruz al-Yusuf* – a newspaper whose original journalistic formula assured its continued success – the new intake of journalists came to learn the tricks of the trade from 'those in the know'. This new generation also had its own vision for journalism and strove to impose it on the newspaper. What changes did this bring to Muhammad al-Tabi'i's old model and what effect did these changes have on *Ruz al-Yusuf*?

The Move from Pure Satire to News-based Satire

The belief that the arrival of a news press was a phenomenon exclusive to the 1940s and specifically to the *Akhbar al-Yawm* of the Amin brothers amounts to plunging the 1930s into a sort of 'media prehistory'.[63] This claim is difficult to accept. The fact that journalists in the 1930s should have competed with each other at all in the search for news probably points towards a change in public taste that no longer only sought the reflection of their convictions and beliefs but attributed to newspapers a principally informative role.

The category of reporter already dates back to the 1920s. Reporters were mainly taken on by daily papers to provide editors with the news they needed to write their articles. Describing his job at the newspaper, Gharib said that he 'would adapt news brought in by reporters to the paper's [satirical] style'.⁶⁴ The fact that al-Tabi'i almost exclusively based his articles on commentary of the week's political events or on his readings of other press sources shows that a lot had already changed since the 1920s.⁶⁵ Examination of the changes at *Ruz al-Yusuf* in the 1920s and 1930s highlights a shift in its treatment of news. While the newspaper was an exclusively satirical publication under Muhammad Mahmud's term as prime minister (1928–9), this satire was increasingly coupled with references to scoops and so to news. The newspaper went from timidly informing its readership of the exclusive nature of its news and declarations to devoting entire articles to the subject, 'very modestly' enumerating the exclusives it had managed to uncover.⁶⁶ *Ruz al-Yusuf* saw itself shift gradually from being a politically engaged publication dealing in short news items to being a politically engaged publication competing with the established newssheets.

The key players of the period attributed this change to a clash between two opposing conceptions of journalism. On the one hand, the partisan wing led by Muhammad al-Tabi'i advocated an image of journalism based on comment and news in brief, while on the other hand, the new generation in particular, headed up by Mustafa Amin, contended that it was a paper's news content and reporting that were fundamental to its success. The latter vision of journalism emerged victorious after Fatima al-Yusuf threw her weight behind the newcomers.⁶⁷ It may be, however, that the collective memory within journalistic circles tended to exaggerate Muhammad al-Tabi'i's aversion to competitive newsgathering, especially as it was Mustafa Amin in particular who popularised this idea.⁶⁸ Although it is indeed undeniable that the trend for publicising scoops in the newspaper increased considerably after Amin's arrival, the fact remains that this practice began well before he joined the newspaper. But were these 'scoops' the same as those that came afterwards? In the majority of cases they were indeed news stories revealed to readers who were left in no doubt as to their exclusive nature.⁶⁹

Journalistic practice had undergone a change, however, in the time between the exclusives of al-Tabi'i and those of Mustafa Amin. Prior to the new generation's rise to power, al-Tabi'i referred to exclusive stories published in the newspaper as being the result of 'the journalist's trenchant analysis of the political situation which allows him to reach conclusions before others'.⁷⁰ Here, the journalist was above all else a skilled analyst. What set newspapers apart from their competitors after that was 'better sources'.⁷¹ News scoops were thus centred on the ability of journalists to publish 'something new' and to be the very first to 'inform'. *Ruz al-Yusuf* placed its editors centre stage and sometimes portrayed them as bona fide detectives, eavesdropping on conversations and unearthing new stories.⁷² One short column was entitled 'From our Reporter Sherlock Holmes' (*Li-mukhbirina* Sherlock Holmes).⁷³ Newspapers were thus engaged in a bitter struggle for all things 'new' and *Ruz al-Yusuf* locked horns not only with satirical newspapers through caricatures and mocking articles (as it had in the 1920s) but also with the big daily papers⁷⁴ by its allegations that these giants were taking news stories first published by *Ruz al-Yusuf* and claiming them as their own.⁷⁵ The race to find news was to have lasting consequences for the format of the newspaper itself, with an increased number of brief news items and pages punctuated with short features at the expense of traditional articles. Although the number of columns remained stable between 1931 and 1934 (nine on average), each was split into separate paragraphs with individual headings. Not even the editorial was spared, and it ended up being scrapped.⁷⁶ Some of the newspaper's content was occasionally pulled 'at the last minute when it no longer squared with the latest political rumours'.⁷⁷ A less welcome consequence of the race for news was news fabrication. The newspaper found itself accused of this many times. Between 31 August 1931, the date which coincided with the mass intake of the new generation of journalists, and 2 July 1934, when al-Tabi'i left accompanied by a large portion of the editing team, *Ruz al-Yusuf* printed no fewer than eighty-one official disclaimers and apologies for editorial mistakes or for the misconduct of one of its journalists. This trend continued, and the newspaper became the subject of numerous investigations carried out by the public prosecutor and appearances before the courts.

Conclusion

No product, however intellectual, can be studied in isolation from those who 'made' it. *Ruz al-Yusuf* began its life during a period of abundant intellectual activity. A 'new and modern Egypt' had to be built. The weekly newspaper brought key players together, such as writers, lawyers, doctors, students and journalists. The most obvious common denominator amongst these groups was their intention to bring cultural renewal to Egypt by reappropriating a sense of the country's 'modernity'. Reappropriation did not, however, amount to imitation. Egypt was, for the most part, defining itself by opposition to the Western model. More specifically, this involved importing elements (such as modes of expression) from abroad and 'Egyptianising' them so that they assimilated seamlessly into Egyptian culture and left no trace of their foreign origins. The generations of men and women in question were all the more capable of achieving their goal thanks to their shared knowledge of European languages and literatures. In its political struggle against colonialism and its reductive discourse, nationalism expressed through culture 'borrowed' in order to form its own counter-discourse that nonetheless avoided accusations of being Western. This borrowing was seen more as an expression of the universality of cultural tools. The same was true of the theatre, of literature and of the press.

Having started out as a newspaper focused on the world of art and literature, *Ruz al-Yusuf* appealed to all manner of people for whom it provided a forum to participate in public debate. These people did not earn a living from press writing. The newspaper's transformation into a successful political publication, however, was to see *Ruz al-Yusuf* become a magnet for a new breed of writer: the journalist who commentated on news, pursued arguments with political adversaries and who saw the newspaper as a 'product'. The more the weekly 'established itself' on the Egyptian media scene, the more numerous these journalists became. Terms like 'sales figures', 'advertising revenues' and 'income' became part and parcel of journalistic vocabulary. Decision-making within the newspaper's very nucleus, its editing team, began to be dictated by the logic of the market. This signalled the emergence of a 'journalistic field' in Egypt, in the sense of a social network functioning according to its very own rules that cannot be ignored in explaining how it evolved.[78] From then on, journalism became a profession and a way to earn a living for those at *Ruz al-Yusuf*. The result was that the issue of the newspaper's political leanings often become a secondary concern. Increasing professional unity came as a result of 'shared experience' and 'common know-how'. The slight change in direction brought about by the triumph of the new generation's vision of journalism and the journalistic profession started to move the newspaper away from being just 'opinion-based' towards being 'news-based opinion', thereby marrying two concepts falsely held to be mutually exclusive. Professional practice was also well ahead of legislation, for although the definition of the journalist had become largely standardised in the 1930s, it was not until the 1940s that journalism gained legal recognition. This perhaps explains why – when approaching the field of journalism – certain industry insiders and academics only date the birth of the modern profession back to when it gained statutory recognition. Only the closest examination of professional practice, however, can provide us with a true picture of how journalism changed and when it evolved.

Notes

1. A weekly magazine founded in 1925 by Fatima al-Yusuf, a theatre actress whose career was faltering, *Ruz al-Yusuf* began as a literary publication but soon turned to politics and became one of the major satirical publications in Egypt from 1928 to 1934, under the direction of Muhammad al-Tabi'i, the editor-in-chief. The magazine continues to be published today but its content is completely different. [This chapter has been translated from a French original. *Eds*]
2. Any historical or sociological study on the composition of the journalistic field is hampered by the lack of information available to researchers and the poverty of archives, particularly from press houses. In the case of *Ruz al-Yusuf*, from a total of 564 signatures listed for the period studied – categorised as 18 journalists, 16 caricaturists, 17 writers, 9 poets, 177 readers, 89 pseudonyms, 196 unknown and 42 people coming from different professions, such as actors, politicians and musicians – we have information on only about 60 people.
3. Uncounted are the tens of cases which start by specifying that the idea of the article was suggested by the reading of a certain European work or publication.
4. *Ruz al-Yusuf* (henceforth *RY*) no. 190 (5 October 1931), p. 6.
5. *RY* no. 193 (26 October 1931), p. 15.
6. *RY* no. 303 (4 December 1933), p. 16.
7. *RY* no. 294 (2 October 1933), p. 25.
8. *RY* no. 328 (4 June 1934), p. 3.
9. *RY* no. 158 (4 February 1930), p. 5; no. 336 (30 July 1934), p. 8.
10. *Akhbar al-Yawm* 13 August 1955; *Sabah al-Khayr* 13 October 1976, in Akhbar al-Yawm Press Files (henceforth AYPF) no. 549 'Fikri Abaza', vol. 2 'Interviews'.

11. *Al-Kawakib* 16 June 1970, in AYPF no. 10649 'Hilmi Halim'.
12. *Al-Musawwar* 28 September 1962, in AYPF no. 184 "Abbas Mahmud al-'Aqqad', vol. 2 'Divers'.
13. Jum'a, *Shahid 'ala-l-'asr*, p. 83.
14. For the evidence of al-'Aqqad, see al-'Aqqad, *Hayat qalam*, p. 41. For more details on the languages of instruction in the Egyptian education system of the time, see 'Ali, *Dawr al-ta'lim*, especially pp. 95–131.
15. Gershoni and Jankowski, *Redefining the Egyptian Nation*, p. 280.
16. For a further critique of Jankowski and Gershoni's work, see Smith, 'Imagined Identities'.
17. Between *RY* no. 178 (24 June 1930) and no. 350 (5 November 1934), 55 articles refer to the 'colonial policy' of either France or Great Britain, and 180 to the interference of the latter in the internal affairs of Egypt against only 21 which stress a common membership of the countries of the East.
18. al-'Aqqad, *'Abqariyyat Muhammad*, p. 294.
19. Jum'a, *Thawrat al-islam*.
20. al-Tuni, *Muhammad fi tufulatih wa sibah*, p. 635.
21. *Al-Ahram* 3 April 1964, in AYPF no. 184 "Abbas Mahmud al-'Aqqad', vol. 2 'Divers'.
22. For example, Jum'a, *Shahid 'ala-l-'asr*, pp. 163, 608.
23. Ibid., p. 164.
24. *Al-Akhbar* 28 April 1993, in AYPF no. 3402 'Muhammad Lutfi Jum'a'.
25. This column appeared between *RY* no. 324 (7 May 1934) and no. 364 (11 February 1935).
26. India particularly held the attention of *Ruz al-Yusuf*, which regularly published articles on Gandhi and made comparisons between his actions and those of Sa'd Zaghlul. Certain writers were also in direct contact with Indian nationalists.
27. Abaza, *Al-dahik al-baki*, p. 147.
28. Ibid., p. 218.
29. On this issue, see Said, *Culture et impérialisme*, p. 558.
30. 'Awadin, *Al-Mazini*, p. 70.
31. See, for example, 'Ma'arik Taha Husayn wa al-'Aqqad, hizban wa thaqafatan' (The Battles of Taha Husayn and 'Aqqad, Two Parties, Two Cultures), *Akhbar al-adab* 8 May 1994, in AYPF no. 184 "Abbas Mahmud al-'Aqqad'.
32. al-Quwisni, *Ihsan 'Abd al-Quddus*, p. 12.
33. Musa, *Al-Sihafa*, p. 50.
34. Jum'a, *Shahid 'ala-l-'asr*, p. 76.

35. This title appears between *RY* no. 328 (4 June 1934) and no. 348 (22 October 1934).
36. This title appears between *RY* no. 349 (29 October 1934) and no. 372 (8 April 1935).
37. *RY* returned to this aspect in practically every issue where the column appeared.
38. *RY* no. 351 (12 November 1934), p. 28.
39. *RY* no. 356 (17 December 1934), p. 28.
40. *RY* no. 351 (12 November 1934), p. 28; no. 356 (17 December 1934), p. 28.
41. On this point, see 'Arif, *Ana wa barunat al-sihafa*, pp. 241–7.
42. 'An individual, who practises his professional activity for one or more bodies of information ... ensures whole or part of the work of collection, treatment and presentation of information relative to facts or contemporary events.' Balle, *Dictionnaire des médias*, p. 134. Ruellan is right to qualify the definition of 'tautological' because it conceals the essence of the practice of the trade. Ruellan, *Le professionnalisme du flou*, p. 62.
43. Charle, *Le siècle de la presse*, p. 143.
44. Martin, *Le canard enchainé*, p. 39.
45. Ibid., p. 122 ('journalistes qui complètent leurs revenus par une activité professionnelle "alimentaire"').
46. *RY* no. 116 (28 February 1928), pp. 3, 18.
47. Ruellan, *Le professionnalisme du flou*, p. 68.
48. Kamil, 'Al-Sihafa al-wafdiyya 1919–1952', p. 508.
49. The column stops after *RY* no. 126 (8 May 1928) but reappears in no. 304 (11 December 1933).
50. See typewritten article of Mahmud al-Badawi, in AYPF no. 41 'Muhammad 'Ali Gharib'; also *Al-Jil al-jadid* no. 129 (14 June 1954), p. 25 (testimony of M. A. Gharib).
51. *Al-Sarkha* no. 53 (16 August 1931), p. 1.
52. Abu al-Magd, *Muhammad al-Tabi'i*, p. 376.
53. al-Shiliq, *Hizb al-ahrar*, p. 153.
54. al-Yusuf, *Dhikrayat*, p. 123.
55. For an overview of where journalists socialised, see *al-Musawwar* no. 456 (7 July 1933), p. 8.
56. al-Yusuf, *Dhikrayat*, p. 127.
57. *RY* no. 3777 (28 October 2000), p. 40.
58. Ibid.

59. *RY* no. 53 (3 November 1926), p. 9; no. 54 (10 November 1926), p. 9.
60. Compare the account of Ahmad Hasan in Abu al-Magd, *Muhammad al-Tabi'i*, pp. 415–16.
61. al-Yusuf, *Dhikrayat*, p. 123.
62. Ibid., p. 124.
63. In his book *al-Thawra fi al-sihafa*, which is dedicated to *Akhbar al-Yawm*, founded by the Amin brothers, Sami 'Aziz speaks of a 'révolution'.
64. *Al-Jil al-jadid* no. 129 (14 June 1954), p. 24.
65. *Al-Musawwar* no. 1806 (22 May 1959), pp. 38–9.
66. *RY* no. 288 (21 August 1933), p. 4.
67. *Akhbar al-Yawm* (25 February 1976), in AYPF no. 49 'Muhammad al-Tabi'i', vol. 1 'Biographie'.
68. See, for example, *Akhir Sa'a* (4 January 1984), in AYPF no. 49 'Muhammad al-Tabi'i', vol. 1 'Biographie'.
69. For example, *RY* no. 156 (21 January 1930), p. 6; no. 175 (3 June 1930), p. 4.
70. *RY* no. 193 (26 October 1931), p. 12.
71. *RY* no. 260 (6 February 1933), p. 4.
72. *RY* no. 256 (9 January 1933), p. 14.
73. The title appears between *RY* no. 366 (25 February 1935) and no. 375 (29 April 1935).
74. *RY* no. 251 (5 December 1932), p. 4; no. 268 (3 April 1933), p. 5; no. 288 (21 August 1933), p. 4.
75. *RY* no. 294 (2 October 1933), p. 10.
76. The last editorial of this period was published in *RY* no. 241 (26 September 1932).
77. *RY* no. 299 (6 November 1933), p. 5.
78. On the conception of an intellectual field and its working, see the works of Bourdieu, 'Champ intellectuel et projet créateur'; 'Champ du pouvoir, champ intellectuel et habitus de classe'; *Choses dites*.

Bibliography

Abaza, Fikri, *Al-Dahik al-baki* (Alexandria: al-Maktab al-misri al-hadith lil-taba'a wa-l-nashr, [1933] 1973).

Abu al-Magd, Sabri, *Muhammad al-Tabi'i* (Cairo: Markaz al-dirasat al-suhufiyya wa tarikhiyya bi-mu'assasat dar al-ta'wun, 1986).

'Ali, Sa'id Isma'il, *Dawr al-ta'lim fi al-nidal al-watani zaman al-ihtilal al-baritani* (Cairo: al-Hay'a al-misriyya al-'amma lil-kitab, 1995).

al-ʿAqqad, ʿAbbas Mahmud, *Abqariyyat Muhammad* (Cairo: Matbaʿat al-istiqamah, 1943).
al-ʿAqqad, ʿAbbas Mahmud, *Ana* (Cairo: Dar al-hilal, 1964).
al-ʿAqqad, ʿAbbas Mahmud, *Hayat qalam* (Cairo: Dar al-maʿarif, 1983).
ʿArif, Jamil *Ana wa barunat al-sihafa* (Cairo: al-Dar al-ʿarabiyya lil-tibaʿa wa-l-nashr wa-l-tawziʿ, 1993).
ʿAwadin, Ahmad al-Sayyid, *Al-Mazini baʿd nisf qarn* (Cairo: Dar al-hilal, 1998).
ʿAziz, Sami, *al-Thawra fi al-sihafa* (Cairo: Matbaʾat misr, 1956)
Balle, Francis, *Dictionnaire des médias* (Paris: Larousse, 1998).
Bourdieu, Pierre, 'Champ du pouvoir, champ intellectuel et habitus de classe', *Scolies* 1 (1971), pp. 7–26.
Bourdieu, Pierre, 'Champ intellectuel et projet créateur', *Les Temps Modernes* 246 (November 1966), pp. 805–906.
Bourdieu, Pierre, *Choses dites* (Paris: Les Éditions de Minuit, 1987), pp. 167–77.
Charle, Christophe, *Le siècle de la presse (1830–1939)* (Paris: Seuil, 2004).
Gershoni, Israel and James Jankowski, *Redefining the Egyptian Nation, 1930–1945* (Cambridge: Cambridge University Press, 1995).
Jumʿa, Muhammad Lutfi, *Shahid ʿala al-ʿasr. Mudhakkirat Muhammad Lutfi Jumʿa* (Cairo: al-Hayʾa al-misriyya al-ʿamma lil-kitab, 2000).
Jumʿa, Muhammad Lutfi, *Thawrat al-islam wa-batal al-anbiyaʾ Abu al-Qasim Muhammad Ibn ʿAbd Allah* (Cairo: Alam al-Kutub, [1939] 2002).
Kamil, Najwa, 'Al-Sihafa al-wafdiyya 1919–1952', in Gamal Badawi and Lamʿi al-Mutiʿi (eds), *Tarikh al-Wafd* (Cairo: Dar al-Shuruq, 2003).
Martin, Laurent, *Le canard enchaîné: Histoire d'un journal satirique (1915–2005)* (Paris: Nouveau monde éditions, 2005).
Musa, Salama, *Al-Sihafa, hirfa wa risala* (Cairo: Salama Musa lil-nashr wa-l-tawziʿ, 1963).
al-Quwisni, Nirmin, *Ihsan ʿAbd al-Quddus, Ams wa-l-yawm wa ghadan* (Cairo: Diyasik, 1991).
Ruellan, Denis, *Le professionnalisme du flou: Identité et savoir-faire des journalistes français* (Grenoble: Presses universitaires de Grenoble, 1993).
Said, Edward W., *Culture et impérialisme*, trans. Paul Chemla (Paris: Fayard, 2000).
al-Shiliq, Ahmad Zakariyya, *Hizb al-ahrar al-dusturiyyin 1922–1953* (Cairo: Dar al-Maʿarif, 1982).
Smith, Charles D., '"Imagined Identities, Imagined Nationalisms: Print Culture and Egyptian Nationalism in Light of Recent Scholarship", A Review Essay of Israel Gershoni and James P. Jankowski, *Redefining the Egyptian Nation,*

1930–1945, Cambridge Middle East Studies (New York: Cambridge University Press, 1995). PP. 297', *International Journal of Middle East Studies* 29:4 (1997), pp. 607–22.

al-Tuni, Muhammad Shawkat, *Muhammad fi tufulatih wa sibah* (Cairo: Matba'at misr, 1959).

al-Yusuf, Fatima, *Dhikrayat* (Cairo: Ruz al-Yusuf, 1953).

PART III
CRITICAL, DISSIDENT VOICES

8

The Anarchist Press in Egypt before World War I

Anthony Gorman

In February 1877 an Italian-language newspaper appeared on the streets of Alexandria announcing itself as an organ of the International, the organisation founded in London in 1864 to represent the interests of working men. Soon suppressed by the authorities, *Il Lavoratore* represented the first of a series of anarchist newspapers published in Egypt over a period of almost forty years but which was particularly active in the decade and a half before World War I. Produced by resident militants and comprising more than a dozen titles, this press testified to the local emergence of an internationalist movement that reflected a multiethnic membership which was predominantly Italian but which in time came to include other linguistic and national communities. Its distinctive mission was to promote a radical critique of the combined evils of nationalism, capitalism and religion through a programme of social emancipation inspired by the new ideas of science, secularism and social justice. At the same time the record of the anarchist press in Egypt demonstrates many of the political and financial difficulties faced by dissident newspapers that attracted the hostility of the authorities and relied on the modest resources of a relatively small group of activists.

Emergence of the Press in Egypt

Apart from a brief appearance during the French occupation, the first local newspaper in Egypt, *al-Waqa'i' al-Misriyya*, an official government publication, was launched in 1828. A number of titles appeared over subsequent decades but it was not until the second half of the nineteenth century that the Egyptian press took on a more dynamic, diverse and privately owned character. The press emerged not only as an important medium of news and communication for the public but also as a forum of expression for the ideas and interests of an increasingly vibrant heterogeneous society.

In this the foreign-language press led the way, a sign of the increasing presence of resident foreign communities in the country and growing international influence. The Italian-language *Lo Spettatore Egiziano* was at the forefront in 1846, and was followed by a series of Italian- and French-language papers in the 1850s and the first Greek-language title, *I Aiguptos*, in 1862. From the 1870s, this phenomenon took on a new energy and dynamism across different language communities, notably in Italian, French, Greek and Arabic. *Le Phare d'Alexandrie* (French, est. 1874), *Il Messaggiere Egiziano* (Italian, est. 1875), *Kairon* (Greek, est. 1873) and the *Egyptian Gazette* (English, est. 1880) became well-established titles among the foreign-language press while the emergence of *al-Ahram* (est. 1875), *al-Muqattam* (est. 1889) and *al-Mu'ayyad* (est. 1889) expanded the offerings to an Arabic-reading audience. By the end of the century, the number of newspapers had multiplied dramatically, speaking to and of diverse audiences and constituencies. They promoted a wide range of social, political, economic and cultural perspectives from official announcements to commercial information, from local news and current affairs to radical social critiques, from serious literary and scientific reviews to illustrated satirical magazines.

In this increasingly polyphonic milieu, the anarchist press appeared, first briefly in the late 1870s, then in a more sustained presence in the decade and a half before World War I. Multilingual and ideologically heterogeneous, it collectively represented a non-elite voice that projected a new, radical vision of social emancipation. Produced and consumed principally by resident foreigners though with aspirations for a wider audience, it was internationalist in imagination and distribution but engaged with local Egyptian conditions in promoting a programme that stood apart from the competing nationalist, colonial and communitarian perspectives of the mainstream press.[1]

Anarchist Origins

The first signs of anarchist activity appear in Egypt amongst resident Italian workers in Alexandria in the 1860s.[2] Many had been drawn to the economic opportunities offered in a country embarking on an ambitious programme of modernisation of military, state administration and public infrastructure. In addition Egypt afforded a place of refuge for political exiles, particularly attractive to a diverse range of Italian nationalists, radical reformers and revolutionaries.[3] This combination of labour and political activists proved a fertile foundation for the emergence of a new radical politics. Established in Alexandria in the early 1860s, the Società Operaia Italiana (Italian Workers Society) represented the first in a series of Italian organisations that embraced the cause of workers. By the middle of the next decade veterans from Garibaldi's campaigns and other militants in exile had formed Pensiero ed Azione (Thought and Action), an association based on Mazzinian principles.[4] Soon after, in 1876, a more radical group in Alexandria split to form an official section of the International. Additional sections were formed in Cairo, Port Said and Ismailia and were represented at the Anti-Authoritarian International held at Verviers in Belgium in September the following year.[5]

The early years of anarchist organisation in Egypt were plagued by the fragmentation, disputation and factionalism that characterised the movement elsewhere.[6] In Italy the defection of Andrea Costa (who had represented the Egyptian sections at Verviers) to legalitarian socialism in 1879 provoked a significant local schism. Ongoing internal divisions based on personalities and ideological faultlines, particularly between anti-organisationalists (or individualists) and anarcho-syndicalists on the role of collective associations in achieving anarchist aims, wracked the movement.[7] By the beginning of the twentieth century the syndicalist tendency was emerging as the dominant element within the movement in Egypt, a development that reflected the transformation of the local labour force and the successful activism in Cairo and Alexandria. The celebrated cigarette workers' strike of 1899–1900 in which anarchists were involved was heralded as a great victory and launched a sustained period of labour militancy. Thereafter anarcho-syndicalists played a crucial role in agitating for the cause of workers, particularly in international unions, such as the International Union of Workers and Employees in Cairo, which presented a broad, multiethnic front in industrial campaigns that called for the respect of workers' rights and social justice, and in 'leagues of resistance'.[8] By 1910, syndicalism had emerged as a significant industrial, even moral, force that would continue to exercise considerable influence in labour organisation and militancy in the lead-up to World War I and subsequently during the upheaval of the 1919 Revolution.

The Press and 'Propaganda of the Word'

In promoting the aims of the movement in Egypt, the anarchist press played a central role. In the period from 1901 to 1914 at least fifteen separate titles, most of them weeklies and in Italian, embraced the strategy (in anarchist parlance) of 'propaganda of the word', taking up the causes of labour militancy, public education and health, social justice and secularism.[9] Along with industrial action itself, the press was a critical means of defining the values and the activities of the anarchist movement. As the editors explained in the first issue of *La Tribuna Libera* in October 1901:

> It is for this [human emancipation] that we begin the publication of *Le Tribune Libre* in order to propagate the doctrines that illuminate the new ideas, the new aspirations; doctrines that are the result of profound scientific studies, of the experience of life and that follow the inclination of our nature.[10]

L'Operaio, a weekly launched the following year, put forward a more detailed case for the fundamental role of a newspaper in disseminating the ideas of the movement and providing a vehicle for the voices of its members:

> We believe a newspaper is necessary: firstly, in order to facilitate communications between workers; secondly, to be able to show the example of work undertaken by others in other similar countries to create also among us here in Egypt the beneficent feeling of emulation; thirdly, in order to have a free organ, of our class, that can have its columns open to whatever protest on our part in defence of our rights and our dignity so often outraged by those on whom we depend against our will; and finally,

because we wish to propagate those ideas of emancipation that must open the way for us leading to the realisation of our desires for peace, well-being and liberty.[11]

In succeeding years a number of titles took up elements of this mission, with varying emphases, even at times competing with one another. In 1909 the anarchist conference held in Alexandria, which brought together activists from all over Egypt, reflected a clearer desire to coordinate these efforts. In a communiqué issued afterwards the role of the press was again emphasised and a resolution passed on how best to organise future efforts:

> All recognise the need to publish an anarchist newspaper. This will contain articles of straightforward propaganda in such a way that the reader can finally learn the first elements of anarchist principles. It must be edited in a simple and easy form within the capacity of all intelligences. It must concern itself with all issues of the day, of labour and social movements, and make comments and criticism from the anarchist point of view spring forth.[12]

Accordingly, it was agreed that the newspaper, to be named *L'Idea*, should in the first instance be issued on a fortnightly basis and be edited by a committee made up of elected members from Alexandria and Cairo. Each issue would be published in a run of 2,000 copies that would be distributed free, with the expenses to be shared equally between members in Alexandria and Cairo.

Anarchism and its Dissident Voices

The appearance of *Il Lavoratore* in 1877 had represented the first local example of this ongoing strategy. Described later by one of its editors as '[leaving] much to be desired from a linguistic and grammatical point of view although it did not lack good material',[13] the newspaper made sufficient impact to attract the attention and hostility of the Italian consulate, which, after only three issues, successfully requested the Egyptian authorities to close it down. The editors responded by publishing under a new title, *Il Proletariato*, but it suffered the same fate as its predecessor after only one issue.

Despite this reverse and the subsequent repression campaign against anarchists internationally, in Egypt the movement regrouped and convened at Sidi Gaber in 1881.[14] Rumours that year of the launch in Alexandria of a new newspaper, *Demoliamo!*, did not materialise but one anarchist group secured an old printing press to produce posters and leaflets promoting its ideas, publicising declarations and calls to action, and commemorating occasions such as the tenth anniversary of the Paris Commune. For the rest of the decade and beyond, the dissemination and circulation of anarchist ideas appears to have been conducted principally through small study groups and occasional announcements rather than any regular periodical.[15]

In 1895, the anarchist *Il Trovatore* appeared briefly in Port Said but it was not until the beginning of the new century that the anarchist press would establish itself in a more significant way.[16] From 1901, it would be a regular and ongoing if often interrupted presence in Egypt in the years leading up to World War I. *La Tribuna Libera/Le Tribune Libre*, a bilingual with two pages each in Italian and French, heralded this new burst of activity with its launch in Alexandria in October of that year. Announcing itself as an 'International organ for the emancipation of the Proletariat', it appeared at a time when the labour movement had scored some notable local successes as a result of strikes by cigarette workers and tailors. While not bound to a strict syndicalist programme, from its first issue the newspaper made clear its condemnation of 'the tyranny of capital' and sought nothing less than the 'complete emancipation of moral-political-economic and social slavery' of the workers of the world.[17]

Over the course of seven issues, *La Tribuna Libera* presented an early template for the local anarchist press to follow in the ensuing years. Composed of four pages of four columns each, the front page carried the editorial announcing the programme followed by a social critique ('Come pensiamo'), and the first instalment in a series 'Comunismo e Anarchia'. International news of the movement from the United States, Argentina and Brazil featured on the second page with some local news items from Cairo (a hanging) and from Alexandria (a labour dispute). A column followed on the Free Popular University, which had opened earlier in the year in Alexandria and provided free evening courses for the popular classes.[18] The second (French) half of the paper provided translations of some of the Italian material but also some additional pieces, such as an article on religious slavery ('L'esclavage religieux') and the first instalment of a series by Dutch socialist

Ferdinand Domela Nieuwenhuis on libertarian education. Subsequent issues would carry letters to the editor and publicity on various anarchist literature.

La Tribuna Libera folded at the end of 1901 principally as a result of financial problems compounded by factional divisions within the movement, chiefly between Jewish and Italian anarchists;[19] however, other titles would take up the role of anarchist mouthpiece even if they emphasised different elements within the ideological spectrum. In Alexandria the weekly *L'Operaio* (The Worker) (1902–3) embraced an explicitly anarcho-syndicalist line with news and discussion on workers' associations, education and public health.[20] *Il Domani* (Tomorrow), launched in Cairo in 1903, adopted a stridently individualist, libertarian position aimed in part at combatting the ideas of the syndicalists. A more up-market fortnightly journal *Lux!* (Light!) (1903), edited by Roberto D'Angio, presented extensive discussions of anarchist theory and practice, while an Alexandrian weekly, *Risorgete!* (Rise Again!) (1908–10), was identified with a strong anti-clerical line.[21] The period ends with the anarcho-syndicalist weekly *L'Unione* that was closed down in October 1914 amidst a campaign of general press repression soon after the outbreak of World War I.[22]

In addition to these ideological nuances, the multilingual aspect of the anarchist press in Egypt reflected the particular character of its membership. Italian and French functioned as its principal languages: the former represented the language of the majority of activists while the latter had come to displace Italian as the lingua franca among many foreigners in Egypt. Of the two other languages known to have been used by anarchists in conferences and featured in anarchist literature, Hebrew does not appear to have been used in the local press, although it was discussed for a section of *La Tribuna Libera* at one point.[23] Greek, by contrast, had a strong profile in local anarchist literature. Greek activists in the broad socialist movement had been present in Egypt since at least the 1880s. When *Sosialistis*, a newspaper published in Athens, appeared in 1890 it very quickly gained subscribers in Cairo and Alexandria.[24] The rise of the organised labour movement, particularly amongst cigarette workers, further served as a basis for substantial Greek participation in militant labour and international unions.[25] During the industrial battles at the end of 1901, the Greek-language Cairo newspaper *Ergasia* (Labour) took a strong pro-worker, if not specifically anarchist, line. Cigarette workers suffered several reverses in the following years but a resurgence of activity in 1908 coincided with the launch of *O Ergatis* (The Worker), the first local anarchist newspaper in Greek, which declared itself an 'organ of emancipation of women and the worker'.[26] *L'Idea*, a product of resolutions at the 1909 anarchist conference, soon appeared with Italian-, French- and Greek-language sections. This Greek-language press was supplemented by a substantial Greek pamphlet literature such as the works of Nicholas Doumas and Stavros Kouchtsoglou, and in periodicals, notably *Grammata* (Alexandria).[27]

The titles of these newspapers referenced the basic values of the anarchist movement. Some invoked the key principles of freedom and liberty, such as *La Tribuna Libera* (1901), *L'Indipendente* and *L'Idea*, or implied the notion of a brighter future, such as *Il Domani* (Tomorrow), *Lux!* (Light!) and *Risorgete!* (Rise Again!). Unity was also stressed as a cardinal virtue (*L'Unione della Democrazia*, *L'Unione*). Other titles such as *Il Lavoratore*, *Il Proletariato*, *L'Operaio* and *O Ergatis* emphasised the centrality of labour. The single-issue *Pro-Ferrer* served as a protest against the trial and treatment of Francisco Ferrer by the Spanish government in September 1909. The subtitles and masthead slogans reinforced these aspirations. *L'Operaio* carried Marx's 'Lavoratori di tutto il mondo, unitevi!' (Workers of the world, unite!) and *L'Idea* called for 'Rivendicazione sociale' (Social rights). Others announced themselves as the 'Organ of emancipation of women and the worker' (*O Ergatis*), or the 'International organ for the emancipation of the proletariat' (*La Tribuna Libera*, 1901). *L'Unione* in its back-page appeal for readers called itself 'a newspaper that strenuously defends the interests of the working class, and is a sword for the weak and a whip for the bully'.[28]

Its polyglottal character notwithstanding, the anarchist press in Egypt does not appear to have produced a dedicated publication in Arabic.[29] The reason may be due in part to the language barrier, most obvious in published form, between the resident foreign and Egyptian working class. Anarchism was not unfamiliar to the Arabophone reader. From the 1890s, anarchism (usually *fawdawiyya* in Arabic) and the activities of its advocates featured in reports and articles in the mainstream Arabic press such as *al-Ahram* and *al-Muqattam*, more often on developments abroad but occasionally on local affairs.[30] Modernist journals such as *al-Muqtataf* and *al-Hilal* also carried pieces discussing the origins and development of anarchist thought and practice, sometimes in the context of the broader socialist movement, such as the short series on socialists and anarchists that appeared in *al-Muqtataf* in the summer of 1894.[31] Indeed, some Arabic-language periodicals engaged with, or were influenced by, a wide range of socialist and anarchist ideas. These included *al-Jami'a al-Uthmaniyya* (est. 1897), edited by Farah Antun, and *al-Mustaqbal* (est. 1914), a weekly that featured the work of writers Salama Musa and Shibli Shumayyil.[32]

Editors and Contributors

The anarchist press in Egypt was the product of the combined efforts of a nucleus of activists supported by a wider circle of contributors and readers. The main figures were, with some exceptions, not professional journalists but came from a range of occupational backgrounds, who by dint of their ideological commitment established a record of advocacy in both word and deed. Icilio Ugo Parrini (1850–1906), a printer by trade from Livorno and a staunch advocate of individualist anarchism, stood as a central figure of the movement from the time of his first arrival in Egypt in 1871 until his death in Mansura.[33] Initially a member of Pensiero ed Azione, Parrini had played a leading role in forming a section of the International in 1876. In 1877, with Giacomo Costa and Giuseppe Messina, he launched the short-lived *Il Lavoratore* and *Il Proletariato* and was responsible for setting up the clandestine printing press in Alexandria in the early 1880s. Expelled from Egypt following the Urabi revolt of 1882, he returned in the early 1890s and continued to act as Egyptian correspondent for many anarchist newspapers in Europe and the Americas. Locally, Parrini launched and co-edited with Romolo Garbati *Il Domani* in Cairo in 1903. A slightly later but no less important figure was Joseph (Giuseppe) Rosenthal (1867–?), a jeweller, born in Safed in Palestine. From the time of his arrival in Egypt in c. 1899, Rosenthal showed himself to be a skilful labour organiser and a particularly influential figure among Jewish anarchists in Alexandria. His role in the anarchist press was seminal: he launched the bilingual *La Tribuna Libera*, served as a member of the editorial committee of *L'Idea* and featured prominently in the protests against the imprisonment (and subsequent execution) of Francisco Ferrer by the Spanish government in 1909, an occasion marked by the publication of a *numero unico* (single issue).³⁴ Another key figure was the Florentine Pietro Vasai (1866–1916), also a printer by trade, who had established a record of distinguished militancy, including two years' imprisonment in Italy, even before his arrival in Alexandria in 1898. An educated man, he had earlier been involved in the publication of *La Questione sociale* in Florence and a cultural magazine, *L'Etna* (1895), in Tunisia.³⁵ In Egypt he was instrumental in setting up a number of anarchist titles, such as *L'Operaio*, *L'Indipendente*, *L'Idea* and *L'Unione*, and he remained a committed militant until his deportation to Italy in 1916. Among Greek activists, Nicholas Doumas, a tanner, and Stavros Kouchtsoglou, a tobacco worker, were prominent editors and pamphleteers with an established record of labour activism.

These figures were veteran organisers and skilled propagandists whose writing skills and experience were put to good effect in promotion of the anarchist cause. Some anarchists who were working journalists also contributed to that effort. Roberto D'Angio (1871–1923) had established a reputation as a skilled journalist as Naples correspondent for the Paris-based *Le Temps Nouveaux* before arriving in Alexandria at the beginning of 1901. Initially hired for Raoul Canivet's progressive newspaper, *La Réforme*, from 1902 he co-edited the weekly *L'Operaio* with Pietro Vasai as well as working for the mainstream daily *Il Corriere Egiziano*. The following year, after the demise of *L'Operaio*, D'Angio edited the anarchist review *Lux!*, arguably the most sophisticated anarchist publication of the period in Egypt. Other editors were or would become established authors in their own right. Romolo Garbati, co-editor with Parrini of *Il Domani*, was a pamphleteer and novelist; Umberto Bambini, editor of *Risorgete!*, a published author; and Giuseppe Ungaretti, editor of *L'Unione della Democrazia*, would establish an international reputation as a poet.

While the early anarchist newspapers of the decade were dominated by particular personalities, there was a noticeable shift to the structure of editorial committees to manage newspapers during the second half of the decade. This new arrangement, which may have been prompted by a realisation of the benefits of cooperation and assisted in part by the death of Parrini (who had been notoriously uncompromising in many matters), combined different anarchist elements and provided a stronger ideological punch. In 1907 the editorial board of the Greek-language *O Ergatis*, for example, brought together anarcho-syndicalists Nicholas Doumas, Stavros Kouchtsoglou, Iosef Chionis and K. Asteriadis (the last had earlier been the force behind *Ergasia* and labour correspondent of the Greek-language *Tilegraphos*) with Dr Georgios Saraphidis and Z. Hatzopoulos, individualist anarchists strongly influenced by the work of Nietzsche. This committee model was endorsed at the anarchist conference in 1909, which agreed on the establishment of a single newspaper, *L'Idea* (1909–11). This was to be managed by two committees drawing on some of the veterans of the movement: Pietro Vasai, Giovanni Brunello, Camillo Brigido and Umberto Bambini in Cairo, and in Alexandria, Francesco Cini, Francesco Donato, Costantino Ungaretti (brother of poet Giuseppe) and Joseph Rosenthal. Funded equally by anarchists in both cities, it offered the potential of a greater readership with articles in Italian, French and Greek. Its successor, *L'Unione*, launched in 1913, bilingual in French and Italian, was similarly co-edited by committees in Cairo and Alexandria.

Across this period, individual editors and editorial teams brought to publication local and international news, theoretical discussions and serialised material from prominent anarchist thinkers such as Peter Kropotkin. There was also a concerted effort to engage the readership itself. In addition to publishing letters to the editor, anarchist newspapers actively solicited and published contributions from readers. Proclaiming itself as a paper 'written by workers and for workers' (*scritto da operaie e per gli operai*), *L'Operaio* encouraged contributions from ordinary workers on topics that concerned their everyday lives: 'All workers can be our collaborators; we do not demand literary works but ideas and facts.'[36] In promoting local content the anarchist press also featured or translated articles from the local press as *L'Operaio* did with *al-Mu'ayyad*,[37] took issue with a rival newspaper such as *L'Oriente*,[38] or recognised the appearance of a new title.[39] Conversely, the appearance of a new anarchist paper was announced in the mainstream press, and certainly followed closely by the authorities.[40]

Readership and Distribution

The core readership of the anarchist press was the members and sympathisers of the movement in Cairo and Alexandria who could be relied upon to support its publications.[41] For these copies could be easily obtained through subscription, personal connections or consulted in small anarchist libraries that served as meeting places for activists. Attested since at least the early 1880s, venues such as the International Reading Room (*Sala di lettura internazionale*) in Cairo held both local and international anarchist newspapers and literature in a variety of languages that were available for consultation.[42] A regular feature of some anarchist publications, the *Piccola Posta*, where readers were answered in very minimalist terms in a collective column, also indicated readers in different parts of the country, such as Mansura, Port Said and Kafr al-Zayyat, as well as abroad.[43]

Newspaper editors were eager to spread their message beyond established anarchist circles, however. When *L'Operaio* appeared in the middle of 1902 its editors sought explicitly to extend its readership beyond the cities of Alexandria and Cairo and connect with workers throughout the country. They appealed to workers in Egyptian villages to subscribe and expressed their wish to penetrate public meetings and the families of all categories of workers.[44] Significantly, the editors of *L'Operaio* aimed to expand its audience beyond the Italian and resident foreign working communities and include native Egyptian workers, characterised in their initial flyer as a 'virgin element'. In pursuit of this aim the paper discussed aspects of the working life of Egyptians in its columns and stressed the importance of the need to organise themselves. When cabdrivers, almost all of whom were Egyptian, went on strike in Alexandria in 1903 the paper pronounced it as 'a great act of rebellion'.[45] Even if the editors would recognise that very few Egyptians were reading the paper, articles such as these represented a significant expression of internationalist solidarity across national lines.[46]

Nevertheless, there were clear obstacles to developing a wider readership. Basic literacy limited its accessibility among local foreign communities, although this was much higher than it was for native Egyptians.[47] That said, the common practice of reading newspapers out loud in cafes and taverns (the latter especially favoured by anarchists) provided access to the communication of news and ideas to the unlettered. The greater difficulty was language. Being for the most part in Italian and French and sometimes Greek, the anarchist press well served the Italian community and those that had functional French, as many Greeks, Armenians and at best certain Egyptian elites. Despite the internationalist sentiments, however, ignorance of European languages severely limited its access to many Egyptians.

Distribution was another important element in determining potential readership. Subscribers received their copies by mail although there appear to have been persistent problems with the postal service, with many subscribers complaining that their copies went missing.[48] In Egypt, especially within the cities, copies were also distributed, probably on a regular basis, by hand.[49] This practice was also used by individuals travelling across the Mediterranean to and from Egypt.[50] In discussions prior to the launching of *Il Domani*, Parrini had suggested that two young Arabs wearing shirts labelled with the name of the paper and crying out, 'Anarchist newspaper of Cairo!' distribute the paper in the streets, although this may not have gone ahead.[51]

In the weeks immediately after its launch, *L'Operaio* used the Libreria Calebotta, a bookshop in Alexandria in Sherif Pasha Street, as an outlet and for a time had a nominated agent.[52] Ultimately, however, the editors turned to their own readers to generate demand and called on them to ask for *L'Operaio* 'in cafes, clubs, restaurants, taverns, patisseries, barber shops and any other shop'.[53] *L'Indipendente* had established outlets in Cairo and Alexandria.

Newspaper circulation figures are difficult to ascertain given the incomplete nature of the evidence but it appears that the anarchist press was produced in significant numbers. The print runs of *La Tribuna Libera* and *Il Domani* were both reported as 1,000 copies, while the printing of 2,000 copies of the unified anarchist newspaper *L'Idea* was proposed in 1909.[54] (By comparison, in 1903 the mainstream daily *al-Muqattam* had a circulation of 3,000–4,000 and the nationalist *al-Liwa'*, of between 1,500 and 2000).[55]

The Local and the International

However the readership of the anarchist press might be characterised and counted, it forged a collective audience for news and communication in its announcements of labour news, discussions of social issues, local affairs, political events and relevant obituaries.[56] More than this, despite some sectarian differences, the press served as a vehicle to foster a sense of community among local activists across the country through its resolute calls for the emancipation of the working classes and an improvement in the fate of the common man.

In addition to communicating this sense of local identity, the anarchist press also engaged with an international network with which it had regular communication and interaction.⁵⁷ Sustained by a sense of international community and global mission, this network served an 'imagined community' created and consolidated not by print capitalism but by print *internationalism* through which disparate elements of the movement were kept connected and informed.⁵⁸ Facilitated by an increasingly developed international transport system, particularly through steamship services, and post and telegraph links, the international anarchist press served as a vital channel for dissemination and diffusion of ideas of a movement that saw itself as international in practice and conception.

These international connections were manifested in two important ways. First, anarchists in Egypt subscribed to a considerable number of international anarchist and radical socialist newspapers. Most often Italian-language publications but also in French and Greek, these are attested from around the world: in Europe (Athens, Milan, Paris, London), North Africa (Tunis) and the Americas (New York, San Francisco, Buenos Aires).⁵⁹ Second, Egyptian anarchists contributed articles and announcements and wrote letters on Egyptian affairs that were published in the anarchist press elsewhere. As early as 1877 Ugo Parrini had reported on the situation in Alexandria in an anarchist newspaper in Italy.⁶⁰ This practice continued throughout the period. Roberto D'Angio maintained his connection with *Les Temps Nouveaux* (Paris) by providing it with regular reports on the Egyptian scene during the period 1902–3. The anarchist *Il Libertario* (La Spezia, Italy), also carried pieces by D'Angio, Vasai and 'Un Vecchio' (a pen name often used by Parrini) that covered the cigarette workers' strike of 1903–4.⁶¹ With the establishment of a local anarchist press in Egypt from 1901, information flowed more freely in both directions. Egyptian newspapers were available to an international readership that could follow labour and social affairs in Egypt, while anarchists elsewhere could contribute articles and letters about the movement to be published in the Egyptian press. In being part of this international press network, anarchists in Egypt were kept informed of the fortunes of the movement abroad, provided with articles apprising them of debates and discussion on matters of labour organisation and strategy as well as theoretical discussions, commentary and serialised literature that promoted a shared sense of the international nature of the anarchist project.

Political and Financial Constraints

The production of a newspaper required both a licence (unless an underground publication) and the means to finance it. In this the anarchist press was significantly restricted in terms of legal space and material resources. Political repression had been a factor from the beginning. The suppression of *Il Lavoratore* and *Il Proletariato* in 1877 represented an early case of state censorship of the press although it is unclear what the legal basis of this action was. The first Egyptian press law legislated in November 1881 was a clear official response to the proliferation of newspaper titles, some of which were becoming increasingly critical of the Egyptian government. Although in the period following the British occupation in 1882 the press law was not applied as rigorously by the authorities in the decade or so after 1894, the government did on occasion take action against an editor who had published work of a politically objectionable nature.[62]

Under the Capitulations foreign nationals enjoyed a privileged legal status, which theoretically granted them greater freedom of speech than Egyptians enjoyed but this depended on the attitude of the relevant authorities. Italian, Greek and French consulates, among others, carefully monitored the activities and output of their respective local citizenry, especially those suspected of subversion. Anarchists were regularly suspected of political conspiracy and of condoning, if not committing, violence and so were often the target for government repression. In response local anarchists stressed the importance of press freedom and were vocal in defending the right to freedom of speech in principle and practice.[63]

Press freedom became increasingly circumscribed from 1909. Early that year the authorities reinstated the press law in response to growing nationalist agitation, and enhanced its reach with the passage of a new Press and Publications Law to curb increasing criticism of British rule.[64] The action provoked widespread protest locally and abroad.[65] There were genuine reasons for such a concern. Nationalist papers, like *al-Liwa'*, were soon closed down as part of a broad government campaign against nationalist opposition, particularly of the Watani Party, and the press law threatened journalists with imprisonment for the first time. Other radical publications were targeted in this increasingly repressive atmosphere. In the summer of 1914 *al-Mustaqbal*, the radical review of Salama Musa and Shibli Shumayyil, was suppressed and soon after the authorities pursued the anarchist weekly *L'Unione* for having published an article by Vasai discussing the assassination of the Italian King Umberto I more than a decade before. At the request of the Italian authorities the Egyptian government ordered the paper closed in October 1914.

This hostile attitude of the authorities to the radical press was part of a broader campaign of repression and caused obvious difficulties.[66] On occasion anarchists found it difficult to find a printer willing to produce their copy and risk the potential repercussions.[67] Sajous, Molco and Co. served as reliable printers for a time,[68] but periodically anarchists discussed the possibility of securing their own printing press to resolve the problem. By 1913 Vasai himself seems to have established his own printing house and produced *Libera Tribuna*. The regular use of pseudonyms by contributors and readers, particularly the case with *Il Domani*, may also suggest an attempt to maintain anonymity with the authorities.

State repression was not the only difficulty for the anarchist press. Like many who produced newspapers, anarchists had to deal with the much more mundane issue of financial viability. Issuing a *numero unico* (single issue), a manifesto or proclamation was a limited financial commitment and much more easily managed; however, the ongoing production of a weekly or fortnightly newspaper required both the start-up capital and continuing means to ensure regular publication. At times this stretched the modest resources of activists and supporters beyond the limit, and more than once newspapers closed down or production was interrupted because of financial reasons.

The financial viability of any newspaper was stronger if it was able to generate its own income. Revenue could come from a number of sources: sales, subscriptions, donations and advertising. While hardly a critical factor in increasing circulation, the cover price of anarchist newspapers was competitive compared with other newspapers. *La Tribuna Libera*, *L'Indipendente* and *L'Unione* all sold for five millièmes (half a piastre) per copy, comparable to the price of mainstream Arabic-language papers of the time.[69] *L'Operaio* sold for only one millième. Some anarchist titles, such as *L'Unione* and particularly *numeri unici* (one-off issues), were often distributed free or invited a voluntary donation, while at the other end of the scale, *Lux!*, a publication of greater substance, bound and stapled on paper of reasonable quality, was relatively expensive at two piastres a copy.

Subscriptions, available to both local and international readers with discounted rates, theoretically offered a steady source of income. In its early issues, *L'Operaio* routinely appealed to its readers to subscribe and, to those financially able, not only for themselves but additionally in favour of an unemployed or low-paid worker.[70] After the first three months, the editors offered subscribers for the second trimester a free set of issues of the first as an incentive.[71] Some subscribers were slow in settling accounts, however, with readers being regularly reminded of their overdue payments. In time this call could become more strident and at times shrill, as editors cajoled readers to make good on outstanding commitments or to renew their existing subscriptions. On a number of occasions the editors of *L'Operaio* even threatened to name and shame those whose subscriptions had lapsed, apparently a particular problem with the readership in Cairo.[72]

Another means of accruing revenue was the subscription fund. Initially the editors of *L'Operaio* had stressed subscriptions as their primary source of income but they had also opened a fund in August 1902 to those who wished to pledge more general financial support. Over subsequent weeks the amounts donated were published in the paper, with sums varying from two to fifty piastres. The names, or more often initials, of donors appeared by way of acknowledgement although many preferred to use pseudonyms, which were alternatively descriptive ('a wine merchant'), whimsical ('the man who laughs'), quasi-epic ('peace and war'), pointedly ideological ('A worker who doesn't want presidents in societies'; 'Man created God'; 'The boss gives me bread and buys beefsteak with my sweat') and even pointedly hostile ('Down with the white scabs!').[73] By the middle of October over five pounds had been collected.

Advertisements were an additional means of generating revenue, although this was not a standard anarchist practice. When used it tended to promote the interests of members. The back page of *L'Operaio*, for example, was given over to commercial notices, most of which were local Alexandrian and Cairo businesses, promoting the virtues of (largely Italian-owned) local restaurants, bars and sellers of alcoholic beverages. Most of these were likely owned by anarchists or by those sympathetic to the cause, since they included Pietro

Vasai's grocery, La Colonia, and the jewellery shop of Joseph Rosenthal (Stone and Rosenthal), the latter unusually advertising in both Italian and Arabic.

Other funding strategies were called on from time to time. Lotteries were a favoured method. After the closure of *La Tribuna Libera* because of financial difficulties its editors unsuccessfully sought to revive the title by running a lottery.[74] In 1903 a lottery was organised to launch *Il Domani* that reportedly sold 3,000 tickets at one piastre each, with prizes that included a watch and watch chain.[75] Subsequent legislation regulating the use of lotteries may have made similar endeavours more difficult. Fundraising events were also organised. In 1902 *L'Operaio* staged a 'fête champêtre' (an outdoor entertainment) to improve its finances,[76] while Umberto Bambini organised a fête for the benefit of his newspaper, *Risveglio Egiziano*, in the Café Grande Giardino Excelsior in Alexandria where poetry and socialist monologues were read, ending with 'une grande loterie humoristique'.[77] The overall impression of the financial viability of anarchist newspapers is of a generally modest and at times precarious arrangement.

Although the individual circumstances of many of these newspapers are not known in any detail, both political and financial considerations figured significantly in the reasons for the closure of a number of titles; however, internal factors could also play a part. After interrupting publication in February 1903 because of financial difficulties, *L'Operaio* resumed in April with its editors defiantly declaring, 'we will not die'.[78] At the same time the libertarian *Il Domani* was launched by Ugo Parrini in Cairo. Known for his hostility towards anarcho-syndicalism and having fallen out with Alexandrian anarchists, Parrini's move undermined the *L'Operaio* readership in Cairo and hastened the paper's closure. Its last issue on 18 April defiantly declared that 'this newspaper is anarchist and not libertarian', no doubt with Parrini and his circle in mind.[79]

Conclusion

After a brief appearance in the late 1870s, from the turn of the century until 1914 the anarchist press functioned as the active mouthpiece of a movement that was to play a significant role in the emergence of local militant labour and radical subaltern politics in Egypt. Serving as a primary means for

Table 8.1 Anarchist newspapers, periodicals and *numeri unici*, Egypt, 1877–1914.[a]

Date and place	Title	Editor	Language	Notes
Feb. 1877[b] Alexandria	Il Lavoratore	Ugo Parrini, Giuseppe Messina and Giacomo Costa	Italian	Organ of the International Weekly; 3 issues only; suppressed by authorities Printer: Ottolenghi; in name of Austrian [FG Urban?]
1 Apr. 1877[c] Alexandria	Il Proletariato	Ugo Parrini, Giuseppe Messina and Giacomo Costa	Italian	Organ of the International Single issue; suppressed by authorities
c. Oct. 1895[d] Port Said	Il Trovatore	Iesse Brandani, Cesare Corsi, Domiziano Lucchi	Italian	Single issue
20 Oct.– 29 Dec 1901[e] Alexandria	La Tribuna Liberal/ Le Tribune Libre	Joseph Rosenthal	Italian & French[f]	'International organ for the emancipation of the Proletariat'; 5 mills. Weekly, 4 pp.; 7 issues Circulation: 1,000 copies (c. 600 sent to Italy); Via Anastasi 41
19 July 1902– 18 April 1903 Alexandria (interr. 21 Feb.–4 Apr. 1903)	L'Operaio	Pietro Vasai and Roberto D'Angio	Italian & French	Anarcho-syndicalist; masthead: 'Lavoratori di tutto il mondo, unitevi!' (Marx) 1 mill. Weekly, 4 pp.; 35 issues; last issue 1,000 copies Owner: AG Bussutil Printer: Carlo Molco (from Nov. 1902)
4 April– 20 July 1903[g] Cairo	Il Domani	Ugo Parrini and Romolo Garbati	Italian	'Periodico Libertario' Libertarian-individualist Fortnightly; 6 issues Circulation: 1,000 copies Darb al-Ibrahimy 18
15 Jun.– 1 Sept. 1903[h] Alexandria	Lux!	Roberto D'Angio	Italian	'Studii e Riflessioni Sociali'; 2 piastres Fortnightly journal; 16 pp. each, 6 issues Printers: I. Della Rocca; V. Penasson

Table 8.1 (cont.)

Date and place	Title	Editor	Language	Notes
1904–8[i] (4 series with interruptions) Cairo–Alexandria	L'Indipendente	I. Pietro Vasai and Roberto D'Angio II. Alfredo Albano; Pietro Vasai (1906)	Italian	Political-literary biweekly; 5 mills Outlets: (1) Cairo: Libreria Popolare, R. G. Lombardi, Piazza dell'Opera (2) Alexandria: Edicola Cauro, Sherif Pasha St.
16 Feb. 1908–10 Oct. 1910+ Alexandria	Risveglio Egiziano/ Risorgete![j]	Umberto Bambini	Italian	Anticlerical weekly; at least 41 issues; 4 pp.; free 'Nous allons à l'humanité, à la verité, à la justice' (Émile Zola) Owner: Umberto Bambini Printer: Nouvelle Sajous, Molco & Co.
1908–9 Alexandria–Cairo	O Ergatis (Ο Εργάτης)	Nicholas Doumas, Dr Georgios Saraphidis, Z. Hatzopoulos, K. S. Asteriadis, Iosef Chionis and Stavros Kouchtsoglou	Greek	'Organ of emancipation of women and the worker' 'a few issues'[k]
c. Jan. 1908–Dec. 1910+ (year II no. 41) [no. 40 also] 10 Oct. 1909 Alexandria; fl. Dec. 1910	L'Unione della Democrazia	Giuseppe Ungaretti	Italian	Weekly; 5 mills; advertising Owner: Ugo Farfara Printer: Sajous, Molco & Co.
18 Mar. 1909–1 May 1911+ Cairo	L'Idea	Committees in Cairo (Pietro Vasai, Giovanni Brunello, Camillo Brigido, Umberto Bambini) and Alexandria (Francesco Cini, Francesco Donato, Costantino Ungaretti, Giuseppe (Joseph) Rosenthal)	Italian, Greek & French	'Organ of Rivendicazione Sociale'; fortnightly, free Circulation: 2,000 copies (first issue) Printer: Joseph Estivalis? Stavros Kouchtsoglou likely to have been on editorial committee in 1911

Date & Place	Title	Editor/Admin	Language	Notes
30 Sept. 1909 Alexandria	Pro-Ferrer		Italian	Numero unico; free 'Dedicato agli onesti di tutti I partiti' In defence of Francisco Ferrer, Spanish anarchist executed 13 Oct. 1909 Printer: Nouvelle Sajous, Molco & Co.
18 Mar. 1913 Cairo	Libera Tribuna	Pietro Vasai	Italian	Critica, Polemica e Propaganda 'Occasional' but possibly only one issue; voluntary donation Printer: P. Vasai, L'Indipendente
6 Jul. 1913– Oct. 1914 Cairo–Alexandria	L'Unione	Leandro Testa (Pietro Vasai from 1 May 1914) (eds) and Giovanni Macri (admin.)	Italian & French	Anarcho-syndicalist weekly; 5 mills c. 65 issues

a For a more detailed if incomplete listing of anarchist newspapers published in Egypt, see Bettini, *Bibliografia*, pp. 81–8. This table does not list anarchist newspapers mentioned in the record as being planned but which cannot be confirmed as having been published. These include *Demoliamo!* (1881), *Il Dromedario* (March 1902) and *L'Indice* (October 1912) (the last probably superseded by *L'Unione*).

b Issues: 11 February (?), 28 February (?).

c Bettini, *Bibliografia*, p. 81 gives this date but ASMAE, Moscati b. 1297, Cairo to Rome, 11 May 1877, suggests a date in early May.

d AIE b. 86 (1900–4) Anarchici, Port Said to Cons Gen of Italy, Cairo, 11 October 1898.

e Issues: 20 October, 26 October, 2 November, (?), 17 November (demi-feuille), 24 November (demi-feuille), 29 December 1901.

f Greek and Hebrew sections were considered but probably did not go ahead.

g Issues: 4 April, 18 April, 9 May, (?), (?), 20 July 1903.

h 15 June, 1 July, 16 July, 1 August, 16 August, 1 September.

i Series I: c. July–December 1904; II: June 1906–; III. 26 January 1908–.

j These two titles appear to be interchangeable. Bettini, *Bibliografia*, p. 85 gives *Risorgete!* but *Risveglio Egiziano* appears more often in the contemporary record.

k Michailidis, *Panorama*, p. 179.

conducting 'propaganda of the word', it was part of a larger production of published material, including books, pamphlets, manifestos and posters, that testified to a vibrant anarchist presence in Egypt during a time of great social and political dynamism. By this means, the movement fostered debates on pressing issues of social identity and economic exploitation, articulating the demands of local labour as well as employing it as a vehicle for the transmission of innovative ideas in public education, science, secularism and social justice among the popular classes. In doing so, it cultivated a sense of community among its readership at a local level at the same time as connecting it to a broader international network of radical activism.

One of a number of emerging subaltern voices of the period that was testimony to the growing prominence of the press and the diversification of the public space, the anarchist press experienced many of the common difficulties of press publications: dilatory subscribers, problems of distribution and modest, if not straitened, resources. Its multilingual character spoke of its ambitions to a wide readership but these constraints and the limitations of language and literacy inevitably restricted its influence. Further, while its radical critique sought to challenge competing notions of nation, class and community, the anarchist press was closely monitored by the local consular representatives and regularly incurred the interference from the political authorities that it denounced.

Notes

1. The anarchist press has been largely overlooked in mainstream accounts of the Middle Eastern press: Ibrahim 'Abduh, for example, lists only one anarchist title (*L'Unione*) in *Tatawwur al-sihafa al-misriyya*. It is mentioned, though hardly discussed, in the literature on the Italian-language press of Egypt. See Rizzitano, 'Un secolo di giornalismo italiano'; Marchi, 'La presse d'expression'. Although limited to Italian-language newspapers, the best catalogue for the anarchist press in Egypt is Bettini, *Bibliografia*, pp. 81–8. I wish to thank the participants of the workshop for their feedback and Ami Ayalon for his comments on a later draft of this chapter. All translations are mine.
2. For the following, see Bettini's short essay, 'Appunti per una storia dell'anarchismo italiano in Egitto', in *Bibliografia*, pp. 281–8, which stands out as the pioneering work on anarchism in Egypt, and Gorman, '"Diverse in Race"'.

3. Michel, *Esuli Italiani*. By the time of the 1907 Egyptian census the Italian population was just under 35,000, 85 per cent of which was domiciled in Cairo and Alexandria.
4. A prominent Italian political figure associated with the First International, Giuseppe Mazzini (1805–72) held democratic, republican and, for a time, radical views.
5. Guillaume, *L'Internationale*, pp. 258, 262. The Anti-Authoritarian International had been set up in 1872 by Bakunin and his allies following the split with Marx at the Hague Congress.
6. Ugo Parrini's own account (republished in Bettini, *Bibliografia*, pp. 303–7) of a movement riven by personal and ideological differences, while no doubt often self-serving, is probably reliable on this point.
7. The former stressed the primacy of individual action and social emancipation, while the latter held that labour organisation was the key to an improvement in the lot of the working classes.
8. For a discussion on this, see Gorman, 'Foreign Workers in Egypt'.
9. For a full listing, see Table 8.1 The term 'anarchist press' is used throughout here to describe those newspapers of an explicit anarchist orientation. Other publications of the time with varying progressive agendas are not included.
10. 'A Nos Lecteurs', *La Tribuna Libera* 20 October 1901.
11. 'Il Nostro Programma', *L'Operaio* 19 July 1902.
12. AIE b. 120, Stampa sovversiva, 'Perche siamo anarchici – Che cosa vogliamo'.
13. Bettini, *Bibliografia*, p. 81.
14. Ibid., p. 282. For the suppression of the International in Italy, see Pernicone, *Italian Anarchism*, pp. 147–57.
15. Bettini, *Bibliografia*, p. 282.
16. *Il Trovatore* apparently appeared only once. AIE b. 86, Anarchici, Port Said to Cons. Gen. of Italy, Cairo, 11 October 1898.
17. *La Tribuna Libera* 20 October 1901.
18. See Gorman, 'Anarchists in Education'.
19. See correspondence AIE b. 87, Stampa anarchica, La Tribuna Libera.
20. See Gorman, 'Internationalist Thought, Local Practice'.
21. Bettini, *Bibliografia*, p. 85. This appears to be the same as the weekly *Risveglio Egiziano* (Egyptian Reawakening) mentioned in a Ministry of Interior memo. AIE b. 111, Anarchici, Min of Interior memo, 16 February 1908.
22. Bettini, *Bibliografia*, p. 88.
23. AIE b. 87, Anarchici, Cons Alex, 25 April 1902.

24. The first issue of *Sosialistis* (3 June 1890) lists representatives in Cairo and Alexandria, and mentions thirty subscribers in Cairo the following month.
25. For a discussion on this, see Gorman, 'Foreign Workers in Egypt'.
26. See *Grammata* 3 (1916), pp. 629–32; Michailidis, *Panorama*, p. 179.
27. Among a number of examples, see Doumas, *Aimata, Aimata, Aimata* (Cairo, 1911); Kouchtsoglou, *Kato I Maska* (Cairo, 1912).
28. *L'Unione* 10 August 1913.
29. Khuri-Makdisi, *Eastern Mediterranean*, pp. 97–107, refers to a radical Arabic-language periodical *al-Nur* published in Alexandria in the years 1904–8 although little detail is provided and its focus seems to have been predominantly Syria.
30. See, for example, Niqula Rizqallah, 'Bayna al-ishtirakiyya wa al-fawdi', *al-Ahram* 16 July 1901.
31. 'al-Ishtirakiyyun wa al-fawdawiyyun', *al-Muqtataf* 18:11 (August 1894), pp. 721–9; *al-Muqtataf* no. 12 (September 1894), pp. 801–7.
32. For a fuller discussion, see Reid, 'Syrian Christians and Early Socialism'.
33. Antonioli et al., *Dizionario Biografico*, s.v. Parrini, Audiberto Icilio Ugo.
34. Despite this record of activity, Rosenthal is probably best known in the literature for the central role he played in the establishment of the Confédération Générale du Travail in Alexandria in 1921 and the Egyptian Socialist Party (later Communist Party) in 1921. Beinin and Lockman, *Workers on the Nile*, pp. 138–41.
35. Antonioli, *Dizionario Biografico*, s.v. Vasai, Pietro.
36. 'Tutti gli operai possono essere nostri collaboratori: noi non domandiamo lavori letterari, ma IDEE e FATTI.' *L'Unione* carried a similar invitation.
37. *L'Operaio* 2 August and 6 September 1902 ('Le Donne Arabe in Provincia').
38. See correspondence AIE b. 87, Stampa anarchica, La Tribuna Libera.
39. *L'Operaio* 20 December 1902. On *L'Oriente*, see correspondence AIE b. 87, La Tribuna Libera, January 1902.
40. See, for example, *Il Corriere Egiziano* 18 October 1901.
41. The editors of *Il Domani* were reported to be reckoning on 350–400 subscriptions from a print run of 1,000 copies. AIE b. 87, Stampa anarchica, Il Domani, Min Interior to Italian Consulate, 17 January 1903.
42. See, for example, AIE b. 86, Circolo libertario anarchico in Cairo, corres., 15 June 1902.
43. See, for example, the *Lux!* nos 1–6 (June–September 1903).
44. *L'Operaio* 26 July and 2 August 1902.
45. 'La Coscienza Indigena', *L'Operaio* 11 April 1903.

46. 'La Gioventu Egiziana', *L'Operaio* 29 November 1902.
47. According to the 1917 Egyptian census, 67 per cent of Italians and almost 60 per cent of Greeks were able to read and write compared with only 13 per cent of Egyptian men and about 1 per cent of Egyptian women (census 1907) who were literate. Quoted in Tignor, *State, Private Enterprise*, Tables A.1–2 and Reid, *Cairo University*, p. 113.
48. *L'Operaio* 29 November 1902, p. 3.
49. AIE b. 87, L'Operaio, Min Interior to Italian Consulate, 20 July 1902, where Rosenthal is said to have taken copies of *L'Operaio* to Cairo.
50. See, for example, AIE b. 84, Min Interior to Italian Consulate, 28 December 1902, where anarchist brochures and newspapers were exchanged by two activists.
51. AIE b. 87, Il Domani, Min Interior to Italian Consulate, 13 January 1903.
52. *L'Operaio* 9 August 1902.
53. *L'Operaio* 4 October 1902.
54. AIE b. 87, La Tribuna Libera, Memo 16 November 1901; AIE b. 87, Il Domani, Min Interior to Italian Consulate, 17 January 1903.
55. Ayalon, *Press in the Arab Middle East*, p. 148.
56. See Gorman, 'Anarchists in Education'; Gorman, 'Internationalist Thought, Local Practice'.
57. This was truer of some titles than others. *La Tribuna Libera*, with a strong internationalist mission, sent 600 copies (of a total of 1,000 printed) to Italy, while *L'Operaio* carried more local content.
58. On Benedict Anderson's thesis of the role of print capitalism in creating the 'imagined' national community, see Anderson, *Imagined Communities*.
59. *Il Libertario* (La Spezia), *Il Grido della Folla* (Milan), *Sosialistis* (Athens), *La Rivoluzione Sociale* (London), *Le Réveil* (Geneva), *L'Operaio* (Tunis), *La Libertà* (New York), *La Protesta Humana* (San Francisco) and *La Nuova Civiltà* (Buenos Aires).
60. In this case for *Il Risveglio* (Siena). Bettini, *Bibliografia*, p. 281 n. 4.
61. Un Vecchio, 'Lettere dall'Estero', *Il Libertario* 7 January 1904.
62. See Gorman, 'Containing Political Dissent', pp. 160–1.
63. Romolo Garbati, co-editor of *Il Domani*, published a pamphlet on the freedom of the press, *La Liberté de la Presse*, in Cairo in 1904. AIE b. 86, Min Interior to Italian Consulate, 20 October 1904.
64. Rizq, 'Laws in Print'.
65. See the mass protest of printers in Cairo in March 1909. Lloyd, *Egypt since*

Cromer, pp. 93–4. For an international response, see Mohamed, 'Il capestro alla stampa in Egitto', *Il Libertario* 15 April 1909.
66. Recall the campaign against the Free Popular University waged by the Italian consulate in 1901. See Gorman, 'Anarchists in Education'.
67. See the correspondence in AIE b. 87, Stampa anarchica, Il Domani. One printer who suffered the consequences of official action was Isacco Ottolenghi, whose business was closed down indefinitely in 1877 after the publication of *Il Lavoratore*. Bettini, *Bibliografia*, p. 81.
68. Constantin Sajous and Carlo Molco were sympathisers, if not anarchists themselves.
69. The nationalist *al-Liwa'* sold for half a piastre, *al-Muqattam* and *al-Mu'ayyad* for one piastre. Ayalon, *Press in the Arab Middle East*, p. 193. At this time the daily wage for highly skilled (usually European) labour was between twenty and forty piastres and for unskilled (most often Egyptian) workmen, about eight piastres. Beinin and Lockman, *Workers on the Nile*, p. 39.
70. *L'Operaio* 19 July 1902.
71. *L'Operaio* 29 November 1902.
72. *L'Operaio* 10 January 1903.
73. *L'Operaio* 30 August 1902.
74. AIE b. 87 La Tribuna Libera, Min Interior to Italian Consulate, 2 March, 31 March 1902.
75. AIE b. 87 Il Domani, Min Interior to Italian Consulate, 28 March 1903.
76. *L'Operaio* 14 October 1902.
77. AIE b. 126 Bambini Umberto, 6 June 1908.
78. *L'Operaio* 4 April 1903.
79. 'Il Libertarii', *L'Operaio* 18 April 1903.

Bibliography

Archives

Italy: Archivio Storico del Ministero degli Affari Esteri, Rome (ASMAE)
Ambasciata d'Italia in Egitto (AIE)
Moscati b. 1297 (Egitto 8 January 1875–22 June 1878)
Polizia Internazionale (PI)

Published Works

'Abduh, Ibrahim, *Tatawwur al-sihafa al-misriyya, 1798–1981*, 4th edn (Cairo: Mu'assasat sijill al-'arab, 1982).

Anderson, Benedict, *Imagined Communities: Reflections on the Origins and Spread of Nationalism* (London: Verso, 1981).

Antonioli, Maurizio et al (eds), *Dizionario Biografico degli anarchici italiani*, 2 vols (Pisa: Biblioteca Franco Serantini, 2003).

Ayalon, Ami, *The Press in the Arab Middle East: A History* (New York: Oxford University Press, 1995).

Beinin, Joel and Zachary Lockman, *Workers on the Nile: Nationalism, Communism, Islam, and the Egyptian Working Class, 1882–1954* (London: I. B. Tauris, 1988).

Bettini, Leonardo, *Bibliografia dell'anarchismo*, vol. 2 (Florence: CP Editrice, 1976).

Gorman, Anthony, 'Anarchists in Education: The Free Popular University in Egypt (1901)', *Middle Eastern Studies* 41:3 (2005), pp. 303–20.

Gorman, Anthony, 'Containing Political Dissent in Egypt before 1952', in Laleh Khalili and Jillian Schwedler (eds), *Policing Prisons and in the Middle East* (London: Hurst, 2010), pp. 157–73.

Gorman, Anthony, '"Diverse in race, religion and nationality . . . but united in aspirations of civil progress": The Anarchist Movement in Egypt 1860–1940', in *Anarchism and Syndicalism in the Colonial and Post-Colonial World 1880–1940* (Leiden: E. J. Brill, 2010), pp. 3–31.

Gorman, Anthony, 'Foreign Workers in Egypt 1882–1914: Subaltern or Labour Elite?', in Stephanie Cronin (ed.), *Subalterns and Social Protest: History from below in the Middle East and North Africa* (London: Routledge, 2008), pp. 237–59.

Gorman, Anthony, 'Internationalist Thought, Local Practice: Life and Death in the Anarchist Movement in 1890s Egypt', in Marilyn Booth and Anthony Gorman (eds), *The Long 1890s in Egypt: Colonial Quiescence, Subterranean Resistance* (Edinburgh: Edinburgh University Press, 2014), pp. 222–52.

Guillaume, James, *L'Internationale, Documents et Souvenirs, 1864–1878*, vol. 4 (Paris: Gerard Lebovici, 1985).

Hartmann, Martin, *The Arabic Press of Egypt* (London: Luzac, 1899).

Khuri-Makdisi, Ilham, *The Eastern Mediterranean and the Making of Global Radicalism, 1860–1914* (Berkeley: University of California Press, 2010).

Lloyd, Lord, *Egypt since Cromer* (London: Macmillan, 1933–4).

Lockman, Zachary, 'Imagining the Working Class: Culture, Nationalism, and Class Formation in Egypt, 1899–1914', *Poetics Today* 15 (1994), pp. 157–90.

Marchi, Alessandra, 'La presse d'expression italienne en Égypte. De 1845 à 1950', *Rivista dell'Istituto di Storia dell'Europa Mediterranea* 5 (December 2010), pp. 91–125.

Michailidis, Evgenios, *Panorama* (Alexandria, 1972).

Michel, Ersilio, *Esuli Italiani in Egitto (1815–1861)* (Pisa: Domus Mazziniana, 1958).

Pea, Enrico, *La vita in Egitto* (Milan: Mondadori, 1949).

Pernicone, Nunzio, *Italian Anarchism 1864–1892* (Princeton, NJ: Princeton University Press, 1993).

Reid, Donald M., *Cairo University and the Making of Modern Egypt* (Cairo: American University in Cairo Press, 1991).

Reid, Donald M., 'The Syrian Christians and Early Socialism in the Arab World', *International Journal of Middle East Studies* 5 (1974), pp. 177–93.

Rizq, Yunan Labib, 'Laws in Print', *al-Ahram Weekly*, 13–19 February 2003, <http://weekly.ahram.org.eg/archive/2003/625/chrncls.htm> (last accessed 16 June 2017).

Rizzitano, Umberto, 'Un secolo di giornalismo italiano in Egitto (1845–1945)', *Cahiers d'histoire égyptienne* 8:2/3 (April 1956), pp. 129–54.

Tignor, Robert, *State, Private Enterprise, and Economic Change in Egypt, 1918–1952* (Princeton, NJ: Princeton University Press, 1984).

9

The Ethiopian War as Portrayed in the Italian Fascist and Antifascist Press in Tunisia

Leila El Houssi

À mon père

The signing of the pact on 7 January 1935 between Benito Mussolini, leader of the Italian government, and French Foreign Minister Pierre Laval led directly to Italy's invasion of Ethiopia later that year. On the diplomatic level, Il Duce had kept the door open to negotiations with France but his principal goal was a 'far-reaching, violent solution' which he had long envisioned in East Africa.[1] It is within this context, and in spite of the initial lack of military progress and the increasingly heavy economic sanctions which followed, that Mussolini's hostility towards the Hoare–Laval compromise and his almost total collusion in seeing it fail can be explained.[2] Meanwhile, on the European front, Hitler's remilitarisation of the Rhineland facilitated Mussolini's unchallenged efforts in Ethiopia, since the attention of France and England had moved considerably away from the Abyssinian conflict. In fact, the Italian aggression against Ethiopia on 3 October 1935 did not represent a simple colonial enterprise. Despite the Fascist regime's attempts to characterise the war in Ethiopia as a domestic matter, in reality it shifted the already precarious European balance of power, creating international tension that was rife with cruel consequences.[3]

In an effort to convince Italians of the merits of the enterprise, Mussolini's regime employed an insistent campaign of propaganda promoting the war in East Africa as the only possible solution to clashes between the Italian colonial troops and Ethiopian forces. Domestically, the simultaneous use of the media to disseminate both information as well as propaganda on the war contributed to creating a consensus in favour of the Italian action, overriding any feelings of agitation or perplexity on the part of the Italian people.[4]

Even in neighbouring Tunisia, home to a large Italian community, the war did not go unnoticed in assiduous press campaigns in the main newspapers and magazines, but they did not have the same positive impact on the domestic level given the mistrust of Mussolini that surfaced after the 1935 agreements in which Il Duce seemed to abandon the Italian promise regarding Tunisia. For the Italians, the political claim had already run its course seeing that the policy of the regime regarding Italians in Tunisia was based primarily on the assertion of an identity between Fascism and 'italianità'.[5]

With the signing of the agreements, most of the Italian community in Tunisia – influenced by antifascist activism in the country – felt betrayed by the regime. Through the contrast between fascist and antifascist positions in the press, which thoroughly reported the different attitudes on the 'Ethiopian question', this feeling became more acute.

Italian fascist propaganda, with the newspaper *L'Unione* and the weekly magazine *L'Alba* at the forefront, while moderate at first, ultimately focused on making Italians forget the famous January 1935 pact between Mussolini and Laval and promoted the Ethiopian invasion as a prelude to more important conquests, including that of Tunisia. The idea put forth was that the agreements were a transitory instrument of Italian policy to gain France's approval, thus allowing Italy to move towards the creation of a larger empire. One could see in the local fascist press, however, the regime's fear that antifascism was capable of creating doubts among the population, which appeared more troubled by the colonial adventure. Mussolini sought to gain the world's attention and gain recognition for Italy via this military intervention.

In this sense the condemnation by Italian antifascists (anarchists, republicans, communists and members of Giustizia e Libertà) working in Tunisia and expressing themselves in the weekly magazine *Domani* and the clandestinely typed newspaper *Il Liberatore* was clear, forcefully denouncing a regime that was more inclined towards the interests of industrial capitalism than towards the Italian citizens resident in the country. In fact, Tunisia was the first country which exported phosphorites, a vital raw material necessary for the production of asphyxiating gases employed by the Italians in the war in Ethiopia.

The Mussolini–Laval Accords

Following the assassination of Louis Barthou in October 1934, Pierre Laval became the French foreign minister under the Doumergue and Flandin governments, the latter of which Rome had hoped to have much better relations with.[6] An extremely pragmatic politician, Laval wanted more than Barthou to reach an agreement with Italy and England in order to stop Germany 'each time that it exceeded the limits'.[7] The new foreign minister might have been the ideal interlocutor for Mussolini concerning the 'Ethiopian question' seeing that he had previously announced in 1932, when serving as prime minister, that if 'Italy gives up any claim in regard to North Africa France will close its eyes on Italian policy and colonial action in East Africa.'[8] Knowing that in order to commence his 'Ethiopian project' an agreement was essential, Mussolini offered concessions to France on a series of issues, particularly regarding Tunisia and its important Italian community. Indeed, Paris did not tolerate Rome's continued claims concerning Tunisia, which it considered merely propaganda. France then proposed that 'the Italian mortgage on Tunisia be foreclosed'.[9]

Following some difficulties at the start of the negotiations, Laval arrived in Rome on 2 January 1935 with the goal of reaching an agreement necessary for both countries. In effect, Mussolini would be free to act in Ethiopia, and Laval would strengthen his personal prestige in addition to his position within the government. The Italian–French agreements signed by Mussolini and Laval on 7 January 1935 contained seven articles, four of which addressed colonial questions including the 'special protocol on the status of the Italian community in Tunisia':[10]

> The two governments are in agreement on the following principles:
> 1. The Convention envisaged in the first article of the Treaty on the regulation of interests of France and Italy in Africa, will be based on the

maintenance until 28 March 1945 of the conventions and appendices currently in force. The return to common law, starting on 28 March 1945, should be progressive.

2. A propos nationality, the aforementioned Convention provides that individuals born in Tunisia to Italian parents prior to 28 March 1945 will be of Italian nationality; individuals born in Tunisia to Italian parents between on 28 March 1945 and 27 March 1965 will be of Italian nationality, but may, during the year following the age of majority, claim French nationality. They will be able, with the assistance of legal guardians, to claim this nationality at 16 years of age; after 28 March 1965, all the individuals born in Tunisia to Italian parents will be subject to the legislation regarding French nationality in Tunisia.

3. A propos the Italian schools in Tunisia, the Convention provides that they be maintained until 28 March 1955, when they will become private schools, subject to French school legislation in Tunisia. It is understood that this legislation will not, in the future, weigh down the situation of the private schools, resulting from the application of the current legislation, and that administrative authorisations for the survival of the royal schools after the change will be granted during desired time, ensuring that their activity does not suffer any interruption.

4. Italians who, before 28 March 1945, would have been allowed to practise professions in Tunisia, especially those of lawyer, doctor, pharmacist, architect, will have the guarantee to be able to practise these professions for life, irrespective of the regime established by the application of the first paragraph.[11]

All the above articles favoured France. The accusation of treason on the part of Il Duce made the rounds in rigorous nationalist circles.[12]

Praise and Rhetoric in the Fascist Press: The Case of *L'Unione* and *L'Alba*

Founded in 1886, *L'Unione*, the most important Italian newspaper in Tunisia, was the expression of a violent response to the establishment of the French Protectorate. Defined by its first editor as a 'newspaper in defence of Italianità', *L'Unione* was characterised by its ties to the Italian bourgeoisie in

Tunis and by its defensive position towards Italian–French disputes. During the fascist dictatorship, it became the official propaganda paper of the regime, which subsidised the publication with a monthly contribution of approximately 25,000 lira.[13]

In 1933 the young journalist Enrico Santamaria was named director, moulding *L'Unione* with this extraordinary description of the paper: 'the rhetoric and truculent standard-bearer of fascist propaganda'.[14] The signing of the Mussolini–Laval Accord in January 1935, however, was not completely understood by the fascist newspaper, at least in the beginning, although admittedly the severe pro-fascist tone of the newspaper was considerably reduced in order to avoid hostility from a community which had received the agreements rather coldly.

The regime sought to win over public opinion amongst Italians of the Regency of Tunis, who were protesting against this 'liquidation'. Indeed, the triumphal moment of fascist Italy in the conquest of its short-lived empire greatly affected the Italian community in Tunisia. In the columns of *L'Unione*, the editor Santamaria wrote that he had a clear perception, 'that the moment lived was not an arrival but rather a departure' ('que le moment on vivait n'était pas une arrivée mais plutôt un départ').[15] The Italians of Tunisia were therefore persuaded that the agreements of January 1935 were necessary because the Ethiopian campaign would be the first of many important conquests, including others in North Africa.

In a surprising development *L'Unione* published two daily editions during the period 15 December 1935–31 July 1936, one in the morning and one in the evening, with a total circulation of approximately 15,000 copies. The evening edition, *L'Unione della Sera*, was presented as a special edition about the Italo-Ethiopian war.[16] It boasted the collaboration of Vittorio Castro and Maurice Soria, who already worked with Santamaria on the regular *L'Unione*.

The Italian newspaper became the semi-official voice of fascism during the conquest of Ethiopia, praising Il Duce with photographs of Mussolini or the military campaigns. This was the position *L'Unione* took: denigrating antifascist forces, while simultaneously exalting national pride, the imperial grandeur of Rome and acts of solidarity of the Italian community. The articles were clearly fascist rhetoric, such as that of 21 July 1935 which 'greeted' the volunteers who left for the front: 'Our hearts depart with them. The

Italians of Tunisia salute the volunteers leaving to show Il Duce the rock-solid solidarity of our people and the certainty of new victories and the luminous destiny of the great fascist fatherland.' The tone of *L'Unione* grew more and more forceful and Santamaria's articles ignited the imagination of the Italian community, convinced that Ethiopia was 'the new Eldorado where each Italian would find a new place in the sun'.[17]

On 3 October 1935, the Italian troops concentrated in Eritrea commenced the attack. The day before, Mussolini had announced the imminent invasion of Ethiopia to all the 'Italian squares'. This announcement quickly reached Tunisia, where there was a general mobilisation of Italian fascists, as the chief of security Simonpoli reported to the chief of the Regency police:

> The fascist civil mobilisation took place yesterday in Tunis, beginning at 7 p.m. The mass of the interested parties was informed through the sale of a special issue of *L'Unione* ... At the Consulate-General of Italy, there was an uninterrupted procession until midnight, the time of the end of the mobilisation ... the Consulate personnel had donned black shirts. This mobilisation resulted in a large amount of activity downtown well into the night ... It is impossible for us to give an even approximate calculation of the number of people, but a considerable multitude was noticed at each location.[18]

The war in East Africa seemed to have ignited patriotism among the Italian community. In connection with the demonstration in Tunis, organised by the Italian consulate and *L'Unione*, the police report spoke of large numbers gathered. According to the report, on 2 and 3 October:

> Gathering: to the roll of drums, to the sound of the volley of all bells and the wail of all sirens, the people of the cities and the countryside of all Italy met in black shirt in the most formidable mobilisation in the history of the world. The compatriots of Tunisia took part with great enthusiasm in rallying forces around the Regime.[19]

In spite of the continuous protests from Italian antifascists, the consulate provided volunteers for Ethiopia, thanks also to skilful dissemination of propaganda by the regime in concert with the consular authorities:

> It is a moral duty to defend – under all circumstances – Italy's position on the question of Ethiopia ... and the delegations' personnel should be considered spiritually and politically mobilised, and everyone, from adults to minors, has the obligation to take every opportunity to contradict unfounded assertions, correct erroneous judgements, explain and illustrate our point of view in the newspapers and private conversations.[20]

November saw the departure of 800 volunteers from Tunis, who were enlisted in the Parini legion, motivated more by unemployment than by true enthusiasm for the effort. Only 300 left for Eastern Africa, only to return when the war was over.

The presence on the battlefield of two 'companies of black shirts of Tunisia: Numidia and Zama'[21] was the pride of the weekly magazine *L'Alba*, a magazine founded along with several others to support *L'Unione*, the official standard-bearer of fascist propaganda. This weekly seemed to distinguish itself from other regime newspapers for its 'cultural mission', with numerous editorials referring to historical episodes obviously revisited and strongly supporting the Ethiopian enterprise.

In support of the campaign in Ethiopia, a rather interesting editorial was published on 6 November 1935, where the author, still unknown, used the anniversary of 4 November 1918 – the surrender of Austrian troops in World War I – to seek support for the war in Eastern Africa:

> So the great historical day has arrived where, 17 years ago, the Italian armies recorded a great victory on the battlefield ... We celebrate the heroic anniversary in our hearts ... But today, it is necessary that the world knows what new spirit and new force animates fascist Italy on this day consecrated by the glorious event, at the moment where, for a monstrous inversion of all the moral and historic values, our allies of yesterday armed the savages of Ethiopia against our soldiers and prepared an economic blockade so that Italy should give in to the will of Great Britain ... Italy cannot be guilty of what might occur. History will not make any effort to blame or identify the responsible parties ... While our legions advance overwhelmingly bringing the light of Latin and fascist civilisations to the barbaric Ethiopian region and thus tearing away an entire population from the misery of a thousand-year-old slavery, we, united around our leader, celebrate with pride and

serenity of spirit the seventeenth birthday of our victory and we stop this relentless selfishness of which our allies of yesterday give us an obvious example.[22]

At this moment of extreme tension with Great Britain the fascist press of Tunisia attacked the British Foreign Minister Anthony Eden, who supported an intransigent policy towards Italy. The condemnation of Italy by the League of Nations and the economic blockade that followed seemed to create a certain nationalistic pride not only in the peninsula but also among the Italian community of Tunisia, which would soon exploited by the propaganda and the organisation of the regime.

What is known about Italian public opinion, however, must be considered in light of a requirement of the government in Rome that called on citizens to joyfully celebrate the Ethiopian campaign. The regime used all its efforts to demonstrate the existence of enthusiastic support for the campaign even among Italians abroad. Admittedly, the image of a people intoxicated by the military effort was 'a part of the fascist plan rather than a consequence of it'.[23] The vibrant protest against the economic blockade was found in a small piece signed by G. Colombo and published in *L'Alba* in November 1935:

> The blockade meant from the beginning: all these economic limitations that our good, dear and generous allies take to put an end to this effort at civilisation in a pandemonium of terror and slavery, in order to starve women, old men, the ill and those weak and without defence . . .[24]

The crusade against the economic blockade continued tirelessly in the pages of *L'Alba* on 14 November:

> The word [i.e. blockade] has become fashionable and the quick threat, we are certain, will garner more laughs than even those who IMPOSED THEM, to see: the unspeakable, very elegant imbecile Eden, and his Coryphées, even if among themselves, there are two nations whose banners are still stained with the generous blood which was spilt on all fronts of France and Albania by the heroic soldiers of Italy to gain with the British, the French and the Belgians: land, gold, estates and incalculable riches . . .[25]

In Tunis, the application of the League of Nations sanctions, decreed on 21 November 1935, met with strong resistance even from the Tunisian authorities. Indeed, Italy was the second trade partner of the Regency after France, and with the economic blockade, trade between the two countries became very weak, greatly affecting the Tunisian budget and the agricultural economy. The growing crisis even led the Maltese, who had also lived for generations in the country, to boycott Italian products:

> the English have made themselves police officers on our sea, the Maltese have begun the boycott of Italian products. If these 'flat feet' were not what they are, incapable of pronouncing the word cretins, we would respond by boycotting their cafes, their shops and their public businesses where our workers have left their money . . .[26]

In retaliation, the weekly magazine *L'Alba* encouraged Italian residents to boycott English businesses, printing a headline on the right-hand side of the front page: 'Italians, buy from Italians'. Publication of the fascist weekly, which seemed to have lost its 'cultural mission' from its early days, was halted after the 4 November 1935 issue because of insults against the United Kingdom and especially the Maltese community, as noted in a communiqué sent by the Chief of Police Pascaud:

> On 2 December last, the Service de la Sûreté notified the director of the printery Gorsse, Bascone and Muscat, 41 Avenue de Londres named Mannino Pietro, guarantor of the Italian newspaper *L'Alba*, the decision, dated November 26 last, of the General Secretary of the Tunisian Government, suspending the publication of this magazine.[27]

By contrast, *L'Unione* was not the victim of legal measures and mobilised against the economic sanctions, publishing on 12 December 1935 the agenda of the Italian Chamber of Commerce of Tunis, where it expressed the great distress of the community:

> Regarding the application of the sanctions in Tunisia, a country not part of the League of Nations, the council of our Chamber of Commerce, met in the presence of the honourable Consul General, closing the meeting with a unanimous vote.
>
> The agenda was as follows
>
> The Council of the Italian Chamber of commerce, agriculture and

the arts, called an extraordinary session on 29 November 1935 – XVI, the twelfth day of the economic assault against Italy on the part of other nations and the third day on the part of Tunisia:

It expresses indignation and pain toward this unjust and unfair treatment towards the fatherland, raising the soul of its members.

It raises, while appreciating the comprehension of which made proof the major part of the French population of Regency, an energetic protest against such a monstrous international injustice which assumes a character even more serious in the reports of Tunisia.

More serious morally because with this measure one constrained the numerous Italian colony of Tunisia to the immoral act and against nature to participate involuntarily in the sanctions against its own fatherland.

More serious legally because in addition to the fact that Tunisia does not form part of the League of the Nations, she denounces in fact, with the decree which applies the sanctions, the commercial treaty of 1896, renewed for ten years by the agreements of Rome of 7 January 1935.

It is certain that all Italians, commercial members and farmers, will unite with their fellow-citizens of Tunisia in supporting their Consul General to fight and resist this harmful measurement by applying counter-sanctions and by offering their gold to the fatherland. To us![28]

The 'inequitable sanctions', as defined by the Grand Council of Fascism, forced the fascist state to seek cash anywhere it could. In addition to a series of financial manoeuvres, the fascist regime took steps to limit consumption in order to better utilise national resources, and the consular authorities in Tunisia encouraged Italians, via the press, to purchase only Italian products.

All this culminated in an impressive demonstration by the Italian community in Tunis on 18 December 1935, which came to be known as the 'Day of the Wedding Ring'. A large part of the Italian community mobilised to donate their gold wedding bands to the Italian consul, Enrico Bombieri. *L'Unione* reported that approximately 15,000 rings were donated, including 12,000 in Tunis. In the months that followed, the fascist newspaper reported that more than 21,000 wedding rings were collected by the Italian consulate. Owing to the campaign's success, Consul Bombieri received ovations from Italians in Tunisia, demonstrating that they 'appreciated the faith and patriotism'.²⁹ Notable in the Italian local fascist press, however, was the regime's alarm regarding antifascist opposition, which had begun to generate doubts and fears amongst the population worried by the colonial adventure in Ethiopia.

The Antifascist Appeal by *Domani* and *Il Liberatore*

In spite of the fascist propaganda which sought to depict the Italian community as being controlled by the fascist regime, there was no unanimous support for the Ethiopian campaign; in fact, there were very strong reservations about it. The agreements of January 1935 weighed heavily on Italians in Tunisia who felt abandoned by Mussolini's renunciation of the community's rights. For Italian antifascists in Tunisia, the real significance of the agreements was revealed in the 'swapping' of the rights of Italian residents in North Africa for French approval for the invasion of Ethiopia.³⁰ As the communist Giuseppe Di Vittorio wrote some years later:

> Admittedly, the conventions of 1896 conceded rights to Italian workers . . . but these rights, obtained by the free negotiation of the Italian government and in 1896 no way fascist, were betrayed by the fascist government and literally sold by Mussolini, with the famous accords of 1935.³¹

Certainly, it was difficult for the opposition press to express dissent shortly after the signing of the agreements, given the repression of the media by Resident-General Peyrouton in 1934.³²

Under the pretext of protecting public order, the French supported the enactment of so-called wicked decrees in April 1933 as part of the Geberal Residence. These decrees led to the abolition of three newspapers and a decrease in Tunisian nationalism. At this juncture, the antifascist movement, through the *Tunis Socialist*, railed against the decrees, arguing that 'through their fascist character, although applied with the severity announced, would have no other effect than to create cheap martyrs'.³³ The repression was also aimed at Italian antifascists, who at this time were increasing their activities. These were the years when many illegal immigrants arrived in Tunisia, from either Italy or France, sparking a growth in the reactionary right and the pro-fascist movements.

In the wake of the Mussolini–Laval agreement, there was an urgency to unite the antifascist forces and build a general consensus in the Italian community to oppose the Ethiopian campaign. The broadening of the antifascist coalition succeeded in drawing in the communists.[34] It was now clear: the struggle against fascism had become a priority, especially in the face of the threat posed by the Ethiopian war. Already since April 1935, on the eve of the signing of the unity of action pact, socialists and communists agreed that:

> the struggle to prevent such a war, to end it as soon as possible, to have it lead to the defeat of Fascism is the duty of all those who love their country in order to spare it of massacres, privations and ruin.[35]

This operation represented an important period in the history of Italian antifascism in Tunisia because it contributed to creating a 'largely democratic platform'[36] and consolidating the fight against the regime. With this new alliance, the mobilisation against the Italian expansion in East Africa resumed, fuelled by the sense of betrayal felt by the Italian community following the agreements signed by Rome on 7 January.

In this context, a new antifascist voice made itself heard even among a plethora of pro-regime newspapers launched in 1934 as instruments of propaganda in the Ethiopian campaign. On 18 August 1935 the weekly *Domani – Rassegna libera di idee, uomini e cose* began publication, with 1,500 copies of each issue printed, which represented for a short period an important tool in the history of Italian antifascism in Tunisia. Edited by Antonino Casubolo,[37] already known for his articles firmly denouncing the regime in *La Voix Nouvelle* – the newspaper of the Tunisian section of the Italian League of Human Rights (LIDU) – *Domani* presented itself as a cartel of the antifascist movement in Tunisia.[38] The new antifascist newspaper became the fruit of this union, by using collaborators such as the lawyer Raffaele Renato Gallico and his son Loris, Dr Nicolo Converti, artist and painter Luigi Damiani, and watchmaker Achilles Luoghi, all notorious Italian anarchists and communists. The communist Pasquale Lentini handled its distribution, sales and subscriptions.[39] The intention of the weekly was clear from the lead article in the first issue:

> [It aims] to break the monotony of singular voices, those of the dictatorial governments. It speaks to all those who, beyond the voice of the master –

who do not consider themselves slaves – want to listen to the voice of one who is not and does not want to be either master or servant, in order to proceed, with full knowledge of the facts, with a confrontation of differing opinions . . .'.[40]

Antifascism challenged the appearance of freedom with evidence of the fact that all Italian institutions on Tunisian territory had fallen under fascist control: associations, cultural circles such as Dante Alighieri, the Dopolavoro, sports clubs, educational establishments and the hospital. It was then essential for the Italian community to come together and it was *Domani* that launched this appeal. It is therefore understandable how important it was for Italian antifascists in Tunisia to find some form of consensus within the community during this period. They found strength in the uncertainty of Italian residents in this North African country, who sensed Mussolini's progressive loss of interest in them following the 7 January accord after years of unwavering support.

Thus the tight-knit antifascist movement in Tunisia denounced, through its weekly magazine, Mussolini's imperialistic desire related to the Ethiopian invasion. Articles also praised the antifascist collaboration of those living outside Tunisia, such as representatives of Giustizia e Libertà like Gianca, writing under the alias Ausonio Agrate, and Bertone. *Domani*'s efforts were designed to put pressure on the portion of the community which really did not feel the war was wanted by the Italian people but rather by the regime. 'Bouleverser le régime' became the condition sine qua non. The weekly outlined the difficulties of the regime and 'called for the rallying of all antifascist forces'.[41]

Starting in September 1935 the winds of war made it possible for *Domani* to gather all the antifascist democratic forces in a joint declaration against the war. It was signed by all the parties and associations, and stated, among other things: 'The conquest of Ethiopia is unjust, unproductive and criminal . . . It invites all forces beyond divisions and political programmes to unite for one purpose: toppling Fascism.'[42] This united declaration against the war was published on 22 September in the last edition of *Domani*, which then ceased publication after being closed down by the authorities. The sudden ban of the weekly magazine did not stop the antifascist movement, however, because the review had been an important experiment in creating a 'public platform for an active antifascism'.⁴³ In spite of its very short life, *Domani* was a rather successful attempt at uniting the efforts of the local Italian antifascism movement. From this experience a single opposition voice challenging fascist supremacy emerged and would continue to work together in future efforts.

On 3 October 1935 the Italian battle against Ethiopia commenced at the same time as the opposition to Italian antifascism in Tunisia. In this regard, two young Italian communists, Maurizio Valenzi and Loris Gallico, wrote a proclamation condemning the fascist aggression in East Africa. The core of Italian antifascists denounced preparations for a new war fought in the name of fascism on the grounds that it sought to defend the interests and the privileges of a handful of exploiters and other senior figures, while throwing into ruin, misery and slavery millions and millions of Italian and colonial workers.⁴⁴

The typed newspaper *Il Liberatore* succeeded *Domani* in representing the Italian wing of the Tunisian Communist Party. The manager and editor of the newspaper were respectively Silvano Bensasson and Michele Rossi, two well-known figures of Italian antifascism, who collaborated with Tunisians in spite of the hostility of the colonial authorities.

It was quite obvious that, even for the Italian core of the Tunisian Communist Party, it was becoming a conditio sine qua non to confront the Ethiopian venture of Mussolini, which as *Il Liberatore* described in its pages was:

> to save the Italian domestic economy and to distract the people from the disastrous economic reality which could not be hidden any longer. Mussolini plays his last card in Abyssinia, at the expense of the people, which will give him their very few pennies, and of the men that the Ethiopian climate does not spare.⁴⁵

The attitude of the Tunisian Communist party vis-à-vis the Ethiopian campaign was to make it clear to Italian residents in the Regency that Mussolini's policy would not change the situation in Tunisia. The appeal of Italian communists to their compatriots in Tunisia was unambiguous: with the agreements of 1935, Italians were considered nothing and they should be aware of it. Moreover, the dispute was played out in economic terms, as they sought to tie poverty to the difficulties felt by all the workers. This was the communists' attempt to reflect on the precarious economic and financial situation in which the Peninsula found itself. It should be noted that, even if the economic situation had improved in 1935, Italy nevertheless was a country that sought a way out of an economic crisis. With the Ethiopian venture, Mussolini hoped to make Italians forget about the difficulties of the Italian economy. According to the communists, to justify the expansion in East Africa:

> We speak about a vital need It is not true that this war is vital for the people, but if it were it would be because of the misery into which the regime has led the working nation. The venture in East Africa is a vital need for Fascism which cannot find any more money in Italy and in order to survive and to assure itself more time rallies the people against a nation.[46]

Furthermore, thanks to sources in Italy, communists in Tunisia revealed on the pages of *Il Liberatore* that an important opposition existed on the Peninsula:

> While middle-class newspapers pronounce the enthusiasm of the Italian people and enlistment of proletarian youth in the divisions departing for Africa, it is our duty to inform [the] Italians of Tunisia of the situation and to make known the demonstrations of the Italian people against the war.[47]

There were protests against the war in many Italian cities such as Florence, Pistoia, Milan and Caltanissetta and they were often broken up by the fascist police force. Italian communists challenged the official propaganda that insisted on nationalistic and imperial myths and proposed to revive Italy by creating an empire which would include Tunisia. In addition, the intensification of the propaganda revealed the regime's fear that antifascism could feed these doubts and fears among the population who were very concerned by the colonial agenda.

Meanwhile, as the war became an inevitability, the communist core in Tunis appealed repeatedly to the Italian population in *Il Liberatore*:

> Workers, jobless, soldiers! . . . war is always in the interest of oligarchies, never of the people. The true war of the people, the war that justice and

necessity sanctify, the only war of the people and by people, we mean people of the whole world, is the Revolution.[48]

Furthermore, after Peyrouton's violent repression, shared both by Italian antifascists in Tunisia and Tunisian nationalists, the two forces joined together to create a platform of common interests. The communist goal apropos the aspirations of the popular masses to rise up out of poverty coincided with the programme of the Tunisian nationalists, which united Islamic solidarity with the 'brothers' in East Africa.[49] News of fascist aggression in Ethiopia raised great concern among Tunisian Arabs due to the manner in which the Italian armed forces waged war against the troops and the population. Opposition to Fascist policies provoked trouble in Cap Bon, Grombalia and Soliman, in which Italian and Tunisian fascists were involved. The point of contention was the provocation of some Italians, who while shouting, 'Long live Il Duce', were beaten by the Néo-destouriens, who responded with shouts of, 'It is France which commands here, not Italy.'[50]

After the battles of Amba Aradam and Amba Alagi in February 1936, the Italian army continued to advance and word of the campaign's success reached the fascists of Tunis very quickly; however, the use of chemical gases in these battles on troops and unarmed civilians outraged Italian antifascists. We know that in December 1935 Mussolini, troubled by the situation in Ethiopia, which seemed adverse for Italy, authorised Badoglio to use all types of gas. Starting on 22 December, Badoglio employed gas – namely *ypérite* (mustard gas), one of the most toxic of gases – on a massive scale in order to eliminate Ethiopian resistance and terrorise the population.[51] The secrecy of the 'gas operation' did not last long, in spite of Badoglio's reluctance and attempts by Dino Grandi to claim that graphic photographs published by English newspapers appearing to document the chemical war in progress were quite simply 'a wretched invention of antifascist propaganda'.[52]

In fact, the war in Ethiopia was a fascist war,[53] which demonstrated the regime's power, and the massive use of gas was the proof. The regime did not make any admission of the use of gas,[54] while antifascists not only denounced chemical warfare but also the interests of industrial capitalism. Relevant to this point was the publication a few years later of an article by Emilio Sereni, in *Lo Stato operaio*,[55] whose title is plainly emblematic: 'Objectives and methods of Fascism in Tunisia', which raised the possibility of a connection between the gases used in Eastern Africa and Tunisia. Sereni explained that:

> Phosphorites constitute, as one knows, the material for the manufacture of phosphates [fertilisers], of which Montecatini has the monopoly in Italy.[56] But their production is, from the technical and industrial point of view, strictly related to that of sulphuric acid and nitrates, essential ingredients of chemical products for war, of explosives and of asphyxiating gases, of which the same Montecatini has the monopoly in our country . . . Almost half the phosphorites – at a value of 45 million liras – was imported from Tunisia; the remainder of this very important material came from Morocco . . .[57]

Conclusion

The Italian community in Tunisia has always relied on the press as an important source of information on the political, economic and social events both in the countries of North Africa and in other Mediterranean nations.[58] For this reason, in addition to the viewpoint of international historiography, an analysis of the Italian periodical press is fundamental for any study on 'Italians of Tunisia'.

It is through this important documentation that we can understand how in the course of two years, 1935 and 1936, Italians found themselves at a crossroads as a result of Italian actions in Ethiopia, a military campaign which should have, in theory, aroused marginal interest. The press, both of the regime and of the opposition, challenged one another by using public emotions and reactions of public opinion. The aim of this research has been to draw attention to the opposition between fascists and antifascists in the Italian community in Tunisia, through the analysis of four political newspapers from among the full panorama of Italian newspapers, namely *L'Unione*, *L'Alba*, *Domani* and *Il Liberatore*, which as this chapter has demonstrated, described the 'daily pulse' of political events of this time period much more than others.

Notes

1. Prior to Laval's arrival in Rome, Mussolini had already issued a secret directive to his armed forces (on 30 December 1934) in which he ordered that

the Abyssinian armed forces be destroyed and Ethiopia conquered. Mussolini used the incident at Ual Ual in Ogaden on 22 November 1934 to accuse Négus of planning to attack Italy, in order to justify his preparation of a military expedition to Ethiopia. The impressive military power shown by Italy revealed the preparation of a national war which required a total victory. See Rochat, *Militari e politici*. [This chapter has been translated from a French original. *Eds*]

2. See Mori, *Mussolini e la conquista dell'Etiopia*. Mori's thesis, which I support, differs from that of De Felice, who believed Mussolini was open to the Hoare–Laval Pact and even after its failure sought a diplomatic compromise. See De Felice, *Mussolini il duce*, pp. 706–10.

3. In the Abyssinian conflict which broke the Stresa Front (signed in April 1935), Pierre Laval displayed an ambiguous attitude. He did not want to take responsibility for compromising the alliance with Italy, considering that Mussolini had the de facto assent of the French Minister of Foreign Affairs at a time when the minister himself could not ignore the military preparations against East Africa. On the other hand, during a speech in the Chamber of Deputies (on 29 December 1935) he affirmed that with the agreements of January, he had no intention of declaring an act of war: thus while recognising Italian influence in Ethiopia, he condemned the military action. Even in the British government there were growing doubts and concerns, which carried Foreign Secretary Samuel Hoare in his policy of appeasement to a revival of a double policy: avoid a conflict with Italy and lead Mussolini to respect 'les obligations collectives sur la base de la collaboration anglo-française' (the collective obligations on the basis of the Anglo-French collaboration). See Mori, *Mussolini e la conquista dell'Etiopia*, p. 50.

4. See Murialdi, *La stampa del regime fascista*.

5. The rose-coloured vision of a Mussolini, who in the eyes of Italian emigrants abroad seemed a staunch defender, increased the consent of the Italians in Tunisia. The operation conducted by the regime in order to emphasise the continuity between fascism and Italian style came to be considered by Italian emigrants abroad, and then Italian citizens, as 'Italians abroad, according to its nationalist rhetoric of fascism, represented a source of pride for the nation, for their courage and their sacrifice.' Colucci, 'L'associazionismo di emigrazione', p. 425.

6. The head of the Italian government was not indifferent to the impending change in Europe. Angered by the politics and war policy of the Great Powers, he

decided to follow the guidance of the Ministry of Foreign Affairs in July 1932. In this climate, the proposal made by Il Duce's 'Four Power Pact' pushed for a new approach between Rome and Paris. At this stage, France was only moderately interested in the Tunisian question; it was beset by the problem of German containment, and believed the agreement with Italy to be an obvious choice.

7. See De Felice, *Mussolini il duce*, p. 519.
8. See ASMAE Fondo Lancellotti, 213.
9. El Houssi, *L'urlo contro il regime*, p. 283.
10. Ibid., p. 133.
11. Ibid., p. 133.
12. See Baer, *La Guerra italo-etiopica*, p. 98.
13. See Serra, 'Appunti sull'immagine della Francia', p. 22.
14. See Brondino, *La stampa Italiana*, p. 98.
15. See Rainero, *La penetrazione fascista*, p. 247.
16. See ANT série E, b. 530, Note d'information du commissaire principal, Chef de la police, Pascaud à la Résidence Générale n. 28351-4 Objet: Presse: A. S. *L'Unione della Sera*, 9 January 1936.
17. Pasotti, *Italia e Italiani in Tunisia*, p. 120.
18. ANT série E, b. 530, Note d'information du Chef de la sûreté Simonpoli au Commissaire principal, Chef de la police, n. 300-D/2: Objet: Mobilisation Civile Fasciste à Tunis. Tunis, 3 October 1935.
19. Ibid.
20. ASMAE Gab., b. 147, Hand and typewritten proof of Mussolini's telegram to embassies and legations abroad of 23 August 1935, in Garzarelli, '*Parleremo al mondo intero*', p. 128.
21. ANT série E, b. 530, *L'Alba*, year 1, no. 8 (Tunis), 6 November 1935.
22. See ANT série E, b. 530, 'La Vittoria (4 novembre 1918)', *L'Alba*, year 1, no. 8 (Tunis), 6 November 1935.
23. Corner, *Il fascismo e il problema del consenso*.
24. ANT série E, b. 530, 'Sanzioni', *L'Alba*, year 1, no. 9 (Tunis), 14 November 1935.
25. Ibid.
26. Ibid.
27. ANT série E, b. 530, Note d'information du Commissaire principal, Chef de la police, n. 19. 166-4 Objet: Suspension du Journal italien *L'Alba*, Tunis, 4 December 1935.
28. ANT série E, b. 530, Note d'information du Commissaire Spécial, Durand, au

Commissaire principal, Chef de la police, Pascaud n. 3541-6 Objet: Article de l'Unione contre les sanctions.
29. Telegram from Mussolini to Consul Bombieri in Cataluccio. Cataluccio, *Italia e Francia in Tunisia*, p. 66.
30. The famous phrase of Laval was pronounced some time later: 'a small grain of Libyan desert served not only to pay for the clauses of the Treaty of London, but also gave the abolition of the Italian rights in Tunisia in exchange'. De Felice, *Mussolini il duce*, p. 529.
31. See Di Vittorio, 'Il popolo Italiano e la Tunisia'.
32. Repression, which targeted the nationalists and the communists in 1934, was not a coincidence. During the same year the split in the Destour Party deepened, with new young and determined elements acting in clear opposition to the former leadership. For the colonial authorities, the Neo-Destour Party, with its political project that looked to the mobilisation of the masses in the struggle for national emancipation, could become closer to the antifascist movement, and especially the Communist Party, which at this time was trying to revive its activities. The repression carried out by Peyrouton was based on the fear of possible political solidarity between the two organisations at a time when people seemed particularly sensitive after the economic crisis that had hit the country.
33. See ASMAE AP TUNISIA 1931–1945, b. 4, Telespresso no. 11653 del Consolato Generale d'Italia al MAE e, per conoscenza, all'Ambasciata d'Italia a Parigi, 15 May 1933.
34. See Archives diplomatiques, Quai d'Orsay b. 1708, Tunisie, Note sur l'activité communiste dans la Régence, April 1935.
35. See 'Azione popolare', 6 April 1935, in Spriano, *Storia del Partito Comunista Italiano*, p. 9.
36. Mattone, *Velio Spano*, p. 62.
37. Born in Favignana (Trapani), Antonino Casubolo was a naturalised French citizen and member of Giustizia e Libertà. See ANT série E, b. 530, Note d'information du Commissaire principal, Chef de la police, Gallois n. 16.715-4 Objet: Presse italienne. Journal Domani.
38. See El Houssi, 'Voci del dissenso', pp. 277–94.
39. See ANT série E, b. 530, Note d'information du Secretariat Général du Gouvernement Tunisien – Police tunisienne – no. 16.715-4. Objet: Presse Italienne. Journal 'Domani'.
40. *Domani* ceased publication after only six issues. See ANT série E, b. 530, Editoriale n. 1, 18 July 1935.

41. See ANT série E, b. 530, *Domani*, 18 August 1935.
42. See ANT série E, b. 530, *Domani*, 22 September 1935.
43. Rainero, *Les italiens dans la Tunisie*, p. 141.
44. Rainero, *La penetrazione fascista*, p. 249.
45. ANT série E, b. 530, Traduction no. 2, *Il Liberatore* 'L'entreprise abyssine', Tunis, 26 June 1935.
46. ANT série E, b. 530, Note d'information du Commissaire principal, Chef de la police, Gallois au Secrétariat Général du Gouvernement tunisien n. 2.460-6. Objet: Traduction du no. 7 de la feuille *Il Liberatore*, 'Le conflit italo-abyssin', 10 September 1935.
47. ANT série E, b. 530, Traduction du no. 2 de la feuille *Il Liberatore*, 'L'opposition du peuple italien à la guerre', 26 June 1935.
48. See ANT série E, b. 530, Note d'information du Commissaire principal, Chef de la police, Gallois au Secrétariat Général du Gouvernement tunisien n. 2.460-6. Objet: Traduction du no. 7 de la feuille *Il Liberatore*, 10 September 1935.
49. Italian antifascism in Tunisia welcomed the call of the Congrès des italiens which took place on 12 and 13 October 1935 in the Matteotti room of la Maison du Peuple of Brussels, where notably the condemnation of the war in Ethiopia was declared. Alatri, *L'antifascismo Italiano*.
50. See Bessis, *la mediterranée fasciste*, p. 178.
51. On the use of poisonous gas see Del Boca, *Gli Italiani in Africa orientale*, pp. 487–96; Del Boca, *I gas di Mussolini*.
52. See Del Boca, *Gli Italiani in Africa orientale*, p. 494.
53. See Labanca, *Oltremare*.
54. As Rochat observes, 'In the correspondence between the political and military authorities from November 1932 to 1935 which prepared the Italian attack on Ethiopia, gas appears only once. In fact, its use was implicit, because already present in the first draft, signed on 29 November 1932 by the Minister of Colonies E. De Bono, the terrorist exploitation of aerial superiority was clearly planned.' Rochat, 'L'impiego dei gas', p 54.
55. *Lo Stato operaio*, the organ of the Communist Party of Italy, was founded in Milan by Palmiro Togliatti and published as a weekly until 1925. On the initiative of Togliatti, it was moved to Paris and published as a monthly periodical from 1927 to 1939 and distributed illegally in Italy. Following the Nazi occupation of France, it was published in New York from 1940 to 1943) under the direction of Giuseppe Berti and A. Donini.

56. An Italian mining and financial company, Montecatini was for a very long period a leading force in the chemical sector. Founded as a company for the exploitation of copper in 1888, Montecatini broadened the scope of its activities in inorganic chemistry, particularly dedicating itself to the production of nitrogen fertilisers. Its history is linked with the people that directed it, such as Guido Donegani and Giacomo Fauser. During the fascist period, the company enjoyed strong development thanks to its close links with political power, which placed it in a monopoly position. Its representative in French North Africa was Gustave Donegani, also the president and director of the Société des phosphates tunisien until his death in 1937.
57. See Sereni, 'Obbiettivi e metodi del fascismo in Tunisia'.
58. Michele Brondino maintains that 'la presse en italien a été l'initiatrice de la presse périodique en Tunisie, précisément le 21 mars 1838, avec la publication du *Giornale di Tunis e Cartagine*' (the Italian-language press had been the pioneer of the periodical press in Tunisia, on 21 March 1838, with the publication of *Giornale di Tunis e Cartagine*). Brondino, *La stampa Italiana*, p. 9.

Bibliography

Archives

France: Archives diplomatiques, Quai d'Orsay, Paris
Italy: Archivio Storico del Ministero degli Affari Esteri, Rome (ASMAE)
Tunisia: Les archives nationales de Tunisie, Tunis (ANT)

Published Works

Alatri, Paolo, *L'antifascismo Italiano* (Rome: Riuniti 1961).
Baer, Gabriel W., *La Guerra italo-etiopica e la crisi dell'equilibrio europeo* (Bari: Laterza, 1970).
Bessis, Juliette, *La mediterranée fasciste* (Paris: Kharthala, 1980).
Brondino, Michele, *La stampa Italiana in Tunisia: Storia e società, 1838–1956* (Milan: Jaca, 1998).
Cataluccio, Francesco, *Italia e Francia in Tunisia (1878–1939)* (Rome: Istituto Nazionale di cultura fascista, 1939).
Colucci, Michele, 'L'associazionismo di emigrazione nell'Italia repubblicana', in Piero Bevilacqua, Andreina De Clementi and Emilio Franzina (eds), *Storia dell'emigrazione italiana* (Rome: Donzelli, 2001), pp. 415–34.
Corner, Paul, *Il fascismo e il problema del consenso negli anni della guerra d'Etiopia*,

paper presented at the conference 'L'Italie e l'Etiopia 1935–1941. A 70 anni dall'Impero Fascista', Milan, 5–7 October 2006.

De Felice, Renzo, *Mussolini il duce: Gli anni del consenso 1929–1936* (Turin: Einaudi, 1974).

Del Boca, Angelo (ed.), *Gli Italiani in Africa orientale* (Milan: Mondadori, 1992).

Del Boca, Angelo, *I gas di Mussolini* (Rome: Editori Riuniti, 1996).

Di Vittorio, Giuseppe, 'Il popolo Italiano e la Tunisia', *Lo Stato operaio* 22:4 (1 March 1938).

El Houssi, Leila, *L'urlo contro il regime. Gli antifascisti italiani in Tunisia* (Rome: Carocci, 2014).

El Houssi, Leila, 'Voci del dissenso tra gli Italiani di Tunisia: la sezione tunisina della LIDU (1930–1934)', *Annali La Malfa* 22 (2007), pp. 277–94.

Garzarelli, Benedetta, *'Parleremo al mondo intero': La propaganda del fascismo all'estero* (Alessandria: dell'Orso, 2004).

Labanca, Nicola, *Oltremare* (Bologna: Il Mulino, 2002).

Mattone, Antonello, *Velio Spano, Vita di un rivoluzionario di professione* (Rome: Della Torre, 2008).

Mori, Renato, *Mussolini e la conquista dell'Etiopia* (Florence: Le Monnier, 1978).

Murialdi, Paolo, *La stampa del regime fascista* (Rome-Bari: Laterza, 1986).

Pasotti, Nullo, *Italia e Italiani in Tunisia: Dalle origini al 1970* (Tunis: Finzi, 1970).

Rainero, Romain H., *La penetrazione fascista sulla Tunisia* (Milan: Marzorati, 1978).

Rainero, Romain H., *Les italiens dans la Tunisie contemporaine* (Paris: Publisud, 2002).

Rochat, Giorgio, 'L'impiego dei gas nella guerra di Etiopia 1935–1936', in Angelo Del Boca (ed.), *Gli Italiani in Africa orientale* (Rome: Editori Riuniti, 1996) pp. 49–89.

Rochat, Giorgio, *Militari e politici nella preparazione della campagna d'Etiopia: Studio e documenti, 1932–1936* (Milan: Franco Angeli, 1971).

Sereni, Emilio, 'Obbiettivi e metodi del fascismo in Tunisia', *Lo Stato operaio* 22:4 (1 March 1938).

Serra, Enrico, 'Appunti sull'immagine della Francia nella propaganda fascista', in Jean Baptiste Duroselle and Enrico Serra (eds), *Il vincolo culturale tra Italie e Francia negli trenta e quaranta* (Milan: Franco Angeli, 1986), pp. 11–49.

Spriano, Paolo, *Storia del Partito Comunista Italiano: I fronti popolari, Stalin, la guerra* (Turin: Einaudi, 1970).

10

A Voice from Below in the 1940s Egyptian Press: The Experience of the Workers' Newspaper *Shubra*

Didier Monciaud

In Egypt during the 1930s and 1940s an influential workers' movement asserted itself through a dynamic syndicalism that also sought official recognition.[1] In doing so, it became an actor in an Egyptian political scene characterised by colonial domination and an authoritarian monarchy.[2] Shubra al-Khayma, a suburb in the north of Cairo, rapidly became an important industrial and labour centre in the textile sector.[3] The General Union of Mechanical Textile Workers of Shubra al-Khayma (GUMTWSK) was the spearhead of this wave. Led by a militant team, it first established itself in the area then expanded its contacts into other industrial zones. Animated principally by nationalist and anticolonialist sentiments, this militant syndicalist current developed an autonomous voice that refused all political patronage. Its leadership was composed of elements from diverse social origins and political sentiments, including nationalists, Muslim Brothers and socialists.

In this context, the union sought to establish its own press organ. In spite of serious difficulties, it managed to lease a weekly, *Shubra*, and transformed it into a 'political workers' weekly', as proclaimed on its masthead. In the period from April 1942 until January 1943 the newspaper established a solid readership, particularly among workers and especially from the textile sector, before the authorities put an end to this unique experiment of a workers' forum run by trade unionists.

The history of workers' and syndicalist newspapers in Egypt is still rather unrecognised but nevertheless, represents a very rich source of social history. This chapter will show how a trade union team was involved in the field of information with the creation of a specific body seeking to mobilise and influence the public. This use of the media weapon reflected a specific desire to build an independent tool. The launching and running of such a newspaper contributed to the development of a militant subaltern network in the social and political field in Egypt during the 1940s. The spirit of the weekly favoured the expression and participated in the crystallisation of a specific workers' political consciousness in a decisive way. The network which carried out this project went through a process of political radicalisation. Progressively, its purely economic perspective expanded to become a form of political consciousness where patriotism and social reform occupied a decisive place. From a matrix of patriotism, a labour consciousness, a certain religiosity and a feeling of social justice, it moved towards a progressive agenda.

This chapter will examine the launch and spirit of this textile workers' newspaper, exploring the centrality of the labour question that it expressed in a political and social consciousness in its political context. Finally it will discuss different dimensions of this unique experiment in the labour press.

Launch and Running of the Project

In 1942 the dynamic and militant team which led the GUMTWSK wished to have its own forum. At this time the union was experiencing a substantial enlargement of its influence in Shubra al-Khayma, other suburbs of Cairo and beyond in the provinces.[4] Its large membership and substantial influence provided a sound financial basis. A newspaper appeared to be a decisive tool to maintain contact with the base and to stabilise its new influence.[5] The difficulties encountered in trade union activity with the police harassment forced such a need.[6] For these trade unionists, the worker's point of view was largely absent from traditional press organs. According to Iskandar Sulayman Salib, labour activists decided to publish their own newspaper following a general experience of injustice and of a press not taking any account of their grievances.[7]

Due to severe legal restrictions, acquiring a licence for a newspaper title at the time in Egypt was very difficult, especially for activists;[8] however, it was possible to bypass the law by renting an existing title from its legal owner. For these activists, there were only two conditions: to fully support its production and to find an affordable rent.[9] In the early 1940s some unions had already published newspapers. *Al-Wagib* was a joint project between the Union of Printers and the GUMTWSK, with unionists renting a regional newspaper from its owner;[10] however, it had a short existence due to differences and the textile unionists soon left the paper.[11] In 1942 *al-Yara'* was launched by the Printers' Union.

Sometime afterwards, two senior workers secured the licence of *Garida Shubra*. On 26 April 1942, at a general meeting of the union, Mahmud al-'Askari announced he had found a solution with the help of Iskandar Sulayman Salib. 'When he informed us that its name was *Shubra*, we were very happy because of the fitting (*munasib*) character of its name for us', Taha Sa'd 'Uthman reflected.[12] In 1937 some leftists around the leftist intellectual 'Isam al-Din Hifni Nasif had taken over the title and turned it into a progressive tribune.[13] Dubbed the 'newspaper of the workers', it promoted what could be called an Egyptian labour agenda.[14]

The owner, Muhammad 'Abd al-Hamid 'Abdullah, was political editor of the newspaper *al-Wafd al-Misri*. A progressive nationalist, he 'belonged to the young intellectuals whose circumstances had allowed them to study in Europe . . . and was a socialist of the Fabian school'.[15] The main concern for the editorial team was its independence. According to 'Uthman, 'The Union has put as a condition on the agreement that the licence owner does not interfere in its content and its management. He only collects the weekly rent and only twenty copies for the subscribers.'[16] A committee responsible for the publication was formed and production transferred to the al-Amal printing shop whose owner was Hagg Senussi, a man of letters, poet and printer.[17] Its launch under the responsibility of workers represented, according to al-'Askari, 'a new era and a former position'.[18]

Shubra was an official publication of the union.[19] Its principal figures were leading officials such as the Administrative Director, Mahmud al-'Askari, and the Editorial Assistant, Taha Sa'd 'Uthman (see Table 10.1). Its editorial staff included textile workers of Shubra al-Khayma but also other lesser-known

Table 10.1 *Shubra* editorial committee, 1942–3. (Source: adapted from 'Uthman, *Mudhakkirat*, p. 56)

Administrative Director and Editor	Mahmud al-'Askari
Editorial Assistant	Taha Sa'd 'Uthman
Secretary of Administration and Editor	Iskandar Sulayman Salib
Editor	Muhammad Ibrahim al-Kafrawi
Editor of Fine Arts	Fathi Ahmad al-Maghribi
Financial Secretary and Social Affairs Editor	Yusuf 'Abd al-Hakam
Editor for Domestic Affairs	Ibrahim Husayn al-Ghazawi

figures such as Iskandar Sulayman Salib, a former Coptic worker turned repair shop owner and prolific author, and Fathi Ahmad al-Maghribi, worker and celebrated labour poet.[20] Based around a core of about a dozen people, the editorial team consisted of educated, skilled workers and foremen who proudly enjoyed the title of effendi and wore the corresponding uniform of a suit and a tarbush, attested by the individual photos of the members of the Committee of the Council of the Union.[21] This expressed the new general political and social climate among textile workers in Shubra al-Khayma at the time. Several committee members, such as Taha Sa'd 'Uthman, al-'Askari and Salib, were prolific contributors, while regular analytical and political contributions appeared, often on the front page, with the signature 'al-Gundi al-Mazlum' (The Oppressed Soldier) although no definite identification of this pen name has been possible.[22]

Shubra first appeared under its new management on 30 April 1942 (no. 303). Printed initially in a tabloid format, it was published on Thursdays, averaged between six and eight pages, and sold for five millim.[23] Correspondence was to be addressed to Mahmud al-'Askari at the GUMTWSK headquarters located in Shubra al-Balad.

The original masthead of the first issue in April 1942 carried the description 'a weekly political newspaper', later changed to 'political workers' weekly', then to 'working-class political weekly newspaper'. Its working-class character was evident in the themes and topics addressed and in its self-definition: '*Shubra*, published by workers which manage its policy.'[24] The editors insisted on this specific profile: 'Worker! Your newspaper *Shubra* disseminates your complaints, cooperates with you for the realisation of your rights. It is published by you, it sacrifices itself for you.'[25] One particular slogan became central: 'Workers are the nerve (*'asab*) of the state. Workers believe in God and in their cause (*qadaya*).' It appeared regularly with the addition of two other terms: justice (*'adala*) and humanity (*insaniyya*).²⁶ Contributions from readers were regularly sought.²⁷

The newspaper defended the worker autonomist orientation of the union. Its aim was to provide 'thoughts, claims and political positions in favour of the labour movement'.²⁸ It was addressed to workers and trade unions: 'Workers, in this paper we find and we say our free opinion, we address our complaints, we demand our rights, we raise our voices, we are in solidarity in our opinions. The (*ittihad*) union is strength.'²⁹ Its objective was to go beyond their stronghold and to connect with other labour sectors. 'The [GUMTWSK] in Shubra al-Khayma is pleased that a new era has begun in the social universe (*muhit*) in general and of the worker in particular. This newspaper has become the voice of the workers.'³⁰

Shubra featured regular features on union news, Egyptian domestic news, 'workers and work', statements by politicians, comments on local and international news, and studies on social issues. The cultural section was important, taking a full page in a newspaper of a modest size, and featured mainly poems and some news.³¹ A few studies were published on Bayram al-Tunsi, 'the prince of the *zagal* of the Orient'.³² Al-Maghribi addressed popular literature in Egypt, including poets such as Mahmud Ramzi Nazim and Shaykh Yunis al-Qadi.³³ The publication of a collection of poetry, *Samir al-'ummal* by Fathi Ahmad al-Maghribi, was announced,³⁴ and cultural competitions were launched with various prizes (such as a fountain pen, clothing, handkerchiefs and subscriptions).³⁵

Shubra appeared regularly until early August 1942,³⁶ when publication was interrupted for the first time because of complaints, according to Mahmud al-'Askari.³⁷ In mid-November it resumed in a smaller format, affirming its creed (*da'wa*) 'for social solidarity between the classes (*tawa'if*) of workers [and] to fight ignorance and social diseases'.³⁸ *Shubra* was then presented as a 'journal of industry and industrial producers' interested in the history of industry. Contributions in this field were again requested.³⁹

The newspaper quickly made an impact. No specific numbers are available regarding distribution and sales but one of its leading figures estimated that between 3,000 and 5,000 copies were printed.⁴⁰ It was distributed beyond Shubra al-Khayma and the number of copies printed increased.[41] According to 'Uthman, 'At the beginning the newspaper was distributed by active members of the union in Shubra al-Khayma, Imbaba, Zaytun, and al-Matariyya (an area of Cairo) but also in other textile sectors including weaving and spinning mills.'[42] It expanded to other textile areas, especially Alexandria and al-Mahalla al-Kubra, influencing other trade unions.[43]

Finally, out of fear of this experience and its dynamism, the Wafdist government put strong pressure on the owner,[44] with the police threatening to suspend his licence and arrest him. They even promised financial support and suggested he focus on legal news. In the end, the agreement was broken and *Shubra* last appeared on 31 January 1943. In all, twenty-three issues were published.

The Centrality of the Labour Question in the Social and Political Conscience

The discourse and the identity of *Shubra* were based on the centrality of labour. For the editorial team, this social group was the heart not only of the trade union movement but of society and the country, according to a true 'labour creed' (*da'wa 'ummaliyya*).[45] 'Workers are the body of the country', affirmed one author;[46] they were fundamental and 'the strongest element in the body of this country'.[47] There were other formulations: 'Workers are the first army of the state, they are the natural basis of its structure (*bunian*), they are the steel (*sulb*) in the life of the country, the carriers of the thesis (*risala*) of civilisation ('*umran*)'; they represented no less than 'the lifeblood of the State ('*asab*)', the 'force', the 'source of life', 'humanity' (*bashar*); they were 'well guided' (*rashidin*), 'patriots' and 'integral' (*kamilun*). A very strong pride was evident because they were 'workers above all else'.[48]

The term 'worker' ('*amil*) was defined as follows: 'every individual of the nation who works in a useful activity (*nafi'*) ... which benefits the honour (*fakhr*) and glory (*magd*) of the nation, is without doubt a worker'.[49] This specific status was based on a conscience, a 'fundamental constitution of humanity',[50] the refusal of exploitation (*istighlal*) and of deception (*taghban*). The industrial worker appears as a central figure.

Textile unionism occupied a particularly significant place. The call to unity was decisive: the union appeared vital because this social group was 'a unit which is not itself divided'.[51] The first edition of *Shubra* discussed the General Assembly of members held in April 1942 with 3,000 people in attendance.[52] The president, 'Uthman, explained the 'policy of the Union' as well as the errors and the needs of 'our young Union'. Fathi Ahmad al-Maghribi recited one of his poems. The Wafdist member of parliament for the district and member of the Parliamentary Labour Commission, 'Abd al-Fattah al-Shalaqani, delivered a speech. Another union member, Mahmud Qutb, presented their demands, while Ibrahim al-Badri discussed the specific literature on labour issues. Delegates of the labour press were present. Slogans that were sung also evoked unity and celebrated labour unions and 'their pure hearts'.[53]

The statutes of the union, published in October 1939, were amended by the General Assembly on 26 April 1942[54] and later printed as a booklet. The visit of the Wafdist Minister of Social Affairs represented both recognition of the union and its influence.[55]

Union meetings were announced and covered in the pages of *Shubra*.[56] On 1 November 1942, a general meeting was held attended by 2,000 workers and Mustafa 'Ashmawi, an inspector in the Department of Labour.[57] In his speech delivered on the occasion, 'Uthman defined 'our foundational politics', based on three stages: 'our self-reform' (*islah anfasina*), the adjustment (*taswia*) and preparation of the ranks, and the reconquest (*istirdad*) of violated rights (*mahduma*). 'Uthman explained the system of finance with notebooks, their presentation to the workers, and the regulations regarding contributions. Articles were again amended and a new administrative committee elected.

The union intervened on many issues, particularly in wrongful dismissals. Mahmud al-'Askari attended a meeting of the conciliation committee for Qalyubiyya governorate that ended in agreement.[58] Links were built with different localities of Greater Cairo, such as Zaytun,[59] and in the provinces (Alexandria, al-Mansura and al-Mahalla).[60] On one occasion, the union intervened directly with the Minister and filed a memorandum at his office.[61] On another, the union president addressed a memo on the conditions of workers in textile mills.[62]

Current political events were not absent. The coming of the Wafd to power on 4 February 1942 changed the political situation in the country.

As the main nationalist current it enjoyed overwhelming support from the popular classes, with the newspaper giving a positive account of government decisions and declarations, such as a communiqué of Makram 'Ubayd, still at that time a central figure of the Wafd and Minister of Supply.[63] A report on the intervention of the prime minister in the resolution of the conflict in the Ghazl al-Mahalla company explained his great interest in the labour question.[64]

Legalisation of trade unions was a longstanding demand of *Shubra*. From its first issue, the newspaper published a bill and its interpretation (*tafsir*),[65] with Zuhayr Sabri,[66] a Wafdist deputy and labour lawyer, presenting a text from the Parliamentary Committee of Proposals and Requests. Transmitted to the Committee of Social and Labour Affairs of the Chamber of Deputies, this document became the basis of Law 85 (1942) which legalised unions. *Shubra* expressed its disagreement with Wafdist Muhammad Bey Mahmud Khalil, who was hostile to such a project, while the Wafdist leader, al-Nahhas Pasha, embodied their hopes: 'We believe that the new president (of the Council) will examine this law with interest.'[67]

Shubra stressed the importance of the project,[68] expressed growing impatience with the slowness of the process and emphasised its urgency.[69] It characterised government agreement on union recognition and on the bill for work contracts as 'progress in the interests of all (*al-gumu'*)'.[70] Accordingly, Law 85 represented a victory obtained from 'the government of the people', as *Shubra* called the Wafd, and a stage towards other legislation because 'that is our right'.[71]

In fact, the impact of this celebrated law remained limited, notably because it prevented the creation of a federation and many categories of workers, such as agricultural workers, functionaries and employees, were not allowed to unionise. This 'height of legislative intervention' represented for Beinin a 'double-edged sword'[72] since the control of the authorities found itself reinforced. The Minister of Social Affairs became a major actor in labour affairs. The law also demanded unions to inform the police of union meetings and forbade all political or religious activity. *Shubra*, however, expressed no criticism of these problematic aspects, perhaps because of self-censorship, illusions, its reformist-statist strategy or from a desire to avoid feuds among its own ranks.

Notwithstanding these limitations, the new law favoured the expansion of syndicalism. In May 1944, 350 unions were officially registered with 120,000 members.[73] Beinin emphasises how these figures in fact underestimate the number of members because they did not take into account members who paid by daily subscription and registered with the authorities.[74] The GUMTWSK would have 271 official members when several thousand people had participated in the General Assembly![75] Nevertheless, the impression of a significant advance predominated, reinforced by a law which imposed work accident insurance on big owners.

Foundations of a Social Consciousness

One particular form of class consciousness rested on a strong feeling of solidarity and pride. This was particularly so in poetry, notably in the *zagal* of Fathi Ahmad al-Maghribi. This worker, trade unionist and pillar of the newspaper was an authority on the labour poetry of the time, often reciting his own compositions during public meetings.[76] *Shubra* itself published poems in almost every issue, as well as an anthem for the workers.[77] Al-Maghribi's work, published here and elsewhere,[78] embraced the central theme of the workers and their struggle and addressed other questions such as the fatherland and daily life. In fact, it expressed a form of working, plebeian patriotism, where the workers were introduced like true heroes with their skills and their knowledge. Another element of this labour pride can be found in the famous poem of Bayram Al-Tunsi 'The Egyptian Workman' (*al-'amil al-misri*).[79]

A deep fascination for industry, 'creative of civilisation (*madaniyya*)',[80] was evident. Muhammad Ahmad Makki evoked the achievements in the textile field, celebrating in particular the project of the Egyptian Federation of Industries (EFI) in 1935.[81] Referring to the role of foreign investment, he advocated industrial expansion, in a patriotic tone. Iskandar Salib called for the expansion of industry, not for private profit but for the public good. On the basis of patriotism, he defended state ownership of industry: 'Egypt asserts its nationalism in the economic and social sphere'.[82]

In 'To the Bosses', Salib addressed the foundations of protest: 'The workers think only of the union after they felt that they were victims of injustice.'[83] Justice was their central claim: 'We (workers) want to live in good (*khayr*), peace and love. We must be moderate in our claims, we must be the community of the workers ... we ask only for life.'[84]

Denouncing the attitude of the EFI towards government projects, al-Gundi al-Mazlum criticised its resistance to social and labour reform, speaking of a genuine 'war of nerves' conducted by the EFI, which did not want to make the least concession.[85] The collective interest must, however, take priority: 'The duty of the individual is sacrificed to the service of the collective.'[86] The legitimacy of the resistance to the reforms was questioned,[87] with al-Gundi al-Mazlum denouncing the Federation of Industry for preaching only 'domestic reform in the fatherland via men of influence'.[88]

According to Salib, trade union organisation was an emanation of the fatherland with the unions themselves representing 'the spirit of the people'.[89] Their role was 'to serve the community (*al-gumu'*)'[90] and to defend the material and moral interests of wage earners. 'The goal (*maqsud*) of the trade union is to act for the good of its sons.'[91] Thus one finds a classic formulation presented in the trade unionism, for example, in the French trade union charter of Amiens (1906) where the interests are not reduced to material or economic dimensions.

A neologism, 'al-niqabiyya'[92] (syndicalism), was used by al-Gundi al-Mazlum. In a speech, the president of the syndicate, Taha Sa'd 'Uthman, invoked the right of workers and the 'duties of the bosses', calling the syndicate 'a kind (*'ibara*) of tribunal where the worker finds his clerk, his advocate, his judge, his advisor (*mustashar*) and all that he needs'.[93] The proposed system of factory delegates was a specific feature of this current. The newspaper advocated not only the strengthening of the union but also the extension of its field of activity, calling for the formation of groups (*jama'at*) and of unions, as much among workers as other social strata such as doctors and lawyers.

Trade union action also participated in the revelation (*wahi*) or the enlightenment of the conscience: 'the voice to (social) peace'.[94] The syndicate introduced a rupture from the classical modes of action. It permitted 'the most joyous days ... before, we rejected injustice (*zulm*) by injustice, oppression by oppression'.[95] It represented the 'voice of the liberty of humanity'.[96] France or Great Britain, Europe itself, seemed like a veritable 'school' in this matter.[97] Taha Muhammad Fawda recalled the history of the first Egyptian

Federation of Labour (CGTE) of 1921–4, which was led by activists of the Egyptian radical left.[98] A regular column also proposed biographical profiles of key unionist figures.[99]

If the accent on class was strong, the content in fact remained rather moderate. Claims should be made 'within the limit of the law' with syndicates proposing 'the correct direction' (*al-tawgih al-salim*).[100] The union declared itself 'for conciliation between the worker and the boss'[101] and insisted on the idea of duty as much of the boss as of the worker. The military decision of not tolerating a work stoppage in key enterprises was even understood: 'There is no doubt that the intention in all of this is the accomplishment (*qiyam*) of their patriotic duty towards the country' with the air raids.[102] It was a question as much of self-restraint as an expression of a patriotic position.

This ethical dimension relying on a strong idealism centred on the idea of social justice. A regular masthead put forward a quote from the Wafdist leader, al-Nahhas Pasha.[103] Society should rest on harmony and stability: this signifies a 'solidarity between the organisms and the groups'.[104] Cooperation (*ta'awun*), the base of society, was perceived as 'the aim (*maqsud*) of the syndicates'.[105] This idea was praised because 'it is the basis of (social) interactions and the basis of the economic awakening'[106] with a Quranic quotation in support. Presented as 'just, practical, material and moral',[107] whoever fought cooperation, fought reform (*Al-islah*), a code of regulation of 'social problems'; trade unions and work contract laws were presented as elements of justice. A profound humanism showed through: 'this humanity (*insaniyya*), partisan and love of the human/e',[108] according to Iskandar Salib, evoked the future of the world.[109] 'Uthman celebrated the cult of friendship 'whatever your profession or trade'.[110]

This moral dimension also appeared when *Shubra* denounced the fact that a great part of the Egyptian industrial production was exported to foreign markets. 'Is this not the same exploitation and same colonialism?' asked Iskandar Salib.[111] His criticism of the employers remained essentially moral: 'They [the employers] are in competition in order to distribute production, then this production is used in the way of war and in favour of ruins (*kharab*) and not for the benefit of the market (*kasb al-aswaq*).'[112] All this explained tension and resentment within the social order.

A utopian dimension was also present, expressing itself in the hope and the search for a 'new life'.¹¹³ An article with an Islamic tone: 'Towards the Light' (*nahwa al-nur*) discussed the dangers of the current situation.¹¹⁴ This religious element has more than a significant role. In the last issue, Muhammad 'Abd al-Fattah Higazi evoked the struggle between the 'shadow' (*zalam*) and 'sun' (*shams*).¹¹⁵ The reference to the 'light' (*nur*) was again used and associated with the figure of the Prophet Muhammad: 'and facing him, the devil' . . .

Religious identity was a fundamental element of this social conscience. From its launch, *Shubra* affirmed that 'Workers believe in God and their cause.'¹¹⁶ When Ahmad 'Afifi evoked the duty of workers towards each other, he hoped that God would not abandon them.¹¹⁷ Prayer was presented as an obligation, and religious formulations were frequently used during public initiatives.¹¹⁸ During a General Assembly, a prayer was said in honour of a deceased,¹¹⁹ – nothing unusual in a society where faith and practice were very present and important in social and individual life.

Taha Sa'd 'Uthman dedicated a series of articles to Islam and workers, wishing to demonstrate the great importance that Islam accorded the economy:¹²⁰ 'This hasn't been the case beforehand on the part of any religion, civilisation, philosophy or law (*shari'a*).'¹²¹ Insisting on the rejection of corruption on earth and on the value of work, he tackled issues of production and work, citing numerous references from the Quran and the Hadith. 'Uthman stressed the 'multiplication'¹²² of exploitation and noted the importance of commercial activity in Islam and the fact that Islam forbade fraud (*ghish*).

Another article tackled corporatism and religion, a restatement of the book of the reformer, Yahya al-Wardani. Religious legitimacy, as much Christian as Islamic, was put forward.¹²³ Without forgetting historical legitimation, ancient Egyptians were offered as an example of cooperative experience.¹²⁴ The role of religious associations was defended, as propagating faith among the young and knowledge of the basics of religion as 'the way of orientation'.¹²⁵

Shubra also addressed the woman question. Taha Muhammad Fawda published several articles where he considered the different views of European women, and Qasim Amin had expressed on this theme.¹²⁶ Since the nineteenth century, a debate existed around the question of the veil. The approach of *Shubra* was rather conformist and conservative.¹²⁷ The work of women in factories was considered as a veritable problem: an 'infamy' (*ar*) as many men were unemployed. It advocated 'giving in addition a job to unemployed men before making women work'.[128] The modern era was denounced because it led to 'this stage of disorganisation of customs'.[129]

On male–female relations, Taha Muhammad Fawda denounced the evolution in progress with freedom to love without families being involved. The need for morality was related as the necessary end of 'this sensible social problem'.[130] Iskandar Salib discussed the marriage of youths and workers, principally because of employment.[131] In discussing the veil, Salib criticised the 'spirit of revolution and revolt' that penetrated society, in response to which he stated that men must follow 'the way of honour in order to guide women' with 'a noble psychological direction (*qiyyada*)'[132] and not by the baton and the whip. 'The crisis of marriage' appeared as one of the great problems of the country.[133] The role of the husband was emphasised. Concerning the phenomenon of the rejection of marriage, Muhammad Musa insisted on the respect of 'rules of Islamic *shari'a*' and the diffusion of responsibilities.[134] The Prophet of Islam was the example to follow.

The tone which predominated, therefore, was conservative. Muhammad Ahmad Makki employed Islamic religious expressions to combat against evil, 'al-amr bil-ma'ruf wa nahi al-munkar',[135] and against tobacco and the water pipe (*nargileh*). This conservatism found itself put on guard against films judged 'licentious' (*ibahiyya*).[136]

Dimensions of a Political Conscience: The Centrality of Nationalism

A vibrant patriotism was at the heart of the approach of these unionists: 'the thing most dear: the fatherland',[137] with the syndicalist network presenting itself as a bearer of genuine patriotism.[138] This patriotism appeared under the banner of duty: 'it is a duty before being a necessity',[139] or further, 'the love and devotion for the fatherland are natural and a duty'. A poem of al-Maghribi defined the love of fatherland as an 'obligation (*fard*)' and a 'duty'.[140] Iskandar Salib Sulayman even compared it to a test.[141]

Regular calls to patriotism were launched. For instance:

> O workers! Be Egyptians before all else. Be patriots before all things. Understand the present situation in its truth. Raise your consciences, your

Egyptianity, your patriotism. The hour is horrifying (*rahiba*). It calls to calm the nerves (*'asab*), to wisdom and to prepare the foundations for a radiant future (*bahir*).¹⁴²

Criticising an *al-Ahram* article dedicated to the textile industry, Iskandar Salib denounced the choice of privilege of silk in place of cotton. He insisted on the weakness of workers' salaries and the need for technical progress. He advocated 'a production of peace', according a 'mission of civilisation' (*risala al-'umran*), denouncing death and destruction.¹⁴³

Shubra embraced democracy, defined as a 'system of equality between people'.¹⁴⁴ Salib called it 'analytical democracy',¹⁴⁵ stating that it should arrange some representative political institutions of the people, which would act in their favour. The country needed stability: 'Egypt, of its army, its just institutions, of magnificent governors [needs] to live in peace and order.'¹⁴⁶

World War II was discussed rather briefly, with the weekly supporting the democracies. Mustafa al-Nahas and Makram 'Ubayd were placed at the side of Churchill, Eden, Roosevelt and Gandhi.¹⁴⁷ This represented a certain boldness given that colonial domination continued and that certain currents in Egypt were leaning more to the Axis, whether because of anti-British sentiment or a fascination for authoritarian experiences. Salib considered the conflict as a 'war of industry and of production, not a war of armour and of sling'.¹⁴⁸ The free world could only obtain peace if it increased the standard of living of the population.¹⁴⁹ War profiteers were actively denounced.¹⁵⁰

A Labour Sensibility in the Political Field

Surprisingly, King Faruq occupied an important place in a newspaper run by a militant worker network in which many cadres later joined the Marxist left. Indeed, the newspaper proposed a positive image of the sovereign, affirming its support and loyalty, and describing him as 'His Majesty the King, the First Worker'¹⁵¹ and further, Faruq, first *nasir* of workers'.¹⁵² The word *nasir* can be taken in two senses, as partisan or defender. He was considered a participant 'with the workers to elevate the ruins (*'anqad*) of his generous hands'.¹⁵³ Their syndicalism committed itself 'on the way of peace under the aegis of his majesty'.¹⁵⁴

The king and his reforming programme expressed in the discourse of the throne were even defended.¹⁵⁵ *Shubra* thus reported that at the General Assembly of the syndicate in the spring of 1942, the name of the king had been chanted many times, such as 'Faruq, *nasir* of workers' and 'Loyalty of workers for their king'.¹⁵⁶ His 'good sentiments towards the workers' were also mentioned.¹⁵⁷ A photo of the sovereign with a tarbush, a breast-pocket handkerchief and a religious symbol appeared on the first page of the same issue. Another issue featured a large photo of al-Nahhas and of the king on the anniversary of his accession to the throne.¹⁵⁸ Elsewhere the newspaper presented its thanks to the king and head of government.¹⁵⁹ Such favourable options towards the monarchy were also expressed in poetry; for instance, Kamal al-Masri wrote a poem for the anniversary of Faruq's accession to the throne.¹⁶⁰ Another author expressed the love of the people for the sovereign.¹⁶¹

Relations with the Wafd were strong but complex. The Wafd still had an immense prestige and remained a key reference.¹⁶² Thus the inhabitants of Shubra al-Khayma thanked the Minister of Social Affairs for his interest in the region.¹⁶³ The use of the expression 'The government of the people' illustrated such a perception, while Mustafa al-Nahhas as 'leader of the nation' was presented as concerned by the labour question.¹⁶⁴ The paper carried a photo of al-Nahhas Pasha captioned 'Minister of the Workers'.¹⁶⁵ The newspaper underlined his profound faith and his devotion (*ikhlas*) in the service of the nation,¹⁶⁶ describing his politics as 'reformist'.¹⁶⁷ An article from *al-Misri* on the government legislative plans was republished,¹⁶⁸ notably on social insurance and the employment of the Arabic language in foreign businesses and shops. The creation of committees of conciliation (*tawfiq*) by military decree was welcomed.¹⁶⁹ During one General Assembly of the union, the Wafdist deputy, 'Abd al-Fattah al-Shalaqani, spoke; a radio message of the prime minister was published,¹⁷⁰ as was as a speech by Makram 'Ubayd, described as 'a courageous minister'.¹⁷¹

The Minister of Social Affairs, 'Abd al-Hamid 'Abd al-Haqq, enjoyed particular prestige among textile workers and unionists. *Shubra* explained that he 'understands perfectly what the workers want'¹⁷² and possessed 'a labour inclination that merits all our consideration'.¹⁷³ He appeared as 'the minister of the society that needs to reform', and was gratified by the very warm appreciation of the 'Great Teacher'.¹⁷⁴ His personality, availability, patriotism and action were praised and his familiarity with the Beveridge

Report on social protection held in his favour.¹⁷⁵ In May 1943 the union expressed its enthusiastic support for 'Abd al-Haqq by organising a great gathering in the presence of more than 20,000 workers.¹⁷⁶ Such a mass initiative aroused the 'anxiety of political and industrial circles' and precipitated his replacement as Minister of Social Affairs by the much more conservative Fuad Sirag al-din, a move that prompted a twenty-four-hour strike in protest in June 1943.¹⁷⁷

This positive posture did not mean unconditional support for the Wafd, however.¹⁷⁸ In spite of their patriotism and attachment to the party, trade unionists refused to be subordinated to it, and a significant difference existed between them on the right to strike. *Shubra* published an 'advertisement' to the workers denouncing those who asserted that the right to strike should not be used when the Wafd was in power.¹⁷⁹ Aimed particularly at some key Wafdist figures including 'Abd al-Hamid 'Abd al-Haqq himself, this was in direct opposition to the official line of the Wafd.¹⁸⁰

The rising Muslim Brothers only appeared in a very short announcement of the launch of a Brotherhood periodical in the Islamic month of Sha'ban dedicated to 'Islamic studies from the pen of leaders of Islamic thought'.¹⁸¹ Yet, a certain influence of the Muslim Brothers was perceptible. Taha Sa'd 'Uthman had belonged to the Brotherhood since 1935. Holding a Diploma of Applied Arts in textiles, he joined the world of industry in January 1938. Because of the non-payment of a promised salary increase, he became involved in syndicalism. An educated, qualified, methodical and organised worker, he was highly appreciated by the Brotherhood Guide Hassan al-Banna who asked him to focus on labour activity.¹⁸² He quickly became a union official: president of the union until 1943, then treasurer and later controller. In 1942, still a Brotherhood member, 'Uthman was still wearing the uniform of the *Gawala*, the Muslim Brothers scouts.¹⁸³

Mahmud al-'Askari may also have been a Muslim Brother,¹⁸⁴ or at least influenced by the organisation. In his memoirs he expresses a certain admiration for Hassan al-Banna, with the Brotherhood Guide described as 'our teacher' (*ustadhuna*) and the 'virtuous Imam Hassan al-Banna'.¹⁸⁵ Certainly a real closeness existed between the Brotherhood and the union, at least through personal links, and al-'Askari mentioned 'the good relations between us and the virtuous imam during his time ('*ahd*)'.¹⁸⁶

Taha Sa'd 'Uthman still largely shared a Muslim Brothers' perspective. His series of articles dedicated to work and workers in Islam corresponded to the views of the Brotherhood on the subject.[187] For 'Uthman, the Quran granted a particular statute to the workers; Islam respected workers and required that people work with diligence and not be lazy. Extremely 'didactic and abstract',[188] these ideas corresponded to the register of social reform of the Islamist literature of the time.[189]

The Brotherhood agenda on labour was not formalised until later in the 1940s.[190] Rejecting the class approach, it perceived society as an organically interdependent entity with group relations relying on the principle of 'social solidarity' (*takafful igtima'i*).[191] This term differs from that of 'solidarity' (*tadamun*) in having a more religious content. Strong advocates of private property, the Muslim Brothers' critique of capitalism only concerned its materialism and excesses. The Islamic state must organise social solidarity. Hassan al-Banna himself considered the unions as humanitarian organisations.[192] The ideas of social solidarity and the union practice of financial aid may have resembled the charitable activities of the Islamist associations.

The vocabulary employed in *Shubra* also indicated an effective affinity with the views of the Muslim Brothers. The caption 'Nahwa al-nur'[193] was used by Hassan al-Banna in his own articles and pamphlets. Muhammad Ahmad Makki employed the term 'politics of the *da'wa*',[194] in order to characterise union activities. As Beinin has emphasised,[195] however, 'Uthman's speech on 1 November 1942 differed from the Brotherhood's outlook on a number of points. While he insisted on the fraternal relations between workers, he stressed the difference of interest existing between the union and the bosses.[196] Such a perception was opposed to the concepts of the Muslim Brothers because it implied the existence of antagonistic interests. Over time, 'Uthman broke with the Brotherhood to join the Marxist left while maintaining his faith and his religious practice and keeping good relations with Hassan al-Banna until 1946. The formal rupture occurred only at the end of 1945 to early 1946 during the great strike of Shubra al-Khayma. Despite this Brotherhood influence on its key organisers, this did not prevent the union from maintaining a genuine autonomy. For instance, the militants always used the de facto secular slogan of 1919: 'Religion is for God; the nation is for all.'

A discrete but not truly elaborated leftist tone started to appear in *Shubra*. The Wafdist deputy, Zuhayr Sabri, was quoted as saying, 'I am a Wafdist socialist, I defend socialism in the Chamber of Deputies with all that I possess as a means of defence!'[197] Mahmud al-'Askari already had a socialist orientation and Muhammad Yusuf al-Mudarrik was already playing a decisive role within the textile unionist milieu. This personality of Egyptian syndicalism, employed by large department stores, was a seasoned militant, influential and respected for his trade unionist autonomist sensibility.[198] He was connected with some fragments of the old Socialist Party involved in the trade union movement, such as the veteran labour activist Sha'ban Hafiz.[199]

Another decisive figure in the political evolution of this trade unionist network was Yusuf Darwish, an Egyptian lawyer of Jewish Karaite origin. After becoming a communist in the early 1930s during his studies in France, Darwish participated in antifascist cosmopolitan circles on his return to Egypt. Influenced by a Swiss resident, Paul Jacquot Descombes, he formed a Marxist circle with two young Egyptian Jewish intellectuals, Sadiq Sa'd and Raymond Duwayk. Involved in the Ligue Pacifiste (*Ansar al-Salam*) experiment,[200] he set up a cultural centre with them, the Groupe Etudes, and slowly and progressively established contacts with these militant unionists.[201]

In spite of these leftist influences, *Shubra* cannot be considered as a leftist newspaper. Its favourable approach to the Wafd was shared by significant fringe elements of the reviving Egyptian left of the time. For instance, the Groupe Etudes affirmed at the same moment, 'it is not false that the Wafd had been responsible for the majority of progressive legislation of recent years'.[202] Numerous articles, notably by Salib, al-'Askari and al-Gundi al-Mazlum, carried a clear socialist, even Marxist, influence but the leftist orientation had still not yet crystallised and so *Shubra* cannot be defined as a Marxist review.[203]

Patriotism, religion and progressivism were the fundamental elements of the *Shubra* credo. A clear fascination appeared for the Wafd, a profound respect for King Faruq and a certain influence of the Muslim Brothers. Its independent stand opened the way for socialist ideas, however, and expressed the political and social conscience of an emerging workers' network. Patriotism and the national question were central, the range of their conceptions rather broad. Nevertheless, a genuine political mutation was taking place: a process of maturation that saw a significant section of the textile union cadres progressively shifting towards leftist perspectives, influenced by Marxism without breaking from a powerful patriotic content.

The Singular Experience of a Radical Syndicalist Newspaper

This section proposes to put this experience in perspective and locate *Shubra* in the field of the labour press and as an object of social, political and cultural history of Egypt in the 1940s (applying the analysis of Christophe Charle[204]) before describing its spirit and its profile.

An Experiment in the Field of the Workers' Press in Egypt

Shubra was not the only attempt to establish a workers' newspaper. Not only *al-Wagib* and *al-Yara*'[205] but subsequently *al-'Alamain* and *al-Gabha*, both Wafdist syndicalist organs, would appear.[206] These attempts remained modest, precarious and were often of short duration. Egypt knew a paradox: the absence of a press for the popular milieu in a country of twelve million peasants and a million workers. As a postwar observer explained, however, 'All the attempts to launch workers newspapers were blocked by the authorities on the basis that a workers publication might become a vehicle of subversive propaganda.'[207]

In his study of the French newspaper *L'Humanité*, Christian Delporte insists 'to limit/define relations, friendly and conflictual . . . with other journals'.[208] In the Egyptian press of its time, *Shubra* situated itself on the periphery of the Wafdist press, with reprints from *al-Misri*, criticisms of *al-Ahram* and a certain proximity with *al-Wagib* and *al-Yara*', yet it still maintained its independence. Although it had no real links with the professional journalist community, it inscribed itself as an independent and radical press, and expressed an affirmation of new opposition sensibilities.[209]

Situating a Newspaper and its Spirit

In this, *Shubra* represented a unique press enterprise. Its management relied on the energy of the syndicalist current in Shubra al-Khayma but its economic and financial dimensions remain unknown since no information concerning the budget or even the cost of an issue is available. The absence of an archive and lack of sources makes it impossible to 'penetrate the hearts of the editing, to look into the professional practice, to follow the modalities of the constitution of information', according to Delporte.[210]

Its dynamism rested on the militant network of professional and skilled workers of the mechanical textile sector. Its leading elements belonged to the world of work but also to the educated if inferior urban layer. They situated themselves between the *effendiyya* (students and graduates), and unskilled or semi-skilled manual workers. Often graduates of technical schools, some found jobs in industry as skilled workers, sometimes even as foremen, where they received training within their company. These workers, educated and skilled, represented the basis of syndicalism and formed the newspaper's coordination team.

Status and recognition remained sensitive questions. In Shubra al-Khayma, discrimination against native Egyptian employees was important in the matter of salaries, promotion and recognition of skills. This situation favoured the emergence of militant activity among native workers. In this industry, unusually compared with other cases, a significant part of the Egyptian foremen considered themselves as belonging to the workers' group.[211] Their cautious or even hostile attitude towards the printers' syndicate illustrated this dimension: they were distrustful towards this 'mixed' syndicate made up of foreigners and 'Egyptianised' local foreign communities, with even some intellectuals.[212]

Their approach in training and in journalism was determined by a militant logic. The editorial committee represented a meeting place for journalists, militants and sympathisers, and its journalistic activity facilitated contacts with political activists and other unions, and afforded them access to information.[213] They were able to establish links, build a support base and search for collaboration and encouragement to write aimed at mobilising and building loyalty around the newspaper.

An Object of Social History

The readership of *Shubra* was strong in Shubra al-Khayma and among textile industry workers of Cairo, and the paper was able to reach other workers in Alexandria and al-Mahalla al-Kubra. Its circulation, between 3,000 and 5,000 copies, was far from insignificant, especially as it addressed itself to a readership mostly composed of industrial workers and trade unionists.[214]

Shubra's readership increased further through redistribution and collective readings, although very little is known of its audience and its attempts at building a regular readership.

We can only focus on what Charle calls 'indirect indexes':[215] the price of the issue, the type of editors, the part of politics or the types of advertisements. The advertisements permit a better understanding of the readership. One finds them for cigarettes and tobacco,[216] a shop of sugar and desserts,[217] a bookshop,[218] a dry cleaners, ironing place and cafe,[219] a modern pedagogical institute, a boutique for the repair of textile machines or a garage.[220] There were also announcements for the publication of a poetry collection, the brochure of the union's statutes[221] and a social study of Iskandar Salib titled 'Secret of Social Civilisation'.[222] These confirm that the readership was centred on the workers' world and consisted especially of educated workers, often qualified or foremen and engaged in the syndicate.

An Actor in Social and Political Life

This 'stable and legal medium of expression of the syndicate'[223] was a true banner, essentially a propaganda tool representing a specific workers' agenda advocating 'the independence of the Egyptian working class and the union movement from personalities and political parties'.[224] The union preserved its autonomy vis-à-vis the Wafd, and demonstrated its own specific spirit by the rupture with *al-Wagib* and the refusal to participate in *al-Yara*'.[225]

A union organ but also a political paper, *Shubra* aimed to enlarge the influence of the union by promoting its political and social views. This tribune of a committed team represented what Ami Ayalon calls 'a tool in the service of opponents'[226] aimed at influencing a specific target: the industrial workers in Egypt. For its promoters, a newspaper remained 'among the most important means of influencing public opinion',[227] allowing them to address wider audiences than the classic militant modes of communication could offer.

Ultimately the newspaper was stopped because of political repression. Pressure from the authorities during the summer of 1942 had interrupted production for a time but it resumed in autumn. New obstacles led to its definitive closing; the constantly increasing printing costs and the lack of paper in wartime doubtless were also significant factors.[228]

An Object of Cultural History

Shubra propagated a new culture with new themes and approaches that corresponded with the level of education, aesthetic tastes, moral and religious agenda and the political conceptions of its editors. It spread ideas and analyses on labour and unionism that favoured the consolidation of a syndicalist milieu. Accordingly, it offers a counter-example to existing elitist approaches to the study of the Middle Eastern press. Rich and original, *Shubra* was neither the work of great intellectual figures nor that 'of secondary intellectuals and writers'.[229] Rather, its leaders, some qualified labour unionists, represent what Antonio Gramsci called 'organic intellectuals'.[230]

In his discussion of modes of transmission, Gershoni has shown the importance of intellectual communities of discourse, of salon intellectuals, of the press, newspapers, books, prose, poetry, drama and other objects of literary culture.[231] The form of message, the choice of title, the role of different rubrics and their development allow a better understanding of the representations of their activists.[232] In *Shubra* a working team functioned as a network, and a circle emerged later following this experience. Yusuf al-Mudarrik, veteran and leader of the autonomist current, and Yusuf Darwish, communist lawyer who began then to weave connections, played a decisive role in building strong links with this militant team and organising its network.

Conclusion

The experience of *Shubra* represents an original and dynamic political adventure: a union periodical run by workers and addressing a public of workers. The weekly favoured the expression of options of the GUMTWSK, far beyond its 'natural' spheres of influence. It propagated trade unionist, social, political and cultural perceptions which influenced large popular and urban sectors. It participated in the affirmation of a critical syndicalist, social and ultimately political thought, where the action and the independence of workers in the struggle for national independence and social reform were central.

Its patriotic dimension was deep-rooted in the social struggle and the general context where a number of factory owners were foreigners, and Egyptian employees were victims of discrimination. The sentiments of dignity, brotherhood and labour self-pride also played a great role, while the wish to build a unionism rid of the guardianship of non-worker elements and political personalities was another crucial element that testifies to the richness of labour culture in Egypt.

Shubra was also a lively example of a rather rare phenomenon: a political mutation in progress. In 1942 the options of a militant labour network developed from its own experience through diverse influences and backgrounds. The Wafd retained real credit; King Faruq was still perceived as a symbol of Egypt and benefited always from a veritable aura. The Muslim Brothers enjoyed a real influence with their moral discourse, the importance of religion and the charisma of their founder. Leftist ideas existed but had not yet crystallised nor become significantly influential. The social and political conscience, far from being homogeneous, relied on a powerful patriotism, a quest for social justice and the will to obtain recognition as workers. In this way, *Shubra* critically participated in their affirmation on the political scene and the building of an independent workers' voice.

Notes

1. This chapter is dedicated to the memory of Taha Sa'd 'Uthman (1916–2004), labour unionist, militant and historian, Yusuf Darwish (1910–2006), labour lawyer and activist, and Ahmad Sharaf al-Din (1953–2006), lawyer and activist. My thanks to workshop participants for their critical comments. [This chapter has been translated from a French original. *Eds*]
2. On Egyptian labour history, see Hamid, *Al-Haraka al-'ummaliyya fi misr*; Beinin and Lockman, *Workers on the Nile*; Couland, 'Regards sur l'histoire syndicale'.
3. See Goldberg, *Tinker, Tailor*; Tignor, *Egyptian Textiles*.
4. 'Uthman, *Mudhakkirat*, pp. 58–61.
5. Interview with Taha Sa'd 'Uthman, Shubra al-Khayma, summer 2001; 'Uthman, *Mudhakkirat*, p. 55.
6. al-'Askari, *Safahat*, p. 120.
7. *Shubra* 7 May 1942.
8. 'Uthman, *Mudhakkirat*, p. 55.
9. Interview with Taha Sa'd 'Uthman, Shubra al-Khayma, summer 2001.
10. al-'Askari, *Safahat*, p. 121.
11. Interview with Taha Sa'd 'Uthman, Shubra al-Khayma, April 2002.
12. 'Uthman, *Mudhakkirat*, p. 56.

13. See al-Sa'id, *Sihafa al-yasar al-misri*, pp. 59–78.
14. See ibid., pp. 59–78.
15. al-'Askari, *Safahat*, p. 121.
16. 'Uthman, *Al-Sihafa al-'ummaliyya* p. 21.
17. al-'Askari, *Safahat*, p. 121.
18. *Shubra* 30 April 1942.
19. See announcement in *al-Wagib* 4 May 1942.
20. See Booth, 'Colloquial Arabic Poetry'.
21. *Shubra* 30 April 1942.
22. Neither Taha Sa'd 'Uthman nor Yusuf Darwish could recall his identity in interviews.
23. *Shubra* 30 April 1942.
24. Ibid.
25. Ibid.
26. *Shubra* 7 May 1942.
27. *Shubra* 11 June 1942.
28. 'Uthman, *Mudhakkirat*, pp. 54–8
29. *Shubra* 30 April 1942.
30. Ibid.
31. *Shubra* 2 December 1942.
32. al-Maghribi, 'Amir zagal al-sharq'. *Shubra* 4 June 1942.
33. al-Maghribi, 'Kitab al-adab al-sha'bi fi misr', *Shubra* 10 December 1942.
34. *Shubra* 28 May, 4 June and 11 June 1942.
35. *Shubra* 10 December 1942.
36. *Shubra* 6 August 1942.
37. *Shubra* 19 November 1942.
38. Ibid.
39. *Shubra* 2 December 1942.
40. Interviews with Taha Sa'd 'Uthman, summer 1999, summer 2001. Yusuf Darwish provided the same evaluation.
41. 'Uthman, *Mudhakkirat*, p. 58.
42. 'Uthman, *Al-Sihafa*, p. 21.
43. Ibid., p. 21.
44. al-'Askari, *Safahat*, p. 121.
45. *Shubra* 18 June 1942.
46. *Shubra* 30 April 1942.
47. al-Gundi al-Mazlum, 'Nida' al-damir', *Shubra* 21 May 1942.

48. *Shubra* 30 April 1942.
49. Taha Muhammad Fawda, 'Ma al-'amil?', *Shubra* 4 June 1942.
50. *Shubra* 14 May 1942.
51. al-Gundi al-Mazlum, 'Kayfa tanajaha al-haraka al-'ummaliyya', *Shubra* 25 June 1942.
52. *Shubra* 30 April 1942.
53. Ibid.
54. *Shubra* 21 and 28 May 1942.
55. *Shubra* 4 June 1942.
56. *Shubra* 2 and 23 July 1942.
57. *Shubra* 19 November 1942.
58. *Shubra* 25 June 1942.
59. *Shubra* 18 June 1942.
60. *Shubra* 18 June, 25 June, 2 July and 6 August 1942.
61. *Shubra* 30 July 1942.
62. *Shubra* 6 August 1942.
63. *Shubra* 30 May 1942.
64. *Shubra* 2 July 1942.
65. *Shubra* 30 April 1942.
66. *Shubra* 21 May 1942.
67. *Shubra* 7 May 1942.
68. 'Abd al-Hamid, 'Qanun al-niqabat', *Shubra* 21 May 1942.
69. 'Abd al-Hamid, *Shubra* 23 July 1942.
70. 'Abd al-Hamid, 'Madha yuridu al-'ummal', *Shubra* 18 June 1942.
71. *Shubra* 19 November 1942.
72. Beinin and Lockman, *Workers on the Nile*, p. 293.
73. See FO 371/41389/J2671/1944.
74. Beinin and Lockman, *Workers on the Nile*, p. 293.
75. See *Shubra* 30 April 1942; *al-Yara'* 24 May 1943.
76. al-Maghribi, *Ana al-'amil*.
77. *Shubra* 18 June 1942.
78. For instance, in *al-Yara'*.
79. For an English translation, see Wayment, *Egypt Now*, p. 24.
80. *Shubra* 2 December 1942.
81. *Shubra* 30 April 1942.
82. *Shubra* 14 May 1942.
83. *Shubra* 7 May 1942.

84. Ibid.
85. al-Gundi al-Mazlum, 'Ittihad al-sina'a wa harb al-'asab', *Shubra* 16 July 1942.
86. Ibid.
87. *Shubra* 23 July 1942.
88. al-Gundi al-Mazlum, 'Madha yuridu ittihad al-sina'at min al-'ummal', *Shubra* 30 July 1942.
89. *Shubra* 16 July 1942.
90. al-Gundi al-Mazlum, 'Kayfa tanajaha al-haraka al-'ummaliyya', *Shubra* 25 June 1942.
91. *Shubra* 6 August 1942.
92. al-Gundi al-Mazlum, 'Min wahi al-damir: al-niqabiyya fi misr', *Shubra* 28 May 1942.
93. *Shubra* 30 April 1942.
94. al-Gundi al-Mazlum, 'Min wahi al-damir: al-niqabiyya fi misr', *Shubra* 28 May 1942.
95. Ibid.
96. Ibid.
97. Ibid.
98. *Shubra* 16 July 1942.
99. 'Shakhsiyyat 'ummaliyya bariza', *Shubra* 8 and 31 January 1943.
100. 'Abd al-Hamid, 'Al-'ummal wa al-gharat al-jawiyya', *Shubra* 16 July 1942.
101. Ibid.
102. Ibid.
103. See, for example, *Shubra* 21 May 1942.
104. *Shubra* 11 June 1942.
105. *Shubra* 6 August 1942.
106. *Shubra* 23 July 1942.
107. *Shubra* 6 August 1942.
108. *Shubra* 28 May 1942.
109. Salib, 'Al-'alam bayna al-hadir wa al-mustaqbal', *Shubra* 28 May 1942.
110. Taha Sa'd 'Uthman, 'Tawjahat min 'amil ila zamilihi al-'amil al-misri', *Shubra* 8 January 1943.
111. Sulayman, 'Al-'alam bayna al-hadir wa al-mustaqbal', *Shubra* 28 May 1942.
112. Ibid.
113. *Shubra* 21 May 1942.
114. *Shubra* 4 June 1942.
115. *Shubra* 31 January 1943.

116. Iskandar Salib Sulayman, 'Misr tutalibu al-wataniyya al-haqqa', *Shubra* 30 April 1942.
117. *Shubra* 25 June 1942.
118. *Shubra* 18 June 1942.
119. *Shubra* 30 April 1942.
120. *Shubra* 10 December 1942.
121. Taha Sa'd 'Uthman, 'Al-'amal wa al-'ummal fi al-islam', *Shubra* 10 December 1942.
122. Taha Sa'd 'Uthman, "Ummal wa al-islam', *Shubra* 8 January 1942.
123. *Shubra* 16 July 1942.
124. 'Al-Ta'awun wa al-misriyyin al-qudama', *Shubra* 23 July 1942.
125. Taha Muhammad Fawda, 'Mashakiluna al-ijtima'iyya wa 'ilaguha', *Shubra* 9 July 1942.
126. Taha Muhammad Fawda, 'Al-mar'a fi al-'asr al-hadith', *Shubra* 11 June 1942.
127. Taha Muhammad Fawda, 'Hawla al-mar'a al-haditha', *Shubra* 18 June 1942.
128. Ibid.
129. Taha Muhammad Fawda, 'Al-mar'a fi al-'asr al-hadith', *Shubra* 11 June 1942.
130. *Shubra* 18 June 1942.
131. Iskandar Salib Sulayman 'Sirr junun al-mar'a', *Shubra* 18 June 1942.
132. Ibid.
133. 'Abd al-Hamid, 'Al-'Ummal wa al-wataniyya', *Shubra* 25 June 1942.
134. Muhammad Musa, 'Al-zawaj wa irada al-shabab tigahu', *Shubra* 17 December 1942.
135. *Shubra* 18 June 1942.
136. Ibn al-Insan, *Shubra* 14 May 1942.
137. 'Abd al-Hamid, 'al-'Ummal wa al-wataniyya', *Shubra* 25 June 1942.
138. *Shubra* 4 June 1942.
139. 'Ali Hifnawi, 'Nahnu wa al-watan', *Shubra* 31 January 1943.
140. *Shubra* 21 May 1942.
141. *Shubra* 16 July 1942.
142. 'Abd al-Hamid, 'al-'Ummal wa al-wataniyya', *Shubra* 25 June 1942.
143. al-Gundi al-Mazlum, 'al-Sina'at al-misriyya ba'd al-harb', *Shubra* 11 June 1942.
144. Iskandar Sulayman Salib, 'al-'Alam bayna al-hadir wa al-mustaqbal', *Shubra* 28 May 1942.
145. *Shubra* 6 August 1942
146. *Shubra* 4 June 1942.

147. al-Gundi al-Mazlum, 'Nida' al-damir', *Shubra* 21 May 1942.
148. *Shubra* 30 April 1942.
149. Salib, 'al-'Alam bayna al-hadir wa al-mustaqbal', *Shubra* 28 May 1942.
150. 'Abd al-Hamid, 'Madha yuricu al-'ummal', *Shubra* 30 April 1942.
151. *Shubra* 14 May 1942.
152. al-Gundi al-Mazlum, 'Min wahi al-damir: al-niqabiyya fi misr', *Shubra* 28 May 1942.
153. *Shubra* 14 May 1942.
154. al-Gundi al-Mazlum, 'Min wahi al-damir: al-niqabiyya fi misr', *Shubra* 28 May 1942.
155. al-Gundi al-Mazlum, 'Madha yuridu ittihad al-sina'at min al-'ummal', *Shubra* 30 July 1942.
156. *Shubra* 30 April 1942.
157. *Shubra* 7 May 1942.
158. *Shubra* 6 August 1942.
159. *Shubra* 30 April 1942.
160. *Shubra* 7 May 1942.
161. *Shubra* 14 May 1942
162. *Shubra* 30 April 1942.
163. *Shubra* 2 July 1942.
164. *Shubra* 30 April 1942.
165. *Shubra* 18 June 1942.
166. *Shubra* 2 December 1942.
167. *Shubra* 30 April 1942.
168. *Shubra* 16 July 1942.
169. *Shubra* 30 April 1942.
170. *Shubra* 21 May 1942.
171. *Shubra* 30 April 1942.
172. 'Abd al-Hamid, 'Madha yuridu al-'ummal', *Shubra* 18 June 1942.
173. 'Nida' ila al-'ummal', *Shubra* 25 June 1942.
174. *Shubra* 19 December 1942.
175. al-'Askari, *Safahat*, pp. 144, 146.
176. Al-Banna, *Al-Haraka al-niqabiyya al-misriyya*, p. 208.
177. al-'Askari, *Safahat*.
178. Ibid., pp. 145–6.
179. *Shubra* 25 June 1942.
180. *Shubra* 9 July 1942.

181. *Shubra* 6 August 1942.
182. Interview with Taha Sa'd 'Uthman, Shubra al-Khayma, 1998.
183. Interviews with Yusuf Darwish, summer 2000, April 2003; and Taha Sa'd 'Uthman, Shubra al-Khayma, 1998.
184. This is claimed by Muslim Brother historian 'Abd al-'Aziz, *Marhala al-takwin*, p. 195. Al-'Askari's daughter, Zaynab, rejects such an assertion. Interviews, Cairo, summer 2005, summer 2008.
185. al-'Askari, *Safahat*, p. 111.
186. Ibid., p. 110.
187. *Shubra* 10 and 17 December 1942; 8 January 1943.
188. See Beinin, 'Islam, Marxism'.
189. Goldberg, *Tinker, Tailor*, p. 160, suggests that Taha Muhammad Fawda was a member.
190. On this particular issue, see Beinin, 'Islam, Marxism'.
191. See analysis in al-Khuli, *Al-Islam la-shuyu'iyya*.
192. See al-'Askari, *Safahat*, p. 110.
193. *Shubra* 4 June 1942.
194. *Shubra* 18 June 1942.
195. Beinin, 'Islam, Marxism', p. 218.
196. *Shubra* 19 December 1942.
197. *Shubra* 14 May 1942.
198. See 'Uthman, *Min turath shaykh al-niqabiyyin al-misriyyin*.
199. al-'Askari, *Safahat*, p. 116.
200. See Monciaud, 'Pacifisme, antifascisme et anticolonialisme'.
201. Sa'd, *Safahat*, pp. 48–9.
202. Wayment, *Egypt Now*, p. 99.
203. For a contrary view, see Yusuf, *Watha'iq wa mawaqif*, pp. 885–6.
204. Charle, *Le siècle de la presse*, pp. 16–21.
205. For *al-Yara'*, see announcement, *Shubra* 14 June 1942.
206. 'Uthman, 'Majalla al-jabha', in *Al-Sihafa al-'ummaliyya*, pp. 33–6; 'Majalla al-alamayn', in *Al-Sihafa al-'ummaliyya*, pp. 29–32. Of this Wafdist press, 'Uthman stated, 'when it [the Wafd] is out of government, it is comprehensively for the interests of the workers and it tries to defend them. However, when it finds itself in power, it tries to control (*ihtawa'*) the labour movement, opposes it, and even fights, sometimes, the essence of its fundamental interests.' 'Uthman, *Al-Sihafa al-'ummaliyya*, p. 36.
207. Benyacov, 'The Egyptian Press Today', p. 16.

208. Delporte, 'L'Humanité, un siècle d'existence', p. 17.
209. See Makarius, *La jeunesse intellectuelle*, p. 33.
210. Delporte, 'L'Humanité, un siècle d'existence', p. 17.
211. Interview with Taha Sa'd 'Uthman, Shubra al-Khayma, summer 1999.
212. al-'Askari, *Safahat*, p. 121.
213. Makarius, *La jeunesse intellectuelle*, p. 33.
214. Benyacov, 'The Egyptian Press Today', p. 14. By comparison, *al-Ahram* sold about 100,000 copies and *al-Damir*, another political labour weekly and organ of the radical Workers Committee of National Liberation, sold 2,000–3,000 copies in 1945–6.
215. Charle, *Le siècle de la presse*, p. 17.
216. *Shubra* 7 and 14 May 1942.
217. *Shubra* 7 May 1942.
218. *Shubra* 14 May 1942.
219. *Shubra* 21 May 1942.
220. *Shubra* 4 June 1942.
221. *Shubra* 2 December 1942.
222. *Shubra* 4 June 1942.
223. Beinin and Lockman, *Workers on the Nile*, p. 214.
224. 'Uthman, *Al-sihafa al-'ummaliyya*, p. 13.
225. Beinin and Lockman, *Workers on the Nile*, p. 213.
226. Ayalon, 'Journalists and the Press', p. 268.
227. 'Uthman, *Al-sihafa al-'ummaliyya*, p. 7.
228. 'Uthman, *Mudhakkirat*, p. 58.
229. See Gershoni, 'The Evolution of National Culture'.
230. See Gramsci, *Selections from the Prison Notebooks*.
231. Gershoni, 'The Evolution of National Culture'.
232. Ibid., pp. 331, 335.

Bibliography

Archives

United Kingdom: The National Archives, London
Foreign Office (FO)

Interviews

Zaynab al-'Askari, Cairo, summer 2005, summer 2008

Yusuf Darwish, summer 2000, April 2003

Taha Sa'd 'Uthman, Shubra al-Khayma, 1998, summer 1999, summer 2001, April 2002

Published Works

'Abd al-'Aziz, Jum'a Amin, *Marhala al-takwin. Istikmal al-bina al-dakhili 1943–1945* (Cairo: Dar al-tawzi' al-islami, 2004).

al-'Askari, Mahmud, *Safahat min tarikh al-tabaqa al-'amila* (Hilwan: Dar al-khidmat al-niqabiyya bi-hilwan, 1995).

Ayalon Ami, 'Journalists and the Press, the Vicissitudes of Licensed Pluralism', in Shimon Shamir (ed.), *Egypt from Monarchy to Republic* (Boulder, CO: Westview Press, 1994), pp. 267–79.

al-Banna, Jamal, *Al-Haraka al-niqabiyya al-misriyya tarikhan wa-tanziman 'abra mi'at 'amm, 1892–1992* (Cairo: Dar al-fikr al-islami al-dawli lil-'amal, 1995).

Beinin, Joel, 'Islam, Marxism and the Shubra al-Khayma Textile Workers: Muslim Brothers and Communists on the Egyptian Trade Union Movement', in Edmund Burke and Ira Lapidus (eds), *Islam, Politics and Social Movements* (Berkeley, CA: University of California Press, 1988), pp. 207–27.

Beinin, Joel and Zachary Lockman, *Workers on the Nile: Nationalism, Communism, Islam, and the Egyptian Working Class, 1882–1954* (Princeton, NJ: Princeton University Press, 1987).

Benyacov, Itzak, 'The Egyptian Press Today', *Middle Eastern Affairs* 1 (January 1950), pp. 13–17.

Booth, Marilyn, 'Colloquial Arabic Poetry, Politics, and the Press in Modern Egypt', *International Journal of Middle East Studies* 24:3 (1992), pp. 419–40.

Charle, Christophe, *Le siècle de la presse (1830–1939)* (Paris: Seuil, 2004).

Couland, Jacques, 'Regards sur l'histoire syndicale et ouvrière égyptienne', in René Galissot (ed.), *Mouvement ouvrier, communisme et nationalisme dans le monde arabe* (Paris: Les Éditions ouvrières, 1978), pp. 173–201.

Delporte, Christian, 'L'Humanité, un siècle d'existence', in Christian Delporte, Claude Pennetier, Jean-François Sirinelli and Serge Wolikow (eds), *L'Humanité de Jaurès à nos jours* (Paris: Éditions Nouveau Monde, 2004), pp. 16–21.

Gershoni, Israël, 'The Evolution of National Culture in Modern Egypt: Intellectual Formation and Social Diffusion, 1892–1945', *Poetics Today* 13:2 (1992), pp. 325–50.

Goldberg, Ellis, *Tinker, Tailor and Textile Worker: Class and Politics in Egypt, 1930–1952* (Berkeley, CA: University of California Press, 1986).

Gramsci, Antonio, *Selections from the Prison Notebooks* (New York: International Publishers, 1971).
Hamid, Ra'uf 'Abbas, *Al-Haraka al- ummaliyya fi misr, 1899–1952* (Cairo: Dar al-kitab al-'arabi, 1967).
al-Khuli, al-Bahi, *Al-Islam la shuyu'iyya wa la ra'smaliyya (1947)* (Cairo: Maktabat al-fallah, 1981).
al-Maghribi, Fathi Ahmad, *Ana al-'Amil* (Cairo: Dar al-fajr, 1946).
Makarius, Raoul, *La jeunesse intellectuelle d'Egypte au lendemain de la Deuxième Guerre mondiale* (Paris: Mouton, 1960).
al-Masri, Sanaa, *Al-Ikhwan al-muslimun wa al-tabaqat al-'amila al-misriyya* (Cairo: Sharikat al-amal lil-tiba'a wa-al-nashr, 1992).
Monciaud, Didier, 'Pacifisme, antifascisme et anticolonialisme dans l'Égypte des années 1930: L'expérience de la ligue pacifiste Ansâr al Sâlam', *Cahiers d'histoire. Revue d'histoire critique* 127 (2015), pp. 51–74.
Monciaud, Didier, *Travail et émancipation nationale: Le Comité Ouvrier de Libération Nationale (1945–46)* (Florence: Robert Schuman Centre for Advanced Studies, European University Institute, 2009).
Sa'd, Ahmad Sadiq, *Safahat min tarikh al-yasar al-misri* (Cairo: Ruz al-Yusuf, 1976).
al-Sa'id, Rifa'at, *Sihafa al-yasar al-misri 1925–1948* (Cairo: Maktabat Madbouli, 1977).
Tignor, Robert, *Egyptian Textiles and British Capital, 1930–1956* (Cairo: American University Press, 1989).
'Uthman, Taha Sa'd, *Min turath shaykh al-niqabiyyin al-misriyyin Muhammad Yusuf al-Mudarrik* (Cairo: Kahraman lil-khidamat, 2001).
'Uthman, Taha Sa'd, *Mudhakkirat wa watha'iq min tarikh 'ummal misr. Kifah 'ummal al-nasij*, vol. 1 (Shubra al-Khayma: Matba'at ikhwan morafiteli, 1983).
'Uthman, Taha Sa'd, *Al-Sihafa al-'ummaliyya fi al-arba'iniyyat* (Hilwan: Dar al-khidmat al-niqabiyya wa al-'ummaliyya, 1999).
Wayment, Hilary, in collaboration with the Groupe Études, *Egypt Now, A Miscellany* (Cairo: Horus, 1943).
Yusuf, Abu Sayf, *Watha'iq wa mawaqif min tarikh al-yasar al-misri, 1941–1957* (Cairo: Sharikat al-amal il-tiba'a wa-al-nashr, 2000).

PART IV
THE PRESS AS COMMUNITY VOICE

11

The Lamp, Qasim Amin, Jewish Women and Baghdadi Men: A Reading in the Jewish Iraqi Journal *al-Misbah*

Orit Bashkin

This chapter deals with a journal entitled *al-Misbah* (The Lamp), a Jewish Iraqi publication which appeared in Baghdad between the years 1924 and 1929.[1] To the best of my knowledge, it is one of the only journals in the Arab world that has been characterised as a Zionist mouthpiece, on the one hand, and also as a testimony to the success of Arab nationalism, on the other.[2] Reading the pages of *al-Misbah* does not resolve the puzzle easily. In what follows, I examine the various issues which dominated *al-Misbah*'s pages in order to highlight the identity of the paper and to enrich our understanding of the nature of the Iraqi press under the British Mandate. I address two discursive circles – the Iraqi and the Jewish one. I propose that the paper conveyed an unmistakable Iraqi and Arab identity. Despite the editor's Zionist inclinations, the conversations between readers and writers acquired a life of their own and the paper had, in fact, promoted a new Arab Jewish identity. The themes dealt with by *al-Misbah*'s readers, moreover, illustrate how Jews sought to use the state's institutions built under the Mandate as venues for the cultivation of non-sectarian and democratic citizenship.

The Jewish community in Iraq at the end of World War I numbered about 87,488 individuals out of a population of 2,849,238. In 1920, 50,000 Jews populated Baghdad; this Jewish Baghdadi community had been relatively affluent as far back as the nineteenth century. The community enjoyed commercial ties with migrant communities of Iraqi Jews in India and England, and boasted a secular education system whose roots date back to the mid-1860s when a school of the Alliance Israélite Universelle was opened in Baghdad. During the 1920s, the number of exclusively religious Jewish schools decreased and more Jews began attending secular schools (either governmental or sponsored by the Jewish community). Their bilingual education enabled many middle-class Jews to integrate into the state's economy under the Mandate, and many worked in British banks and commercial companies.[3]

Jews began to affiliate themselves with the Iraqi community subsequent to the Young Turk Revolution in 1908. This process was culturally marked by the abandoning of Judeo-Arabic (Arabic written in Hebrew characters) and the adoption of Arabic and Ottoman Turkish in its stead. Indeed, Iraqi Jews were involved in the publications of bilingual (Ottoman–Arabic) journals printed in Baghdad immediately after the Young Turk Revolution. In the 1920s, Arabic language was introduced into all Iraqi schools as a means of inculcating new notions of Iraqi-Arab nationalism among all the subjects of the new Iraqi state. Jews in this period gradually adopted Arabic as their written language, a process that accelerated to a much greater degree during the 1930s and 1940s.[4]

Analysing the pages of *al-Misbah* and, more broadly, of Jewish Iraqi history, necessitates reading against the grain of two national historiographies. The first is a Zionist historiography that had tended to emphasise the failure of the Jewish community to become fully integrated in Iraqi state and society. Although Jews had aspired to become equal members in Iraqi society, this narrative argues, anti-Jewish sentiments and hostility were generated by the growth of the radical branch of Iraqi Pan-Arabism, the radicalisation of national elites during the 1930s, and the unfolding conflict in Palestine. This process had culminated in the *Farhud*, a wave of anti-Jewish riots in 1941, during which over 180 Jews were killed. The influence of certain pro-fascist and authoritarian voices in the Iraqi public sphere had been used to underscore the anti-Semitic nature of some groups identified with Iraqi-Arab nationalism. The activity of the Zionist underground in Iraq in the 1940s and the final migration of Iraqi Jews to Israel in the early 1950s mark the final result of this long process.[5] Ultranationalist Iraqi historiography, on the other hand, pointed to Zionist conspiracies that began in the 1920s and culminated in the late 1940s, which allowed the Zionist movement to win its share of supporters among the Jewish community.[6] Both historiographies, however, de-contextualise the realities of the Jewish community in the 1920s by projecting the realities of the post-1948 era onto the early history of the Iraqi state and of Arab Iraqi nationalism. Both, moreover, overemphasise the extent of influence of the Zionist movement in Iraq. Finally, both narratives have recently been rejected by a host of Iraqi, Arab and Israeli scholars who searched for new ways of exploring the world of the Arab Jews.[7]

Contextualising *al-Misbah* also necessitates a new reading of the 1920s in Iraqi history. Peter Wien has pointed out the enormous differences between the 1920s and 1930s in Iraq, cautioning historians not to lump together the two time periods under the comfortable rubric of 'the interwar period'.[8] Much scholarship has emphasised the radical, Pan-Arab elements of the Iraqi intellectual history during the interwar period. Most attention was paid to Ottoman bureaucrats and officers turned Iraqi nationalists and to voices of intellectuals affiliated with the state. During the 1930s the dominant national discourse was Pan-Arabism as evident in the important works of Sati' al-Husri, Fadhil al-Jamali and other prominent Pan-Arabists. In addition, authoritarian and antidemocratic voices became very prominent in public debate during this period.[9]

In contrast, the 1920s represent an entirely different era. The state had indeed espoused a Pan-Arab identity which was influenced by narratives shaped in the Arab Revolt, and spoke of the great contribution of the Hashemites to the Arab and Islamic nation. Nevertheless, essays concerning political theory of the early 1920s dealt with such themes as the virtues of constitutionalism, republicanism and democracy. Such themes typified the discourse of the constitutional revolutions in Iran and in the Ottoman Empire as well as the prevailing Wilsonian ideology. Significantly, one of the most important media to discuss democracy and parliamentarianism was the budding Iraqi press, whose editorials from the early 1920s all addressed these themes.

Furthermore, a review of the intellectual production of poets, writers and journalists in the 1920s reveals an interest in a variety of topics, not necessarily affiliated with Pan-Arabism. Iraqi Shi'i poets from the south, for example, dealt with the land regime in Iraq and the suffering of poor tribesmen and peasants.[10] During the 1920s, Iraq had only a few major dailies like *al-'Iraq*, *al-Istiqlal* and *al-'Alam al-'Arabi*. The print culture, however, allowed local writers to express concerns specific to their religious, ethnic or regional communities or to use newspapers to promote their personal agendas.[11] Popular Shi'i poet 'Abbud al-Karkhi utilised his journal *al-Karkh*, written in rhymed colloquial Iraqi Arabic, to reflect on a plethora of topics ranging from his wife's lovers to praise of *Ahl al-Bayt*.[12] The Sunni neoclassical poet Ma'ruf al-Rusafi examined issues like women's emancipation and the urban poor in his poetry and discussed cultural themes in his journal *al-Amal*.[13] The themes discussed in the public sphere, in other words, were highly diverse and mirrored the interests of various segments within the nation. It is in this context that we should scrutinise a journal like *Al-Misbah*.

Al-Misbah's editor and publisher was Salman Shina (1899–1978), a Jewish law student and the founder of the Hebrew Literary Society of which he served as secretary.[14] Anuwar Sha'ul (1904–84), a Jewish writer, lawyer and poet, served as editor for the first ten months and then resigned, apparently due to disagreements with Shina.[15] The paper was published once a week in a Christian publishing house (al-Matba'a al-Siriyaniyya al-Kathulikiyya), although Jews owned publishing houses themselves (most notably the Dangur publishing house that had been active since 1904).

Most of the writers and readers of *al-Misbah* were young Jewish men who belonged to the Baghdadi middle class; however, among the subscribers were also readers from Basra and Hilla as well as from Iran, Lebanon and India. In the 1920s, a number of Jewish literary societies such as al-Saff al-Adabi and al-Jam'iyya al-Iqtisadiyya were active in Baghdad and sought to bring progress and equality to Iraqi society. The members of these organisations constituted a major and substantial group that both subscribed to the paper and contributed items to it.[16] Based on the contents of the paper and biographical details of its writers, it seems that most writers were educated (with a high school diploma or higher). Advertisements published in the paper (mostly by Jewish businessmen) also indicate the upper- and middle-class background of writers and readers. The paper advertised fashion products (for both men and women), as well as bicycles, cars, bookstores and journals, insurance companies, the Iraqi Casino and products unique to the needs of the Jewish community like kosher meat. Like other Iraqi nationalists, Jews believed that the modern subject should have a healthy physique; thus we find in *al-Misbah* a few sports stories and advertisements for a fitness gym (*mahal tanshit al-abdan*) in which young Jewish men exercised. In addition, *al-Misbah* published medical advice to young men and women in the column 'Fawa'id sihhiya'. The advertisements, then, reflect the leisure practices and literary interests of bourgeois men as well as the products they consumed.

The Iraqi Nation State and its Arab Culture

Readers and writers showed a growing interest in Arabic language and literature as *al-Misbah* frequently published original poems and translated others. Some were romantic verses which dealt with the beauty of nature or the torments of lovers; others addressed sociopolitical dilemmas pertaining to the unjust Iraqi social structure and the gaps between different social groups. The paper also published poems written by Egyptian and Lebanese poets such as Iliya Abu Madi and Jubran Khalil Jubran, while young Jewish writers like Murad Mikha'il challenged conventional neoclassical norms in their romantic poetry. Evidence of *al-Misbah*'s literary success can be found in a letter sent to the paper by the poet Ma'ruf al-Rusafi in which he expressed his support of Mikha'il's poetry. *Al-Misbah* also included short stories in its issues, again a new addition to the Iraqi literary canon. Early works in the field of theatre appeared in the first issue. The paper likewise reported at length on various plays performed in Iraq, and profited from advertisements for shows and theatrical plays. As early as 1921, the Jewish Literary Society introduced the play *Salah al-Din al-Ayubi*. Since it was not accepted for females to act in plays in those days, Sha'ul was chosen to play the leading heroine. In 1926, the play *al-Sid* was shown in Iraq, directed by Khaduri Sharabani and performed by the members of the Iraqi Literary Society.[17]

The interest in new literary genres should come as no surprise to those familiar with the Iraqi literary scene of the 1920s. In these years, neoclassical poetry dominated the Iraqi poetic scene with the works of Rusafi and Jamil Sidqi al-Zahawi published frequently. Other writers, nonetheless, began introducing new literary genres. Socialist writer Mahmud Ahmad al-Sayyid, who published in *al-Misbah*, experimented with the writing of short stories and plays. Egyptian and Lebanese literary products that assumed a central role in the Iraqi print market impressed readers with their thematic and literary innovations. *Al-Misbah*, in this respect, responded to its readers' fascination with new phenomena in the Arabic literary field and appropriated many of the literary genres current in the Arabic periodical literature.

Arab culture was highly relevant to the readers of the journal. The 'Arab proverbs' section (*hikam 'arabiyya*) of *al-Misbah* is a good example of the journal's commitment to the preservation and cultivation of Arab culture and Arab history. This section quoted sayings of medieval writers like al-Jahiz or Ibn al-Muqaffa'; famed Arab political or religious leaders like 'Umar ibn al-Khattab, Mu'awiya and imam 'Ali (ibn Abi Talib – the word 'imam' appeared in the original); and contemporary Muslim reformers like Muhammad 'Abduh.[18]

The selection of past and present heroes was constructed in a non-sectarian fashion and included historical figures that were viewed very negatively in Shi'i historiography (Mu'awiya) as well as the Shi'i imams. Interwar Sunni intellectuals were noted for their penchant for frequently referencing the *futuhat* era (the period in which the Middle East was conquered by the Muslims) as a model for young Iraqi Arabs.[19] The writers in *al-Misbah*, it seems, followed this pattern by referencing the second Muslim righteous Caliph 'Umar. Nonetheless, in their attempt to appear non-sectarian, they quoted writers identified with the *shu'ubiyya* as well as those who critiqued it and venerated Sunnis and Shi'is, Arabs and Persians equally. In doing so they marked the fact that all things Arab, and all things related to Arab Islamic culture, were relevant to their lives. Even reformer Muhammad 'Abduh's suggestions for revitalising Islam so that it would be compatible with the demands of the modern world struck a chord in Jewish readers, who posed similar queries regarding their own religion.

The identification with Arab culture had implications concerning the self-image of the Iraqi Jewish community. One effect was a conceptual change with respect to time, in which Jews came to regard Arab and Islamic history as their own. For example, one article hailed the munificence of Islam in general, and the Ottoman Empire in particular, for providing refuge to Jews who were expelled from Spain in 1492. Moreover, the religious harmony between Jews and Muslims in the Middle Ages was celebrated and positioned vis-à-vis medieval European (and hence Christian) fanaticism.[20]

These narratives are worthy of note. First, they appropriate a position articulated by many a Muslim reformer, namely that concepts of tolerance and equality did not originate in modern Europe but in Islam. While Europe was in the darkness of the Middle Ages, Islamic empires cultivated religious coexistence. These narratives, however, were now imbued with a Jewish meaning as it was suggested that this tolerance enabled medieval Jewish communities to flourish. Second, the construction of the positive image of the Ottoman Empire refers to common themes within the Iraqi print media. Hashemite Iraq of the 1920s commemorated the great achievements of the Arab Revolt as one of the main legitimising narratives of the ruling elites. The Hashemites were hence represented as liberators of Iraqis, and indeed of all Arabs, from the repressive Ottoman yoke. Nonetheless, the print media of interwar Iraq was full of praise for Turkey and the Ottoman Empire. Iraqi Sunni elites, schooled in the bilingual (Ottoman–Arabic) system and accustomed to reading in Ottoman-Turkish, did not forget their past easily and continued to reference Ottoman works in their writings.[21] In addition, Kemalism represented a positive model of reform and change. Thus, positive reference to the Ottoman past, in particular when juxtaposed with British colonialism, was not uncommon in this period. *Al-Misbah*, whose editor Shina worked as a translator for the Ottoman army during World War I, reproduced such narratives and adjusted them to the Jewish context.

Writers' perception of time relates to their understanding of the term 'revival', or 'awakening', signified by the Arabic term *al-nahda*. The *nahda* in the Arab world denoted the process of Arabic literary and cultural renewal which occurred during the second half of the nineteenth and early years of the twentieth centuries. In Iraq, the Hashemites viewed the Iraqi state as the outcome of the Arab *nahda*. The *nahda* holiday (*'id al-nahda*) was commemorated in Iraq on the ninth of Sha'ban to associate it with the Arab Revolt.

The Jewish writers of *al-Misbah* were also interested in the concept of revival. Writer Ezra Haddad noted that the period in which Iraqis lived was an era of scientific and literary innovations. Yet the spread of *nahda* in the East, he argued, was conditioned upon the expansion of education and culture, namely an increase in libraries and schools, which would provide Iraqis with the tools needed to live in a modern world. He likewise bemoaned the fact that Iraqis had internalised only the superficial components of Western culture, especially Western clothing, without internalising the more meaningful scientific and philosophical currents attached to Western modernity.[22] Other essays called on Iraqis to awaken from the state of stagnation (*jumud*) which characterised the East and, instead, mimic the Japanese model of bilingual education and expansion of educational missions.[23]

The arguments proposed by *al-Misbah*'s writers were never marked by great originality. On the contrary, they mirrored the countless debates in the Arab press of the time regarding the success and poetical failures of the Arab *nahda*, its relationship to the projects of the Enlightenment and secular modernity, and its nationalist implications. All the arguments produced by *al-Misbah*'s writers were expressed in the Arab press of the period. Instead, the significance of the journal was that it demonstrated that Iraqi Jews had come to view their history in non-religious terms. The revival of Arab culture during this period of renaissance and reawakening was connected in these articles not to specific events in the history of the Iraqi-Jewish community, or even to the Jewish community at all. Rather, Jews saw themselves as part of the Arab community whose cultural revival was theirs and whose achievements they shared and appreciated.

Al-Misbah did not directly express views on political issues such as the struggle for independence, since its editors were not permitted to take political sides in a journal that was defined as a literary cultural magazine. Even within these restraining parameters, however, Anuwar Sha'ul attacked the privileges granted to foreign companies in Iraq in one of his editorials.[24] Noticeably, this piece had nothing to do with cultural affairs, and very clearly articulated the national desire to have full control of the nation's capital and to attain economic sovereignty.

Al-Misbah displayed considerable interest in the political arena. Writers were proud of the new institutions created by the state, such as the new parliament and the Iraqi elections, and hoped that such institutions would ensure equality to all members of the Iraqi nation regardless of their religious affiliations. *Al-Misbah* took great pride in the Jewish members of parliament and the senate, especially the Jewish Minister of Finance, Ezekiel Sasson, as well as the Jews who played a leading role in the state's judicial institutions like Da'ud Samara or Ibrahim al-Kabir.[25] The inclusion of Jews in such institutions was perceived as testimony to their non-sectarian, democratic nature. Young writer (and future gifted short story writer) Shalom Darwish likewise bemoaned the lack of non-sectarian Iraqi national holidays in which all members of the community could participate.[26] The very existence of *al-Misbah* was linked to the Iraqi national revival as writers argued that their goal was to serve the nation and called on all Iraqi youths to awaken and come to the assistance of the Iraqi homeland (*watan*).[27]

The articles about the Iraqi state and its new institutions speak, again, to a larger Iraqi context. At the time, Iraqi nationalists and intellectuals (Sunni and Shi'i alike) expressed growing suspicions that the institutions created by Britain in Iraq were merely a democratic façade while in effect, British colonial interests dominated the politics of the new Iraqi state. They felt that the parliament, the constitution and the senate were devoid of democratic merit as they did not truly represent the desires of the Iraqi electorate.[28] *Al-Misbah*'s writers, in contrast, expressed their hopes that the new institutions – the parliament, senate and Iraqi electoral system – would be able to fulfil their democratic potential and allow Iraqis to enjoy a true democracy. Whilst these hopes might be deemed extremely unrealistic and naïve, they indicate that even if the British and King Faysal viewed such institutions as convenient venues to secure their interests, elements within the Iraqi community had actually hoped to imbue them with democratic meanings, and, moreover, use them as important bridges to build new non-sectarian and democratic notions of citizenship and civic consciousness.

In Iraqi and Arab history, nationalists were often divided into Pan-Arabists, on the one hand, and local or territorial nationalists, on the other. While the former group consisted of individuals who cherished the shared cultural features of the Arabic-speaking peoples, and often desired a unity of some sort between Arabs divided into artificially created nation states, the latter group tended to emphasise the unique territorial, historical and geographical features that emerged in *each* nation state (Egyptian, Lebanese, Iraqi, etc.). These divisions were meaningful for many Arabs, and had momentous political repercussions on their lives, as the Pan-Arab/territorial binary coloured Arab politics, cultural considerations and print markets during most of the twentieth century.[29] Nonetheless, the boundaries between the Pan-Arab and the local were not always clear-cut. In fact, they were fluid, adaptable and highly unstable, and their meanings fluctuated from context to context and from time to time.

Al-Misbah's readers did display a sense of an Iraqi identity. Stories in the newspaper expressed their authors' pride in the fact that they belonged to a political unit named Iraq. These writers, moreover, genuinely hoped that the new nation state and its institutions, in the present political borders, would grant them citizenship rights and equality. Nonetheless, these writers lived in a state governed by a Hashemite monarchy whose systems of cultural patronage promoted narratives of Pan-Arab ideology as a legalising mechanism that authenticated the Hashemite right to rule Iraq. The state educational elites promoted Arab education and culture while Iraqi poetry, composed by such poets as Muhammad Mahdi al-Basir, 'Ali Sharqi, Ahmad Safi al-Najafi and al-Zahawi, commemorated both Arab and Islamic symbols and the great achievements of the Arab Revolt.[30] These means were effective. Writers in *al-Misbah* cherished Arab culture; they saw themselves as active participants in the formation of a modern Arab culture and in the constant deliberations about its components and historical narratives. Based on their readings of Arabic literature, culture and history, however, they produced their own version of Pan-Arabism, which appropriated many narratives and metaphors current at the Arab and Iraqi literature of the day and yet fitted the needs of the Jewish Iraqi community. Other religious and ethnic communities in Iraq followed the same path, and used the Arab Iraqi press to articulate their unique cultural needs, on the one hand, and their shared vision of Arab Iraqi nationalism, on the other. Importantly, the policies adopted by Pan-Arabists, like Sati' al-Husri, which insisted on the teaching of Arabic to minority groups, had consolidated both the Arab *and* the Iraqi identities of minority groups since their knowledge of Arabic enabled them to read and write in Arabic and take an active part in the Iraqi public sphere and its press.

Representing Minority Voices: Social Issues and Jewish Affairs

A large proportion of items in *al-Misbah* dealt with the endemic inequality in the Iraqi society. Articles referred to the wrongs inflicted on the poor segments of society, the condescending attitudes of the rich towards the poor, and the ways in which education could change the lot of the poor, themes which were all discussed in Iraqi neoclassical poetry and the contemporary press. A topic which appeared in many issues of *al-Misbah* was the emancipation of Iraqi women. The influence of Qasim Amin's (1863–1908) writings is evident in these articles. A frank discussion of the issue started as early as July 1924 with a letter sent by a girl called R. S. Alias, who complained about the obstacles confronted by a young Jewish girl. Her parents were disappointed at her birth that she was not a boy and later on they deprived her of a proper education, a tool with which she could still have had some opportunity to better her miserable lot. This letter promoted a spate of responses – letters, articles and poems – all written by men, most of them calling for the revival of the Iraqi woman (*al-nahda al-nisa'iyya*). Anuwar Sha'ul summarised his position by arguing that the nation would progress if it enjoyed the efforts of both genders. In fact, he said, those who object to the emancipation of women should be honest and admit that they do not want the nation to progress at all. These views were strengthened by articles reproduced from Iraqi, Egyptian and Lebanese papers that reported and debated various activities of women in Iraq and the Middle East.[31]

Women's emancipation was relevant to the realities of 1920s Iraq. The heated dispute about veiling, especially in 1924 (the year in which the letter by Alias was published), encompassed numerous journals and featured the positions of leading intellectuals. Both Rusafi and Zahawi stood at the forefront of a camp which called for unveiling, ending women's seclusion and promoting education amongst the female members of society. Both reproduced, in poetic form, the arguments of Qasim Amin and publications that appeared in the Ottoman journal *Ictihad*. Shi'i *mujtahids*, like Hibat al-Din al-Shaharstani, expressed opinions in favour of permitting women's education, although they still objected to unveiling and supported polygamy. More radically, Shi'i intellectual Fahmi al-Mudarris suggested emulating the reforms occurring in Egypt and Turkey, saying that such steps were necessary if the nation was to experience a true revival. Iraqi women, moreover, took the initiative themselves. Asma' al-Zahawi's Baghdadi club al-Nahda al-Nisa'iyya (Women's Revival), which included mostly upper- and middle-class women, protested seclusion and advocated women's education in order to facilitate the running of modern households. Similar positions were addressed in the journal *Layla* (1923–5), edited by Pauline Hassun. The majority of intellectuals, however, objected to women's unveiling and supported seclusion.

'Abbud al-Karkhi, for instance, lampooned those Muslims who abandoned their traditional values only to replace them with the lifestyle of Egyptian scientists, doctors and philosophers which mimicked the European ways.[32]

The articles on the revival of Iraqi Jewish women should be understood within this context. The essays written by the Jews who contributed to *al-Misbah* associated the transformation of Jewish women into modern educated citizens with the revival of the Arab Iraqi nation. Jewish women, moreover, were praised for their education, their knowledge of Arab culture and their command of the Arabic language. Most of the writers' arguments for liberating Jewish women were reproduced from Arabic publications, especially the representation of women as the educators of the next generation. They, like other Arab writers, claimed that if marriages were to be based on love, both men and women would be enriched, and the nation would enjoy the existence of productive and successful households.

On the other hand, the essays about Jewish women dealt with specific Jewish themes such as the call to reform the practice of dowry in the community or to reduce its financial burden. In fact, these essays sparked intense debates within the Jewish Iraqi community. One reader even suggested cancelling all forms of dowry completely. These discussions, more than indicating the Jewish nature of the paper, designate the kind of Jewish identity the paper promoted: it appealed to reform-minded, secularising young elites who not only adopted Arabic as their written language and embraced Iraq's new national culture but also sought to reform the Jewish community itself along the same lines suggested by Muslim and Western reformers. The connections made between household and nation, mother and educator, in other words, were now re-narrated to fit the needs of Jewish readers and the changes in the Jewish community.[33]

Writing about the inequalities typifying Iraqi society forced writers to locate the Jewish community within this discourse of rights and new notions of citizenship. *Al-Misbah* focused on issues relevant specifically to the Jewish community and devoted considerable space to discussing its desires and dilemmas. In the same way that writers of *al-Misbah* sought to bring change to the Iraqi society as a whole, and to its oppressed groups in particular, they also wanted to apply their concepts of modernity, nationalism and equality to the Jewish context. Thus, the paper took an active role in a campaign calling for uniting all Jewish schools under one national management, and preached for the abolition of outdated religious customs in Jewish society such as the ritual slaughter of animals.

Al-Misbah offered a stage to the Jewish voice to fight against discrimination and anti-Jewish publications. When Shakespeare's *Merchant of Venice* was translated into Arabic, *al-Misbah* featured a long essay explaining the historical background which produced the false stereotype represented by Shylock.[34] In 1924, an Iraqi officer by the name of Rasul al-Qadiri, who had served in the Russian White army, published his memoirs in the Baghdad journal *al-'Alam al-'Arabi*. Al-Qadiri told readers of the existence of a multinational Jewish conspiracy to take control of the world's economic resources through a series of political revolutions, the most recent of them being the Bolshevik Revolution. Anuwar Sha'ul attempted to counter Qadiri's charges in the paper in which they were published, but the editor of *al-'Alam al-'Arabi* refused to print Sha'ul's response. Undaunted, Sha'ul published several articles in *al-Misbah* explaining the absurdity of al-Qadiri's accusations: 'Allah will judge you, oh Qadiri, for the abominable lies you have written . . ., for this despicable fabrication! . . . for such malicious slander!!!', Sha'ul fumed. At the end of the affair, al-Qadiri apologised. He explained that his intention was to discredit only the Russian Jews, whereas Iraqi Jews were definitely loyal citizens who posed no danger to anyone. The success of *al-Misbah*'s campaign illustrates that its criticisms resonated beyond the confines of the Jewish community and were effective in the general Iraqi domain as well. Al-Qadiri's 'original' defence also demonstrates that he could not produce any anti-Semitic remarks with respect to Iraqi Jews.[35]

Al-Misbah served as an important medium of informing the local community of the life of the other Jews in the Diaspora. It presented reports on the lives of famous Jews such as Albert Einstein; on the activities of Jewish organisations such as Hadassa and B'nei Brith; and on the anti-Semitism to which Jews were exposed around the world – from the pogroms in Russia to the Ku Klux Klan in the USA (aptly described as *al-jam'iyya al-sharira*, 'the evil society').[36] In fact, articles about the status and circumstances of Jews in places like Italy and Russia suggest that the writers seemed to think that the lot of Jews in Russia was far worse than theirs and that Iraqi Jews, unlike their Ashkenazi brethren, enjoyed a certain measure of security, success and emancipation.

Al-Misbah described the activities of the Zionist movement and reported on the lives of Jews who lived in mandatory Palestine. The paper covered the opening ceremony of the Hebrew University in Jerusalem in 1925; reported on the activities of the Zionist poet Haim Nahman Bialik; quoted from Hebrew papers appearing in Palestine such as *Davar* and *Haaretz*; and reported on the meetings of Chaim Weizmann with the Amir 'Abdullah.[37]

Salman Shina addressed several Zionist organisations both as publisher of *al-Misbah* and as the secretary of the Hebrew Literary Society. He noted that although he and his colleagues could not publish anything which was openly connected to Zionism, their paper *al-Misbah* was still a victim of many attacks because of its Zionist leanings; however, depicting the paper as a 'Zionist' paper would be a grave mistake since most of its articles dealt with the Jewish community in Iraq and with Iraqi and Arab issues. In spite of Shina's argument that the paper was identified with Zionism, the readers of *al-Misbah* seemed not to have been aware of any such leanings. To them, *al-Misbah* was mostly a journal written in Arabic which discussed matters of the Jewish and Iraqi community, and they related to it as such. Even when writing about Zionism, articles in *al-Misbah* called for cooperation between Palestinian Arabs and Jews, 'the children of Abraham', in building a just society in Palestine. Therefore, they recognised the importance of *both* communities and hoped for coexistence and peace between them. As naïve and unrealistic as this vision might seem today, it indicates that the paper's writers projected their own hopes for a society based on equality for Jews and Muslims in Iraq onto the Palestinian arena as well. Since the Jewish writers identified themselves with Arab culture, they could not typify the Arab culture as degenerate or backward since in doing so, they would be denigrating their own culture. Similarly, as denizens of the Arab Middle East, they could not have imagined Palestine as a land without a people.

Al-Misbah closed in 1929. As the conflict in Palestine escalated after 1929, the Jews were impelled to take sides in the conflict. In the 1930s, most chose to side with the goals of Arab nationalism and adopted anti-Zionist positions. During the 1920s, when the identities of the Iraqi state as well as those of Iraqis, Arabs, Jews and Muslims were constantly negotiated, the existence of *al-Misbah* was almost a necessity. It ceased to be so towards the end of the decade.

The trans-regional links between Iraqi Jews and other Jewish communities across the globe, as expressed in *al-Misbah*, might cast doubt on the paper's national commitment. Yet, in the Iraqi context, trans-regional networks existed for other non-Jewish groups. Since the Iraqi press was quite modest in the 1920s, Iraqi writers and readers (many of them Sunnis) read Arab publications produced outside of Iraq. Iraqi students also acquired higher education in other Arab countries during this decade. The movement of students, teachers, journalists and intellectuals to and from Iraq consolidated these Arab trans-regional bonds. Many Sunnis, moreover, continued reading Turkish publications even after World War I. Iraqi Shi'is read publications produced in Lebanon (especially the journal *al-'Irfan*) and Shi'is from Jabal 'Amil resided in Iraq for periods of time and integrated into its public sphere. Family connections, pilgrimage to the shrine cities of Najaf and Karbala', and movement of journals and books strengthened the trans-regional aspects of Shi'i culture, which included such states as Iran, India, Lebanon and Iraq. Iraqi Kurds read publications in Kurdish produced in Syria, and a lively, albeit modest, Kurdish public sphere existed in the north of Iraq. These trans-regional networks did not necessarily jeopardise the national character of the Iraqi nation. The existence of this system, however, meant that while Iraqis considered themselves loyal citizens, they did care for other groups situated outside of Iraq. Nonetheless, many a time they articulated their concerns for such groups as *Iraqis* and compared their fortunate location with that of their brethren. The periodical literature thus maintained a system of hyphenated identities in which one could be an Iraqi and a member of a religious or ethnic community.[38]

Conclusion

Al-Misbah appeared during a crucial stage in the history of the Iraqi Jewish community when the community desired to become fully integrated in the Iraqi nation, on the one hand, while preserving its Jewish identity, on the other. *Al-Misbah* reflected a growing propensity among Iraqi Jews to read Arabic material and to write in Arabic. Jewish history and cultural life were relevant to readers' lives, yet the language in which to think about Jewish life and the encounter of the Jewish community with modernity was Arabic, and the conceptual tools used to reflect upon processes related to modernity were borrowed from the realm of Islamic reform and Arab nationalism. The Iraqi press generated the sense that all readers belonged to the Arab Iraqi nation, yet Iraqi Pan-Arabism was not an ideology imposed on an ethnically divided population from above, but was rather a system of thought which was constantly negotiated according to the needs of different communities.

Those who wrote in the paper perceived themselves as the intellectual elite of their society. A journalist was a pioneer, a person with a noble mission – to change his or her society. Yet, despite this image, *al-Misbah* was a male, bourgeois product. It called for women's equality and for helping the poor, yet such demands were mostly articulated by middle-class Baghdadi men. Nonetheless, *al-Misbah* did allow some new voices in Iraqi society to be heard, above all that of the young generation who proclaimed their agenda for the Jewish and Iraqi community on the paper's pages.

Both readers and writers regarded themselves as members of the Iraqi nation. They felt that this nation was being shaped before their eyes and yearned to participate in the process. They likewise hoped that the new nation state would provide equality for all minorities, including Jews. The great hopes affiliated with the concept of nationalism might call into question certain assumptions regarding the experiences of Jews in the modern Arab world. In *The Jews of Islam*, Bernard Lewis purports that while Jews and Muslims were able to coexist and enrich each other's cultures during medieval times, Jewish–Arab relations were irreversibly changed with the rise of Arab nationalism and with the adoption of certain anti-Semitic motifs coming from Western sources.[39] Other writers have likewise emphasised the proclivity of Arab nationalists, especially due to the Arab–Israeli conflict, to adopt European anti-Semitic discourses.[40] The somewhat concealed Orientalist presumption of such arguments is that Arab nationalism was unable to adapt from the religious 'dhimma' concept to the modern Western notion of equal citizenship, and thus turned instead to Western anti-Semitic rhetoric and stereotyping.

The experience of *al-Misbah*, however, shows us another option. Iraqi Jews saw the advantages of the democratic nation state and believed that this political framework was the most beneficial to their interests. Moreover, the participation of Muslims in the newspaper and more broadly, the openness of the Arab literary field to the integration attempts of these Jews confirm that their hopes, at least in the context of the 1920s, were not unfounded. This is by no means an attempt to idealise the concept of nationalism or to ignore its authoritarian dimensions in Iraq. It is meant, however, to highlight the fact that in the context of the 1920s, the combination of Arab nationalism and a functioning democratic constitutional system seemed like a workable option for Iraqi Jews, as well as for Iraqi Muslims.

Finally, *al-Misbah* attests to the problematic historiography of the Iraqi press produced under the British Mandate. It has been assumed that this press was preoccupied mainly with national issues, especially the unfolding 1930 Treaty with Britain, and was dominated by the politics of leading personalities. Nevertheless, moving beyond the content of Baghdadi dailies, we see that the anticolonial struggle was only one issue that occupied the journals of the time. Just as the unique universe of Iraqi Jews comes to life through reading *al-Misbah*, many other intriguing microcosms could emerge from reading analogous newspapers published in Najaf, Kirkuk and Baghdad itself. *Al-Misbah*, furthermore, illustrates how Iraqi subjects attempted to come to terms with the British Mandate and its institutions. In the Jewish context, it seems that regardless of the colonial machinations that accompanied the creation of Iraqi state institutions, groups within Iraqi society hoped to imbue these institutions with democratic substance that would facilitate the creation of new notions of citizenship and nationhood.

The vision promoted by *al-Misbah*'s writers did not survive the turbulent late 1940s and the realities created in the Middle East following 1948. Yet *al-Misbah*'s failure should not obscure the significance of its vision and the tolerant, inclusive view of Arab nationalism it offered. Today, as the Iraqi state itself is torn apart by civil war, and relations between Arabs and Jews in Israel and Palestine have reached a new nadir, the writings of *al-Misbah* might offer us all some comfort, hope and an alternative vision.

Notes

1. A brief version of this chapter was presented at MESA 1999. I warmly thank Anthony Gorman, Didier Monciaud and Ami Ayalon.
2. al-Ma'adidi, *al-Sihafa al-yahudiyya fi al-'iraq*; 'Abd al-'Aziz, 'al-Nashat al-sahyuni fi al-'iraq'; 'Abd al-Mushin, 'Majallat *al-Misbah*'; Moreh, 'Anuwar Sha'ul'; Kazzaz, "itoma'im yehudim be-'iraq'; Snir, *'Arviyut*.

3. On the Iraqi Jewish community, see Bashkin, *New Babylonians*; Schlaepfer, *Les intellectuels juifs de Bagdad*; Kazzaz, *He-Yehudim be-'iraq*; Rejwan, *Jews of Iraq*; Ben Ya'qov, *Yehudey Bavel*; Ghunayma, *Nuzhat al-mushtaq* (*Nostalgic Trip*).
4. Kazzaz, "itoma'im yehudim be-'iraq'; Me'ir, *Hitpathut tarbutit hevratit shel yehudey 'iraq*.
5. Atlas, *Be-Zel 'Amud ha-teliya*; Moreh and Yehudah, *Sin'at yehudim u-fera'ot be-'irak*; al-Peleg, *Ha-mufti ha-Gadol*, p. 59; Cohen, *Ha-Pe'ilut ha-zionit be-'iraq*.
6. 'Abd al-'Aziz, 'al-Nashat al-sahyuni fi al-'iraq'; al-Ma'adidi, *al-Sihafa al-yahudiyya fi al-'iraq*; al-Barrak, *al-Madaris al-yahudiyya*.
7. Snir, *Arviyut*; Snir, "'My Heart Beats with Love of the Arabs'"; Shiblak, *Lure of Zion*; Rejwan, *Jews of Iraq*; Shenhav, *Arab Jews*; Levi, "'From Baghdad to Bialik with Love'"; Somekh, *Baghdad, Etmol*; Rejwan, *Last Jew in Baghdad*.
8. Wien, *Iraqi Arab Nationalism*.
9. Ibid.; Dawn, 'The Formation of Pan-Arab Ideology'; Marr, 'The Development of a Nationalist Ideology'; Cleveland, *Making of an Arab Nationalist*; Suleiman, *Arabic Language*, pp. 126–46; Simon, *Iraq between Two World Wars*; Epple, *Palestine Conflict*.
10. Izzidien, *Modern Iraqi Poetry*.
11. F. Butti, *Sihafat al-'iraq*; R. Butti, *al-Sihafa fi al-'iraq*.
12. The poems were later collected in al-Karkhi, *Diwan 'Abbud al-Karkhi*.
13. Matlub, *al-Naqd al-adabi*.
14. On Shina, see Shina, *Mi-Bavel le-Zion*.
15. Sha'ul, *Qissat hayati*; al-Khalili, *al-Qissa al-'iraqiyya*, pp. 207–35; 'Abd al-Ilah, *Nash'at al-qissa*, pp. 237–51.
16. Me'ir, *Hitpathut tarbutit hevratit shel yehudey 'iraq*, pp. 422–3.
17. *Misbah* 17 April, 8 May, 17 July, 31 July, 18 August and 11 September 1924; 28 May and 11 June 1925; 22 April, 29 April and 3 June 1926; 19 August 1929.
18. *Misbah* 28 June and 4 February 1925.
19. Dawn, 'The Formation of Pan-Arab Ideology'.
20. *Misbah* 22 April and 6 October 1926.
21. On the Ottoman background of Iraqi ruling elites, see Bashkin, *Other Iraq*, pp. 177–82.
22. *Misbah* 10 April 1924.
23. *Misbah* 1 May 1924; 10 July 1926.
24. *Misbah* 7 May 1924. See also 14 May 1924.
25. *Misbah* 30 October 1924; 11 June, 18 June and 25 October 1925.
26. *Misbah* 6 December 1928.

27. *Misbah* 7 May 1924
28. See, for example, the poems published by Ma'ruf al-Rusafi, *Diwan al-Rusafi*, vol. 2, pp. 403–5 and Muhammad Mahdi al-Jawahiri, *Diwan al-Jawahiri* (see the poems *Thawrat al-'iraq* (1921), *al-Thawra al-'iraqiyya* (published in the Lebanese journal *al-'Irfan* in 1921), *Bayn al-qalb wa'l Istiqlal* (published in *al-'Irfan* in 1921), *al-'Alam wa'l wataniyya* (published in the Iraqi daily *Dijla*): vol. 1, pp. 50–4, 55–9, 69, 77–8, 87–8; al-Najafi, *al-Amwaj*, pp. 108–11; Basir, *Ta'rikh al-qadiyya al-'iraqiyya*. For a general discussion, see Izzidien, *Modern Iraqi Poetry*.
29. On the binary territorial Pan-Arab in the interwar period, see Gershoni, 'Rethinking the Formation of Arab Nationalism'.
30. On narratives of Iraqi Pan-Arabism and unique territorial features of the nation, see Bashkin, *Other Iraq*, pp. 125–93.
31. *Misbah* 11 July, 24 July, 31 July, 7 August and 6 November 1924; 2 April, 7 May, 18 June, 27 August and 10 October 1925; 11 February and 3 March 1926.
32. Bashkin, 'Representations of Women'; Efrati, 'The Other "Awakening" in Iraq'; Efrati, *Women in Iraq*; Masliyah, 'Zahawi'; al-Shaykh Da'ud, *Awal al-tariq ila al-nahda al-nisawiyya fi'l-'iraq*; Wiebke, 'From Women's Problems'; al-Mudarris, *Maqalat*.
33. *Misbah* 14 August, 21 August, 11 September, 18 September and 2 October 1924; 9 March, 7 May and 11 September 1925; 13 May, 17 June and 12 August 1926.
34. *Misbah* 24 April 1924.
35. *Misbah* 25 September, 2 October and 16 October 1924; Kazzaz, *He-Yehudim be-'iraq*, pp. 211–12; Sha'ul, *Qissat hayati*, p. 108.
36. *Misbah* 15 May and 18 June 1925.
37. *Misbah* 26 March, 23 April, 30 April, 7 May and 10 October 1925; Sha'ul, *Qissat hayati*, pp. 95–7.
38. On Iraqi trans-regionalism, see Bashkin, *Other Iraq*, pp. 157–93.
39. Lewis, *Jews of Islam*.
40. Particularly disturbing examples are Podhoretz, *World War IV*; Küntzel, *Jihad and Jew-Hatred*. See also Cohn-Sherbok, *Anti-Semitism*, ch. 20.

Bibliography

'Abd al-'Aziz, Hisham Fawzi, 'al-Nashat al-sahyuni fi al-'iraq fi dhill al-intitabd al-baritani', *Shu'un filastiniyya* 180 (March 1988), pp. 41–60.

'Abd al-Ilah, Ahmad, *Nash'at al-qissa wa tatawwuriha fi al-'iraq, 1908–1939* (Baghdad: Dar al-Shu'un al-Thaqafiyya al-'Amma, 1986).

'Abd al-Mushin, 'Majallat *al-Misbah* wa dawruha al-sahayuni fi al-'iraq', *al-Jumhuriyya*, 1979, pp. 55–6.

Atlas, Yehuda, *Be-Zel 'Amud ha-teliya* (Tel Aviv: Ma'arakhot, 1969).

al-Barrak, Fadhil, *al-Madaris al-yahudiyya wa'l iraniyya fi al-'iraq: dirasa muqarana* (Baghdad: n.p., 1985).

Bashkin, Orit, *New Babylonians: A History of Jews in Modern Iraq* (Stanford: Stanford University Press, 2012).

Bashkin, Orit, *The Other Iraq: Pluralism and Culture in Hashemite Iraqi* (Stanford: Stanford University Press, 2009).

Bashkin, Orit, 'Representations of Women in the Writings of the Iraqi Intelligentsia in Hashemite Iraq, 1921–1958', *Journal of Middle East Women's Studies* 4:1 (2008), pp. 52–78.

Basir, Muhammad Mahdi, *Ta'rikh al-qadiyya al-'iraqiyya* (Baghdad: Matba'at al-Fallah, 1924).

Ben Ya'qov, Avraham, *Yehudey Bavel mi-sof tekufat ha-ge'onim ve-ad yemeynu – 1038–1960* (Jerusalem: Yad Ben Zvi, 1965).

Butti, Rafa'il, *al-Sihafa fi al-'iraq* (Cairo: Bulaq/Jami'at al-duwal al-'arabiyya, 1955).

Butti, Fa'iq, *Sihafat al-'iraq* (Baghdad: Maktabat Baghdad, 1969).

Cleveland, William L., *The Making of an Arab Nationalist: Ottomanism and Arabism in the Life and Thought of Sati' al-Husri* (Princeton, NJ: Princeton University Press, 1971).

Cohen, Haim, *Ha-Pe'ilut ha-zionit be-'iraq* (Jerusalem: Ha-Sifriya ha-zionit, 1969).

Cohn-Sherbok, Dan, *Anti-Semitism: A History* (Stroud: Sutton, 2002).

Dawn, Ernest C., 'The Formation of Pan-Arab Ideology in the Inter-war Years', *International Journal of Middle East Studies* 20:1 (1988), pp. 67–91.

Efrati, Noga, 'The Other "Awakening" in Iraq: The Women's Movement in the First Half of the Twentieth Century', *British Journal of Middle Eastern Studies* 31:2 (2004), pp. 153–73.

Efrati, Noga, *Women in Iraq: Past Meets Present* (New York: Columbia University Press, 2012).

Epple, Michael, *The Palestine Conflict in the History of Modern Iraq: The Dynamics of Involvement, 1928–1948* (London: Frank Cass, 1994).

Gershoni, Israel, 'Rethinking the Formation of Arab Nationalism in the Middle East, 1920–1945: Old and New Narratives', in James Jankowski and Israel Gershoni (eds), *Rethinking Nationalism in the Arab Middle East* (New York: Columbia University Press, 1997), pp. 3–25.

Ghunayma, Yusuf Rizq Allah, *Nuzhat al-mushtaq fi ta'rikh yahud al-'iraq* (Baghdad: al-maktaba al-'arabiyya, 1924). Also published in English as *A Nostalgic Trip into the History of the Jews of Iraq* (Lanham, MD and Oxford: University Press of America, 1998).

Izzidien, Yousif, *Modern Iraqi Poetry* (Cairo: The Cultural Press, 1971).

al-Jawahiri, Muhammad Mahdi, *Diwan al-Jawahiri*, 5 vols (Beirut: Dar al-'awda, 1982).

al-Karkhi, 'Abbud, *Diwan 'Abbud al-Karkhi* (Baghdad: Matba'at al-ma'arif, 1955).

Kazzaz, Nissim, *He-Yehudim be-'iraq ba-me'a ha-'esrim* (Jerusalem: Yad Ben Zvi, 1991).

Kazzaz, Nissim, "itoma'im yehudim be-'iraq', *Kesher* 7 (1990), pp. 36–40.

al-Khalili, Ja'far, *al-Qissa al-'iraqiyya, qadiman wa-hadithan* (Baghdad: Matba'at al-ma'arif, 1957).

Küntzel, Matthias, *Jihad and Jew-Hatred*, trans. Colin Meade (New York: Telos Press, 2007).

Levi, Lital, '"From Baghdad to Bialik with Love": A Reappropriation of Modern Hebrew Poetry', *Comparative Literature Studies* 42:3 (2005), pp. 125–54.

Lewis, Bernard, *The Jews of Islam* (Princeton, NJ: Princeton University Press, 1984).

al-Ma'adidi, 'Isam Jum'a Ahmad, *al-Sihafa al-yahudiyya fi al-'iraq* (Cairo: al-Dar al-dawliyya li'l istithmarat al-thaqafiyya, 2001).

Marr, Phebe, 'The Development of a Nationalist Ideology in Iraq, 1920–1941', *The Muslim World* 75:2 (1985), pp. 85–101.

Masliyah, Sadok, 'Zahawi: A Muslim Pioneer of Women's Liberation', *Middle Eastern Studies* 32:3 (1996), pp. 161–71.

Matlub, Ahmad, *al-Naqd al-adabi al-hadith fi al-'iraq* (Cairo: Ma'had al-buhuth wa'l dirasat al-'Arabiyya, 1968).

Me'ir, Yosef, *Hitpathut tarbutit hevratit shel yehudey 'iraq me'az 1830 ve 'ad yemeynu* (Tel Aviv: Naharayim, 1989).

Moreh, Shemu'el, 'Anuwar Sha'ul, rishon ha-meshorerim ha-'iraqiyim ba-safah ha-'aravit', *Pe'amim* 22 (1985), pp. 129–31.

Moreh, Shemu'el and Zvi Yehudah (eds), *Sin'at yehudim u-fera'ot be-'irak* (Or-Yehudah: Merkaz moreshet yahadut bavel, ha-Makhon le-heker Yahadut Bavel, 1992).

al-Mudarris, Fahmi, *Maqalat Fahmi al-Mudarris* (Baghdad: Matba'at as'ad, 1970).

al-Najafi, Ahmad Safi, *al-Amwaj* (Beirut: Dar al-'ilm li'l-mala'iyin, 1971).

al-Peleg, Zvi, *Ha-mufti ha-gadol* (Tel Aviv: Misrad ha-bitahon, 1989).

Podhoretz, Norman, *World War IV: The Long Struggle against Islamofascism* (New York: Doubleday, 2007).

Rejwan, Nissim, *The Jews of Iraq: 3000 Years of History and Culture* (Boulder, CO: Westview Press, 1985).

Rejwan, Nissim, *The Last Jew in Baghdad: Remembering a Lost Homeland* (Austin: University of Texas Press, 2004).

al-Rusafi, Ma'ruf, *Diwan al-Rusafi*, 2 vols (Beirut: Matba'at dar al-ma'rad, 1931).

Schlaepfer, Aline, *Les intellectuels juifs de Bagdad. Discours et allégeances (1908–1951)* (Leiden: Brill, 2016).

Sha'ul, Anuwar, *Qissat hayati fi wadi al-rafidayn* (Jerusalem: Manshurat rabitat al-jami'iyin al-yahud al-nazihin min al-'iraq, 1984).

al-Shaykh Da'ud, Sabiha, *Awal al-tariq ila al-nahda al-nisawiyya fi'l-'iraq* (Baghdad: Al-Rabita, 1958).

Shenhav, Yehouda, *The Arab Jews: A Postcolonial Reading of Nationalism, Religion, and Ethnicity* (Stanford: Stanford University Press, 2006).

Shiblak, Abbas, *The Lure of Zion: The Case of Iraqi Jews* (London: al-Saqi Books, 1986).

Shina, Salman, *Mi-Bavel le-Zion* (Tel Aviv: n.p., 1956).

Simon, Reeva, *Iraq between Two World Wars: The Creation and Implementation of a Nationalist Ideology* (New York: Columbia University Press, 1986).

Snir, Reuven, *'Arviyut, Yahadut, Zionut: Ma'vak Zehuyot bi-Yeziratam shel Yehudei Iraq* (Jerusalem: Yad Ben Zvi, 2005).

Snir, Reuven, '"My Heart Beats with Love of the Arabs": Iraqi Jews Writing in Arabic in the Twentieth Century', *Journal of Modern Jewish Studies* 1:2 (2002), pp. 182–203.

Somekh, Sassom, *Baghdad, Etmol* (Tel Aviv: Ha-Kibutz ha-Me'uhad, 2004).

Suleiman, Yasir, *The Arabic Language and National Identity* (Washington, DC: Georgetown University Press, 2003).

Wiebke, Walther, 'From Women's Problems to Women as Images in Modern Iraqi Poetry', *Die Welt des Islams* 36:2 (1996), pp. 219–41.

Wien, Peter, *Iraqi Arab Nationalism: Authoritarian, Totalitarian and Pro-Fascist Inclinations, 1932–1941* (New York: Routledge, 2006).

12

From a Privileged Community to a Minority Community: The Orthodox Community of Beirut through the Newspaper *Al-Hadiyya*

Souad Slim

The period following the Allied victory of 1918 was one of dividing up the Arab provinces of the Ottoman Empire and political trade-offs between Britain and France, as set down by the Sykes–Picot agreement and the Hussein–McMahon Correspondence. These new states would be governed by the system of Mandates, under the auspices of the newly formed League of Nations.[1] The fall of the Ottoman Empire and the dismemberment of its territories left the Greek Orthodox of the city of Beirut in a state of apprehension, insecurity and uncertainty. Soon after the war many Orthodox families moved to Beirut, followed by large communities who came from Anatolia and Cilicia in 1922 in the wake of the withdrawal of the French armed forces from southern Anatolia and those from Hauran in the wake of the Druze revolt in southern Syria in 1925. These refugees moved into a very precarious livelihood in the hill regions of territories belonging to the waqf of the Orthodox community.[2] Their mass arrival from Alexandretta, Adana, Hauran and Cilicia disturbed the balance of social forces in favour of a middle-class commercial bourgeoisie.

The decline of the Ottoman Empire had changed the modes of coexistence of peoples and communities drastically. Formerly a majority among the Christian communities of the empire and protected by Tsarist Russia, the Orthodox were now reduced to a minority in Greater Lebanon, cut off from their traditional geographic concentration which was vital to their business and trade. Deprived of the benefits of Russian protection, the choice of cultural Arabism drew an important faction of this community to support British policies. The Beirut bourgeoisie remained faithful to the concept of supporting the official pro-French government, and it was from this bourgeoisie that the Mandate power chose an Orthodox intellectual journalist and lawyer, Charles Debbas, to become the first president of the new Lebanese republic.

The Khati-Humayun issued in 1856 had demanded the Christian communities of the empire use the laity for the management of internal affairs of the Church, resulting in the formation of the community councils (Majlis al-Milli) in the dioceses of the big cities of Beirut, Damascus, Tripoli and Homs. Considered as the urban notability, they were chosen by the bishop from the so-called seven families (Jubayli, Trad, Bustros, Tabet, Daghir, Fi'ani and Tueni). The councils operated successfully and led to a renaissance in the ranks of the Orthodox communities, both in the administration of waqfs and in education and creation of new schools.[3] They ran the community institutions with incomes from waqfs and had no hesitation in paying taxes owed by the community or in acquiring new waqfs. Despite their nomination by the bishop, their initiatives and decisions did not always agree with those of the clergy, and conflicts often occurred between lay people and clergy concerning issues of property management or designation of officials.[4] This period of recovery was also helped in 1870 by the election of an Arab bishop in Beirut (the first case of requiring the appointment of an Arab instead of a Greek bishop).

At this time of great change, the population of the former Arab provinces of the Ottoman Empire were trying to define their attitude towards the new state. Patriarch Gregory IV of Antioch, which covered part of Bilad al-Sham, favoured a kingdom ruled by Faysal bin al-Husayn al-Hashimi.[5] By contrast, the Orthodox community of Beirut with their bishop, twice exiled by the Ottomans, sought support from the Mandate to run their businesses. Other Orthodox of Lebanon voted according to their particular regional interests. Those of both Mount Lebanon, who since 1901 had a bishop appointed from Damascus, and Tripoli supported the Patriarch and the Arabs. By contrast, those in the Kurah supported a Greater Lebanon like their co-religionists in Beirut. Most of the community, according to the King–Crane Commission, asked for a united Syrian state and a political arrangement which would recognise their presence in the different regions of Syria and Lebanon.[6]

Some scholars hold that the Greek Orthodox in the region did not need Russian protection. Being part of the urban bourgeoisie, their professions as traders and middlemen, their jobs as secretaries and farm tax collectors under local Ottoman governors, and their role as dragomen for the European ambassadors and consuls gave them a very appreciable political and economic power in the urban Ottoman world.[7] The situation of rural people was not as favourable, however. In Syria, villagers were subject to the raids and the abuses of Bedouin and were indebted to the notable elders of their towns, their supposed protectors. In the mountain villages of Lebanon, the peasants were overwhelmed by multiple tax collections and snubbed by the *muqata'ji* families designated by the Sublime Porte as tax farmers and governors of Mount Lebanon.

The late nineteenth and early twentieth centuries had been a period of transition and rebirth for the Orthodox of Beirut. Lay associations founded institutions with help from the clergy. Asylums, schools, hospitals and public libraries were run by associations whose members often sat on the community board and, when needed, propped up budgets.[8] These charitable community activities were supported by intellectual, cultural and religious actions in which newspapers played an important role.[9] Reviews published by the diocese of Beirut and community associations hitherto had been primarily religious and cultural. *Al-Hadiyya*, a newspaper owned by the Bishop of Beirut, instead focused its leading articles on an astonishing range of contemporary political and social questions: the position of minorities, the participation of immigrants in political life, the migration of populations, the Bolshevik Revolution, and local and international economic problems. The analysis of the problems of the Orthodox world such as communism in Russia, Greco-Turkish relations, the question of Cilicia, the revolt of Hauran and the difficulties of the Ecumenical Patriarchate all expressed feelings of revolt and rout.

The Newspaper and its Dissemination

During the Nahda, Cairo and Beirut became poles of attraction of cultural life with literary and political clubs, publishing houses and newspapers gaining an unprecedented importance in the East. A new category of intellectuals was born, who had a culture that was not specifically based on religious training but on a modern mastery of Arabic. They were also distinguished by their encyclopaedic knowledge and their desire to work for the development of the societies in which they lived.[10] Cities in each diocese had their own periodical: *al-Ni'ma* was published in Damascus, *al-Karmeh* in Tripoli and *Homs* in the city of Homs.

In Beirut, the printing house of St George had been founded to publish essentially religious and liturgical books in the eighteenth century. At the end of the nineteenth century, it published three periodicals: *al-Manar, al-Mahabba* and *al-Hadiyya*. The last, although the oldest (it first appeared in 1890), was relaunched after the war in 1921 as a political publication rather than the mainly religious one it had been before. For the time, it appears that *al-Hadiyya* was well distributed. Exhaustive accounts recorded subscriptions, exchanges with other periodicals, monthly payments, dating of receipts and changes in addresses for forwarding mail. These were registered in a special account book.[11] Officers were appointed to monitor the newspaper's affairs in each district of Beirut. Distribution was by post, with American immigrants constituting a third of all readers. This was the beginning of a period where remittances from immigrants began to arrive in Lebanon. This windfall ended with the 1929 crisis, and a small percentage of these families returned to settle in the country.[12]

The main subscribers were the Orthodox of Beirut distributed across three main districts, namely Ashrafiyya including Sayfi and Jemayze, Mazra'a including Muṣayṭbe and Btina, and Ras Beirut. Until the nineteenth century, these areas were regarded as rural suburbs populated by migrants from the mountains and from Damascus who took advantage of opportunities offered by the expansion of the city.[13] Eighty issues were exchanged with journals and newspapers in Beirut and in other capitals: twenty-two in Syria, forty-seven in Beirut, five in Palestine, and six in Egypt and the Sudan.

The distribution of subscribers in the register was recorded in great detail.

In Lebanon, this was by district (*qada'*) and village or diocese. Large villages had the greatest number of subscribers: al-Hadath, Baskinta, Marja'iun, Zahle, Hasbayya, Amiun and Batrun each received at least ten copies but even the most distant villages of the mountain or the Biqa' received the newspaper. The villages of Husn and Wadi al-Nasara in Syria were included with 'Akkar in Lebanon. Other lists designated Mount Lebanon as Old Lebanon (*Lubnan al-qadim*) and also mentioned the *mutasarrifiyya* of Biqa'. Syria was divided into cities of the interior and coastal cities but no issues of *al-Hadiyya* reached the villages of Syria. Was it because of transport difficulties, lack of mail services or illiteracy?[14] In addition, internal quarrels and divisions in the community had started to emerge between Syria and Lebanon, a situation which had an impact on the distribution of the newspaper in Syria. Still, several issues of the journal were sent to the main Greek Orthodox monasteries. The Syrian city with the largest subscriptions was Latakia, known for the commitment of its inhabitants to the Orthodox community and its ties of kinship and common interests with the cities of Tripoli and Beirut.

A peculiarity in the lists of subscribers was the change of address registered with each name. At the beginning of the century, emigration to the New World and internal migration increased particularly towards Beirut and its outskirts, as well as between cities and between the Syrian villages or between the hinterland and the coastal city.[15] Travel between Tartus, Safita, Marmarita, Tripoli and Husn al-Akrad was frequent, as well as from Damascus to Beirut or Latakia. The United States of America had the most subscribers among migrant countries with 177, divided according to the different states or cities, thus: Los Angeles, San Francisco, Oakland, Texas and Oregon. Latin American countries were also listed, with Argentina having the most subscribers (forty-nine). Despite the relative importance of these subscribers, *al-Hadiyya* did not play the role of intermediary or link between immigrants and their communities of origin, as was the case with the journal *Homs*. The latter, published by the Ḥomṣ diocese since 1907, reported news of Homs residents who had migrated to Latin America and published their articles.

At this time North America attracted the majority of migrants from Lebanon, with few Lebanese and Syrians settling in Africa. Later, the Lebanese in Marseille, encouraged by the French presence on the continent, set up their businesses more sustainably in various African colonies. The Latin American countries that had the greater number of immigrants from Syria, mainly the towns of Homs and Ḥama, were Argentina and Chile, while Lebanese immigrants seemed to have been more numerous in Brazil. At that time, a prelate from Beirut, Ignatius Abūrrūṣ was the Episcopal delegate in Argentina and remained in contact with the diocese of Beirut and Beiruti families living in Argentina. These emigrants from the second half of the nineteenth century were fleeing poverty, Ottoman atrocities, religious massacres and the lack of freedom in an East which began to open up to the West.[16]

An annual subscription for *al-Hadiyya* was only 500 Syrian piastres, a low price which suggests that the publication of the newspaper was partly funded by the church and community council. In the countries of migration, a subscription sometimes covered three years. In villages, however, subscribers would pay for only a semester or trimester. Subscriptions were offered as gifts between different cities or countries in the region and the New World, with copies sent for free to members of the clergy, other journals and the various city administrative authorities such as the municipality, water office, dioceses and the Ministry of Public Works. Lists were compiled regularly of the names of those in arrears and the amount owing. Other lists included the names of subscribers together with the name of the officer in charge of their subscription and the date of payment. Each amount was recorded on a receipt with a number and signed by the director of the newspaper, Jirji 'Atiyya, with the date of the duration of the subscription.[17] The total number of subscribers, according to one of these lists, reached 740 without counting Mount Lebanon and America, with postal expenses registered next to the addresses.

Other equally detailed accounts concerned the advertisements. The fourth page of the newspaper was devoted entirely to these, one of its main sources of revenue. Beirut had become an important trading port; markets were flooded with European goods. The advertisements featured products such as fabrics for women, furniture and construction materials. Luxury products included furniture and crockery. The page emphasised the new professions such as doctors, lawyers and engineers, with praise of their knowledge and expertise mentioned in framed advertisements. Some advertisements were placed on other pages, informing readers of the newspaper of the return of a doctor or engineer or the arrival of new merchandise and models.

Al-Hadiyya: A Reflection of the Internal Situation

Al-Hadiyya mirrored the internal situation of the country, which was heavily influenced by the international context. The press had been playing a political and cultural role for some decades as a privileged means of expression.[18] As all economic, administrative, political and cultural policies were generally decided by the mandatory authorities, *al-Hadiyya* adopted a positive attitude towards the French Mandate, expressing its nuances in relation to certain vital problems for the country in well-written articles. These ranged from disapprobation to criticism. The newspaper did not stop at this stage but presented solutions. Articles provided fairly lengthy analyses of such problems as the budget, agriculture and the Ottoman debt.

Attitude towards the French Mandate

The attitude of *al-Hadiyya* towards the Mandate followed the official League of Nations justification that underdeveloped countries must be administered by advanced countries to prepare them for independence after a number of years.[19] During its first years, the newspaper reported the measures taken by the authorities to administer the country. 'Umar Beyhum, a Sunni notable and president of the municipality of Beirut, thanked the city government for its efforts to organise the elections.[20] Similarly, we learn that General Gouraud, High Commissioner from 1919 till 1923, established a court for the trial of foreigners in Greater Lebanon and Syria, a measure intended to encourage the settlement of officials or foreign families and to protect them.[21] Later articles began to demand a constitution to prepare the country for independence. The issue was raised regularly, especially after the return of High Commissioner General Weygand. The High Commissioner met with parliamentary representatives, with whom he reviewed the administrative and financial measures with a view to preparing the necessary institutions to establish the country's constitution in accordance with Article 22 of the Treaty of Versailles and Article I of the Mandate agreement. One article stated that the current situation should not last long: 'We must accelerate the process leading the country to the ultimate goal of independence.'[22]

High Commissioner General Sarrail oversaw more practical projects for the development of the country, such as the provision of electricity for Beirut and other regions, the widening of the Litani, the culture of mulberry trees to promote silk production, a post and telegraphs centre, and the expansion of the equestrian and the aeronautical clubs. The most positive aspects of the Mandate were highlighted. On the eve of his departure, the Governor of Aleppo, General Billiot, was reported as speaking in the following terms: 'France had three goals when declaring war on Germany: to liberate Alsace and Lorraine, to preserve the sovereignty of Poland and to rescue Syria.'[23] He further assured his audience:

> We leave Syria as we left Poland when we have accomplished our mission. We are not here to civilise, Syria has its own civilisation, but you lack the practical applications and technologies. We are in Syria to exercise and introduce you to these technologies that circumstances did not let you gain.[24]

Such assertions were a response to the rebellion that had broken out in Syria. In 1925, revolts had raged in the region of Jabal al-Duruz, Hauran and northern Syria. The new borders, created by the Mandate, had affected the affinity between man, social groups and the land. It resulted in complicating commercial routes, dismantling the traditional trips of rural exchange and truncating the areas of tribal movement. These sectors of the population were directly affected by the creation of 'national' borders, causing much of the first resistance in the countryside between 1919 and 1925.[25]

We find several articles demanding that France finalise the constitution which should lead Syria and Lebanon to independence. This was to be carried out by mutual agreement between France and the country under Mandate. One article recalled Article 1 of the Mandate, which distinguished this system from colonialism and direct occupation. It was not until 1926, however, that the Lebanese deputies took advantage of the events of the Druze revolt and voted a constitution for the Lebanese Republic, whose articles cleverly mixed the French parliamentary model with established community representations as practised in Levantine society.[26]

Al-Hadiyya constantly raised the dilemmas of the French presence, such as the human and financial cost, which reached unexpected proportions. It reported that in the French parliament, certain political parties might have succeeded in persuading the government to resign from its mandatory responsibilities at the League of Nations towards the countries Syria and Lebanon but two reasons led France to maintain its position: French interests in the region and the balance of international forces in the Mediterranean, in which France had a strategic role. One article attested that Syria could not do without French assistance to recover its past glory and to achieve its independence.[27]

Two policies aimed at reducing the cost of the Mandate had already been initiated: the authorities had begun to create a local army in order to reduce military spending and taxes were raised. On these measures *al-Hadiyya* seemed pessimistic, noting people in the region were very reluctant to participate in military service and preferred to flee or emigrate. Moreover, people already complained of the tax increases that had already been implemented since the beginning of the Mandate.[28]

The Domestic Situation

Rich in studies on the internal situation of the country, *al-Hadiyya* provided a fascinating picture of the country's economic situation, with articles by well-informed journalists on the budget, foreign debt, agriculture, industry, summer tourism and emigration. While the ever present issue of fiscal policy and taxes was the main complaint of residents, the most serious problem was emigration. Already in his early articles, Athanasius Sayqali, one of the most important economic journalists, had suggested statistics be used as in Egypt to assess the situation and the needs of the country, arguing that the cost of this operation was very low.[29] Comparisons with Egypt were very frequent, an Arab country occupied by a power (Britain) that was both an ally and rival of France, and which thus constituted an important reference point for Syria and Lebanon under the French Mandate.[30] Moreover, many Lebanese-Syrians lived in Egypt, and local readers were interested to know the situation in that country.

From the village of Aynab, Athanasius Sayqali wrote several articles on the country's budget deficit caused by the number of employees and the expenses incurred by infrastructure. He suggested a series of solutions for the reform of taxation and agriculture. Sayqali began by proposing taxes on uncultivated lands (*salikh*), which would oblige owners either to sell or to cultivate them. He also proposed to reduce the presence of goats, which had resulted in damage to forests, which he viewed as necessary to improving olive tree cultivation. Regarding vineyards, he suggested adopting the method of the Jesuits, who removed vines and planted new crops. He also proposed the production of alcohol from carob.[31]

Sayqalī deplored the situation in agriculture – the traditional methods of irrigation and labour, the lack of raw materials and sources of energy such as oil and coal, and the scarcity of forests are factors still cited today to explain the weakness of the economy – and urged the authorities to increase the farmland acreage. In order to do this, the exact population needed to be determined, a land registry set up and tax reforms undertaken. He also invoked the threat of emigration suspended over the head of the country like the sword of Damocles. The suggested reforms were a balance between two conflicting measures: a reduction in taxes and a salary increase for civil servants, who, Sayqalī pointed out, were the only ones to pay taxes and yet their salaries were ridiculous (for example, the Director of Public Health received fifty-two Syrian pounds per month). In this way, he sought to avoid corruption and convince the most able to opt for the civil service rather than the liberal professions. Further, he suggested the construction of a drainage system to collect rainwater, the installation of sewers, and that the city be cleaned up by spraying for mosquitoes and trapping rats, noting that they could transmit disease to humans. Other criticisms addressed the 1925 budget of 2.5 million Syrian pounds, two-thirds of which was designed to pay the civil servants and the private tutors of the state and only a third spent on public works.[32] The repayment of the Ottoman debt, as determined by the Redistribution Commission of Financial Debt, was an additional burden.[33] Of a total of 57.5 million Ottoman gold pounds, Lebanon and Syria were estimated to owe 15 million pounds.

Al-Hadiyya was a measure of public opinion and a reflection of the changes that occurred in the wake of the collapse of the Ottoman Empire. Changes in social life were crucial. Customs and habits were heavily Westernised, with everyday products primarily imported from European countries. The arrival of the Allied armies eventually convinced the most reluctant who challenged these changes. *Al-Hadiyya* presented a criticism of the liberalism emerging in the Eastern mentality and pointed to the excesses in this new consumer society, warning readers of threats to the family and talking of the century of social hysteria.³⁴ It held that the main enemy of society was the search for entertainment among the ranks of the younger generation, and the expenses and life of pleasure a scourge for the values of society.³⁵

Al-Hadiyya voiced particular concern about the changes in the lives of women. Women who belonged to the bourgeois elite used to hire nurses to feed and care for their newborn children, while they fulfilled their worldly obligations. The newspaper was scandalised and accused those corrupted mothers of wanting to preserve the shape of their bodies and their breasts at the expense of the health of their children.³⁶ One article cited the benefits of breastfeeding for women and children.³⁷ The only article that celebrated the efforts of women and their role in the economy discussed the French losses during World War I and how France had been able to upgrade its economic role and recover its losses thanks to women who had taken over the affairs of their husbands and revived the economy.³⁸

This criticism of social change and habits raised matters of cultural identity that particularly concerned the issue of language. *Al-Hadiyya* strongly believed in the need to preserve and strengthen the Arabic language, which united the people but was being replaced by the foreign language (without naming it) that became the official language. Yet Arabic had survived all attacks throughout the centuries and persisted even in the fields of science and literature. It was therefore essential to preserve it in order to preserve Arab heritage and culture. Another author stated that other languages were equally important for dialogue and communication with other people.³⁹ These concerns were not limited to *al-Hadiyya*. Elsewhere in the region, the questions of national identity, culture and language became crucial public issues. The new intellectual elite, with the advent of research and the growth of publications in Arabic, sought to perpetuate their literary heritage in the context of a modernised Arab world affected by the ideas of reform and progress.⁴⁰ Arabic language underwent a crucial change in its structure and vocabulary. It became a way to discuss topics as delicate as religion, women and politics. The newspaper went even further, noting various problems of translation and suggesting that it would be better if France could require all officials to know Arabic to avoid misunderstandings and misinterpretations in the administration of the country.⁴¹

Confessional Conflicts and National Revolts

The issues that seemed to have most affected the Greek Orthodox and *al-Hadiyya*'s readers, however, were the setbacks of the mandatory power that took place in the northern region of Cilicia and Adana and in the region of Golan and Hauran. These events took on a serious confessional aspect and resulted in a great exodus that particularly affected the Orthodox villages of the two border regions.[42] The difficulties endured by the Lebanese and Syrians from Cilicia residing in Turkey increased, with entire communities being exiled and their properties confiscated.[43] The Treaty of Lausanne had already considered these people as Ottomans. Discussions in the columns of *al-Hadiyya* wondered if these people were to benefit from the protection of France.[44] Already part of the population had withdrawn from the region with the arrival of the French army in 1922. In the war against Turkey, the Greek Orthodox in the region of Cilicia and Anatolia, even ethnic Arabs, were identified as Greeks. Between 1922 and 1928, 125,000 Orthodox Arabs left Antioch and its regions, with 16,000 of them arriving in Beirut.[45]

In the south, the Christian villages of Hermon and Julan Huran had been attacked by the Druze since 1921. Feuding or family disputes over the ownership of agricultural land degenerated into armed attacks under the command of Sultan al-Aṭrash. The villages of Hineh, Tissia, 'Ayha, 'Ayn Hirsheh and Qal'at Jeandal were looted and the small towns of Hasbayya, Rashaya and Dar'a attacked and their inhabitants assaulted. The newspaper accused the security forces in the region of not reacting strongly enough to punish the perpetrators of these crimes.[46]

In 1925, the Druze revolt against the French developed on a much larger scale. Initially a political revolt, like those that broke out all over Syria, it rapidly degenerated into a confessional conflict which had economic causes as well. Agricultural mismanagement and recurrent taxation by the Mandate authorities were the direct reasons for the revolt. Statistics show that wheat crops had declined steadily from 1921 until 1925. Due to drought, crop yields further declined in 1924 and 1925, and heavy taxation exacerbated an already bleak situation.[47] Further, dozens of villages were emptied of their inhabitants as clashes between the Druze of Jabal al-Duruz and the French troops occurred on the plains of Hauran.[48]

Al-Hadiyya reported on the debate about the name given to the revolt: was it a Druze revolt or a revolt of the Druze of Jabal al-Duruz in Hauran, or a Syrian revolt? The local press challenged the name 'Druze revolt' because Druze in other regions remained calm; the Egyptian press used the term 'Syrian revolt'; *al-Watan* denied that name because the events against the Christians concerned only Hauran, and the rest of Syria remained calm. *Al-Hadiyya* responded with great vehemence and affirmed that Druze elsewhere were not calm and in fact participated in numbers that exceeded the army of Mount Lebanon during the *mutasarrifiyya* and even the army of Sparta.[49]

The attitude of *al-Hadiyya* could be justified by the fact that most who fled the region were Greek Orthodox Christians, estimated at 350 families from Hauran and 50 from Antioch. Aid was provided by the communities and they were sheltered in schools, with the families later permanently installed in the neighbourhoods of Karm al-Zaytun on the steep slopes of Ashrafiyya for the people coming from Hauran and St Dimitri for the people of Antioch.[50] Some associations had been created to help the refugees from these regions and to send aid to the parishes of Beirut.[51] The Orthodox support for the mandatory forces became increasingly lukewarm with the arrival of the displaced, and articles became more critical. The Orthodox writers of *al-Hadiyya* realised that the gains made by their communities were not the ones they had expected. Several articles believed that the rights of their community were stripped away and that they were being discriminated against and treated, as the Arab saying goes, as 'children of maids as opposed to children of the elite'.[52] The injustices they felt came from the new voting laws and from the number of delegates to represent the community, estimated to be far less than the importance of the community, economically and demographically.[53]

These injustices were experienced particularly by the city of Tripoli, which had a large Orthodox community. The choice of Beirut as the capital had already disadvantaged the bourgeoisie of Tripoli since the creation of the *wilaya* of Beirut in 1888. Most of this bourgeoisie had settled in Beirut after the establishment of the French Mandate and moved their businesses to the capital, although many family members remained in Tripoli. In *al-Hadiyya* they found a forum in which to express their disappointment as Orthodox.

The newspaper published a list of grievances, and a series of reforms was called for: the reinstalling of the appellate courts in the city, the lowering of rail transport costs, a reduction of taxes on land and cargoes, exemption from export taxes as in Beirut, and for Tripoli to become again the centre of the northern district it once had been.[54] There was also the matter of clean drinking water in the city.[55] The latter project was to be executed in the vicinity of the town but the people of Zghorta felt that the project encroached on the territory of two mills that supplied the village with grain and cereals, a matter that clearly showed the emergence of the confessional division between Zghorta, a Maronite village, and Tripoli, a Sunni/Orthodox city.[56]

The spectre of confessional competition and conflict surfaced in an article where the newspaper complained that the community did not receive the donations and the aid of other communities. It seems that the mandatory authorities had dispensed some subventions to charity associations around the country but that the Greek Orthodox had been forgotten in this operation. Listing community institutions and charitable enterprises, namely St George Hospital, a home for the elderly, and the school and orphanage at Zahrat al-Ihsan, among others, the author wondered if it was possible that the High Commission had forgotten the Orthodox share of aid. If the omission was an oversight, he continued, then the authorities should consider the article as a reminder; if it was intentional, then the High Commission practised confessional discrimination.[57]

This tougher attitude towards the Mandate represented a crucial change in the views of the Orthodox community in Beirut. Although it derived not from a position of principle but a confessional attitude, it would be the beginning of a malaise of misunderstanding and disappointment between both parties.[58] The Orthodox community realised that the French Mandate was applying a policy of discrimination in favour of the Maronites and that they were losing their traditional advantage in the city.

Religious Problems

Although owned by a religious authority, *al-Hadiyya* carried little of importance relating to religious education. It was rather the sociological aspect of religious community that interested the editors more than the theological. The key focus of its articles was the Greek Orthodox community in Lebanon

– and more precisely that of Beirut – and it reported on the activities of its institutions and associations. Lay notables and clergymen were responsible, but the writers were essentially drawn from the new intellectual bourgeoisie who sought to play a role in Arabic literature and in a political revival.

In publicising Church events and the affairs of individuals, *al-Hadiyya* aimed at strengthening community solidarity. Diploma ceremonies and school theatrical productions, funded by community associations, were most important occasions in its columns. The festivities of bishops and patriarchs were also featured. In February 1922, two articles were devoted to the celebration of the feast of the Patriarch Gregory IV of Antioch. The first recounted the celebrations in Damascus, while the second covered those of the St George's monastery in Humayra in Northern Syria. The aspect of duality in the relations between the country and city within the Greek Orthodox community in Syria and Lebanon was clear in these items. In Damascus, the celebration of the mass by the patriarchal representative was attended by the associations with their official trappings (insignia, flags), the students of the schools of Midane and Qassa' (Christian quarters of Damascus), state officials and church dignitaries.[59] At Humayra Monastery, speeches were delivered after mass by the school director, and by students and inhabitants of the regions.[60] A few weeks later, *al-Hadiyya* reported on the festivities in Beirut for Bishop Gerasimos Masarrah. The editor-in-chief spoke at the ceremony, giving a thorough report of the bishop's activities and achievements since his enthronement.[61]

The most important religious issue taken up by *al-Hadiyya* was the polemic against the Greek Catholics. The Orthodox perceived the Mandate as an encouragement to proselytism by Greek Catholics and Latin missionaries, even though this sectarian conflict had already been settled in the second half of the nineteenth century. The Greek Catholic community had been founded during the first quarter of the eighteenth century with the help of Latin missionaries and European consuls in many cities of Bilad al-Sham. It believed in the *filioque* (the procession of the Holy Spirit from the Father and the Son), recognised the authority of the Pope of Rome and declared itself united to Rome. Many other practical and liturgical divisions emerged later, sustained by local and other sociopolitical considerations.[62] During the Mandate period, several Orthodox villages in 'Akkar converted to Catholicism in an act of revolt against the Greek Orthodox *muqataʿji* families, a practice directly encouraged by the mandatory powers.[63]

Several articles took up this anti-Catholic polemic in 1924 after the publication of an article issued by the Greek Catholic Patriarch of Antioch, Dimitrios al-Qadi. The Patriarch, who resided in Damascus, had begun a programme of radical reform in the patriarchate and prepared to convene a new council.[64] In May 1924, *al-Hadiyya* reported on its principal themes, namely that religious authority was independent from the temporal, and the contrary was the result of human weakness and circumstance. The Patriarch added that the separation of churches from Constantinople was due to the loss of its status as a Christian capital. He attested to the primacy of the local church on the basis that every church had the right to be independent. Asserting that the Great Schism happened due to reasons linked to papal authority and other dogma, he held that the issues that caused the Great Schism were political and no longer existed. This tolerant view, which minimised the reasons behind the disunity of churches, provoked a general outcry in the Orthodox community.[65] Several articles signed 'Ibn al-Batriq' responded by focusing on the rites issue and confirming that having the same liturgy did not imply the realisation of church unity. The Orthodox attachment to their traditional liturgy was a proof of their loyalty to their Church's faith. The other Oriental rites (Armenian, Syriac and Copt) had overcome the hardships in their history and the persecutions they experienced by preserving their languages and the traditions related to their mass celebrations.[66]

Rome had claimed to accept the Eastern rites only to attract the Eastern communities. The books of liturgy in Rome were printed and distributed to the communities united with Rome in the first half of the seventeenth century. This vociferous defender of Orthodoxy denied the Patriarch's affirmation that Rome threatened to excommunicate missionaries who attracted the Eastern people to the Latin rite. He recalled to this effect the latest events of Tripoli, when the conversion of an Orthodox doctor to the Latin rite had caused some unfortunate confrontations. The great susceptibility of the Greek Orthodox towards the Greek Catholics was fuelled by the persistence of proselytism practised by the latter. Religious questions in Lebanon took a sociological turn very far from the free choice of personal faith. Notable families, commercial competition, the balance of power and political patronage were often the main causes of feuds and religious conflicts in the region.⁶⁷

In response, Father Kyrillos Rizq published an article in *al-Ahwal* that affirmed 90 per cent Orthodox wished to celebrate their religious holidays with Catholics. Under the motto that one should be correcting errors and not changing them, *al-Hadiyya* denied the right of the Catholic priest to speak on behalf of the Orthodox, since only the Patriarch was entitled to do so. We also find the same emphasis on the unification of the liturgy as less important than the unity of doctrine and faith.⁶⁸ This dispute was the most vehement because it occurred between two close communities. By keeping the style of vestments for their clergy and maintaining relatively the same liturgy, Greek Catholics continued to attract the Greek Orthodox to Uniatism.⁶⁹

Ironically, the speech pronounced by Monsignor Matar, the Greek Catholic Bishop of Beirut, which covered almost the same subject, did not provoke the same reactions or cause as many responses since there existed a proximity and civility among the members of the local clergy in Beirut.⁷⁰ Family relationships, business associations and social events in a growing capital city made ecumenism more realistic and relevant than the polemics of the clergy.⁷¹

Moral issues took up little space in the pages of *al-Hadiyya* and were only indirectly approached. In 1922, 'Abd al-Rahman Majzub wrote an article on religious education in which he noted that religion is the strongest tie between people and dictates the principles of justice and equality and gives everyone their rights. He called upon his readers to preserve the religious feeling in their hearts and to encourage religious education.⁷² Another article reported on the activities of an Egyptian association of Egyptian writers whose goal was to practise virtues to prevent sins and evildoings in society. The article invited all Lebanese, from whatever religious group, to do the same.⁷³

International Politics

World events were of great importance to *al-Hadiyya*, particularly those relating to the Orthodox world, especially the Soviet Union and Orthodox Russia, with articles on the Bolsheviks the highest in number in the international politics section during the six years of the newspaper's publication. It reported in detail on Soviet life, stressing its negative aspects and the tribulations of the revolution. The term 'revolution' was not used; the newspaper was mainly concerned with the political side of the 'Bolshevik Government'. Most articles were translated from French publications like *Le Matin* and *Le Temps*, or from English newspapers such as *The Times*, and generally deplored the slow but certain progress of the Soviet presence in Europe.[74] The Genoa Conference of 1922 was given special attention, with the European powers who accepted the Soviet attendance accused of taking part in the spreading of communist ideas in Europe.[75]

Other pieces published between 1922 and 1924 exposed Soviet economic difficulties: the problem of famine, the situation of the Church, European conferences and Soviet participation in European treaties after the war. A great deal of information was provided on the country's economy.[76] Interviews with key Soviet figures such as Leonid Krasin and Christian Rakovski were published with long commentary and criticism.[77] The most frequent subject was the famine, with its problems of humanitarian aid and international relations, with even the Pope calling upon the European states and Christians to help the Russian people. The newspaper described how each European state provided aid to the newly established power: Italy provided food and took advantage of the situation to sign an agreement with the USSR, while England took part in a European commission, whose goal was to provide aid to the Russian people,[78] and France organised its own aid of up to six million francs and only recognised the new Soviet government in October 1924.[79]

Every help to Russia, however, without consideration of conditions, was regarded as deference by Europe and encouragement of the spread of 'Bolshevism'.[80] *Al-Hadiyya* went further and accused the Soviets of putting international aid money aside to spend on spreading communist principles and ideas in the donor countries. The Soviet financial and economic situation was exposed in detail, such as the currency, the gold reserves, and the natural and agricultural resources. This country began, at that time, accepting help from external companies to exploit its resources, essentially coal, and to organise the means of transportation in the country. Competition among the European countries resulted in increasing the number of international agreements between them and the Soviet Union, with talks not progressing in accordance with European interests.[81] Famine, which affected the international community, was considered by the Soviets as a cyclic event, occurring every twenty years.[82] The newspaper was interested in the Russian Church's reaction towards the famine. After accusing the Jews of causing the revolution in order to end Russian civilisation, both on the religious and temporal levels, those Jews were disappointed. The Russian Church showed solidarity with its people and worked by all means to bring relief to the community. Bishop Arsene of Novgorod, for example, sold the liturgical objects of churches and monasteries to feed people in his diocese.[83]

After 1924, the tone of articles changed from criticism to concerns on how to combat the threat of Bolshevik policies. The newspaper described their evolution in Europe and their activities in the colonies. Bolshevism was their pet hate and the reason for all subversion. Soviet ambassadors in Europe, the activities of syndicates and demonstrations of all kinds were presented as signs of the danger. The negotiations of the Russians with the European countries were discussed as Soviet attempts to avoid the payment of debts of the *ancien régime*.[84]

According to *al-Hadiyya*, the danger of Bolshevism was especially imminent in the British and French colonies. For Britain, this never came from the local popular revolts or their aspirations to independence but from communist plots. Russian expansionism in Asia – particularly in India – could be traced to the Tsar's regime, but the misery and illiteracy of the Indian people were of great help to Bolshevik propaganda.[85] The same reasoning applied to Egypt, where the communist newspaper *al-Hisab* strove to spread ideals against property and religion. For France, the danger threatened in Morocco, and *al-Hadiyya* proposed an alliance between Lebanon and France to fight against communist principles.[86]

We might assume that a pro-Mandate newspaper would keep its readers abreast of the latest news on the mandatory country; however, *al-Hadiyya* was much more concerned with Britain than France. In fact, after the collapse of the Ottoman Empire, the Orthodox turned to England since Russia, their traditional protector, was under the grip of communism. France was the ally of the Maronites so it was obvious to the Orthodox that they should turn to the closest power to their community on a religious level. Locally, a reconciliation took place between the Protestants and the Orthodox during the patriarchate of Gregory IV, who paid a visit to the American University of Beirut in 1927.[87] Gregory had been a student at the Syrian Protestant College in the village of 'Abay, which later became the famous American University of Beirut (AUB). Orthodox intellectuals continued their studies at AUB without converting to Protestantism. On the international level, the Anglican Church started talks with the Orthodox Church after calls from the Patriarch of Constantinople at the beginning of the twentieth century.[88]

Ministerial crises, official decisions, cabinet formation, the problems of commerce, unemployment and the prices of goods in Britain were subjects in which the editors of *al-Hadiyya* kept their Lebanese and Syrian readers informed. It also reported on international congresses, treaties and talks of the postwar settlement. The fate of entire regions was unknown. Decisions taken by the Great Powers concerning Palestine, Mosul and Cilicia were not definitive. People in the Middle East – newly informed of their right to decide their fate – were stripped of this right even before experiencing and exercising it. Relations between the two Great Powers were described as tense; competition and exaggeration were the lot of the local news. After World War I, the door was open to local wars in the Middle East – in Arabia, in Anatolia and in Mosul – leaving destruction, massacres, devastation and refugees.[89]

The efforts made by *al-Hadiyya* to describe these different situations expressed the apprehension and perplexity of the local population. Contradictory situations were explained, lies were justified, and the value of declarations was enhanced as coming from superior authorities. The Orthodox, upset by the setbacks of their co-religionists in Anatolia and Cilicia, were challenged to justify the position of France and England. These two powers had to take into consideration the feelings of the colonised Muslims under their authority and avoided a conflict with the newly established Turkish state, even at the expense of the Christian and Muslim minorities. Armenians, Orthodox, Syriacs, Assyrians, and even Alawites and Kurds were shunted around constantly and at the mercy of armies which advanced or retreated. All these affairs were subject to interventions from all sides. The conflict between Britain and Turkey in the region of Mosul had causes such as oil wells, Kurdish autonomy, and the threats of an alliance between the Soviets and the Turkish government.[90] Other issues concerning Britain, such as the Egyptian situation, were reported on.[91] By contrast, the affairs of French colonies were rarely cited to the same extent.

Conclusion

Did the Orthodox of Lebanon receive recompense for their attitude towards the Mandate by having Charles Debbas, a Beiruti lawyer from the community, appointed as first president of the Republic in 1926? Described in consular letters before the war as a fanatic, Debbas supported the Ottomans and demanded the cancellation of the Capitulations since the new Ottoman state considered all its subjects to be equal citizens. *Al-Hadiyya* no longer existed to tell us about it. Debbas was the first and the last Orthodox president of the Lebanese republic. Was it for this reason that the newspaper folded, considering that the new president, with the new constitution, needed no more complaints and popular grievances from his own community? Rather, in fact, it was for economic reasons. Did *al-Hadiyya* express the traditional reaction of the authorities in facing up to religious evolution and modernity out of control? Yet these authorities had paved the way for modernity in the Eastern communities through their schools, the participation of the laity, associations and the press. Did it merely take up a position against the Arabism of the Patriarch Gregory IV, the friend of King Faysal? But this was the same publication that defended the Arabic language and advised the French to teach it to their superior officials. Although a friend of the French, *al-Hadiyya* urged them to give a constitution to the country and carry out the necessary reforms to put it on the road to independence. Many articles asked for representative elections, in view of the formation of the parliament and the establishment of democracy.

Disappointed by the Russian Revolution, by the setbacks of the French Mandate, by economic problems and increasing emigration, the Orthodox of Beirut adhered to the old mentality of the Capitulations. From the Russians to the Ottomans, from the French to the British, they did not know from whom to seek protection. Internal problems, entangled with the religious and external situation, had complicated things. The Orthodox of Beirut, aware of their economic and political power during the Ottoman period, saw their city becoming a capital of refugees arriving from all regions of the Middle East, of Armenians, Antiochians, Syriacs, Anatolian Greeks, Syrians from Hauran and later Palestinians. *Al-Hadiyya* provides us with a valuable perspective on how the community faced up to these hardships, somehow constituting a buffer between the popular classes and the political authorities and a means of expressing political and social grievances.

Notes

1. Méouchy, 'Introduction thématique', p. 34.
2. Juraydini and Allam, *Awda' al-rum al-urthuduks*, p. 41.
3. Mayeur-Jaouen, 'Les chrétiens d'orient'.
4. Davie, 'La millat grecque-orthodoxe', p. 153.
5. Longrigg, *Syria and Lebanon*, p 44.
6. Mitri, 'Conscience de soi', p. 83.
7. Jabir, 'al-Siyasa al-rusiyya fi al-qarn al-tamin wa al-wusul ila al-miyah al-hara'.
8. Slim, *Greek Orthodox Waqf*, p. 170.
9. Between 1918 and 1939, 490 newspapers titles were published in Syria and Lebanon, principally dealing with political issues but many were also interested in cultural, scientific or feminist subjects. See Méouchy, 'La presse de Syrie', p. 55.
10. Dupont and Mayeur, 'Monde nouveau, voix nouvelles', p. 32.
11. Catalogue of the Archives of the Greek Orthodox Bishopric of Beirut (henceforth CAGOBB), University of Balamand 1995, Bey 2031.
12. Touma, *Un village de montagne*, p. 85.
13. Slim, *Greek Orthodox Waqf*.
14. Transportation and communications services constructed by foreign companies in the late Ottoman period favoured coastal regions and large cities in the interior. Ducruet, *Les capitaux européens*, p. 19.
15. Davie, 'La millat grecque-orthodoxe', p. 321.
16. Courbage and Fargues, *Chrétiens et juifs*, p. 276.
17. CAGOBB, Bey 2031.
18. Dupont and Mayeur, 'Monde nouveau, voix nouvelles', p. 11.
19. According to Gérard Khoury, the Mandate system was a variant on the colonial regimes of direct administration, the protectorate and internal administration, and represented a form of neo-colonialism. Méouchy, 'Introduction thématique', p. 34.
20. *Al-Hadiyya* no. 84 (16 February 1922).
21. *Al-Hadiyya* no. 95 (1 March 1922).
22. *Al-Hadiyya* (10 June 1924).
23. *Al-Hadiyya* no. 731 (18 November 1924).

24. Méouchy, 'Introduction thématique', p. 36.
25. Méouchy, 'La presse de Syrie'.
26. Chevallier and Miquel, *Les arabes*, p. 484.
27. *Al-Hadiyya* no. 732 (20 November 1924).
28. *Al-Hadiyya* no. 736 (26 November 1924).
29. *Al-Hadiyya* no. 89 (22 February 1922).
30. Louis, 'A Note on the British Colonial Archives'.
31. *Al-Hadiyya* no. 271 (29 October 1922).
32. *Al-Hadiyya* no. 709 (17 October 1924).
33. *Al-Hadiyya* no. 719 (1 November 1924).
34. *Al-Hadiyya* no. 778 (30 January 1925).
35. *Al-Hadiyya* no. 749 (16 December 1924).
36. Slim and Dupont, 'La vie intellectuelle des femmes', p. 381.
37. *Al-Hadiyya* no. 783 (6 February 1925).
38. *Al-Hadiyya* no. 792 (19 February 1925).
39. *Al-Hadiyya* (16 May 1924).
40. Dupont and Mayeur, 'Monde nouveau, voix nouvelles', p. 32.
41. *Al-Hadiyya* no. 719 (1 November 1924).
42. Juraydini and Allam, *Awda' al-rum al-urthuduks*, p. 27.
43. Tachjian, 'Les grecs orthodoxes', p. 7.
44. *Al-Hadiyya* no. 738 (28 November 1924).
45. Jabir, 'al-Siyasa al-rusiyya'.
46. *Al-Hadiyya* no. 1033 (10 September 1925).
47. Provence, 'An Investigation', p. 382.
48. 'Atiyya and Khlat, *Al-Sihafa*, p. 65.
49. *Al-Hadiyya* no. 1034 (11 September 1925).
50. Juraydini and Allam, *Awda' al-rum al-urthuduks*, pp. 27–8.
51. CAGOBB, Bey 264, 266.
52. *Al-Hadiyya* no. 900 (1 March 1925).
53. *Al-Hadiyya* no. 75 (5 February 1922).
54. *Al-Hadiyya* no. 730 (16 November 1924).
55. 'Atiyya and Khlat, *Al-Sihafa*, pp. 66–78.
56. *Al-Hadiyya* no. 740 (30 November 1924).
57. *Al-Hadiyya* no. 900 (1 March 1925).
58. Slim and Dupont, 'La vie intellectuelle des femmes', p. 404.
59. *Al-Hadiyya* no. 74 (4 February 1922).
60. *Al-Hadiyya* no. 77 (8 February 1922).

61. *Al-Hadiyya* no. 97 (3 March 1922).
62. Hajjar, *Les chrétiens uniates*.
63. Issawi, *Economic History*, p. 238.
64. Descy, *Introduction à l'histoire*, p. 72.
65. *Al-Hadiyya* no. 698 (5 June 1924).
66. *Al-Hadiyya* nos 698, 699 (5 and 6 June 1924).
67. *Al-Hadiyya* no. 701 (10 June 1924).
68. *Al-Hadiyya* no. 758 (2 January 1925).
69. Descy, *Introduction à l'histoire*, p. 75.
70. *Al-Hadiyya* nos 661, 662 (29 and 30 May 1925).
71. Another critical problem was the vacancy of the Ecumenical Patriarchate, which had been vacant since the end of World War I.
72. *Al-Hadiyya* no. 86 (18 February 1922).
73. *Al-Hadiyya* no. 768 (16 January 1925).
74. *Al-Hadiyya* no. 90 (23 February 1922).
75. *Al-Hadiyya* no. 76 (7 February 1922); no. 95 (1 March 1922).
76. *Al-Hadiyya* no. 86 (18 February 1922).
77. *Al-Hadiyya* no. 84 (16 February 1922).
78. *Al-Hadiyya* no. 696 (3 June 1924).
79. *Al-Hadiyya* no. 710 (18 October 1924).
80. *Al-Hadiyya* no. 93 (26 February 1922).
81. *Al-Hadiyya* no. 85 (17 February 1922).
82. *Al-Hadiyya* no. 86 (18 February 1922).
83. *Al-Hadiyya* no. 94 (28 February 1922). Almost until the present day, the idea that the Jews were the principal architects of the Bolshevik Revolution has been very widespread in popular circles in Lebanon.
84. *Al-Hadiyya* no. 690 (21 May 1924).
85. *Al-Hadiyya* no. 792 (19 February 1925).
86. *Al-Hadiyya* no. 658 (20 May 1925).
87. 'Absi, 'Grigorius al-rabi' Batrik Antakia'.
88. Issawi, *Economic History*, p. 274, Habib, 'Al-Urthuduks wa al-ingiliyun', p. 305. Ultimately, this resulted in the establishment of the World Council of Churches and the Middle East Council of Churches many years later in 1965.
89. *Al-Hadiyya* no. 778 (30 January 1925).
90. *Al-Hadiyya* no. 696 (31 May 1924).
91. *Al-Hadiyya* no. 749 (16 December 1924).

Bibliography

'Absi, Frida Haddad, 'Grigorius al-rabi' Batrik Antakia wa sa'ir al-sharq', in Issam Khalifeh (ed.), *Baldat Abayh fi al-tarikh*, Proceedings of the First Historical Conference for Balada Abayh (20–1 November 1999) (Beirut: Lajna ihya turath 'Abayh, 2001), pp. 451–91.

'Atiyya, Atif and Lutfallah Khlat, *Al-Sihafa bayna al-din wa al-siyasa* (Beirut: Dar al-nahar, 1999).

Chevallier, Dominique and André Miquel, *Les arabes, du message à l'histoire* (Paris: Fayard, 1995).

Courbage, Youssef and Philippe Fargues, *Chrétiens et juifs dans le monde arabe et turc* (Paris: Fayard, 1997).

Davie, May, 'La millat grecque-orthodoxe et la ville de Beyrouth – Structuration interne et rapport à la cité, 1800–1940' (PhD thesis, University of Paris-Sorbonne Paris IV, 1993).

Descy, Serge, *Introduction à l'histoire et l'ecclésiologie de l'Église melkite* (Beirut: Saint-Paul, 1986).

Dick, Ignatius, *Al-Sharq al-masihi* (Beirut: Al-Maktaba al-bulsiyya, 1950).

Ducruet, Jean, *Les capitaux européens au Proche-Orient* (Paris: Presses universitaires de France, 1964).

Dupont, Anne-Laure and Catherine Mayeur-Jaouen, 'Monde nouveau, voix nouvelles: Etats, sociétés, islam dans l'entre-deux-guerres', in Anne-Laure Dupont and Catherine Mayeur-Jaouen (eds), *Débats intellectuels au Moyen-Orient dans l'entre-deux-guerres. Revue des mondes musulmans et de la Méditerranée*, 95–8 (2002), pp. 9–39.

Habib, Gabriel, 'Al-Urthuduks wa al-ingiliyun fi majlis kana'is al-sharq al-awsat', in *Al-Urthuduks wa al-ingiliyun : fi al-mashriq al-'arabi: qira'a tarikhiyya wa afaq mustaqbaliyya* (Balamand: Manshurat Jami'a Balamand, 2004), pp. 301–12.

Hajjar, Joseph, *Les chrétiens uniates au Proche Orient* (Paris: Seuil, 1962)

Issawi, Charles, *The Economic History of the Middle East* (Chicago: University of Chicago Press, 1966).

Jabir, Mundhir, 'al-Siyasa al-rusiyya fi al-qarn al-tamin wa al-wusul ila al-miyah al-hara', in A. F. Nazarnikof (ed.), *Russia wa urthuduks fi al-sharq* (Balamand: Manshurat Jami'a Balamand, 1998), pp. 233–86.

Juraydini, Ra'id Nihad and Dina al-Asmar Allam, *Awda' al-rum al-urthuduks al-wafidin ila Bayrut mutalla' al-qarn al-'ashrin* (Balamand: Manshurat Jami'a Balamand, 2000).

Khoury, Gérard and Nadine Méouchy (eds), *Etats et sociétés de l'orient arabe en quête d'avenir 1945–2005*, vol. 1 (Paris: Geuthner, 2007).

Longrigg, Stephen Hemsley, *Syria and Lebanon under the French Mandate* (Oxford: Oxford University Press, 1958).

Louis, Roger W., 'A Note on the British Colonial Archives', in Gérard Khoury and Nadine Méouchy (eds), *Etats et sociétés de l'orient arabe en quête d'avenir 1945–2005*, vol. 1 (Paris: Geuthner, 2007), pp. 173–7.

Mayeur-Jaouen, Catherine, 'Les chrétiens d'Orient au XIXe siècle: un renouveau lourd de menaces', in Jean-Marie Mayeur (ed.), *Histoire du christianisme*, vol. XI (Paris: Desclée, 1995), pp. 793–849.

Méouchy, Nadine, 'Introduction thématique', in Nadine Méouchy (ed.), *France, Syrie et Liban 1918–1946. Les ambiguïtés et les dynamiques de la relation mandataire* (Damascus: Institut français d'études arabes de Damas, 2002), pp. 17–33.

Méouchy, Nadine, 'La presse de Syrie et du Liban entre les deux guerres (1918–1939)', in Anne-Laure Dupont and Catherine Mayeur-Jaouen (eds), *Débats intellectuels au Moyen-Orient dans l'entre-deux-guerres. Revue des mondes musulmans et de la Méditerranée* 95–8 (2002), pp. 55–70.

Mitri, Tarek, 'Conscience de soi et rapport à autrui chez les orthodoxes au Liban 1942–1975' (PhD thesis, Paris X Nanterre, 1985).

Provence, Michael, 'An Investigation into the Local Origins of the Great Revolt', in Nadine Méouchy (ed.), *France, Syrie et Liban 1918–1946: Les ambiguïtés et les dynamiques de la relation mandataire* (Damascus: Institut français d'études arabes de Damas, 2002), pp. 377–408.

Slim, Souad, *The Greek Orthodox Waqf in Lebanon during the Ottoman Period* (Beirut: Orient-Institut Beirut, 2007).

Slim, Souad and Anne-Laure Dupont, 'La vie intellectuelle des femmes à Beyrouth dans les années 1920 à travers la revue *Minerva*', in Anne-Laure Dupont and Catherine Mayeur-Jaouen (eds), *Débats intellectuels au Moyen-Orient dans l'entre-deux-guerres. Revue des mondes musulmans et de la Méditerranée* 95–8 (2002), pp. 381–406.

Tachjian, Vahé, 'Les grecs orthodoxes libanais et syriens de Cilicie: La fin d'une vie communautaire', *Chronos* 8 (2003), pp. 7–61.

Touma, Toufic, *Un village de montagne au Liban (Hadeth el-Jobbé)* (Paris: Mouton, 1958).

Notes on the Contributors

Orit Bashkin is Professor of Modern Middle Eastern History in the Department of Near Eastern Languages and Civilizations at the University of Chicago. After her initial studies at Tel Aviv University, she graduated with a PhD from Princeton in 2004. She has since published on many aspects of the history of Arab Jews in Iraq, Iraqi history and Arabic literature. Among her recent publications are *The Other Iraq – Pluralism and Culture in Hashemite Iraq* (2009) and *New Babylonians: A History of Jews in Modern Iraq* (2012).

Marilyn Booth holds the Khalid bin Abdallah Al Saud Chair in the Study of the Contemporary Arab World, Oriental Institute and Magdalen College, Oxford University. In 2014–15 she was Senior Humanities Research Fellow, New York University Abu Dhabi and before that, Iraq Professor of Arabic and Islamic Studies at the University of Edinburgh. Her most recent scholarly book is *Classes of Ladies of Cloistered Spaces: Writing Feminist History in fin-de-siècle Egypt* (Edinburgh University Press, 2015). She edited and contributed to *Harem Histories: Envisioning Places and Living Spaces* (2010) and co-edited and contributed to *The Long 1890s in Egypt: Colonial Quiescence, Subterranean Resistance* (with Anthony Gorman, Edinburgh University Press, 2014). She is writing a monograph on Zaynab Fawwaz, early Arab feminisms and gender polemics. She also writes on nineteenth-century genres (novel, auto/biography, conduct literature, newspaper essays), vernacular Arabic writing, and practices and politics of literary translation. She has translated many works of fiction from the Arabic, most recently *The Penguin's Song* and *No Road to Paradise*, both by Lebanese novelist Hassan Daoud (2015; 2017).

Leila El Houssi is Adjunct Professor of History of Islamic Countries at the University of Padua. After completing an MA in Intercultural Studies at the University of Padua, she received her PhD at the University of Pisa, where she prepared a thesis on the role of Italian antifascism in Tunisia in the period between the two world wars. Since November 2011, she has been the coordinator of the MA Mediterranean Studies at the University of Florence. She specialises in history, culture and gender issues in the contemporary Mediterranean, and in particular on the relations between Italy, Tunisia and other countries in North Africa (Maghreb). Among her publications are *Il Risveglio della democrazia. La Tunisia dall'indipendenza alla transizione* (2013) and *L'urlo contro il regime. Gli antifascisti italiani in Tunisia tra le due guerre* (2014), which was recently awarded the prestigious Giacomo Matteotti prize and Francesco Saverio Nitti prize.

Kaïs Ezzerelli is a historian specialising in the contemporary history of the Middle East. After obtaining MAs in History and Arabic Literature from the University of Paris-Sorbonne and the National Institute of Oriental Languages and Civilizations in Paris, he held scholarships at the French Institute of the Near East (IFPO) and at the Oriental Institute of Beirut. His PhD at the School of Higher Studies in Social Sciences (EHESS) in Paris is focused on the life and thought of the Syrian scholar Muhammad Kurd 'Ali (1876–1953). Among his publications are an edition of the memoirs of Muhammad Kurd 'Ali (fifth volume), an edited book on autobiographies in Bilad al-Sham and, most recently, *Diplomatie Occidentale et dissidence arabe* (2014), a study on the relationships between French diplomats and Syrian Arabists before World War I. He has also published on the history of the Hijaz railway and the reformist movement of Muhammad 'Abduh.

Anthony Gorman is Senior Lecturer in Islamic and Middle Eastern Studies at the University of Edinburgh. He has taught at universities in Australia, Egypt and Britain and is the author of *Historians, State and Politics in Twentieth Century Egypt: Contesting the Nation* (2003) as well as a number of articles on the resident foreign presence in modern Egypt. He is co-editor (with Marilyn Booth) of *The Long 1890s in Egypt: Colonial Quiescence, Subterranean Resistance* (Edinburgh University Press, 2014) and (with Sossie Kasbarian) of *Diasporas of the Modern Middle East: Contextualising Community* (Edinburgh University Press, 2014). He continues to work on his history of the prison in the Middle East as well as aspects of the anarchist movement in the Eastern Mediterranean before 1914.

Mustafa Kabha is Professor in the Department of History, Philosophy and Judaic Studies at the Open University of Israel. He completed his PhD, titled 'The Role of the Press and Journalistic Discourse in the Arab Palestinian National Struggle, 1929–1939', under the supervision of Israel Gershoni in the History Department at Tel Aviv University in 1996. He publishes in English, Arabic and Hebrew. Among his publications are *The Press in the Eye of the Storm: The Palestinian Press Shapes Public Opinion 1929–1939* (in Hebrew, Yad Ben-Zvi, 2004); *The Palestinian Press as Shaper of Public Opinion: Writing Up a Storm* (2007); and (with Dan Caspi) *The Palestinian Arab In/Outsiders: Media and Conflict in Israel* (2011).

Gül Karagöz-Kızılca is Assistant Professor in the Department of Journalism at Ankara University. She received her PhD in the Department of History at Binghamton University, SUNY (State University of New York). Trained in nineteenth-century Ottoman history, with specialities in Ottoman press history, social history, nationalism and imperialism, her primary research interests include the history of communication and the media history of the Ottoman Empire and Turkey. She addresses these issues in both English- and Turkish-language publications.

Fred H. Lawson is Senior Fellow of the Centre for Syrian Studies at the University of St Andrews. He has served as president of both the Syrian Studies Association and the Society for Gulf Arab Studies and is author of a number of works including *The Social Origins of Egyptian Expansionism during the Muhammad 'Ali Period* (1992) (subsequently translated into

Arabic); *Constructing International Relations in the Arab World* (2006); and *Why Syria Goes to War* (1996).

Didier Monciaud is an Associate Research Fellow at GREMAMO (Groupe de recherche sur le Maghreb et le Moyen Orient, University Denis Diderot Paris VII, Paris). Since 1999 he has served as a member of the editorial board of *Cahiers d'Histoire, revue d'histoire critique* (https://chrhc.revues.org). His main research interests and publications deal with political commitments, social mobilisations, and intellectual and cultural debates in contemporary Egypt. He has edited an issue of the *Cahiers d'Histoire, revue d'histoire critique* on the history of the Left in Egypt and is currently working on a biographical study of Injy Aflatoun, an Egyptian painter and progressive woman activist.

Odile Moreau is Associate Professor of History at the University of Montpellier, France, and researcher at the French National Research Centre (CNRS), Institut des Mondes Africains (IMAF) and Paris 1 University. Her most recent books are *Subversives and Mavericks in the Muslim Mediterranean: A Subaltern History* (2016) and *La Turquie dans la Grande Guerre, de l'Empire ottoman à la république de Turquie* (2016).

Souad Slim is Director of the Centre of Documentation and History at the Institute of History, Archeology and Near Eastern Studies at the University of Balamand and Professor of History, Cultural Studies and Methodology at the Faculty of Art and Social Sciences at the Institute of Theology of the University of Balamand (Lebanon). She completed her first PhD at the Sorbonne Paris IV in History in 1984 and her second one at the University of Birmingham in Islamology in 2000. She was the first scholar to introduce the methodology of serial and quantitative history to the History of Lebanon and the Near East. She is the author of three books: *Le métayage et l'impôt aux XVIII et XIX siècles* (1987); *Balamand, histoire et patrimoine* (1995); and *The Greek Orthodox Waqf in Lebanon during the Ottoman Empire* (2007).

Sonia Temimi is Assistant Professor of History at the University of Tunis and research fellow at the Temimi Foundation (Fondation Temimi pour la Recherche Scientifique et l'Information), Zaghouan, in Tunisia. She completed her PhD on *Ruz al-Yusuf* at the University of Provence in Aix-en-Provence in 2008. She specialises in the press and intellectual history of Egypt. Among her publications are 'D'un journalisme l'autre: contours d'une identité professionnelle et évolution de son rapport au pouvoir politique 1923–1970', *Égypte/Monde arabe* 2nd series, 4–5 (2001); (with Racha Hanafi), 'La "Loi sur le voile" en France: un regard égyptien', *Maghreb-Machrek* 182 (Winter 2004–5), pp. 101–7; and 'Ottomanisme, pharaonisme et égyptianité', in Fatma Ben Slimane and Hichem Abdessalmad (eds), *Penser le national au Maghreb et ailleurs* (2012), pp. 253–63.

Index

Ababil (Beirut), 182
Abaza, Fikri, 211, 213, 222
'Abbas, Kamil, 114
'Abbas Hilmi II Pasha (Khedive), 157–8, 161, 168–9n, 171
'Abd al-'Aziz, Sultan (Morocco), 157, 168n
'Abd al-'Aziz, H., 217
'Abd al-Hafidh, Sultan (Morocco), 156, 157, 159, 162, 167n, 168n, 170n, 171n
'Abd al-Hamid II (Ottoman Sultan), 4, 162, 177, 191
'Abd al-Haqq, 'Abd al-Hamid, 302–3
'Abd al-Raziq, 'Arif, 103
'Abd al-Razzaq (Iraqi Sufi), 62
'Abduh, Ibrahim, 8, 22n, 64, 92n, 258n
'Abduh, Muhammad, 172n, 179, 185, 328
'Abduh, Sa'id, 222–4
Abdülaziz (Ottoman Sultan), 39
'Abdullah, Amir (of Jordan), 336
'Abdullah, Muhammad 'Abd al-Hamid, 290
'Abdullah, 'Umar, 106
Abu Durra, Yusuf, 103, 121n
Abu Madi, Iliya, 327
Abu Shadi, Muhammad, 180
Acre, 107, 112–13, 123n
Adana, 356
Adham, A., 217
adib (pl. *udaba*') (men of letters), 183, 220
advertisements, 47, 118–19, 136, 138–9, 181, 184, 224, 228, 252–4, 303, 308, 326–7, 350
Agadir Crisis (1911), 155, 162
agriculture, 64, 99–101, 129, 131, 136, 142, 147n, 273, 351, 353–4, 356, 362
Ahl al-Bayt, 326
al-Ahram (Alexandria, Cairo), 22n, 93n, 118, 161, 183, 222, 224, 238, 244, 301, 306, 317n
al-ahrar
  liberals, 183
  respectable women, 70, 75, 77–9
al-Ahwal (Beirut), 361
Αιγυπτιώτης-'Ελλην-al-Yunani al-Mutamassir (Alexandria), 26n
Aiguptos, I (Alexandria), 238
'Ain Karim, 134, 145n
'Ajjur (Ajur), 129, 142
Akhbar al-Yawm (Cairo), 225, 232n
'Akkar, 349, 359
al-'Alam al-'Arabi (Baghdad), 326, 335
Alawites, 364
Alba, L' (Tunis), 266, 268, 271–3, 281
Albano, Alfredo, 256
Aleppo, 50, 178, 182, 200n, 352
Alexandretta, 345
Alexandria, 69, 74–5, 79, 81, 94n, 219, 237, 239, 241–50, 253–4, 255–7, 260n, 293–4, 307
Algeciras Conference (1906), 155
Algeria, Algerians, 74, 154, 161, 163–5, 171n, 187
'Ali (ibn Abi Talib), imam, 328
Ali Kararname (Sublime Decree) (1867), 52n
Ali, Maulana Mohamed, 132
Ali, Maulana Shaukat, 132, 141, 143
Ali Suavi, 51–2n
Alias, R. S., 333
All Palestine Arab Labourers' Congress, 130
All Palestine Arab Villagers' Congress, 129
Alliance Israélite Universelle (AIU), 155, 324
al-Amal (Iraq), 326
al-Amal (printing shop), 290

America (North, South America), 141, 245, 250, 349–50
American University in Cairo (AUC), 8
American University of Beirut (AUB), 113, 127, 363–4
Amin, Ahmad, 217
Amin, 'Ali, 223, 225, 232n
Amin, Mustafa, 207, 223, 225–6, 232n
Amin, Qasim, 27, 157, 299, 333
anarchist conferences
  (1881), 242
  (1909), 244, 247
anarchist press, 237–64
  international, 250, 261n
anarchists, 18
  anti-organisationalists (individualists), 239
  in Egypt, 237–64
  Greek, 243–4, 246–8
  Italian, 237–64
  in Tunisia, 266, 276
anarcho-syndicalism, anarcho-syndicalists, 239, 243, 247, 254, 257
Anderson, Benedict, 10, 261n
Anglican Church, 364
Anglo-Iraqi Treaty (1930), 130
Anglo-Ottoman Trade Convention (1838), 34
Anti-Authoritarian International (Verviers, 1877), 239, 259n
Antifascists, 266, 270, 277–8, 280–1
Antioch, Antiochians, 345, 346, 356–7, 359–60, 365
anti-Semitism, 324, 335, 338
anti-Zionism 128, 133, 140–1, 336
Antun, Farah, 245
al-'Aqqad, 'Abbas Mahmud, 17, 211–12, 215, 217, 220, 225
al-'Arab (Jerusalem), 104–5, 109–11
Arab Advocates of Palestine, 128
Arab Bank, 104
Arab Club, 192
Arab Economic Congress, 129
Arab Executive Committee, 100, 102, 104, 114–15, 121n
Arab Higher Committee, 115, 137
Arab Jewish identity, 19, 323
Arab nationalism, 19, 323–4, 336, 338–9
Arab proverbs (*hikam 'arabiyya*), 328
Arab Syrian Congress (1913), 194
'Arabeh, 106
Arabic Academy of Damascus, 178
Arabic language, 6, 67, 72, 177, 187, 198, 211, 302, 324, 327, 332, 334, 348, 355, 365
  colloquial, 106–7, 216, 326
Arabic language press, 4, 6, 8, 10, 12–13, 15–16, 20n, 71, 99–125, 136–7, 156–7, 162–3, 181–2, 238, 244–5, 252, 336
Arabism, 4, 110, 186, 198, 346, 365; *see also* Pan-Arabism
Armenian, Armenians, 6, 248, 364–5

Arslan, 'Adil, 183
Arslan, Shakib, 179, 196–7
artisans 38, 46, 50n
al-'Asali, Shukri, 176, 181, 183, 192–3, 195, 197
'Ashmawi, Mustafa, 294
al-'Askari, Mahmud, 290–2, 294, 303, 305
Assyrians, 364
Asteriadis (or Asteridis), K. S., 247, 256
Atatürk, Mustafa Kemal, 132
'Atiyya, Jirji, 350
Austria-Hungary, 160, 196
Ayalon, Ami, 8
al-Azhar, 158, 208
  College, 113
al-'Azm, Haqqi, 183
al-'Azm, Rafiq, 183
'Azmi, Mahmud, 8, 224

Babil, Nassuh, 199
Badoglio, (Marshal), 280
Baghdad, 6, 19, 62, 105, 178, 323–4, 326, 333, 335, 338–9
Baghdad Pact, 5
Bakunin, (Mikhail), 259n
al-Balagh (Cairo), 224
Balfour Declaration, 128, 140
Balkans 40, 186
Bambini, Umberto, 246–7, 254, 256
al-Bandak, 'Isa, 103
Banha, 67
Bani Suwayf, 67, 78–9
al-Banna, Hassan, 303–4
bars, 67–8, 71, 73, 82, 93, 222, 253; *see also* taverns
Barthou, Louis, 267
al-Barudi, Fakhri, 183
al-Basir, Muhammad Mahdi, 332
Basra, 40, 194, 326
Baudrillard, Jean, 66
Bedouin, 100, 133, 347
Beirut, 3, 19–20, 105, 113, 130, 182, 192, 196, 200n, 345–70
Belghiti, Muhammad, 161
Bensasson, Silvano, 278
Berkowitz, Daniel Allen, 33
Berlin, 105
Bethlehem, 112, 139
Beyhum, 'Umar, 351
Bialik, Haim Nahman, 336
Bilad al-Sham, 200n, 346, 359
bilingual (press), bilingualism, 26n, 157, 180, 208–9, 242, 245, 247, 324, 329–30
Billiot, Gen. (Governor of Aleppo), 352
Biqa', 349
Bishara, Salih ('Hawwasa'), 118
Bishop Arsene of Novgorod, 363
Bishop Gerasimos Masarrah, 359
Bishop (Orthodox) of Beirut, 346–7, 359

Bishop (Greek Catholic) of Beirut (Msgr Matar), 361
black shirts, 270–1
B'nei Brith, 335
Bolshevism *see* communism
Bombieri, Enrico, 274
bookshops, 249, 308
Brandani, Iesse, 255
Brigido, Camillo, 247, 256
Britain, 15, 59, 80, 101, 113, 127, 177, 186, 211, 271–2, 282n, 297, 331, 339, 345, 353, 363–4
British government, 127, 282n
Brunello, Giovanni, 247, 256
Butaji, Imil, 107

cafes, 59, 66–8, 74, 108, 117, 181, 222, 248–9, 254, 273, 308
Cairo, 3, 6, 14, 18, 58, 60–1, 68, 70, 78, 80, 89, 105, 130, 159–64, 176, 179–80, 185–6, 219, 222, 224, 239–43, 245, 247–9, 253–4, 255–7
Cairo University, 8
Cameroon, 155
Canivet, Raoul, 246
Canning, Capt. R. G., 129, 140
Capitulations, 35–6, 51n, 251, 365
caricatures, caricaturists, 2, 7, 13, 110, 208, 216, 227, 229n
Castro, Vittorio, 269
Casubolo, Antonino, 276, 284n
censorship, 6, 12, 47, 52, 106, 165, 179, 199, 251; *see also* banning of newspapers
Central Bank of Co-operative Institutions in Palestine, 135
Chancellor, Sir John, 127
Charles, Christophe, 219
Chionis, Iosef, 247, 256
Chirqas, Muhammad, 114
Christians, Christian communities, 34–5, 50n, 102, 109, 112, 116, 187–8, 193, 345–6, 357, 362, 364
cigarettes, cigarette workers, 139, 239, 242–4, 246, 250, 308
Cilicia 345, 347, 356, 364
Cini, Francesco, 247, 256
Clancy-Smith, Julia, 153
Clot Bey, 78
clubs, 249, 277, 348, 352
    Arab, 192
    journalists', 222
    women's, 333
Cohen, Levy Abraham, 166n
Collomb (French official), 178, 187, 189–90
Colombo, G., 272
colonialism, 3, 6, 155, 166n, 167n, 187, 213–15, 228, 288, 298, 329, 352, 366n; *see also* imperialism
columns, columnists, 7, 61, 105, 217–18, 221–3, 227, 248, 298, 327; *see also hawadith*
commerce du Maroc, Le, 167n
Committee of Union and Progress (CUP), 156, 158, 187
communism, communists, 26, 100–1, 133–5, 266, 275–6, 278–80, 284n, 285n, 305, 309, 347, 362–3
Communist Party of Palestine, 133
Constantinople, 360, 364; *see also* Istanbul
Constitutional Liberals (Egypt), 10, 222
constitution, constitutionalism, 5, 21n, 156, 160, 164, 196, 198, 325, 331, 351–2, 365
Converti, Dr Nicolo, 276
Copts, 72–3, 360
correspondents, 7, 14, 16, 39, 40, 59–60, 62–4, 5, 67–8, 71, 75, 81, 83, 85, 87–8, 126, 160, 163, 217, 222, 245–7
Corriere Egiziano, Il (Alexandria), 246
cosmopolitan, cosmopolitanism, 155, 305
Costa, Andrea, 239
Costa, Giacomo, 245, 255
counter-elites 48, 54n
Cretan insurrections (1866–9), 34
crime, 59, 61, 64–6, 81, 86–7, 89, 91n, 133, 135
Crimean War (1853–6), 33–4
Cromer, Lord, 168n, 181

Dahdah, Ni'met Allah, 156, 168n
al-Dajani, Hasan Sidqi, 115
Damascus, 16, 80, 176–83, 185–7, 189–93, 196–8, 200n, 346, 348–9, 359–60
Damiani, Luigi, 276
D'Angio, Roberto, 243, 246, 250, 255–6
Dar al-Niyaba, 161, 170n
Dar al-Taraqqi (publishing house), 193
Dar'a, 356
Darnton, Robert, 40
Darwish, Shalom, 331
Darwish, Yusuf, 305, 309
Davar (Tel Aviv), 336
'Day of the Wedding Ring', 274
de Tarrazi, Filip, 8
Debbas, Charles, 346, 365
Demoliamo!, 242, 257
Demolins, Edmond, 188
Di Vittorio, Giuseppe, 275
diaspora, 13, 335, 349
al-Difa' (Jaffa), 102, 104–8, 110–11, 113–14, 116–17, 121n
divorce, 58, 81, 87, 91n
Diwan al-Muhafaza, 84
Djemal Pasha, 183, 193, 196–7
doctors, physicians, 7, 39, 78, 81, 85, 87, 130, 227, 268, 297, 334, 350, 360
Domani (Tunis), 18, 266, 275–8, 281
Domani, Il (Cairo), 243–6, 249, 252, 254, 255, 260n
Donato, Francesco, 247, 256

INDEX | 379

Donegani, Guido, 286n
Donegani, Gustave, 286n
Doumas, Nicholas, 244, 246–7, 256
Doumergue, Gaston, 195, 210, 267 (government)
dowry, 334
drugs, 68, 93n
Druze, 112, 356
Druze revolt (1925), 345, 352, 356–7; see also Great Syrian Revolt
Dughman, Peter, 140
al-Dustur, 194

Eastern Question, 36, 50n
Ebüzziya Tevfik, 37, 42, 44–6
Ecumenical Patriarchate, 347, 368n
Eden, Anthony, 272, 301
editorial committees, 16, 218, 225, 245–7, 290–1, 293, 307
editorials, 14, 31, 39–40, 42–3, 46, 63, 66, 72–3, 105, 111, 129–33, 136–7, 140, 142, 162–3, 165, 181–4, 197–8, 227, 242, 271, 325, 330
editors, 6, 8, 10, 19, 31–3, 36–48, 49n, 51n, 53n, 59, 61, 63, 64, 89, 176–84, 192, 198, 207–11, 213–15, 217–18, 221, 223–5, 240–1, 245–9, 251, 253–4, 255–7, 268, 278, 290–1, 308–9, 323, 326, 329–30, 358–9, 364
  Palestinian, 100–9, 111–15, 120n, 122n, 126–7, 130–2, 136, 140–4
Effendiyya, 107, 307
Egypt, 3, 5–9, 11, 13, 15–19, 58–63, 66–7, 71–4, 78–80, 83, 86, 88, 110, 118, 130, 132, 153, 154–62, 164, 168n, 171n, 179–83, 192–3, 207, 210, 212–15, 227–8, 229n, 237–46, 249–50, 254–5, 288–90, 292, 296, 301, 306, 308, 310, 333, 348, 353, 363
Egyptian Gazette (Alexandria), 6, 238
Egyptian Socialist (Communist) Party, 260n, 305
Emergency Regulations (Palestine), 5
English College of Jerusalem, 113
English language press, 6, 12, 15, 126–7, 131, 136–43, 166n, 238
Enver Pasha, 193, 197
Ergasia (Cairo), 243, 247
Ergatis, O (Alexandria-Cairo), 244, 246, 256
Eritrea, 270
Ethiopia, Ethiopians, 265–7, 269–72, 275, 277, 278, 280–1
  Italian invasion of, 265–81

faits divers, 14, 61–6, 68, 73, 78, 85, 88–90, 92n
al-Fajr (Tangiers), 156–7, 168n
Fakhreddine Bey, 189
Falastin (Jaffa), 126–143
Farah, Bulus, 101
fard, 72, 300
Farhud, 324
Farmers' Conference ('Ajjur, 1920), 129
Faruq I (King of Egypt), 301–2, 305, 310

al-Faruqi, Shaykh Sulayman al-Taji, 106, 113–15
Fascism, Fascists, 265–81
Fauser, Giacomo, 286n
fawdawiyya (anarchism), 244
Fawwaz, Zaynab, 85
Faysal (bin Husayn al-Hashimi), 132, 143, 198, 331, 365
Fayyum, 70–1, 76, 79
Ferrer, Francisco, 244–5, 257
Fez, 156–7, 160, 162, 168n, 169n
Filastin (Jaffa), 15, 100–6, 108–9, 113–14, 116–17
Flandin government, 267
Fleischmann, Ellen, 142
Foucault, Michel, 78–9
France, 71, 88–9, 154–5, 159–60, 162, 166n, 177, 185–6, 193–5, 198, 210, 229n, 265–8, 272–3, 275, 280, 283n, 297, 345, 352–3, 355–6, 362–4
Free Popular University (Alexandria), 242, 262n
freelance writers, 218, 220, 225
French authorities, 80, 113, 156, 160–5, 186–96, 199, 265–87, 345–70
French note (1867), 34
French Press Law (1852), 52n

Gallico, Loris, 276, 278
Gallico, Raffaele Renato, 276
Gandhi, Mahatma, 132, 230n, 301
Garbati, Romolo, 245–6, 255
Gazette de Cologne, 163
General Islamic Conference, 132
General Union of Mechanical Textile Workers of Shubra al-Khayma (GUMTWSK), 288–92, 296, 309
Genoa Conference (1922), 362
Germany, 131, 155–6, 160–2, 165, 177, 196, 267, 352
Ghali, Butrus, 171n
Gharib, Muhammad 'Ali, 207–8, 221, 223–4, 226
al-Ghuri, Emil, 113, 115–16
Gianca (Ausonio Agrate), 277
Giustizia e Libertà, 266, 277
al-Glawi, Madani, 162
Golan, 356
Gorsse, Bascone and Muscat (printers), 273
Gorst, Sir Eldon, 157
Gouraud, Gen. (High Commissioner), 351
Grammata (Alexandria), 244
Grandi, Dino, 280
Great Syrian Revolt (1925–7), 199, 345, 357; see also Druze revolt
Greco-Turkish relations, 347
Greek Catholics, 359–61
Greek language press, 10, 238, 243–4, 246–7
Greek Orthodox (community), 345–70
Gregory IV, Patriarch of Antioch, 359, 363–5
Groupe Études, 305
guilds 34, 50n

Gulf States, 9
Gülhane Rescript (*Hatt-ı Sharif* of Gülhane), 34
al-Gundi al-Mazlum (The Oppressed Soldier), 291, 297, 305

Haaretz (Tel Aviv), 336
Habermas, Jürgen, 10
Hadassa, 335
Haddad, Ezra, 329
Hadika (Istanbul), 14, 31–2, 36–7, 41–8
al-Hadiyya (Beirut), 19–20, 345–70
al-Haffar, Lutfi, 183, 191
Haifa, 101, 107, 112, 118
hakawati, 117
Halim, Hilmi, 211
Hama, 350
al-Hamamsi, Galal al-Din, 223
Hammad, Muhammad 'Ali
Hanna, Yusuf, 15, 105, 114
al-Haqq (Tangiers), 161, 163, 165
Hardegg, Loytved (German consul), 197
Hartmann, Martin, 8, 182
Hasan I, Mawlay (Moroccan Sultan)166n
Hasan, Ahmad, 223
al-Hasani, Shaykh Taj al-Din, 197, 199
Hasbayya, 349, 356
Hashemites, 325, 329
Hassun, Pauline, 333
Hatzopoulos, Z., 247, 256
Hauran 345, 347, 352, 356–7, 365
hawadith, 14, 59–62, 64, 66, 73, 89
Haykal, Muhammad Hasanayn, 10
Haykal, Muhammad Husayn, 10
Hebrew Literary Society, 326–7, 336
Hebrew language press, 6, 136, 243, 257, 336
Hebrew University, Jerusalem, 336
Herman, Edward, and Noam Chomsky, 47, 54n
High(er) Muslim Council, 100, 104, 111, 115, 120n, 121n, 122n, 137
al-Hilal (Cairo), 63, 108, 180, 182–3, 244
al-Hisab (Cairo), 363
Hizb al-Islah al-Dusturi (Constitutional Reform Party, Egypt), 157
Hoare–Laval Pact, 265, 282n
Holmes, Sherlock, 228
Homs (Homs), 348
Homs, 346, 348, 349–50
Hürriyet, 52n
Husayn, Taha, 215
al-Husayni, Haj Amin, 111
al-Husayni family, 104, 107, 113–16
al-Husayni, Jamal, 107, 115
al-Husayni, Munif, 115, 117
al-Husri, Sati', 325, 332

Ibn al-Athir, 62
Ibn al-Batriq, 360
ibn al-Khattab, 'Umar, 328
Ibn al-Muqaffa', 328

Ibrahim al-Kabir, 330
al-Ibrashi, Z., 210
İbret (Istanbul), 14, 31–2, 36–7, 41–6, 48, 49n, 51n, 53n
Ictihad, 333
Idea, L' (Cairo), 241, 244–7, 249, 256
illiteracy, 349, 363; *see also* literacy
al-Imam, Ahmad, 107, 121n
Imbaba, 293
imperialism, 1, 6, 12, 17, 59, 64, 157, 164, 188–9, 193, 198, 269, 277, 279; *see also* colonialism
India, Indians, 93n, 112, 130, 132, 141, 143, 157, 213, 230n, 324, 326, 337, 363
Indian nationalist movement, 132, 230n
Indipendente, L' (Cairo-Alexandria), 244, 246, 249, 252, 256
al-Inglizi, 'Abd al-Wahhab, 183, 193, 195, 197
Institute for Editing, Translation and Journalism (Cairo University), 8
intellectuals/ intelligentsia, 7, 13, 17, 38, 59, 61, 69, 80, 88, 89, 100–1, 105–7, 116, 119, 167n, 171n, 180, 215, 217, 219–20, 232n, 290, 305, 307, 309, 325, 328, 331, 333, 337, 348, 355, 364
International, The (First), 237, 239, 256, 259n
International Reading Room (Cairo), 248; *see also* libraries
International Union of Workers and Employees in Cairo, 240
Iqbal, Muhammad, 132
Iran, 4, 9, 213, 325–6, 337
Iraq, 9, 323–44
al-'Iraq (Iraq), 326
Iraq Times (Baghdad), 6
Iraqi Casino, 326
al-'Irfan (Sidon), 337
al-'Isa, family, 104, 122n
al-'Isa, 'Isa (Da'ud), 103–4, 112, 114–15, 126
islahiyyun, 183
Islam, 4, 110, 158–9, 212, 299–300, 304, 328
Islamic press, 9, 161–4, 303
Islamiyyats, 211–12
'isma, 71, 77, 93n
Ismailia, 239
Isma'il, Khedive, 68
Istanbul, 3–4, 14, 31, 39, 41, 156–8, 160, 164, 189, 191–2, 196; *see also* Constantinople
İstikbal (Istanbul), 14, 31–2, 36–7, 39, 41–4, 46–8, 51n
al-Istiqlal (Baghdad), 326
al-Istiqlal Party (Palestine), 109, 115–16, 121
Italian Chamber of Commerce (Tunis), 273
Italian community, 6, 18, 248, 259n, 261n, 265–87
Italian (local) authorities, 132, 241, 251, 252, 262n
Italian language press, 6, 10, 12–13, 18, 237–8, 242, 244, 247, 250, 258n, 286n

Italian League of Human Rights (LIDU), 276
Italy, Italians, 6, 18, 239, 248
İttihad, 52n
al-Ittihad al-Islam, 158–9
al-Ittihad al-Maghribi (Maghribi Union), 16, 154, 159, 161–5, 171n, 172n
al-Ittihad al-'Uthmani (Beirut), 182
Izzet Pasha, 162

Jabal 'Amil, 337
Jabal al-Duruz, 352, 356–7
Jabotinsky, Vladimir, 130, 144n
Jaffa, 15, 101–2, 107, 110, 112–13, 118, 125, 129
al-Jahiz, 328
al-Jamali, Fadhil, 325
al-Jami'a al-'Arabiyya, 104, 110
al-Jami'a al-Islamiyya (Jaffa), 111, 117
al-Jami'a al-'Uthmaniyya, 245
al-Jam'iyya al-Iqtisadiyya (Baghdad), 326
Janissaries, 34, 36, 50n, 51n, 52n
Jankowski, James and Israel Gershoni, 211–12
Jara'id (website), 8
al-Jarida (Cairo), 68
al-Jawa'ib (Istanbul), 4
al-Jaza'iri, Shaykh Tahir, 183, 185, 191
Jenin, 106, 112, 118
Jerusalem, 107, 111–13, 128, 130, 132–4, 136–7, 200n, 336
Jerusalem Post (Jerusalem), 146n
Jewish Agency, 101–2, 116, 139
Jews, Jewish communities, 6, 130, 135, 140, 187, 305, 363, 368n
    Iraqi, 19, 323–44
Jewish Advocate (Bombay), 141
Jewish anarchists, 243, 245
Jewish press, 9–10, 19, 141, 155, 166n, 323–44
al-Jihad (Cairo), 225
Jordan, 5, 112
journalism, 7, 219
journalists, 7, 10, 16–17, 32, 65, 89, 108, 215, 220, 223, 227–8, 251, 307
    anarchist, 245–6
    associations, 7, 218
    bilingual, 324, 329–30
    economic, 353
    educational background of, 112–14
    foreign language, 7
    imprisonment of, 5, 190, 192, 194, 222, 251
    Lebanese, 353
    memoirs of, 179, 181, 207
    Iraqi, 325, 337–8
    Moroccan, 166n
    Ottoman, 32–3, 36–40, 44, 48, 52n
    Palestinian, 100, 105, 107–8, 111–18
    political, 7, 10, 160, 222

    as profession, 7, 13, 105, 218–20, 222, 228–9, 246
    salaries of, 113, 223–5
    socialisation of, 231n
    Syrian, 102, 114, 156–7
    women, 7
Jubran, Jubran Khalil, 327
Judeo-Arabic, 6, 324
Jum'a, Muhammad Lutfi, 212–13

Kafr al-Zayyat, 248
Kairon (Cairo), 238
Kaiser Wilhelm II, 155
Kalifa, Dominique, 64, 66
Kamil, Mustafa, 110, 157–8, 168
Kamil, Najwa, 220
Karbala', 337
al-Karkh (Baghdad), 326
al-Karkhi, 'Abbud, 326, 334
al-Karmeh (Tripoli), 348
al-Karmil (Haifa), 99–101, 103, 105, 108–9, 115, 117, 120n
Kasap, Teodor, 37, 42, 51n
Kashkul (Aleppo), 182
al-Kashkul (Cairo), 220
al-Kattani, Sharif Muhammad, 156, 168n
Kautsky, Karl, 133, 140
Kawkab al-Sharq (Cairo), 224
kayd al-nisa' (women's cunning), 70–1
Kemal, Namık, 37, 42, 45, 51n, 52n
Kemalism, 329
Khalifa, Ijlal, 9
Khalil, Muhammad Mahmud, 295
al-Khamis (Jaffa), 110
Khati-Humayun, 346
al-Khatib, Muhibb al-Din, 177, 183, 191
al-Khatib, Shaykh Yunis, 107, 120n
Khizran, Shaykh Subhi, 107
Khulusi Bik, *wali*, 196
al-Khuri, Faris, 183
King–Crane Commission, 347
Kolstrup, Søren, 66
Kouchtsoglou, Stavros, 244, 246–7, 256
Kozma, Liat, 88
Krasin, Leonid, 362
Kropotkin, Peter, 247
Ku Klux Klan, 335
Kurd 'Ali, 'Adil, 176, 199
Kurd 'Ali, Ahmad, 176, 181, 190, 192, 194, 197, 199
Kurd 'Ali, Muhammad, 176–99
Kurds, 337, 364

labour *see* workers
al-Lahab (Jerusalem), 111
Latakia, 349
Laval, Pierre, 265–7, 281n, 282n, 284n
Lavoratore, Il (Alexandria), 237, 241, 244–5, 251, 255, 262n

laws *see* press laws
lawyers, 7, 8, 107, 113, 128, 219, 227, 268, 297, 350
Layla, 333
Le Bon, Gustave, 188
Le Chatelier, Alfred, 180, 200n
League of Nations, 128, 272–3, 345, 351, 353; *see also* Mandates
Lebanon, 9, 19, 23n, 130, 190, 326, 337, 345–70
  Civil war (1860), 34–5
Lentini, Pasquale, 276
letters to the editor, 50n, 54n, 100, 104, 118, 128, 140–1, 181, 243, 247, 327, 333
Levine, Philippa, 80, 84
Lewis, Bernard, 338
Libera Tribuna (Cairo), 244, 252, 257
Liberal Arab Party, 114
Liberatore, Il (Tunis), 18, 266, 275, 278–9, 281
Libertario, Il (La Spezia), 250
Liberty and Entente Party, 186, 192
libraries, 5, 141, 177–8, 247, 329, 347
Libreria Calebotta, 249
Libya, 132, 154, 159
Lisan al-Maghrib (Tangiers), 156, 167n, 168n
literacy, 2, 4, 248, 258, 349, 363
al-Liwa' (Cairo), 110, 161, 171n, 249, 251, 262n
al-Liwa' (Palestine), 107, 113, 117
London, 51n, 52n, 105, 111, 237, 250
lotteries, 254
Luoghi, Achilles, 276
Lux! (Alexandria), 243–4, 246, 252, 255

al-Madi, Muhammad, 107, 120n
al-Maghrib (Marrakesh), 156
al-Maghrib al-Aqsa (Tangiers), 166
al-Maghribi, Fathi Ahmad, 291–2, 294, 296, 300
al-Mahabba (Cairo), 348
al-Mahalla al-Kubra, 293–4, 307
Mahmud, Muhammad, 220, 226
Majlis al-Milli, 346
Majlisiyyun, 114, 121n
Majzub, 'Abd al-Rahman, 361
Makhzan, The, 154–6, 162, 166n, 167n, 169n, 170n
Maktab Anbar, 183
Maltese, 273
al-Manar (Cairo) 161, 171n, 179, 183
al-Manar (Beirut), 348
Mandates (League of Nations), 128, 345, 366n
  British, 19, 102, 105, 111, 139, 323, 339
  French, 19, 199, 346, 351–3, 357–8, 365
Mannesmann bros, 162
Mannino Pietro, 273
Mansur, 'Ali, 114
Mansura, 245, 248, 294
Mardam Bik, Jamil, 183
Maroc, Le, 167n
Maroc commercial, Le, 167n
Marrakesh, 156, 170n

Martin, Laurent, 219
al-Matariyya, 293
al-Matba'a al-Siriyaniyya al-Kathulikiyya (printing house), 326
Matba'at al-Muqtabas (printing house), 176, 180
Matbuat Nizamnamesi (Publication Act) (1864), 52n
Matin, Le, 362
al-Mazini, Ibrahim 'Abd al-Qadir, 215, 217
Mazzini, Giuseppe, 259n
Mecca, 178, 187
men of letters, 13, 183, 220
Meşrutiyet, 160
Messagiere Egiziano, Il (Alexandria), 238
Messina, Giuseppe, 245, 255
Midane, 359
Mikha'il, Murad, 327
Minister of War (Ottoman), 159, 170n
Ministry of Foreign Affairs
  French, 193–5
  Italian, 283n
Ministry of Interior (Egypt), 67, 78, 88, 171, 222
Ministry of Justice (Ottoman), 43
Ministry of Public Works (Lebanon), 350
minorities, 20, 338, 347, 364
Mir'at al-Sharq (Jerusalem), 110, 113, 117, 119n
al-Misbah (Baghdad), 323–44
al-Mishkat (Damascus), 182
al-Misri (Cairo), 302, 306
al-Misri Effendi, 213
missionaries, 359–60
el-Mokri, El Hadj Hammed, 159
Moniteur ottoman (Istanbul, 1831), 3
Montecatini (mining company), 281, 286n
Morocco, 4, 16, 153–72, 281, 363
Morokko Aktion, 164
Mosul, 40, 364
Mu'aridhun [opposition] newspapers (Palestine), 137
Mu'awiya, 328
al-Mu'ayyad (Cairo), 14, 16, 58–98, 157, 160–2, 165, 168n, 180, 238, 247
al-Mudarris, Fahmi, 333
al-Muddarik, Muhammad Yusuf, 305, 309
al-Mufid (Beirut), 182
al-Muhajir (Damascus), 182
Muhammad, 'Abd al-Rahim al-Haj, 103
Muhammadist movement, 191
Muhbir (Istanbul, London), 51n
Muhibb al-Din al-Khatib, 177, 183, 191
mujtahids, 333
mukhbirun, 222; *see also* reporters
mülkiyye, 184, 201n
muqata'ji families, 347, 360
al-Muqattam (Cairo), 161, 238, 244, 249, 262n
al-Muqtabas (newspaper and review), 176–206
al-Muqtataf (Beirut, Cairo), 179, 182–3, 244–5
Musa, Salama, 216, 245, 252
Musamarat al-Sha'b, 180

al-Musawwar, 108, 118
Muslim Brothers, Brotherhood, 215, 288, 303–5, 310
Muslim Mediterranean, 153, 158, 164–5
Mussolini, Benito, 265–7, 269, 270, 275, 277–80, 281n, 282n
Mussolini–Laval Accords, 18, 266–9, 275
al-Mustaqbal, 245, 252
mustard gas, 280

Nabi (Nebi) Musa, 134, 145n
Nablus, 112–13, 118, 139
al-nahda (Nahda), 199n, 329, 330, 348
al-Nahda al-Nisa'iyya, 333
Nahdat al-Maghrib, 163
al-Nahhas, Mustafa, 295, 298, 302
Najaf, 337, 339
al-Najafi, Ahmad Safi, 332
al-Naqib, Sayyid Talib, 194
al-Nashashibi, 'Azmi, 127, 144n
al-Nashashibi, Fakhri, 116
al-Nashashibi, family, 114–16
Nasif, 'Isam al-Din Hifni, 290
Nasif, Malak Hifni, 11, 68
Nasr, 'Abd al-Rahman, 223
Nassar, Najib, 100, 108, 114–15
National Arab Party, 114
National Bloc (Syria), 199
nationalism, 72, 90, 111, 138, 142, 158, 228, 237, 275, 300–1, 323–5, 332, 334, 336, 338–9
Nawfal, Sara, 85
Nazim, Mahmud Ramzi, 292
Nazim Pasha (wali of Syria), 182, 190–3, 195
networks, Pan-Islamic 153–75
  subaltern, 11, 16, 153–75, 254–5, 289
  translocal, 16, 164

newspapers
  banning, suspension of, 5–6, 162, 164, 150–2, 194–5, 243, 251, 273; *see also* censorship
  circulation of, 4, 10, 49n, 54n, 89, 104, 107, 117–18, 120n, 127, 144n, 157, 161, 181, 220, 247–9, 261n, 269, 276, 292–3, 307, 317n, 349
  dailies, 16, 59–60, 90, 99, 103, 183, 326, 339
  distribution of, 39, 52n, 104, 106, 247–9 348–50
  educational purpose, 44
  finance of, 104, 156, 163, 194, 252–4
  monthlies, 99, 103, 109
  periodicity of, 11, 32
  price of, 252–3, 262n, 350
  weeklies, 99, 103, 108–9, 156, 166n, 228, 240
Nietzsche, 247
Nieuwenhuis, Ferdinand Domela, 243
al-Ni'ma (Damascus), 348
Nimr, Faris, 179
niqabiyya (syndicalism), 297
Nord, Debora Epstein, 80

Nuri, 37, 45
Nusaibah, Anwar bin Zaki Effendi, 136
Nuwayhid, 'Ajaj, 114–15, 122n
nuzala' (incomers), 73

Operaio, L' (Alexandria), 240, 243–4, 246–9, 252–4, 255
oranges, 131, 142, 143
orientalists, 180, 188–9
Oriente, L' (Alexandria), 247
Ottavi, Paul, 178, 193–5
Ottoman constitution (1908), 198
Ottoman Empire, 4, 14, 34, 37–41, 177, 181–2, 186–90, 325, 328–9, 345–6
Ottoman finances, 31–57
Ottoman non-ruling elites 38, 48
Ottoman press, 31–57, 52n, 160, 182
Ottoman publics, 31–57
Ottomanism, 186–8

Palestine Arab Women's Congress (1929), 128
Palestine Bulletin (Jerusalem), 136, 146n
Palestine Post (Jerusalem), 146n
Pan-Arabism, 158, 324–5
Pan-Islamism, 132, 140, 154, 157–8, 161–4, 171n, 186–9
Paris Commune (1871), 38, 242
Parrini, Icilio Ugo, 245–6, 249–50, 254–5
peasants 36, 38, 48, 87, 99–103, 107, 131, 185, 191, 306, 326, 347
Pensiero ed Azione, 239, 245
Permanent Mandates Commission, 141
Peyrouton, Resident-General, 275, 280, 284n
Phare d'Alexandrie, Le (Alexandria), 238
phosphorites, 267, 281
photographers, photography, 7, 92n, 132
Piccola Posta, 248
plays, 73, 85, 119, 214, 216–17, 219, 228, 327
poets, poetry, 63, 73, 85, 110, 229, 246, 254, 290–2, 296, 302, 308–9, 325–7, 332–3, 336
Poincaré, Raymond, 186
police, 31, 65, 68–71, 73–8, 80–1, 84, 88–9, 133, 135, 138–9, 192, 270, 273, 279, 289, 293, 295
Port Said, 79, 83–4, 88, 239, 242, 248
Porte, Sublime Porte, 31–48, 194, 347
press
  bilingual, multilingual, 6–7, 22n, 26n, 160, 242, 245, 247, 324
  clandestine, 18, 52n, 245, 266
  foreign language, 2, 10, 155, 238
  nationalisation of, 6, 7
  private (non-state) 3, 5, 7, 31–3, 36, 39, 41, 44, 48, 238
  see also individual entries under languages (Arabic, English, French, Greek, Hebrew, Italian); *and also* anarchist, Islamic, Jewish, Ottoman, socialist, Wafdist, women's, workers' press

Press Bureau
    Iraq, 5
    Morocco, 166n
Press Club (*Nadi al-sihafa*), 222
press laws, 2, 290
    Ali Kararname (1867), 52n
    French (1852), 52n
    Matbuat Nizamnamesi (Publication Act) (1864), 52n
    Press and Publications Law (Egypt): (1881), 63, 251; (1909), 251
    Press Ordinance (Palestine) (1933), 5
press symbols and slogans, 109–11, 137, 142, 244, 292, 302, 304, 332
printers, 245–6, 252, 261n, 262n, 273, 290, 307
printing houses, 113, 116, 166n, 176, 179–80, 191, 193, 197, 252, 326, 348
Pro-Ferrer, 244–6, 257
Proletariato, Il (Alexandria), 241, 244–5, 251, 255
prostitutes, prostitution, 60, 65, 75–84; see also sex workers
public health, 31, 39, 243
public opinion, 1, 14–15, 99, 141, 156, 167n, 168n, 184–5, 193, 198, 214, 218, 269, 272, 281, 308, 354
    Ottoman, 31–57
public sphere, 10, 14, 48, 324, 326, 332, 337
publishing houses, 155, 193, 326, 348
Punch (London), 216

al-Qabas (Damascus), 182, 194, 199
al-Qadi, Dimitrios (Greek Catholic Patriarch of Antioch), 360
al-Qadi, Shaykh Yunis, 292
al-Qadiri, Rasul, 335
al-Qalqili, 'Abdullah, 102, 113, 115
Qaraman, Tahir, 107
al-Qasimi, Salah al-Din, 183, 191
Qasiri, Sami, 180
Qassa', 359
al-Qassam, Shaykh 'Iz al-Din, 101

radio, 103
al-Ra'id al-Misri, 179
Rakovski, Christian, 362
Ramadan, Hafiz, 222
Ramses Café, 222
Rangoon, 80
Rashaya, 356
al-Rayyis, Najib, 199
reading, readership, 4–6, 33, 41, 46, 87, 117–19, 143, 167, 178, 181, 183, 185, 187, 198, 212, 216, 226, 247–50, 253–5, 288, 307–8, 326–8
Redistribution Commission of Financial Debt, 354
Réforme, La (Alexandria), 246
reporters, 7, 13, 41, 46, 100, 105, 107, 222, 225–6

Reşad, Kayazade, 37
Rescript of Reform (*Islahat Fermanı*), 35, 346
réveil du Maroc, Le (Tangiers), 155–6
Revolution, al-Buraq (*Thawra al-Buraq*) (1929), 126
Rida, Rashid, 179, 191
Rif'at, 'Abd al-Azim Ahmad, 163, 172n
Risveglio Egiziano, Risorgete! (Alexandria), 243–4, 246, 254, 256, 257n
Rizq, Father Kyrillos, 361
Rosenthal, Joseph (Giuseppe), 245, 247, 254, 255–6, 260n
Rossi, Michele, 278
al-Rusafi, Ma'ruf, 326–7, 333
Russia, Russians, 335–6, 345–7, 361–3, 365
Ruz al-Yusuf (Cairo), 17, 207–34

al-Sa'ada, 156, 167n, 168n
Saba, Ya'qub, 113
al-Sabah (Tangiers), 156–7, 168n
Sabri, Hasan, 210
Sabri, Zuhayr, 295, 305
Sadiq, Khalil, 180
al-Saff al-Adabi, 326
St George Hospital, 358
St George's monastery (Humayra), 359
St George (printing house), 348
Sajous, Molco and Co. (printers), 252, 256–7, 262n
Saladin, 137
Salah al-Din al-Ayubi (play), 327
Salame, Hassan, 103
salaries, 301, 307
    of civil servants, 50n, 354
    journalist, 113, 224–5
Salib, Iskandar Sulayman, 289–91, 296–8, 300–1, 305, 308
Samara, Da'ud, 330
Santamaria, Enrico, 269–70
Saraphidis, Dr Georgios, 247, 256
al-Sarkha (Cairo), 221, see *Ruz al-Yusuf*
Sarrail, Gen. (High Commissioner), 351
al-Sarraj, Sami, 102, 105, 114
Sarruf, Ya'qub, 179
Sarukhan (illustrator), 221, 223–5
Sasson, Eliyahu, 116
Sasson, Ezekiel, 330
satire, satirical poetry, 191–2, 208, 215–16, 218, 220, 225–6
Saudi Arabia, 9
Sawt al-Sha'b, 103, 117
Sayqali, Athanasius, 353–4
al-Sayyid, Mahmud Ahmad, 327
Seignobos, Charles, 188
Sereni, Emilio, 280–1
Serph, V. A., 167n
sex trade (Bombay), 60, 80, 88–9
sex workers, 67, 73, 75–80, 83–5, 89
al-Shabab (Jerusalem), 111

al-Shaharstani, Hibat al-Din, 333
Shahbandar, 'Abd al-Rahman, 183
Shahin, Raghib ('Reuter'), 118
Shakespeare (*Merchant of Venice*), 335
al-Shalaqani, 'Abd al-Fattah, 294
al-Sham (Damascus), 179
al-Sham'a, Ahmad Pasha, 193
al-Sham'a, Rushdi, 183, 192–3, 197
al-Shanti, family, 102, 122n
al-Shanti, Ibrahim, 102, 104–5, 113, 115
Sharabani, Khaduri, 327
al-Shara'i, Muhammad Pasha, 159, 161–2, 171n
al-Sharq (Damascus), 197
Sharqi, 'Ali, 332
Sha'ul, Anuwar, 326–7, 330, 333, 335
Shaw Commission, 127–9
Sherif Pasha, 160, 170n
Sherlock Holmes, 227
al-Shidyaq, Ahmad Faris, 4
Shifman, Jacob, 133
Shihada, Bulus, 113–15
Shihada, Nicolas, 179
Shi'is, 187, 325–6, 328, 331, 333, 337
Shina, Salman, 326, 329, 336
al-Shinnawi brothers, 223
al-Shinnawi, Kamil, 208
al-Shuqayri, Ahmad, 114
al-Shuqayri, As'ad, 115
short stories, 209, 216, 327, 331
Shubra (Shubra al-Khayma), 288–319
Shubra al-Balad, 291
Shubra al-Khayma, 18, 288–93, 302, 304, 306–7
Shumayyil, Shibli, 245, 252
shu'ubiyya, 328
Şinasi, İbrahim, 4, 37, 39, 43–5, 51n
Singer, Mr (Director of Deutsche Orient Bank), 162
al-Sirat al-Mustaqim, 102, 110–11
al-Siyasa (Cairo), 224
socialism, socialists, 239, 242, 243, 245, 276, 288, 290, 305, 327
socialist press, 250, 275
Società Operaia Italiana (Italian Workers Society), 239
societies, literary, 326, 327, 336; *see also* clubs
Society for Arab Renaissance (Jam'iyyat al-nahda al-'arabiyya), 177, 183, 191–2, 202n
Soria, Maurice, 269
Sosialistis (Athens), 243, 260n, 261n
South Africa, 140
South Asia, South Asians, 132, 140–1, 143
Soviet Union, 135, 361–2
Spettatore Egiziano, Lo (Alexandria), 238
Stato operaio, Lo (Milan), 280, 285n
strikes, 101, 130–1, 239, 242, 248, 250, 303–4
   Great /General strike (1936), 15, 102, 117, 123n, 128, 138
students, 85, 141, 143, 160, 208, 211, 227, 307, 337, 359

Subaltern studies, 153–4, 165n
subscribers, 100, 107–8, 141, 162, 193, 243, 249, 253, 258, 290, 326, 348–50
subscriptions, subscription funds, 171n, 180–1, 184, 247, 252–3, 260n, 276, 292, 296, 348–50
subsidies, 6, 184
Suez, 67
Sufis, 62, 84, 131
suhufi (journalist), 220
Sunni intellectuals, 328, 331
Surat Yusuf, 71
Suriyya al-Janubiyya, 110
syndicalism, syndicalists, 18, 239–40, 242–3, 288–9, 296–7, 300–1, 303, 305–7, 309; *see also* anarcho-syndicalism
Syria, Syrians, 5–7, 9, 16, 53, 67, 110, 130–1, 176–200, 213, 337, 345–65
Syriac, Syriacs, 360, 364–5

al-Tabi'i, Muhammad, 17, 214, 216–17, 221–7, 229n
Taher Bey, Aref, 16, 154, 157–65, 169n, 170n, 172n
tailors, 242
Takvim-i Vekayi (Istanbul), 3, 31
Talaat Bey, 193
Tambe, Ashwini, 60, 88, 90
Tangiers, 155–7, 161, 163, 165, 166n, 167n, 168n
Tanzimat, 32–3, 35–7, 49n
Tasvir-i Efkar (Istanbul), 14, 31–2, 36–7, 39–41, 43–6, 48, 49n, 159, 170n
al-Ta'un (Fez), 156
taverns, 67, 73–4, 248–9; *see also* bars
tax farmers, 42, 347, 360
taxation, 39, 353, 356
Taymur, 'A'isha, 85
teachers, 7, 113, 119, 123n, 172n, 219, 337
Tel Aviv, 130, 134
Temps Nouveaux, Les (Paris), 246, 250
Tercüman-ı Ahval (Istanbul), 4, 44
Testa, Leandro, 257
Tetouan War, 154, 166n
textile industry, workers, 18–19, 288–310
Thabit, Karim, 223, 225
The Times (London), 140, 362
trade unions, unionists, 18, 289, 292–3, 295–8, 303, 305, 307, 309; *see also* unions
translations, 2, 67, 134, 136, 141, 171n, 180–1, 188, 208–9, 355
Tribuna Libera, La / Le Tribune Libre, (Alexandria) (1901), 57, 240, 242–5, 249, 252, 254, 255
Tripoli (Lebanon), 346, 348–9, 357–8, 360
Tripoli (North Africa), 159, 163
Tripolitania, 161, 163–5, 186
Trovatore, Il (Port Said), 242, 255
Tulkarm, 112, 118
al-Tuni, Muhammad Shawkat, 212

Tunis Socialist (Tunis), 275
Tunis, Tunisia, 17–18, 154, 161, 163–5, 187, 246, 250, 265–81, 282–3n
al-Tunisi, Salah al-Din, 191
Tunisian Communist Party, 278, 284n
al-Tunsi, Bayram, 292, 296
Turkification, 187, 192

'Ubayd, Makram, 132, 295, 301–2
ulama, ulema, 51n, 168n, 185
al-Umma (Damascus), 190
Ungaretti, Costantino, 247, 256
Ungaretti, Giuseppe, 246, 256
Unione, L' (Cairo-Alexandria), 243–4, 246–7, 252, 256, 258n, 260n
Unione, L' (Tunis), 18, 266, 268–71, 273–4, 281
Unione della Democrazia, L' (Alexandria), 246, 256
Unione della Sera, L' (Tunis), 269
unions, 7, 18–19, 101–2, 218, 240, 243, 288–310
al-Uskubi, Shaykh Ibrahim, 192
'Uthman, Taha Sa'd, 290–1, 293–4, 297–9, 303–4, 310

Vahiddetin, Sultan 164, 172n
Vakit (Istanbul), 169n
Valenzi, Maurizio, 278
Vasai, Pietro, 246–7, 250, 252, 254, 255–7
veiling, 299–300, 333
Voix Nouvelle, La (Tunis), 276
von Oppenheim, Baron Max Freiherr, 162, 171n
Vorwärts (Germany), 133, 140

Wadi al-Hawarith, 133
Wadi al-Nasara, 349
Wadi Karam, 156, 168n
Wafd, Wafdists, 9, 209, 220, 222–3, 293–5, 298, 302–3, 305, 308, 310, 316n
al-Wafd al-Misri, 290
Wafdist press, 220, 222, 290, 306, 316n
al-Wagib (Cairo), 290, 306, 308
Wailing Wall riots, 126
al-Waqa'i' al-Misriyya (Cairo), 3, 238
waqf, 345–6
al-Wardani, Yahya, 299
Wasif, Mahmud, 180
Wasif, Mustafa, 179
al-Watan (Cairo), 357
watan ('homeland'), *wataniyya*, 111, 331
Watani Party, 171n, 213, 222, 251
Weber, Eugen, 66
Weizmann, Chaim, 336
Weygand, Gen. (High Commissioner), 351
whistle blower, blowing, 170n, 185, 218
Wien, Peter, 325
women, 128, 142, 244, 299–300, 326, 333, 338, 355

Jewish, 334
journalist, 7
and literacy, 261n
press, 9,11, 14
readers, 118
representation of, 14, 58–90
'respectable', 67, 70–1, 75–7, 79, 81–2
Women's Arab Executive, 129
workers, 17–18, 36, 46, 50n, 53n, 54n, 239–40, 242–4, 247–8, 250, 273, 275, 278–9
Egyptian, 17–8, 248, 288–310
Italian, 239
Palestinian, 101–2
press, 243–4, 247, 288–319
wages of, 224
see also sex workers
World Muslim Congress, 132

Yahya, A. F. ('Abd al-Fattah), 210
al-Yara' (Cairo), 290, 306
al-Yarmuk (Haifa), 104, 110, 121n, 123n
Yemen, 9
Yeni Gazete, 159
Young Ottomans, 7, 13, 37–9, 49n, 50n, 51n, 52n
Young Turk Revolution (1908), 158, 176, 324
Young Turks, 177–8, 190–1, 196, 198–9
youth, 37, 76, 79, 105, 111, 116, 119, 122n, 136, 138, 214, 279, 300, 331
Yusuf, Shaykh 'Ali, 64, 93n, 157–8, 162, 169n, 171n, 180
al-Yusuf, Fatima, 17, 220, 222–6, 229n

Zagazig, 76, 79
Zaghlul, Ahmad Fathi, 188
Zaghlul, Sa'd, 157, 230n
al-Zahawi, Jamil Sidqi, 327, 332–3
al-Zahir (Cairo), 180
Zahle, 179, 349
Zahrat al-Ihsan, 358
Za'tar Effendi, Abu Qasim, 213
Zanzibar, 157
Zaydan, Jurji, 180
Zayn al-'Abidin, Mawlay, 162
Zaytun, 293–4
Zghorta, 358
al-Zibawi, Shaykh Yusuf, 101
Zionism, Zionists, 9, 15, 19, 99, 102, 119, 128, 130–1, 133–4, 136–7, 140–1, 143–4, 323–5, 336
al-Zirikli, Khayr al-Din, 102, 105, 110, 114, 183
Ziwar, A., 210
Zu'aytir, 'Umar, 113
Zu'aytir, Akram, 113–15, 119, 123n
al-Zuhrawi, 'Abd al-Hamid, 195
al-Zumur (Acre), 107, 110

EU representative:
Easy Access System Europe
Mustamäe tee 50, 10621 Tallinn, Estonia
Gpsr.requests@easproject.com